IN THE
COMBAT ZONE

IN THE COMBAT ZONE

Special Forces since 1945

ROBIN NEILLANDS

Weidenfeld & Nicolson
LONDON

This one is for Derek 'Lou' Lucas of Chakola,
New South Wales, Australia
and 40 Commando, Royal Marines.

A good friend and a good soldier.

First published in Great Britain in 1997
by Weidenfeld & Nicolson

A CIP catalogue record for this book is available
from the British Library

ISBN 0 297 81673 X

Typeset by Selwood Systems, Midsomer Norton

Set in Trump Medieval

Printed in Great Britain by
Butler & Tanner Ltd, Frome and London

Weidenfeld & Nicolson

The Orion Publishing Group
Orion House
5 Upper Saint Martin's Lane
London, WC2H 9EA

CONTENTS

ILLUSTRATIONS

PREFACE

This is the story of Special Forces since 1945, with a look back at the development of Special Forces since they were first created during the Seven Years War, in the middle decades of the eighteenth century. The book concludes with a look forward to the possible role of Special Forces in the next century. Large parts of this account are oral history, in which the story is told in the words of the men who were in Special Forces and there at the sharp end when Special Force history was made.

With the current worldwide interest in Special Forces such a book seemed called for, and although the main concentration is on the development and deployment of such forces since the end of the Second World War, I have called it a story, rather than a history, because following the disbandment or rundown of Special Force units at the end of that conflict – and a decade in the doldrums – Special Forces went through a rapid revival and then expanded across the world. Their history has not been constant but varies from place to place, and the term Special Forces can mean different things in different countries. As the list in the Appendix reveals, there are now a vast number of Special Force units and to cover them all in adequate detail would require a multi-volume history, not a single book.

This book therefore concentrates on British and US Special Force units and since – as the Appendix again demonstrates – these two countries have a great many such units, and a long tradition of Special Force activity, they provide the bulk of the relevant text. But other units in other countries – the Israeli paratroopers at Entebbe, the Italian Leatherheads rescuing General Dozier, the German GSG9 ending the aircraft hijack at Mogadishu, Argentine Special Forces in the Falklands, the Foreign Legion's crack 2nd REP parachute formation at Kolwezi, for example – are not left out.

The central theme is to show not only how Special Forces have developed, expanded, changed and been employed since 1945, but also how their central role or roles – long-range reconnaissance, raiding, intelligence gathering – have remained constant, though augmented in recent years with hostage rescue, counter-terrorism and co-operation with the intelligence community, these last two being activities about which this author has several reservations.

The other intention was to examine the growing Special Force 'legend' and see how far the popular image of the Special Force soldier –

described by one parachute veteran as 'the kick down the door and bung in a grenade school of history' – varied from the reality. Most of the veterans who contributed their stories to this book did so on the understanding that 'professional heroes' and 'would-be Rambos' were excluded and, since that was my original intention, that has been the broad thrust of the book. No one who appears in or contributed to this book has ever carried a knife between his teeth. The picture of the Special Force soldier presented in this book is light-years away from the lurid image offered in some recent accounts of Special Force warfare.

The final result, I hope and believe, is to present an accurate, entertaining picture of the Special Force soldier and Special Force activity in all its aspects, from recruitment and training to actual operations, in various roles, by a wide variety of units, in a dozen theatres of war. Special Force units are nothing if not diverse. It also shows the development of the Special Force spirit, based from the beginning on the trained, expert, tenacious fighting man. Fighting men have not changed a great deal down the centuries, and we can trace this story from Rogers' Rangers in the eighteenth-century French and Indian War to the SAS troopers hunting Scud missiles in the deserts of Iraq in 1991.

The Special Force soldier, however, is far more than a killing machine. He is, first and foremost, a good soldier, a man trained to use his brains as well as his weapons. He has to have guts, but his distinguishing asset is a great, if somewhat dry, sense of humour: 'Remember the old rule, Robbie: "If you can't take a joke, you shouldn't have joined,"' as one Old Sweat reminded me. The Special Force field of operations is usually behind the lines and always at the sharp end, and that is the way he likes it. I like them a lot and I commend their story to you.

A book of this nature could not be written without a great deal of help from people in every corner of the world, who sent in their accounts of Special Force life and provide much of the detail on various aspects of the Special Force story since 1945. Thanking all these people for their help is one of the most enjoyable parts of writing a book and I only hope they are pleased with the final result.

In this particular case I must first acknowledge the tremendous and expert assistance of Scott di Marco of the King Library, Miami University, Oxford, Ohio, USA. Scott heard of this project and wrote in offering to help, and his assistance has been unstinting and most useful, both in finding information on US Special Force units and in commenting on the text. His knowledge and academic expertise has been invaluable and I am greatly indebted to him for it. Scott's dedication to the task even extended to his honeymoon in Mexico in 1996, when the village near his hotel was attacked by rebels, who killed eight Mexican Marines before withdrawing. As he wrote to me later, 'this was interesting, to say the least ... I am used to studying this sort of thing, not living it.'

Generous assistance also came from Lieutenant-Colonel Landon K. Thorne III, USMC, of Key Biscayne, Florida, and Steve Richmond, Lt, USMC, of West Union, Ohio, and the CAP programme in Vietnam. In the UK Major-General Julian Thompson, CB, OBE, was as always extremely helpful and I am grateful for his support and advice. Thanks also to two 'old muckers,' Terry Brown of 42 Commando RM, and Sid Ward of Z Troop, 45 Commando RM.

Special thanks also to Gary Linderer of *Behind the Lines* magazine of Festus, Missouri, who supplied accounts of his own experiences with the F Company LRRPs, 101 Airborne in Vietnam, and generously opened the magazine files for me, and to Mike Nibbs of *Strike Swiftly*, the magazine of the Australian Commando Companies and Association.

Among many British Special Service soldiers I should like to thank Major Denis Aldridge, 41 Independent Commando, Korea; Cecil Blanche of 12 Commando; Brigadier Christopher Bullock, OBE, MC, 2/2nd Gurkhas, Borneo; Victor Stevenson, 5 Commando; Joe Cartwright, Royal Marines Commandos, of Johannesburg, South Africa; Ted Kelly of 2 Commando; my old section corporal in 45 Commando, Arthur Derby of 41 (Independent) Commando RM, Korea; Colonel Robin McGarel Groves for accounts of Palestine; Fred Heyhurst, also of 41 Independent Commando RM and a veteran of Korea; Fergus McCartney of Kenya, for his account of fighting Mau Mau gangs in the Kenya Emergency; Fred Musson, 5 Commando; Lieutenant-Colonel Andrew Whitehead and Captain Ian Gardiner of 45 Commando RM for their accounts of the Falklands War.

I must also thank Lieutenant-General Sir Frank Kitson, for his advice on counter-terrorism and on the setting up of the Mau Mau 'pseudogangs' in Kenya; Ron Pocock and Bryan Ricketts, for accounts of soldiering in Cyprus; Brigadier Joe Starling, the Parachute Regiment for his accounts of the Parachute Regiment in Aden and Northern Ireland; Bill Sculthorpe, Para Squadron, 22 SAS Regiment, Malaya; R. W. Strickland, 33 Field Regiment, Parachute Gunners, for his accounts of operations in Aden and at Suez; Lieutenant-Colonel Euan Southby Tailyour, Royal

Marines, for his views on amphibious warfare and on the Falklands campaign; John Grebby, of Canada, for accounts of his service in the Parachute Regiment and the Royal Marines; Chuck Tilley, 2nd Independent Pathfinder Company, the Parachute Regiment; Major Philip Neame, 2 Para, for his account of Goose Green.

In the USA, thanks to Bob Bunnell MSG, USSF, for his accounts of Vietnam; James E. Butler of Vietnam 'Team Python', now of Carmel Valley, California, and a descendant of a man who served in Rogers' Rangers; Lieutenant-Colonel Bradley Biggs of the 555 Parachute Infantry Regiment (the Triple Nickels), America's first-ever black Parachute unit; David Hackworth, author and soldier; Albert P. Frechette of the First Special Service Force, 'The Devils Brigade'; Dr Donald Goodwin, of US Special Forces Vietnam and now of Yangon, Myanmar (Burma).

I am grateful also to Richard Hale of Merrill's Marauders, Burma; Lionel Hebert of CCRAK, Special Operations, Korea; Tom Harvey, USMC, now of Bangkok, Thailand, who served in a USMC Combined Action Programme and kindly sent me the CAP Newsletter; Matthew Kaye, of the Navy Scouts and Raiders for sending me his memoirs; Mike 'Machine Gun' Kelley, of the 101 Airborne, Vietnam and Sacramento, California, for finding me books and the generous gift of an autographed sketch of a Vietnam operation; Leslie 'Bill' Kick, 82nd Airborne; and an old friend and associate in other books, Jack Capell, 4th US Infantry Division, Normandy and North-West Europe.

Thanks too, to Corporal Frank Kulak, USMC, Korea; Richard Marcinko, US Navy SEALS; Master-Sergeant Charles H. Owens, USMC, who served in the Second World War, Korea and Vietnam and provides perspective for this work; John McLeod, of Texarkana, Texas; Bob Sales of the 29th Rangers and the 29th US Infantry Division; Morton I. Silver, of the 'Chosin Few' Veterans for permission to quote at length from his excellent account of the USMC at the Inchon landings and the Chosin Reservoir in Korea; Bob Singer, Sergeant-Major, USMC, for his help in contacting US veteran organizations and putting me in touch with sources for USMC and Force Recon records.

In Australia I thank Derek Lucas of Chakola, New South Wales and formerly of 40 Commando; Alison Yamasaki for her help at the Canberra Memorial; Brigadier W. H. 'Mac' Grant, former CO of 1 Commando Company; Davil Aldea for his help and advice on the Argentine Special Forces, the Buzo Tactico and Argentine Special Forces in the Falklands War of 1982; Captain Mike Wells of IRNSWR (Commando) for his account of Australian Special Force soldiers in Vietnam.

Among clubs and associations, libraries and museums, I should like to thank the 'Chosin Few' Veterans of the United States Marine Corps and 41 Independent Commando, Royal Marines; Merrill's Marauders and Mars Force Veterans Association; Bob Bunnell of the Vietnam Veterans of America; the Delta Raiders of Vietnam Association; the Parachute Association; the Commando Association; the US Special Forces Association; Franklin D. Gross, the Defenders of Wake Island, Independence, Missouri; the Association of Polish Paratroopers, USA; the Royal Marines Historical Association; the London Library; the Mississippi Chapter of the Vietnam Veterans of America; the USMC Air and Ground Museum, Quantico, Virginia; the Imperial War Museum, London; the Combined Operations Museum, Inverary, Scotland; the Commando Museum, Spean Bridge, Scotland; the Royal Marines Museum, Eastney, Portsmouth, England; the Marine Corps Historical Center, Washington DC.

Useful magazines have included *Strike Swiftly*, the official journal of 1 Commando Association, Australia; *Commando*, the Australian Commando Regiment; *Fortitude*, the US Marine Historical Association; *The Globe and Laurel*, the Royal Marines; the US *Marine Corps Gazette*; *Behind the Lines*, US Military Special Operations; *Pegasus*, the Parachute Regiment; the US Airborne *Static Line*; *Military*, Press of Freedom, USA; The *Empire State Marine*, the Marine Corps League; *The Old Breed*, the 1st Marine Division USMC.

A great many Special Force soldiers have helped me with this book, on the understanding that I told it straight, avoided bullshit and did not use their accounts to produce yet another 'gung-ho heroes' epic. This is what I have tried to do and, since many of the contributors are fearsome gentlemen, I hope I have succeeded.

Robin Neillands
Beckhampton, Wiltshire
June 1997

LIST OF ABBREVIATIONS

ACC	Army Catering Corps
AFPC-TU	Australian Federal Police Counter-Terrorist Unit
AFSOCCENT	Air Force Special Operations Command
AK47	Kalashnikov rifle
ALN	Army for National Liberation
ANZAC	Australian and New Zealand Army Corps
AO	Area of Operations
APC	Armoured personnel carrier
APL	Aden Protectorate Levies
APS	Australian Protective Service
ARSOFT	Army Special Operations Task Force
ARVN	Army of the Republic of Vietnam
ASU	Active Service Unit (IRA)
AU8086	Army Unit 8086 (South Korea)
BATT	British Army Training Team
BBE	Dutch anti-terrorist unit
BEF	British Expeditionary Force
BJ	Beach Jumper
B Specials	Protestant police reserve (Northern Ireland)
CACO	Combined Action Company
CAF	Combined Action Force
CAG	Combined Action Group
CAP	Combined Action Platoon/Civil Action Program
CB	Construction Battalion
CCRAK	Combined Command for Reconnaissance Activities, Korea
CIA	Central Intelligence Agency
CIDG	Civilian Irregular Defense Group
CMF	Citizens Militia Force
CO	Commanding Officer
COPP	Combined Operation Pilotage Party
CQB	Close-Quarters Battle
CRW	Counter-Revolutionary Warfare
CSM	Company Sergeant-Major

CSRM	Commando School, Royal Marines
CT	Communist Terrorist (in Malaya)
DA	Direct Action
DI	Drill Instructor
DMIO	District Military Intelligence Officer
DMRLA	Democratic Revolutionary Movement for the Liberation of Arabistan
DMZ	Demilitarized Zone
DST	French secret service
DZ	Dropping Zone
ELAS	Greek Communist guerrillas
EOKA	Cypriot terrorists
ETA	Basque terrorists
FAC	Forward Air Controller
FA-MAS	French rifle
FARC	Revolutionary Armed Forces of Colombia
FARELF	Far East Land Forces
FCO	Fire Control Officer
FLN	Front for National Liberation (Algeria)
FLOSY	Front for the Liberation of South Yemen
FOB	Forward Operating Base
FOO	Forward Observation Officer
Force X	pseudo-Huk force
Force 116	SEAL unit, Mekong Delta
Force 136	Far East unit, SOE
GEOS	Grupos Especiales de Operaciones (Spain)
GIGN	Group d'Intervention Gendarmerie Nationale (France)
GIS	Grupo di Intervention Speciale (Italy)
GPMG	general-purpose machine-gun
GRU	Soviet Military Intelligence
GSG9	Grenzesshutzgruppe 9 (German anti-terrorist unit)
H&K	Heckler & Koch
HILO	High-exit, Low-opening
HMS	Her Majesty's Ship

IDF	Israel Defence Forces
IRA	Irish Republican Army
IS	Internal Security
JEHU	Joint Experimental Helicopter Unit
JTF2	Joint Task Force 2 (Canadian counter-terrorist)
JUSMAPG	Joint US Military Advisory and Planning Group (Greece)
KAU	Kenya African Union
KGB	Soviet secret service
KSK	Kommando Spezialkraft
L Detachment	SAS
LAW	British rocket-propelled grenade
LCA	landing craft – assault
LLDB	Lac Luong Dac Beit (South Vietnamese SF)
LRDG	Long-Range Desert Group
LRRP	Long-Range Reconnaissance Patrol
LST	landing ship – tanks
LZ	landing zone
M60	machine-gun
M79	grenade-launcher
MA&WC	Mountain and Arctic Warfare Cadre (RM)
MACV-SOG	Military Assistance Command, Vietnam – Studies and Observations Group/Special Observation Group
MAGV	Military Assistance Group, Vietnam
MI5	British Security Service
MI6	British Secret Intelligence Service
MIKE	Mobile Strike Forces (US, Vietnam)
ML	Mountain Leader
MM	Military Medal
MMG	Medium machine gun
MPAJA	Malayan People's Anti-Japanese Army
MRABA	Malayan Races Anti-British Army
MSR	Major Supply Route
MTB	motor torpedo boat
MTT	Military Training Team

NATO	North Atlantic Treaty Organization
NCO	Non-Commissioned Officer
NLF	National Liberation Front (Aden)
NOCS	Nucelo Operativo Centrale di Sicurezza (Italy)
NSWTG	Navy Special Warfare Task Group
NVA	Army of North Vietnam
OC	Officer Commanding
OP	Observation Post
OR	Other Ranks
OSS	Office of Strategic Services
P9S	H&K 9mm pistol
PF	Popular Force (South Vietnam)
PFLP	Popular Front for the Liberation of Palestine
PIRA	Provisional IRA
PLO	Palestine Liberation Organization
POW	prisoner-of-war
PPA	Popski's Private Army (Western Desert)
PSG1	H&K rifle
PSP	People's Socialist Party (Aden)
PT	physical training
QM	Quartermaster
RA	Royal Artillery
RAAF	Royal Australian Air Force
RAF	Royal Air Force
RAPC	Royal Army Pay Corps
RASC	Royal Army Service Corps
RCMP	Royal Canadian Mounted Police
RE	Royal Engineers
REME	Royal Electrical and Mechanical Engineers
REP	Régiment Étranger de Parachutiste (French Foreign Legion)
RM	Royal Marines
ROK	Republic of Korea (South Korea)
RPG	rocket-propelled grenade
RT	Recce Team
RTU	Return to Unit
RUC	Royal Ulster Constabulary

S-1	Administration (US, Vietnam)
S-3	Operations Officer (US, Vietnam)
S&R	Scout and Raider (US)
SAPS	South African Police Service
SAS	Special Air Service
SBS	Special Boat Service
SD	Nazi Security Service
SEAL	Sea, Air, Land special forces
SERT	Special Emergency Response Team
SF	Special Force(s)
SOC	Special Operations Capable unit
SOCCE	Special Operations Command and Control Elements
SOCCENT	Special Operations Command, Central Command
SOCOM	Special Operation (Unified) Command
SOE	Special Operations Executive
SOF	Special Operation/Operating Forces
Spetznaz	Spetzialnoje Naznachenie (Russian SF)
SQMS	squadron quartermaster sergeants
SRS	Special Raiding Squadron
SS	German army units drawn from Nazi party members
SS	Special Service (British)
SWAT	Special Weapons and Tactics (US police)
TL	Team Leader
TLO	Tactical Liaison Operations
UAR	United Arab Republic
UDT	Underwater Demolition Team
UN	United Nations
Unit 101	OSS Far East guerrilla unit
USCENTOM	US Central Command
USMC	US Marine Corps
USS	US Ship
VC	Vietcong
VCP	Vehicle Check/Control Point (Ireland)
Waaf	Women's Auxiliary Air Force
WO	Warrant Officer
Wren	member of WRNS, Women's Naval Service
Z Special Unit	Australian naval SF

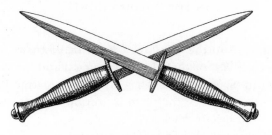

Commando fighting knives

CHAPTER ONE

Special Soldiers, Special Tasks

Are you TOUGH? If so, get out.
I need f—ers with intelligence.

Captain Roger Courteney,
Folboat Section SBS, 1942

S pecial Forces are not new. Those who comb the pages of the Old Testament will find tales which would fit neatly into any account of modern Special Force operations. King David harried the Philistines, conducted night raids and sudden assaults, and sent his men on countless forays behind the enemy lines, and examples of what would now be called Special Force operations can be found in all the histories, from the time of the Vikings to the day before yesterday. The times may have changed but the role of the Special Force soldier has remained surprisingly constant.

In the Middle Ages the Mongol leader Genghis Khan had his 'special forces', bands of irregular horse led by the warlord Yasotay. Yasotay, who was never promoted to the ranks of the Khanate in spite of his scouting skills, knew the value of his work, warning his fearsome lord, 'You do not need more generals but when the hour of crisis comes remember that forty selected men can shake the world,' a sentence that sums up the fundamental attitude of the Special Force soldier: numbers are not everything, and much can be done by having the right soldier in the right place. Every age has produced its special soldier, from the Greek hoplite to the English archer, from the American

Minuteman of 1776 to the US Green Beret of Vietnam and the SAS trooper in the Gulf War of 1991. In the closing decade of the twentieth century, the term 'Special Forces' has taken on a distinctive meaning, but Special Forces, even as the term is commonly understood today, can still trace their origins back over 200 years.

The popular concept of a Special Force soldier is of a tough, crop-haired young man, draped with weapons, clad in an exotic uniform, with paint on his face and a knife between his teeth. Thus garbed for war, he parachutes into the night, abseils down cliffs, or swims ashore through shark-infested seas, a 'one-man wave of destruction', wreaking havoc on his country's enemies. This is the public image of the Special Forces soldier, typified by the cinematic creation *Rambo*. This image bears no resemblance to the truth, is an image that all true Special Force soldiers have come to dislike, an image that this book aims to dispel. As for the 'elite' title, a word often used for Special Force units, all well-trained, well-led and well-disciplined units can claim that distinction. Infantry or cavalry, artillery or logistical, any unit can be an elite, provided they do the job they have to do and do it well. The Brigade of Guards, the German Afrika Corps, General Lee's Army of Northern Virginia in the American Civil War, the Israeli Defence Force and half a hundred other units in a dozen armies over the past century can all justifiably claim to be elite.

Most Special Force soldiers will freely admit that the only 'special' elements in Special Force soldiering are the task that the unit has to do, the training necessary to do it, and the type of man such soldiering attracts. They tend to be the older, more mature professional soldier, rather than the glory-seeker or the badge-draped 'professional hero', whose antics and boasting do true Special Force soldiers nothing but harm. 'I have to say that those of us in the 101st Airborne were not over-impressed with the Green Berets,' says Mike Kelley of Sacramento, California, once a machine-gunner with the 502nd Parachute Infantry Regiment, 101st Airborne Division in Vietnam. 'We heard a lot about how good they were and it may well be true, but I guess they put their pants on one leg at a time, just like everyone else.' John Grebby, who served in the Parachute Regiment, agrees with this viewpoint: 'I was a lance-corporal in the Battalion Orderly Room of 2 Para from 1956 to 1958 and it always struck me that our efficient battalion owed a lot of credit to its supporting arms, the REME vehicle mechanics, ACC cooks, RAPC pay clerks, even REME armourers. We could not have done what we did without them.'

The very term 'Special Forces' can mean different things in different places and it is necessary at the start to divide Special Force units into two forms, Special Forces (SF) and Special Operation or Special Operating Forces (SOF) – though these terms can mean different things in different countries. In Britain, for example, 'Special Forces' can include the Royal Marine Commandos and the Special Boat Service, the Parachute Regiment and the SAS. Historically, it can also include units like the Chindits, who operated in Burma during the Second World War, and has included clandestine organizations like the Second World War Special Operations Executive (SOE), which aided the French Maquis in the fight against the German occupation. These links are relevant, for the Chindits' US equivalent, Merrill's Marauders, form part of the history of the US LRRPs (Long-Range Reconnaissance Patrols) who fought in Vietnam in the 1960s, and the SOE's US counterpart the OSS (Office of Strategic Services) was the forerunner of the US Special Forces, the Green Berets, and so the historic links are forged.

The term 'Special Forces' can also embrace those specially trained units of artillery, engineers and logistical troops who provide the 'teeth' units with the necessary support, and even Royal Marine units like the Commachio Troop, which is charged with guarding Britain's nuclear submarine bases, oil rigs and nuclear power plants and the movement of fissionable material about the UK.

In the United States, the term has a much narrower definition. There it refers only to units designated as 'Special Forces' – or more popularly as 'Green Berets' – and such units as the Navy SEALs (sea, air, land special forces), and the highly secret Delta Force. These units are tasked with reconnaissance and patrolling duties, with small-scale raids, intelligence gathering and escape and evasion, with the training and support of irregular indigenous resistance movements and, in the case of Delta, with hostage rescue.

These definitions are not always clear-cut, and there is a good deal of overlap, but to clarify the position, at least in this book, SF units will include Green Berets, SEALs, SAS, SBS, Delta and similar units, while SOF will cover the USMC, US Ranger and Parachute units, the Royal Marine Commandos, all British Parachute units and all other such units in all other armed forces. These are SOF in that they have a special task, amphibious warfare for the USMC and the Royal Marines, airborne assault for the Parachute units, though they are large enough to play a role in conventional infantry warfare and skilled and fit enough to handle behind-the-lines operations and special tasks. Units like the LRRPs and the US Marine Force Recon and the Arctic and Mountain Warfare Cadre of the Royal Marines are also SOF, in that they are raised from, and used by, their parent units for particular purposes and are not entirely separate formations.

The units referred to in this book are all either SF or SOF and the aim is not only to tell the story of Special Forces since 1945 but to explain, largely in the words of the soldiers themselves, exactly why Special Force soldiers are 'special'.

The Special Force soldier – SF or SOF – is defined by his role and his training. He is a soldier who tends to operate cin small groups, often at night, behind the lines or in the amphibious or parachute assault role. He uses technology appropriate to the task in hand, from the rifled musket of the eighteenth and early nineteenth centuries to the parachute, submarine or attack helicopter of today. He is highly skilled in the necessary military techniques, though his training is mainly directed towards irregular warfare, reconnaissance and raiding operations. He may be a Marine, a paratrooper, a Ranger, a trooper in the Special Air Service Regiment, an LRRP, an SBS frogman or a member of the US Navy SEALs. He may be German, Australian, Argentinian, Italian, Israeli, British or American, or a Foreign Legionnaire.

The nation, unit or title hardly matters: the special force soldier is defined by his role. There is, however, one element that links any Special Force soldier with all other Special Force soldiers, past or present, domestic or foreign: the Special Force soldier is, first and foremost, a well-trained fighting man.

'We only had lunatics in the Commandos really,' recalled Brigadier Peter Young, DSO, MC and Bar, of No. 3 Commando, one of the elite infantry units of the Second World War. 'I don't really mean that, but some of them were fiends, just aching for a fight. I can name half a dozen from the early days, who were always thirsting for action – Algy Forrester, Denis O'Flaharty to name but two, both killed later and superb leaders, and of course the soldiers will follow officers like that. In the Commandos I had the company of men who hated peacetime ... they thought peacetime was too bloody dull, and it is dull, believe me.

'So what makes a good Commando soldier? Well, a restless nature ... no, all sorts, we had all sorts. You had to know them, and play on their natures, tweaking them into action. I was cut off for a week, behind the German lines in Italy, with just four soldiers and they looked after me so well ... you know? They'd get their shot in first, relieve you of all fear of surprise or ambush. I was always lucky and I didn't get a lot of soldiers damaged and the young sods liked that ... they stick with you if you are lucky. You also have to be on the lookout for good people. A Commando is like a good club and you have to keep up the membership. I remember an infantry battalion coming into Termoli, just as it was getting hectic, with the Germans pushing us back into the town, and there was a young sergeant in the first platoon, with the MM [Military Medal] on his chest and the light of battle in his eye; I remember him and it is years ago ... I'd have had him in 3 Commando if the time had been right ... but I expect he bought it. Good people die quickly in war, you know.

'Training? Well, you have to breed them into a state of alertness, always on their toes. Otherwise you are no bloody use to me, as officer, sergeant or private soldier – and I'll break your back if you have a slack attitude. I looked for a man who could soldier, that's all ... and that's a lot. How do you pick them? Well, you look at them, talk to them, don't you? Make up your mind if he is a bullshitter or has something to offer – you can usually tell. I was wrong sometimes but not often. Young soldiers are good; they will follow you into the fire out of innocence. A good old soldier is a good soldier ... but a bad old soldier is worse than useless.'

Another, equally personal view comes from General Sir Peter de la Billière, an SAS soldier who served in Malaya and the Oman before commanding the British troops in the Gulf War of 1990–1: 'The only reason I joined the Army in the first place was to go on operations and I spent most of my life looking for trouble spots. Fortunately for me, I always managed to find unrest somewhere in the world...'

Lieutenant-Colonel Euan Southby Tailyour, Royal Marines, an experienced Commando officer, who served in the Army of the Sultan of the Oman and in the Falklands War, has another view on the necessary qualities for a Commando soldier: 'Leadership, individuality and eccentricity are the keys; you have to avoid being predictable. When I was in the Oman I discovered that the Arabs liked eccentrics, and getting them to follow you is the trick. If you were dull or dour not only would they not follow you, they would either mutiny or more probably kill you. Marines are not crash-bash soldiers; Marines, well, Royal Marines anyway, are trained to sit down and think through a crisis, not go on beating their heads against the opposition's brick wall. Had a Commando unit fought the action at Goose Green in the Falklands, victory would probably have taken longer but it would have been equally successful and we would have taken fewer casualties. We go on raids in much the same way – four or five men slip ashore from a frigate, take out a radar station or whatever, kill a few people in exotic and silent ways, and fade away back to sea. It takes training, yes, but you need the right men to begin with.'

A Special Force soldier is a man on the lookout for adventure. He is usually a volunteer, accepting a harsh selection and training process and a higher-than-average chance of death or injury in the field, for the chance to serve in a unit that offers him opportunities for front-line soldiering. Volunteering is one of the first actions of a Special Force soldier today, but historically not all SF soldiers have been volunteers.

The majority of the Royal Marine Commando units in the Second World War and a large number of British parachute and glider battalions were regular Army or Royal Marine battalions transferred to the parachute or Commando role. The subsequent training soon weeded out the sick, lame, lazy or unwilling, and there is little evidence that such units had an inferior battlefield performance to the all-volunteer units. The USMC had to abandon its traditional insistence on regular volunteers during the Vietnam War and soon found that the draftees – conscripts – were every bit as good and just as tough as the regular enlisted Marines. A large number of men who served in Vietnam parachute units like the 101st Airborne were not even parachute-trained, but they knew how to soldier.

It will already be apparent that the true Special Force soldier has little in common with the fictional *Rambo* version of the Commando, Ranger, SEAL or Green Beret. A Special Force soldier needs certain personal qualities: a sense of humour, tenacity, intelligence and guts – this last not least to endure the training and subsequent discomforts. He must be fit, but fitness alone will not be enough if a willingness to keep going, though tired, wet and heavily laden, is not there. He must have maturity and common sense, be able to live and fight with others in small groups but be equally content to work on his own. He must possess all the relevant military skills to a high degree of expertise, but these can be taught. The personal qualities must be there to begin with, though they will be enhanced by training.

Volunteers for Special Force soldiering come from all kinds of other units. Few SF units recruit directly, though many SOF units do. The British SAS Regiment tends to receive a great many volunteers from the Parachute Regiment, and when the US Ranger Companies were reformed for Korea in 1950 they obtained many volunteers from the 82nd Airborne Division. But soldiers from the service and technical arms are always well represented in Special Force units. This is one reason why SAS training includes a complete infantry training course, to bring successful volunteers from the technical arms up to the required standard in infantry weapons and tactics. Lieutenant-Colonel

Durnford Slater, who formed No. 3 Commando, the first British Commando unit in 1940, and Colonel William Derby, who formed the first US Ranger battalion in 1942, were both artillery officers and had to learn infantry tactics as they went along.

Special tasks do not in themselves make a special unit, or create a need for a specially trained soldier. To clarify the term we have to go back at least as far as the eighteenth century, when Special Forces first made a major impact on the military scene. This will also reveal that before you can have 'special soldiers' you must first have regular soldiers, a fact that was not lost on Colonel Charlie Beckwith, the founder and first commander of the modern US anti-terrorist unit, the Delta Force: 'I had to articulate that before a soldier could become a good unconventional soldier he'd first have to be a good conventional soldier. He had to understand what a rifle squad was all about, what a platoon could do, what a rifle company needed to know. To break the rules you have to know what the rules are. You can't be unconventional until you are conventional first.'

To find regular conventional soldiers, in the recognizable modern pattern, it is necessary to go back to the New Model Army formed by Oliver Cromwell in the 1640s, during the English Civil War, a force which laid down that foundation of sound training, specialization and harsh discipline which provided the bedrock for later European armies. Many modern armies still contain regiments founded in those distant days, and this includes the three British Royal Marines Commandos, which can trace their origins through that of their parent Corps to the Duke of York and Albany's Maritime Regiment of Foot, formed in 1664 from the Trained Bands of the City of London. This Regiment began with a special task defined in its Mustering Order, which called for '1,200 soljers to serve in His Maj's Fleet and equipped for sea service'. The mighty cousin of the Royal Marines, the United States Marine Corps, mother of Force Recon, the USMC Special Force unit, was founded in a public house, the Tub Tavern, in Philadelphia on 10 November 1775, and the US Marines have been the elite troops of the Republic ever since.

In the eighteenth century, armies gradually became more professional, more rigidly disciplined, more 'conventional', and were slowly standardized into three main arms – cavalry, infantry and artillery. Battles between regular armies became a set routine: the opening blast of artillery, the advance of the infantry into musket range, the murderous exchange of volleys at ranges of 200 yards or less, the bayonet charge and the pursuit by cavalry. Victory in these battles went to that side which could best train and discipline its soldiers to endure the blast of close-range musketry and artillery.

However, a force that used sensible tactics, like concealment and skirmishing, could cut a regular army to pieces, a fact first demonstrated in North America by a force of French irregulars and Indian warriors at Fort Duquesne – the present Pittsburgh – in 1755, during the French and Indian Wars, the North American phase of the Seven Years War. The British Commander at this débâcle was General Edward Braddock, an officer of the Coldstream Guards, a soldier described by Benjamin Franklin as 'a brave man, who might have made a good figure in some European War. But he had too much self-confidence, too high an opinion of the value of regular troops; too mean a one of both Americans and Indians.'

Braddock's task was to take Fort Duquesne as part of a concerted effort to drive the French back into Canada. For this task he had a force of some 1,500 men, made up of two battalions of British Redcoats recently arrived from England and a number of colonial militia; one of the young officers serving in this militia was George Washington. Braddock's little army advanced through the woods towards Fort Duquesne and had crossed the ford on the Monongahela river, some miles from the fort, when it was attacked by a strong force of Indians, French soldiers from the Duquesne garrison and French-Canadian woodsmen, about 900 men in all.

Braddock was not ambushed. He had scouts and he used them well, sending them ahead to check out the route as his axemen chopped a path through the forest for his cannon and the infantry column. What defeated Braddock was a fresh form of tactics, the skirmishing fire of skilled marksmen. Those marksmen, using cover and rifled muskets, cut Braddock's force to pieces. The first intimation of attack came when the advance guard saw an Indian wearing a French officer's gorget running towards them through the woods. Behind that man, actually a French officer in Indian garb, came scores, then hundreds, of painted warriors. On sighting the British advance guard the Indians spread out and opened a sharp fire on the Redcoats from the cover of the trees. The Redcoat column, following established European tactics, wheeled into line and commenced firing volleys, the men cheering and crying 'God Save the King!'

Many of the French and Canadians fled before these volleys, but the Indians, armed with muskets, hatchets and knives, swarmed around the flanks of the column, firing into the Redcoat line, rushing out under cover of the thick smoke produced by musket fire to stab and hack at any soldier left wounded or alone. Within minutes the British position began to crumble as the soldiers came under fire from an enemy they could not even see. 'We would have fought', said one of the surviving soldiers, 'if we had seen anyone to fight with.' A few of the Redcoats broke ranks and attempted to take cover behind trees, but General Braddock, dismounting from his horse, drove them back into line with the flat of his sword. The artillery opened fire, 'doing great damage to the trees and none at all to the enemy', according to Francis Parkman, until the gunners were shot down. The infantry stood in confused groups, firing into the trees or into the air, sometimes into their own comrades, until the path and the edges of the forest were carpeted with dead bodies and wounded men.

Four horses were shot from under General Braddock as he rode about in the confusion and finally an Indian sniper marked him down and put a ball into his body. Of the eighty-six officers in the British and American line that day, sixty-three were killed. Out of 1,373 NCOs and private soldiers who went into action, only 459 survived. The rest were killed with the musket or the hatchet or taken back to Fort Duquesne to be tortured and burned in the Indian fires. French and Indian losses totalled fewer than fifty men.

The lesson of Braddock's defeat on the Monongahela, on 9 July 1755, that it was stupid to stand in the open attempting to engage men in cover, was not learned. British armies continued to stand in rank and to be shot down by hidden foes for another hundred years. However, if the lessons of the Monongahela were not appreciated in the European armies, they were absorbed in North America and used with telling effect against the British during the American War of Independence.

One man who made good use of Indian tactics in the French and Indian War and in the War of Independence was Major Robert Rogers, a man regarded in America as the 'Father of Special Forces'. Rogers has a good claim to that title and he left a mark on the history of irregular warfare that endures to this day. Born in Metheun, Massachusetts, on 7 November 1731, he was only twenty-four when, in September 1756, he arrived at Ticonderoga in command of a band of New England scouts, bringing with him three Canadian prisoners and a great deal of useful information.

Rogers was described as 'a strong, well-knit figure, in dress and appearance more woodsman than soldier, with a clear bold eye and an ungainly nose'. Before the outbreak of war he had earned a precarious living as a smuggler, trading across the Canadian border, and that had taught him a great deal of cunning and considerable skill in woodcraft. Rogers' information turned out to be accurate and the British commanders at Ticonderoga naturally wanted more of it. Within months, raised to the rank of major, Rogers had nine 'scouting companies' under his command, the men armed with hatchets and muskets and clad in buckskins, not in the scarlet uniforms of the line battalions. This scouting force needed a name and since they were always ranging ahead of the regular forces they become known as Rogers' Rangers.

James E. Butler, of Carmel, California, who served ten years with Special Forces in Vietnam and who will appear again in this book, can trace his family history back to the American Revolution, when two of his ancestors served with the Rangers: 'My family is one of the oldest English families in America. They came over on the *Mayflower* and fought for the Massachusetts Bay Colony in the Narragansett Indian Wars. I am descended from Mildred Files Walton and the Butlers, two families that epitomized early unconventional warfare in America, though the families hated each other.

'Walter Butler, Captain of Rangers, was born in 1753 and grew up with the Iroquois Indians. He was a Royalist in the War of Independence and led many expeditions against the Rebels and was hated by all. He saved the life of and later married Abigail Cilley and they had a son, John. Walter never saw his son for he [Walter] was run down, killed and scalped by American Rangers in April 1777. John's son, William, was a privateer in the War of 1812, and died of yellow fever while serving with Simon Bolivar in South America.

'William Files was born in England in 1728. He went to America, joined the English Army and ended up in Rogers' Rangers. He was at the fall of Fort William Henry in the French and Indian War, where he was taken prisoner by the Indians, but later overpowered his captors and escaped. He fought in the Revolution, against his old Commander, Major Rogers, who was leading raids into Maine from Canada, and as late as 1812, aged eighty-two, he shot a "Lobsterback" [a British Redcoat] when the British fleet attacked his home town of Falmouth near Portland, Maine, and burned it to the ground.'

In 1759, Major Rogers drew up a List of Instructions for his Ranger Companies, and this List, virtually unchanged, is displayed in US Ranger barracks to this day:

1. Don't forget nothing.
2. Have your musket as clean as a whistle, hatchet scoured and sharp, sixty rounds of ball ready. Be ready to move at a minute's warning.

3. When on the march, act as if you are hunting a deer. Get your shot in first.
4. Tell the truth on what you see and do. The Army depends on us for information. Never lie to a Ranger officer.
5. Don't take any chance you don't have to.
6. When on the march go single file, far enough apart that one shot won't kill two men.
7. On soft ground, spread out so it's hard to track us.
8. When we march we keep moving until dark, so the enemy can't get at us.
9. When we camp, half sleep while the other half watch.
10. Don't ever march home the same way; take a different route to avoid ambush.
11. In big parties or little ones, keep a scout twenty yards ahead or behind and to either flank, so we won't be surprised.
12. Every night you will be told what to do if attacked by a superior force.
13. Don't sit down to eat without posting sentries.
14. Don't sleep beyond dawn; that's when the enemy likes to attack.
15. Don't cross rivers by the regular ford.
16. Ambush the folks that are trying to ambush you.
17. Don't stand when the enemy is coming against you; kneel down, lie down, get behind a tree.
18. Let the enemy come close, close enough to touch. Then let him have it and finish him off with your hatchet.

Practically every method and tactic used by Rogers' Rangers in that long-ago Indian war in the woods of North America was used by the American LRRPs and the USMC Force Recon in the jungles of South Vietnam more than 200 years later.

After the Seven Years War Rogers got into financial difficulties and had to flee to England. He returned to America on the outbreak of the War of Independence, but George Washington refused to employ him and he eventually joined the British forces and became colonel in a Loyalist force called the Queen's Rangers. This service brought him no particular distinction and when the War ended, unable to settle in the United States, he returned to England, got into debt again and died in a debtors' prison in 1795.

The British were not entirely unaware that the forest wars in North America called for fresh tactics. King George III was also the Elector of Hanover and a large number of German troops were recruited from his Continental domains to fight for the Elector in America. This 20,000-strong force – 'Hessians' to the colonials – contained 260 *Jägers*, men who normally worked as gamekeepers or foresters on the Elector's estates. Excellent shots and trained woodsmen, these *Jägers* did so well that a further 2,000 were recruited from the other German principalities and sent to fight in North America.

A good example of amphibious warfare also comes from this period, in General James Wolfe's campaign along the St Lawrence in 1759, which culminated in a night landing and a dawn victory over the French on the Plains of Abraham outside Quebec. This was an example of early Army–Royal Navy co-operation, but the first attempt at an organized, properly equipped and trained amphibious raiding force on modern lines may be found in the British brigade formed by Colonel Eliot, later Lord Heathfleld, in 1758. This was a cavalry force mustered to work with the Royal Navy in making raids on the French coast. This they did with some success, destroying shipping and shore facilities in Cherbourg and St Servan by St Malo in Brittany, as well as riding inland to attack other towns. The significant fact about this force is that it experimented in Portsmouth Harbour with various types of landing craft, some designed to carry troops and horses and put them ashore without the need for ports or quays.

Some lessons were learned from these irregular wars in North America, not perhaps in the field of tactics, but certainly in the need to train soldiers to fight as thinking individuals, able to take care of themselves and kill the enemy at little cost to themselves. In Britain, the leading figure in the move to improve infantry training was Lieutenant-General Sir John Moore, a soldier of the Light Infantry. Moore entered the British Army in 1777 at the age of fifteen. By the time he was forty he had reached the rank of lieutenant-general, and was regarded as a thinking soldier by Prime Minister Pitt and by the head of the British Army, the Duke of York. But he was a fighting soldier as well as a thinking one. He had seen service against the French in Egypt and the Baltic, collecting five wounds and a great deal of practical experience in the process.

Moore is remembered by the British public as the tragic hero of the Retreat to Coruña. In the British Army he is best known as the 'Father of the Light Infantry', but he was much more than that. He altered the very nature of the British Army, changing it on from a brutish, sullen force, ruled by the lash, into that well-balanced fighting machine that thrashed the French in battle after battle of the Peninsular War, and he did it by example and by the force of his personality. He believed in the well-trained, well-led, alert, enthusiastic soldier. He believed that such a man, if told what to do, and trained how to do it, could and should be trusted to get on with it. He insisted that respect had to be earned and did not come with rank, that the most effective form of discipline was self-discipline, that soldiers should be encouraged to show initiative, that praise and kindness was more effective than blind obedience enforced with the fear of punishment.

In 1803 the Duke of York told Moore to open a camp at Shornecliffe in Kent and put his revolutionary theories into effect in a unit known as the Experimental Rifle Corps. Moore's philosophy was backed with intensive training in drill, marksmanship and in those skirmishing tactics practised by the American woodsman. The results were little short of miraculous, not least in terms of discipline and morale. In the Light Division, desertion was unheard of and punishment rare. Those battalions of the Light Infantry, the 95th, 43rd and 52nd Foot, which passed through Shornecliffe and became rifle regiments, were soon noted as among the most efficient in the Army and were composed of formidable soldiers.

In July 1809, after Moore had been killed and when Sir Arthur Wellesley, later Duke of Wellington, was in command of the British Army, the Light Division, fully armed and equipped for battle, marched forty miles in twenty-four hours, on unmade roads and in the full heat of the Spanish summer, to join the rest of the Army at Talavera; not one man fell out. When the Light Division held the fords of the River Coa on the Portuguese border, Wellington could sleep undisturbed, for no enemy force could move without being spotted by these green-clad soldiers. The example they set spread throughout the Army, and the Light Infantry methods and tactics were widely adopted, as Special Force tactics are today. In the 1960s, the US Army sent officers and men from 'heavy' infantry units through the US Ranger School because the lessons they learned there were useful to the Army as a whole, just as the training and example of Moore's men had inspired the British Army 150 years before.

It is tempting to infer from this that irregular forces are invariably successful and can fight and win battles, however long the odds. That claim has been made by Special Force members and their numerous admirers from time to time, but it is not true. Special Forces have their limitations. Irregular forces can win skirmishes and influence campaigns, but they are most useful when their skills are combined with the operations of efficient, regular forces. Used like that they can help to win wars, a fact that can be illustrated by another example from the early history of irregular warfare.

During the Napoleonic Wars, General Wellesley took Britain's only field army out of Portugal to fight the French in Spain. Wellesley found that his allies, the Spanish Regular Army, could achieve very little in open battle against the French, but that the rugged terrain of the Spanish peninsula, 'where small armies are defeated and large armies starve', proved ideally suited to the activities of the Spanish guerrillas. It is from the Spanish word *guerrilla* – or 'little war' – that generations of irregular soldiers took their name. Wellesley did not have enough regular soldiers to engage the French in full-scale campaigns, but he used his army and the Spanish *guerrilleros* in combination, until he was strong enough to take the field and fight conventional campaigns.

The French had an overwhelming number of troops in the Peninsula, quite enough either to smash Wellesley's small army of Redcoats or stamp out the scourge of the Spanish guerrillas, had they been able to devote all of them entirely to either task. Unfortunately for the Emperor Napoleon, the French had to do both, and the effort was beyond their military capability. To muster sufficient forces to crush General Wellesley's small but highly trained army, the French commanders had to deplete their garrisons and guard posts. As soon as they did so, the Spanish guerrillas descended from the hilltops to overwhelm their positions, wipe out their patrols and kill their couriers. Equally, when the much harassed French dispersed their forces and turned to campaign against the guerrilla bands, Wellesley came marching out of Portugal, laid siege to frontier cities in French hands and defeated those smaller armies the French could put in the field.

Much the same tale can be told of the 1812 Retreat from Moscow, when the Cossacks harried the retreating French Army, cutting off stragglers, allowing the survivors no rest. A combination of Cossacks and terrible weather did more damage to Napoleon's Grande Armée than all the Russian regular soldiers put together. This combination of guerrilla and regular forces shattered the Grande Armée, and was to prove equally effective in many other wars thereafter.

So, slowly, in the early decades of the nineteenth century the word spread that light troops – of the kind that would now be known as Special Forces – operating in small parties, using cover carefully to approach the enemy lines, could play a significant role in battle and in the conduct of campaigns. But it also became clear that such troops had to be of high quality, well trained and well led, if they were to be fully effective. During the greater part of the nineteenth century, many wars took place on the frontiers of the expanding European empires, in India or Africa, or in the islands of the Far East, where skirmishing tactics were constantly employed, not least by the local fighting men who had no wish to be colonized. From these campaigns, the regular, Western armies learned painful but useful lessons, among them the need to work with local forces and recruit local fighting men. The French fought Arabs in the Moroccan Riff, and pirates in the swamps and creeks of Indo-China. The British found themselves fighting wars with the Afghans or hotly engaged by the Pathan tribesmen on the North-West Frontier of India. The US Army fought for decades against the Indian tribes on the plains and mountains of the Far West. All these armies found that one good way to defeat adversaries skilled in irregular warfare was to recruit native tribesmen into their armies and send them out to scout or fight against their own people.

This tactic has proved relevant in the present century. A British officer, Major Frank Kitson, another Light Infantryman, used 'pseudo-gangs' of loyal Africans and European settlers in heavy disguise, in the fight against Mau Mau terrorists in Kenya in the 1950s. The British recruited former headhunters, Iban trackers from Borneo, to hunt Communist bandits during the Malayan Emergency of 1950–60, besides 'turning' many captured Chinese terrorists to fight against their old Communist comrades in the jungle. After the Malayan Emergency ended, the British were soon raising the Border Scouts in Borneo, local tribesmen who were trained and equipped by SAS 'advisers', and used to guard the frontiers of Borneo during the 1960s 'Confrontation' with Indonesia. In Vietnam, the US Special Forces, the Green Berets, made equally good use of Montegnard tribesmen mustered into CIDG (Civilian Irregular Defense Groups) in the fight against the Vietcong, and recruited North Vietnamese deserters, the so-called Kit Carson Scouts, to lead patrols against their former comrades.

It will be seen from this chronicle that in Special Force soldiering only the technology changes, and those who are already familiar with modern Special Force operations will have noted many historic parallels. The problems, and the solutions, remain much the same down the centuries, for Special Force soldiering is soldiering at its most basic and is very dependent on the skills and intelligence of the man at the front.

As technology developed and was increasingly employed in military operations, so the opportunities for special operations increased, for technology, though useful, is also vulnerable, a fact borne out more than a century ago by the raids on enemy bases, factories and railway lines by regular and irregular cavalry during the American Civil War of 1861–5. Among the most famous of these was Grierson's Raid, the deep cavalry sortie behind the Confederate lines conducted by Colonel Grierson, later commander of the all-black 10th Cavalry. Grierson took two cavalry regiments well into Confederate territory and destroyed the railway line supplying the Southern armies, before leading his much depleted force out through the Confederate lines to Baton Rouge. Large armies needed a great deal of logistical support even in the last century, and their supply bases and lines of communication are often open to attack by irregular units. Raids led by cunning guerrilla fighters like Mosby and Quantrill in Virginia and Kansas played a significant part in the Confederate South's ability to fight on against larger and better equipped Union forces.

Another example of successful guerrilla warfare comes from the early years of the present century, during the South African War of 1899–1902. After some initial successes, when the Boer Commandos – units of irregular horse – shot down the British infantry in quantity, the Boer irregulars found themselves unable to defeat the ever-increasing power of the British Army in regular engagements. The indomitable Boers therefore went 'on Commando', taking with them nothing but horses and rifles and a knowledge of how to live off the land. Thus equipped, they were able to keep up the war against the full might of the British Empire for another three years. In 1940, the British Prime Minister, Winston Churchill, who had been captured in South Africa when a Boer Commando wrecked a British armoured train, elected to call the British raiding forces 'Commandos' out of respect for the doughty opponents of his youth.

These wars offered a constant reminder that Special Forces and special tactics can prove decisive, but there is no evidence that this point was taken seriously by the military establishment. Even the longest-running form of Special Operations, amphibious warfare, went on for centuries without any noticeable improvements in equipment, training or techniques. The soldiers or Marines tasked with an amphibious assault went ashore in rowing boats and gigs pulled by the sailors and got what support they could from naval gunfire. The obvious fact that amphibious operations are always complicated, often hazardous and therefore worthy of special attention never seems to have occurred to the powers-that-be at all.

The Great War of 1914–18 provides two outstanding examples, one disastrous, one successful, of amphibious operations. The first was the landings at Gallipoli in the Turkish Dardanelles on 25 April 1915. The

British, French, Australian and New Zealand forces got ashore but the advantage of surprise – the most useful military asset – had already been lost. The invaders met with firm resistance and were soon checked and penned up in narrow bridgeheads, where they remained, at a great cost in lives. This landing force maintained itself ashore until the end of the year but made no progress inland before being withdrawn under cover of night on 8/9 January 1916. Nothing of significance was achieved at Gallipoli and the losses were considerable: 30,000 troops were killed, 74,000 wounded, 8,000 missing or taken prisoner. Winston Churchill, then First Lord of the Admiralty, the man who had thought of this operation as a way of outflanking the stalemate on the Western Front, was forced to resign, and from then on the British military establishment became very wary indeed of amphibious operations. Fortunately, the next amphibious operation, if much smaller in scale, was more successful in execution.

On St George's Day, 23 April 1917, a force of Royal Marines drawn from the 4th Battalion of the Corps carried out a raid on the Belgian port of Zeebrugge. Zeebrugge was a major German submarine base, and the task of the Royal Marines was to block the main channel of the harbour and destroy the port facilities. The raid was carried out with great *élan*, the Marines going ashore on the mole from two converted ferries; by the time they left, the harbour was completely blocked and the Corps had earned two Victoria Crosses.

Special operations did not flourish on the Western Front, where the network of defences running from the North Sea to the frontier of neutral Switzerland proved hard to pierce and impossible to outflank. The British and French failed to penetrate the German lines for any distance in three and a half years of frontal assaults, but in the March Offensive of 1918 the German Army did succeed in breaking the Allied line by using 'stormtroops', well-trained infantrymen who infiltrated into the Allied lines.

The use of stormtroops, plus incessant and costly trench raids, was about the limit of infantry tactics on the Western Front but mobile warfare and action 'behind the lines' was common in the Middle East, where another British officer, later known as Lawrence of Arabia, raised and equipped a force of Bedouin tribesmen, captured the port of Aqaba by assault, destroyed trains and overran Turkish outposts around Damascus, working with regular infantry and cavalry forces under General Sir Edmund Allenby to defeat the Turkish armies and bring about the downfall of the Turkish Empire.

This short survey of Special Force history has carried the story swiftly from the actions of King David against the Philistines to a coastal raid in the closing years of the Great War. That war ended on 11 November 1918, and for the next twenty years most of the world's military forces – except those of Nazi Germany – quietly stagnated. Given 2,000 years of history and countless examples of all that an amphibious strategy could achieve, or, as at Gallipoli, what disasters it could cause, it is surprising that Britain's military establishment still saw no need to raise a properly trained and equipped amphibious force. Since 1664 Great Britain had, at least in theory, maintained a force designed for small coastal raids and amphibious assaults, the Corps of Royal Marines, but the duties of the Corps had become more naval than amphibious, their opportunities for shore training were limited and their continued existence was often in doubt. In 1922 the functions of the Corps were defined by the Admiralty as 'to provide in manning their share of the main armament, and to be trained to provide a striking force ... for amphibious operations, such as raids on the enemy coastline, or for the seizure and defence of bases for the use of our own Fleet'. No steps were taken to train or equip the Corps properly for any of these designated tasks, although the problems of assault landings had been outlined by a joint Army–Navy Committee as far back as 1913. The Committee's findings had been published in *A Handbook of Combined Operations*, which laid out the problems of amphibious warfare very clearly, not least in the areas of training and the provision of suitable craft. But nothing was done to tackle the problems, provide the necessary craft or train the men. The modern form of Special Forces had not yet been thought of; the big military argument in the inter-war years centred on that controversial invention, the tank.

As a result, when the Second World War broke out in 1939, Britain was woefully unprepared for 'Combined Operations'. One of the most obvious shortcomings was in landing craft. In 1930, the Royal Navy, then the largest maritime force in the world, had exactly three prototype landing craft in service. The best of these had a top speed of five knots and drew four feet of water. In the next ten years, the number of landing craft available expanded to six, none of which was of a noticeably better design. The United States Navy had no landing craft at all in 1930, though nine years later it was experimenting with a small troop-carrying craft known, from the name of its designer, as a Higgins boat.

When war broke out on 3 September 1939, the British Expeditionary Force departed for France, as its predecessor had in 1914, and with the BEF already established on the Continent, there was thought to be no need for an amphibious or a 'Combined Operations' capability. Nine months later came Dunkirk, and it would be four long years before the British Army returned to France. In that time a large Special Forces and Combined Operations organization was developed and flourished among all the Allied nations, one brought into existence by sheer necessity rather than deliberate calculation.

Special Forces have a long, colourful and distinguished history. This chapter has taken the story forward some 200 years, from Rogers' Rangers fighting the French and Indians in the 1750s and 1760s to the opening days of the Second World War in Western Europe. Some of the units created during that time survive to the present day but all modern Special Force units can trace at least part of their *esprit de corps*, their training techniques and their skills in combat to the campaigns listed in these opening pages.

Combined Operation badge

CHAPTER TWO

The Nursery of Special Forces
1940–1945

I have a young son and I tell him, stay away from
war. The pay is lousy, the hours are long, and it
can get you killed.

Robert L. Sales, 29th Ranger Battalion, 29th
Infantry Division, United States Army, 1944

The Second World War was the nursery of the modern Special
Forces. That war spawned scores of SF units, but this chapter
will be largely devoted to those which were the forerunners of
post-1945 Special Forces, or played a significant part in creating the SF
role and character. This still represents a considerable number of units
and covers a varied range of tasks.

The reasons for the rapid development of Special Forces in the Second
World War are obvious. It was a world war, fought on land, sea and air,
in every kind of terrain, from Arctic tundra to desert, from European
coastal waters to the jungles of the Far East. This variety of terrain, the
growing size and complexity of armies and the increasing use of military technology gave increasing scope for Special Force units.
The Second World War was fought, with certain exceptions in the
South Pacific and Burma, by large, mechanized armies, which needed

bases and a long logistical train, a supply route vulnerable to attack by raiding forces. Technical developments – troop-carrying aircraft, gliders, parachutes – also provided the means by which Special Forces could get into the battle and deliver a blow behind the enemy lines.

The use of gliders by the German airborne forces who captured the Dutch fort at Eban Emael in 1940 and the *coup de main* by which major John Howard's glider-borne soldiers took the Caen canal and Orne river bridges on D-Day 1944 are just two examples of new military technology used in the attack role by Special Service troops. Though the list is endless, the use of aircraft and gliders, of landing craft, submarines, of handy all-terrain vehicles like the Willy's jeep, added to existing methods of transport like the canoe and the small boat. All increased the scope of Special Force operations, and led to the creation of SF units which could exploit these inventions and technologies. Many of these units were created or recruited from conventional military forces.

They included the British Army and Royal Marine Commandos, the American Army Rangers, the parachute forces of Germany, Britain, Canada and the United States, the USMC Raider battalions, the Special Air Service Regiment, which contained French and Belgian elements as well as British troops, jungle intruder units like the British Chindits of Orde Wingate, and, in the US Army, Merrill's Marauders. In addition there were units such as the Long-Range Desert Group (LRDG) of North Africa, the clandestine Special Operations Executive (SOE), which operated in Western Europe and the Balkans, Force 136, an SOE guerrilla unit that fought in the Far East, the OSS, the American equivalent of SOE, and Unit 101, the OSS equivalent of Force 136. Britain took the lead in creating many of these units, but the United States was never far behind.

If a new problem was discovered, new units were often created to deal with it. When amphibious landings were contemplated, swimmers and canoe parties from the American UDT (Underwater Demolition Teams) and the British COPP (Combined Operation Pilotage Parties), which specialized in breach reconnaissance and obstacle clearance, were sent in first to assess and then to remove the beach defences. When enemy blockade runners could not be attacked by conventional means, they became targets for Special Force attacks. Three famous units formed for this task were the Special Boat Squadron, the Special Raiding Squadron, which operated in the Aegean, and the Royal Marine Boom Patrol, forerunner of the modern SBS, which sent a dozen canoeists to paddle up the Gironde river and sink German ships in Bordeaux harbour.

Parachute units were used for the first time in the Second World War and took part in various actions which established the reputation of the parachute soldier as a superb fighting man, a reputation that endures to this day. 'What you get by stealth and guts,' General Gale told the British 6th Airborne Division before D-Day, 'you must hold with skill and determination,' and parachute soldiers of every nation still abide by that instruction. German parachute troops fought with distinction in Crete; British, Canadian and American Airborne soldiers seized the flanks of the invasion front in Normandy, and spearheaded the Rhine Crossing; the US Airborne fought with great gallantry at Bastogne. But a lasting example of what parachute soldiers can do was provided by the British 1st Airborne Division at the Battle of Arnhem in September 1944, a battle which remains the definitive parachute action.

Ordered to land by parachute and glider, take the Arnhem Bridge and hold it for two days until the Second Army could reach them, 1st Airborne said they could hold it for four. In the end they held it for nine days, fighting off everything the German Army could hurl against them.

Seven days into the Battle of Arnhem, Major Dickie Lonsdale of the Parachute Regiment assembled the remnants of the 1st and 3rd Battalions in the church at Oosterbeek. These were haggard men, many of them wounded, all weary from days without sleep; 'not in their Sunday best', says Lonsdale, 'but still defiant, still unbroken'. Lonsdale climbed into the minister's pulpit, told them that this was a fight to the last man and the last round and finished with some words the Parachute Regiment would remember: 'This is by no means the first time we have fought the Germans. We fought the cream of their Army in North Africa, in Sicily and in Italy. We defeated them in those campaigns and now we are up against them again here. Well, they were not good enough for us then – and they are bloody well not good enough for us now. In one hour's time you will take up defensive positions on the Oosterbeek–Arnhem road. Make certain you are well dug in. Make certain your weapons and ammunition are in good order. We are getting short of ammunition, so conserve it and, when you shoot, shoot to kill ... and good luck to you all.'

The history of Special Force warfare is composed of deeds performed by men commanded by officers like Dickie Lonsdale, men who wrote a fresh chapter in the history of their regiments and laid down many of the traditions that have inspired SF soldiers to the present day, sometimes by a simple statement of that essential but elusive military quality, unit pride. This quality is often created by the ability to survive hard training. Anders Lassen, the fighting Dane of the Special Boat Service in the Aegean, who won a posthumous VC at Lake Commachio in Italy in 1945, explained his Commando training methods to a regular Army general. 'The men march and when they can march no more, we march further ... and when we have marched further, we march again.'

Men like Lonsdale and Lassen are part of the Special Force tradition. Another such man was Tom Durrant, a sergeant with No. 1 Commando who took part in the St Nazaire Raid of March 1942. Sergeant Durrant was on a motor launch, ML 306, one of the few still afloat after the raid had destroyed the large repair dock in St Nazaire harbour. ML 306 was well out into the Loire estuary and heading home when it met a group of three German destroyers heading upriver. The last destroyer detected the ML and illuminated it by searchlight. The launch and the destroyer both opened fire, the destroyer with her main armament and heavy machine-guns, the troops on the ML with rifles, Tommy guns and the launch's twin Lewis machine-gun, which was manned by Sergeant Durrant.

Circling each other in the grey dawn, this unequal battle went on until twenty of the twenty-eight men on the ML were dead or seriously wounded. Sergeant Durrant, who was himself gravely wounded, was standing alone on the open deck of the launch, engaging the destroyer as she closed in for the kill, sending one final burst into the German bridge. At this the destroyer pulled back, raking the ML again with shell and machine-gun fire. Durrant continued to reply with the Lewis until he died of his wounds. Only then were the Germans able to close with the launch and board, taking off the wounded and carefully removing the body of Sergeant Durrant from the straps of the gun.

There is a sequel to this tale. Some weeks later the Captain of the German destroyer, Kapitanleutnant F. K. Paul, went to the prison camp near St Nazaire where the raiders were being held and called on Colonel A. C. Newman, the CO of 2 Commando. Paul told the Colonel of the great fight put up by Sergeant Durrant, 'whom you may wish to recommend for a high decoration'. Durrant eventually received a posthumous Victoria Cross, Britain's highest award for valour, the only one ever awarded to a soldier for a naval action ... and on the recommendation of an enemy officer.

The Special Forces Hall of Fame from the Second World War – if there was one – would include many soldiers like these, and their names should be remembered. There was David Stirling and the fighting

Ulsterman Blair 'Paddy' Mayne of the SAS, John Durnford Slater, who formed and led the first Commando unit, and Peter Young of 3 Commando, Colonel 'Red Mike' Edson of the US Marine Raiders, Brigadier Derek Mills-Roberts of 6 Commando and the 1st Commando Brigade, 'a soldier if ever there was one,' according to Peter Young, himself no mean soldier. There was Orde Wingate of the Chindits, a mystic but a fighting man. There were men like Colonel Merrill of the US Marauders, who fought so hard and well in Burma, Bill Derby, who formed the first American Ranger battalions and led them into battle, and Colonel Rudder of the 2nd US Ranger Battalion, which scaled the cliffs of the Point de Hoc to silence the German batteries that threatened the landings on Omaha. Not all of these men survived the war but they created the spirit, even the legend, of Special Forces. They raised the units, trained the men, led them into battle and proved what well-trained, well-led fighting men could do when inspired by the belief that anything is possible if the will is there.

The story of Special Forces in the Second World War really begins in June 1940. When war swept Europe in 1939, only the German Army was really prepared for battle and their *Blitzkrieg* – lightning war – tactics, employing fast-moving tanks with close air support, swept all the other armies aside, in campaign after campaign, until they reached the Channel coast in June 1940 and drove the British Army back to Britain.

Two other nations, Denmark and Norway, were invaded on 9 April 1940, and France and Britain promptly sent forces to Norway, including the first Independent Companies, forerunners of the British Commandos, the first major SF unit of the Second World War. Ken McAllister was one of the original Independent Company volunteers: 'One Sunday in early 1940, just after church parade, the Sergeant-Major asked me some very odd questions ... "Was I in a fighting mood? ..." and so on. Then he took about nine or ten of us aside and a captain came along and told us we had been picked for a "Special Unit" because we appeared to be the type they wanted. "Men who would not be squeamish at seeing their mate's head blown off." Don't ask me how they could tell we wouldn't be, or indeed how anybody wouldn't be, but we all volunteered and became part of No. 4 Independent Company, the nucleus of the original Commandos. It was a small unit, with no transport, and we did a bit of training before being sent to Scotland for embarkation, destination unknown, but which turned out to be Norway.'

After the Dunkirk evacuation in June 1940 some soldiers from No 6, 7, 8 and 9 Independent Companies formed No. 11 Independent Company under the command of Major Ronnie Tod, later CO of No. 9 Commando. These Independent Companies were soon disbanded and the men were told they could either return to their parent units or revolunteer for 'Special Service'. Many ended up in No. 1 SS (Special Service) Battalion, a unit designated as a raiding force. The 'SS' designation was, not surprisingly, very unpopular with British troops and within weeks the Special Service battalion was broken up to form No. 1 and No. 2 Commandos. No. 3 Commando, the first of these Commando units, had already been formed by Lieutenant-Colonel Durnford Slater. The task of these Commandos was to get back across the Channel, raid the coast of France and show the German Army that the British were still full of fight. The first Commando raids, on the French coast and the island of Guernsey, were small affairs that achieved very little, but they provided some useful training in irregular warfare.

The first British parachute forces were also created at this time by the Prime Minister, Winston Churchill, who ordered the formation of a 'Corps of at least five thousand parachute troops', using selected volunteers from all the corps and regiments of the British Army. The first parachute school, the Central Landing School, was established at Ringway near Manchester in June 1940, and the RAF training staff were endowed with every parachute that could be found, provided with six obsolescent Whitley bomber aircraft and told to get on with it.

Parachute forces were not new. The British General Wavell had attended the Soviet Army summer manoeuvres in 1936 and was amazed to see a complete battalion parachute on to the 'battlefield', 1,200 men, complete with machine-gun detachments and light artillery. The German Army had used airborne forces to overcome the Dutch defences at Eban Emael during their drive into Holland, and the image of hordes of paratroops descending behind the lines, to sow alarm and despondency among the defenders, was a potent force in the early days of the Second World War and certainly attracted the attention of Winston Churchill.

However, the British military establishment had a lot on its mind in the summer of 1940 and the creation of parachute and glider forces was not regarded as a top priority. The Air Ministry saw it as a waste of resources and the War Office was not keen to see the best men taken from the front-line battalions and sent off to join *ad hoc* formations of 'paratroops' or 'Commandos', with the German Army already at the gates.

There was also a certain confusion about how these paratroopers or Commandos were to be used. Admiral of the Fleet Sir Roger Keyes, the first Chief of Combined Operations, believed that 'Commandos' should be sent into battle by air and it was decided that No. 2 Commando should be parachute-trained. Both paratroopers and Commandos were to be involved in raiding and assault landings but their methods of getting to the battlefield soon diverged. Commandos took over seaborne raiding and amphibious assault, paratroopers took over air assault and airborne raids by parachute and glider. As the war went on Commando units and parachute battalions spent more time in the line, fighting as normal infantry, the outstanding individual skill of their soldiers compensating for their lack of numbers.

In 1941, David Stirling, a Scots Guards officer of No. 8 Commando in Egypt, created 'L' Detachment of the SAS and, after some early disasters in parachute attacks, commenced raiding behind the enemy lines in jeeps. Stirling saw the SAS role as raiding rather than reconnaissance, and led his men in attacks behind the enemy lines, concentrating on supply dumps and airfields. Vladimir Peniakoff, leader of another Western Desert raiding force, PPA, or Popski's Private Army, and himself no mean soldier, described Stirling as 'the romantic soldier of the war in the Middle East. He raised his first SAS regiment first for parachute operations, then for land fighting in jeeps. With Mayne and a band of friends they had ravaged the German airfields before Alamein, and spread panic among the enemy troops after that battle. With a light heart and cool courage he inspired in his men a passionate devotion and led them to thrilling adventures. Where we plodded, he pranced.'

So, slowly, by land, sea and air, the Special Forces went to war, learning how to do it as they went along. Some of the ways they learned their trade were very dangerous indeed.

The first recorded military parachute drop in the British Army was made at Ringwood on 13 July 1940 by the 'pull-off' method, which was then regarded as a gentle way of introducing soldiers to what parachute instructors came to call the 'second greatest thrill'. For the 'pull-off' method the soldier climbed out on to a platform created by removing the rear gun turret of a Whitley bomber. Once out there, battered by the aircraft slipstream, he pulled the ripcord of his parachute, the canopy deployed and the soldier was plucked off the aircraft into space. Amazingly enough, there was no shortage of people willing to do this, though the process was not without risk. The first fatal British military parachute accident took place just twelve days later, when Driver Evans of the Royal Army Service Corps (RASC), a soldier with 2 Commando, fell to his death after his parachute 'candled', or failed to open. Before long the basic course, initially three jumps for the award of the coveted parachute 'wings', had been increased to eight jumps, the first two from a captive balloon, the last one at night, the majority with a full set of equipment, including platoon weapons. Parachute troops were being formed in other countries, and these alarming experiences were shared by the paratroopers of Australia, as Brigadier John Blanco White of the Australian Army recalls: 'I was instructing Independent Companies at Darby in Victoria, when I was given the task of raising and training a parachute force. The instructor was Flight-Lieutenant John Milne of the RAAF [Royal Australian Air Force], formerly a barnstorming pilot, and our equipment was one staff car, one Tiger Moth biplane, carrying one pilot and one passenger, and a Demon Tiger aircraft which we could peg down before revving up the engine to produce a wind. None of us had ever seen a parachute at this time.

'After six weeks of PT [physical training], rolling about practising landings, the great day arrived; we received our parachutes and we all ran to our DZ [dropping zone], a mile from the hangar, to see our first parachute jump, which would be made using a dummy from a Dragon Rapide. The course was drawn up on parade, the aircraft flew over and the dummy was dropped. It thundered down and landed with a crash into the ground in front of the squad, with no sign of the parachute opening. The course was given the order, "About Turn", and we all doubled away, back to the hangar. After that we all spent a great deal of time carefully packing our parachutes, and our first jumps were successful, except for one man, Eric Johnson, who became hooked up on the tailplane. He courageously unhooked himself over the local dam, but was killed on impact with the water.'

British soldiers flocked to join these new Commando and parachute units. Apart from the two shillings (10p) a day parachute pay there was no special inducement to join the Parachute Regiment, but there was never any lack of volunteers. Very few of those who started the parachute course failed to go through with it, though a good number failed to measure up to the physical standards required and fell out in training. Those who volunteered for the Commandos got no extra pay at all and had to pass the gruelling course at the famous Commando School at Achnacarry in Scotland.

The Commando School later trained the first of the American Ranger units, and one of those American soldiers was Bob Sales from Madison Heights, Virginia, then a soldier in the 29th Infantry Division, a unit destined to land on Omaha beach on D-Day: 'I expected to go to France with the 29th Ranger Battalion. This was formed at Tidworth in Hampshire, England, from picked troops of the Division, and we went to Achnacarry, which was then the toughest battle school in the world. The discipline was unbelievable and we were on British rations up there ... if you don't think you will ever eat and starve to death you have not tried British Army food. We started at seven-mile speed-marches when we got off the train, full kit, and just went on up, and if you fell out you got kicked out, no second chances. But I was young and fit and passed the course, and then got a week off in London, where a young guy just had to have a good time.

'The 29th Ranger Battalion went on some raids across the Channel from Dover with British Commandos, but we were broken up before D-Day and sent back to our companies. I tell you, that near broke my heart. I really wanted to fight with the Ranger Battalion, but I became personal bodyguard to Captain Zappacosta, the CO of B Company, 116 Infantry Regiment, and landed with that company on D-Day. Most of the men I landed with were killed on the beach.'

The great attraction of the new parachute or Commando units was the red or green beret and the prospect of action. The men knew that they had been specially chosen, but they had no illusions about their future role. Those accepted had probably seen active service already, were physically fit, had clean conduct sheets – mostly – and could display maturity and common sense. These last qualities were necessary, for the men still had a lot of lessons to learn and a lot of training to do, not least in discovering how to plan, organize and conduct Commando and parachute operations, which were a new form of warfare in the early 1940s. These were the early days, of 'one man, one rifle, fifty rounds of ball and a bag ration', but this simple soldiering was not to last. Before long, Special Force units started to grow.

The great contribution of the parachute was in the creation of the Allied parachute divisions. These were large units, many thousands strong, which spearheaded most of the Second World War assaults. Apart from the Russian parachute corps, the Western Allies raised seven full divisions of airborne troops, the British 1st and 6th and the US 82nd, 101st, 17th, 11th and 13th Airborne Divisions. These divisions were composed of both parachute and glider troops and were to establish the basic tenets of airborne warfare in which the Allied armies remained dominant throughout the war after the German parachute divisions were decimated in the attack on Crete in 1941.

Landing thousands of men by parachute, on time and in the right place, with all their weapons, was not always easy, as Chuck Tilley of the 2nd (Independent) Pathfinder Company recalls. His unit's task was to parachute on to dropping zones before the assault and mark the DZ for the main-force landings, using a radio system called 'Eureka': 'More than half the radio sets were dud. There was nothing we could do if they didn't work, apart from check the connections and jiggle the on-off switch. They were totally enclosed and we hadn't a clue what was inside them. There was a test button we could press, and we should have got a coded buzz in the headphones to let us know if it was working and ready to start. While the Eureka operator was doing this the main force would be some eighty miles away coming in to drop the paratroops or launch the gliders. While the operator was getting his set ready, other chaps were laying out the yellow cloth strips in either a "T" or an "F" shape, or whatever the code was for that dropping zone. Other members took up "all-round protection" for the rest of the Company to secure the DZ ... well, that was the theory anyway.'

Even getting to the DZ could be hazardous, if it involved flying over the Allied warships, heading for the seaborne assault. Leslie 'Bill' Kick, of the 82nd Parachute Division, who fought in Africa, Sicily and France, recalls some of his experiences: 'I joined the Army in 1940 and in September 1942 I took the four-week parachute course at Fort Benning, followed by a two-week course in parachute communications. In November I was assigned to HQ 82 Airborne Division artillery at Fort Bragg, and from there I went with the Division to North Africa, arriving there in May 1943. Two months later I was in the belly of an aircraft heading for the parachute drop into Sicily. As we flew in over the US Fleet, we received heavy anti-aircraft fire from the warships and both the engines on our C47 were hit. The pilot managed to nurse the aircraft till we crossed the coast, losing height, but we all got out ... except the pilot and co-pilot, who were killed when the aircraft crashed.'

Amphibious operations also had their hazards and it soon became clear that the chances of a successful landing by the conventional landing force would be increased if the beach was recce'd beforehand by Special Force units. Units created for this purpose included the British COPP teams, which sent men ashore from submarines, to swim about just offshore and examine beach obstacles. One of the COPP team members was Sub-Lieutenant Jim Booth of the Royal Navy: 'COPP was formed after the Dieppe Raid of 1942, which was a disaster partly because the troops could not find the beach exits and the tanks could not get up the shingle – no beach survey beforehand, you see. Anyway, our job was pre-invasion recce and we did a lot of them in Italy and Sicily. We went over in big submarines which surfaced offshore at night and then we paddled to the beach in canoes, or swam in from the canoes if there were enemy about. A team was two men, a naval surveyor who did his stuff below the tide line and a Royal Engineers officer who did the beach above the low-water mark. We would put in a peg on the water line and then swim out taking offshore depths and sand core samples at twenty-five yard intervals. I suppose the Army chaps did the same, as well as studying any beach obstacles. Then we would paddle back out and rendezvous with the submarine. I really enjoyed it – jolly good fun.'

The US Navy created UDT (Underwater Demolition Team) units, which performed the same function in the South Pacific. There were other units with similar tasks like the US Scouts and Raiders, which operated in Europe and North Africa. Matthew Kaye was in this unit: 'During the Big War I was a Scout and Raider (US Navy). My particular unit [Group One] did not reach Africa until it was secured. However, Group One did arrive before the Torch invasion, scouted the beaches and led the first few waves to their proper beaches. Following this operation, Group One participated in the invasion of Sicily, Anzio and Salerno. At Anzio we lost two officers.

'At that period Unit 2 arrived from the States, along with a group called the Beach Jumpers [BJs]. After assembling in Ferryville, North Africa, they, along with two S&R teams, left to join Marshal Tito's partisans in Yugoslavia. With deceptive radar and radio they tied two German divisions to the Adriatic coast. Their CO was Douglas Fairbanks Jr, the Hollywood actor. Another member was Sterling Hayden, also a Hollywood actor. The two German divisions were slated to go to Normandy and the D-Day operation might not have ended the way it did had they been there.

'The Head of Group One was Lieutenant Phil Bucklew, who was recalled to the service during the Korean War and then organized the cream of all covert groups, the US Navy SEALs. The Underwater Demolition Teams claim the SEALs as their grandchild but Bucklew was first and last a Scout and Raider. Their training schedule is right from our S&R manuals and their home base today is in Coronado, California. Bucklew scouted the Normandy beaches some weeks before the invasion like the COPP boys did. He anticipated sceptics not believing our information and the story goes that he once produced a bucket of Normandy sand and dumped it on the desk of a British intelligence officer. The COPP guys were just as capable.'

Special Force units were not always small. Few of them came out of the Second World War with a higher reputation than the mighty United States Marine Corps, which fought an amphibious war in the South Pacific, seizing island footholds ever nearer to Japan. Charles H. Owen of Lafayette, Georgia, who retired as a master-sergeant after thirty years in the Marine Corps, served in the Second World War, Korea and Vietnam. At the assault on Peleliu in 1944, he was a sixteen-year-old Private, first class – and he had already been in the Marine Corps for two years: 'I guess there were not many who enlisted at the age of fourteen, but there were certainly some who came in at sixteen years of age and I had no trouble as long as I did my job. I was placed on guard duty at first and then I got myself in the Marine Detachment on the battleship USS *New York*. This duty I hated because it was so strict, with many regulations. Being a young lad, I thought I needed to see combat and when I joined the 1st Marine Division there were troops who had seen combat at Guadalcanal, New Guinea and New Britain. When you are placed in a platoon with veterans such as these it is better than any training.

'I was in an Amtrac [amphibious tracked vehicle] in one of the first waves at Peleliu, 15 September 1944. When we hit the beach I went over the side. It was a long jump … like falling into hell. The beach was being hit by heavy small-arms fire and mortars and artillery. There were bodies and part of bodies all around. I was terrified.

'We had always been told to get off the beach. It was the most dangerous place to be. But many troops were still there and not moving. Out of nowhere came a major I never saw before or again. He ignored all the torrent of enemy fire and was busy kicking ass and screaming at us. All I could think of was to get off the beach before that crazy son-of-a-bitch shot me. Years later, while I was serving as a senior drill instructor at "boot camp" (our recruit training center) in San Diego, I had a fellow DI who babied and talked his recruits through training. I was told this was psychology. All those years, I had thought what that Major on Peleliu was using was psychology. But whatever it was, he saved our lives.'

Peleliu was a small island, just six miles long and two miles wide. It was garrisoned by 10,000 Japanese troops and it took the US Marines a week and 6,000 casualties, including 1,200 killed, to take it. The 10,000 Japanese defenders fought to the last man.

In 1945 Charles Owen was in action again at Okinawa: 'The landing at Okinawa was nothing like the Peleliu landing. At Peleliu we were under heavy fire. The Okinawa landing was quiet, but we were well trained and ready. We landed at 0830 with only a few shots fired in anger. In my regiment, the 7th Marines, only one Company Commander was killed by mortar fire and several other men wounded. By April we had killed 122 Japanese with a loss of 35 Marines. We took the northern part of the island by the end of April.

'The most fierce fighting I remember was on the Dakeshi ridge. My 1st Battalion lost 125 men in eight hours while crossing a shallow draw. This was in May. In June the other fierce fighting was for Kunisha ridge on 12 June. Our Regimental Commander had sent two rifle companies on the ridge at night, because of the heavy casualties we had taken because of enemy fire coming from the front and flanks while going over a long open area. The next day my Company was sent in tanks. All but one of the crew was removed from a tank and then six men from A Company were placed in a tank with just the driver. The records say a "reinforced" Platoon was sent from A Company – that was all that was left of A Company. Kunisha ridge was like being on an outpost in Korea. You could not get off and were under heavy fire with the Japs all around you.'

Other than the USMC and some embryo parachute units, the US had no Special Force elements when the Japanese attacked Pearl Harbor in December 1941 but such forces were clearly needed and were soon created. The USMC raised a strike force, the US Marine Raiders, commanded by Lieutenant-Colonel Mike Edson, and the US Army swiftly followed suit. American troops went into action on European soil for the first time in the war in August 1942, when a party of the newly formed American Rangers took part in the Canadian and British Commando raid on the French port of Dieppe.

The first Ranger battalion was formed in Northern Ireland in the spring of 1942 on the orders of General Lucian Truscott, who wanted a raiding unit on the lines of a British Commando. The man chosen to raise the 1st Ranger Battalion was Major William O. Derby, a thirty-one-year-old West Point graduate. Derby called for volunteers and took 700 men to the British Commando School at Achnacarry for the seven-week course; about a third fell out but the rest ran the course in record time and the 1st US Ranger Battalion was passed for duty on 19 June 1942.

Just forty-two US Rangers went on the disastrous Dieppe Raid in August 1942, but from that time on the Rangers were in action in every corner of the world. In October 1942, Colonel Derby led his men ashore at Arzew in Algeria, as part of the American invasion of North Africa.

With the British Commandos, they later spearheaded the seaborne assaults on Sicily and at Salerno and Anzio on the Italian mainland. On 6 June 1944 Colonel Earl Rudder took 355 men of the 2nd and 5th Ranger Battalions to assault the Pointe de Hoc in Normandy, losing nearly 200 men in the first day of the D-Day landings.

The US Rangers also fought in the Far East, where, in January 1945, the 6th Rangers made an epic raid forty miles behind the Japanese lines to rescue the emaciated inmates of a Japanese prison camp, killing over 200 Japanese before fighting their way back to the American lines with the joyful POWs. Six Ranger battalions were raised in 1942–5 and by the time the war ended they were regarded as among the elite units of the US Army. Colonel Derby was killed just before the European war ended, while commanding a regiment in the 10th US Mountain Division.

Italy was the battleground for another unique Second World War regiment, the 1st Special Service Force – the 'Devil's Brigade' – a unit composed of American and Canadian soldiers, commanded by an American officer, Lieutenant-Colonel Robert T. Frederick. The Special Service Force was composed of three regiments, each of two battalions, and trained in rock climbing, amphibious techniques, skiing and airborne warfare. The Force served in North Africa, Italy and the South of France before being disbanded at the end of the war. However, the Special Service Force is now listed by the US Special Forces, the Green Berets, as one of their parent units.

Other SF units were being formed to fight the Japanese in Burma where a British force, the Chindits, under Brigadier-General Orde Wingate, made some long-range penetrations behind the Japanese lines. From the strategic point of view these first operations achieved very little, but they proved that European troops, if properly trained and led, could fight and win in the jungle.

Orde Wingate, the commander of the Chindits, was a strange man. A passionate Zionist, an occasional nudist and a semi-Marxist, he had an unusual amount of experience in Special Force operations, for while serving with the British Army in Palestine before the war he had formed a clandestine unit, the Special Night Squads, to counter Arab attacks on Jewish settlements. Working with the squads, Wingate learned what small groups of well-trained, well-led men could do, and he put these lessons to good use behind the Japanese lines in Burma.

The Chindit example was followed by an American force, formed with the uninspiring title of the 5307th Composite Unit (Provisional), commanded by Brigadier-General Frank D. Merrill, and therefore better known as Merrill's Marauders. This unit and its successor, the Mars Force, put up a great fight against the jungle, disease and the Japanese during the war in Burma, culminating in a battle for the Japanese airfield at Myitkyina. Richard Hale, who served in the Mars Force, recalls those days: 'General Merrill allegedly told the Chiefs of Staff that he could not make mule skinners out of soldiers so could they send him some mule skinners and he would turn them into infantrymen. The Marauders and Mars Force used mules to carry our heavy equipment, radios, artillery, machine-guns and ammo, so looking after the mules was important. I was in the cavalry, at Fort Riley in Kansas, and that is how I got volunteered for the war in Burma, as it seemed logical that if we could look after horses we could take care of mules.

'We kicked off from Myitkyina in November 1944, down part of what would become the Burma Road into China. We had minor skirmishes with Jap patrols, then turned east, and ran into their 18th Division and they tried to get us out with shelling and banzai attacks, infantry charges with the bayonet, led by Japanese officers carrying samurai swords. The banzai attacks were never a problem; we had the firepower and we let them come on and just shot them down. Some of us frankly enjoyed the slaughter, considering it a form of revenge.

'Their artillery was more of a problem, as their 105mm and 155mm far outranged our pack 75mm. Finally they gave up and we were exfiltrated out, everyone from general to private marching out ... and I'm sure that we were all very happy to get out of the jungle. We were supposed to go on to China, but the atomic bomb ended the war before that could happen. Having walked more than 500 miles in the last few months, across some of the worst terrain in the world, I was pretty happy I did not have to walk across China.'

The Marauders were first employed in northern Burma, clearing he Japanese away from the Burma Road, which brought in supplies from China. From January 1944 until February 1945, the Marauders were in almost continual action behind the Japanese lines and scored a great success by capturing the airfield at Myitkyina in May 1944. After more months of combat the unit was finally stood down in July 1945, by which time it had earned the rare distinction of a Presidential Unit Citation, a rare award for a 'provisional' unit, originally established for just ninety days. Both these units, the US Rangers and Merrill's Marauders, are regarded as the forerunners of both the post-war US Rangers and the many LRRP (Long-Range Reconnaissance Patrol) units formed for Vietnam.

Other US Special Force units can trace their origins to Second World

War creations, including the somewhat mysterious OSS – the Office of Strategic Services – which in spite of its somewhat formal title was raised for special operations behind the enemy lines. The OSS was created by President Franklin Roosevelt in July 1941, before the United States entered the war, and was placed under the command of Colonel William 'Wild Bill' Donovan. Colonel Donovan defined the tasks of the OSS as 'espionage, propaganda, subversion and related activities under the aegis of a centralized intelligence agency'.

During the Second World War the OSS was engaged in the more orthodox forms of irregular warfare, including the dropping of the so-called 'Jedburgh' teams to provide the Maquis resistance fighters in German-occupied France with weapons training and radio contacts. In this the OSS much resembled the British SOE, and both have links with the modern SAS and US Special Forces. While SOE teams could and did take part in actual operations, their prime task was to work with the local or indigenous people, providing the weapons and explosives, and training local resistance groups in their use.

Every Allied nation involved in the war played some part, large or small, in the Special Force story. The New Zealanders and Rhodesians were very active in the Western Desert, serving with the LRDG and the SAS. The Australian Z Special Unit mounted canoe raids against Japanese shipping in Singapore, including Operation Jaywick in 1943 and Operation Rimau a year later. Operation Jaywick was a great success for a very small unit. Fourteen men, Australian and British, commanded by a British officer, Major Lyon, made their way to Singapore in a small trawler, the *Krait*, and attacked Japanese shipping in the harbour using canoes and limpet mines. Seven ships were sunk and the men returned to Australia without losing a man. Operation Rimau in September 1944 was much larger and far less successful. This time there were twenty-six men, including six of the Jaywick party. What went wrong has never been entirely clear but the party, having been taken by submarine to a point near Singapore, captured a fishing boat for the final approach. The party were then detected, men were lost in a series of actions with the Japanese and the ten who survived were executed.

Captured Special Force soldiers were frequently executed. The Australian raiders captured after Operation Rimau were beheaded on 7 July 1945, just forty days before the end of the war. Nine US Marines from Lieutenant-Colonel Carlson's Raiders, captured by the Japanese after a raid on Makin Island in 1942, were also beheaded. Such executions were not confined to the Far East or Pacific theatres.

The constant harassment by Allied raiding forces so infuriated the Germans that soldiers captured on Special Force operations in Europe were often shot or sent to concentration camps for *Nacht und Nebel* – Night and Fog – treatment, summary execution. The Royal Marines captured in Bordeaux by the Germans after the Operation Frankton canoe raid of 1942 were executed under the terms of Hitler's infamous Commando Order of 1942, which decreed that all raiders caught behind the lines were to be handed over to the SD, effectively the Gestapo, for 'special treatment', which meant interrogation and execution. This fate befell the British paratroopers sent on an abortive raid against the German heavy-water plant in Norway, where material for a German atomic bomb was being prepared. This heavy-water plant and its product were eventually destroyed by Norwegian resistance fighters.

Among the Axis forces – German, Japanese, Italian – SF units were less common. The principle exponent of irregular warfare in the German Army was an SS officer, Otto Skorzeny, who in September 1943 would lead a group of SS men on a daring raid by glider and light aircraft on to the Gran Sasso plateau in Italy to rescue Benito Mussolini, the deposed Italian dictator, and bring him to Germany. SS troops also engaged in deception programmes during the Ardennes counter-offensive of 1945, 'the Battle of the Bulge', dressing up in American uniforms to drive about behind the Allied lines, spreading confusion. Those Germans captured in American uniforms were shot.

One feature of Second World War soldiering that was to have repercussions in the post-war years was the use of Special Forces to support resistance movements in the German Occupied Territories in Eastern and Western Europe. OSS and SOE in France have already been listed, but there were many more such units. The partisan forces of Marshal Tito waging war on the Germans in Yugoslavia were strongly supported by the British Commandos of 40 and 43 (Royal Marine) Commandos and No. 2 Army Commando, who established a base on the Yugoslav island of Vis in 1943 and used it to harry the Germans in Yugoslavia for the rest of the war.

In the Greek islands the task of harassing the enemy was in the care of the Special Boat Squadron and the Greek Sacred Squadron, operating from motor torpedo boats (MTBs) or Greek caiques, landing by night on German-occupied islands, attacking supply boats, calling in Allied aircraft to attack German shipping. The war against the Germans in Russia was especially hard, but here too irregular units were at work with the partisans, raiding behind the German lines, attacking convoys, blowing up supply dumps, allowing the enemy no rest.

As the war went on, many of these Special Force units changed. They changed their personnel, as the founder members were killed or captured or promoted, or went on to other challenges. They changed their fields of operations as the battle-lines of the war shifted. Most of all, they changed their composition and their role. By 1944 the free-wheeling small-scale raiding days gave way to a more organized kind of irregular warfare, often in support of regular Army operations. As the Axis powers were driven back, raiding activity faded away and the parachute, Commando and Ranger units were often employed in a regular infantry role, for which they were ill-prepared. Meanwhile, as the enemy learned how to cope with Special Force harassment and beat off guerrilla attacks, artillery, armoured cars, even aircraft, came into Special Force use. In the Mediterranean, for example, the Raiding Support Regiment provided artillery support for Commando raids and other units acquired field artillery and mortars.

So, gradually, those small, lightly equipped bands of cheerful guerrilla fighters that had sprung up in 1940–1 were transformed into regiments and brigades – even divisions in the Airborne Corps – all with the inevitable logistical tail. The days when Major Brian Franks, Brigade Major of 2 Commando Brigade, kept all the Brigade papers in a pocket of his battledress trousers were fading away by the end of 1943, but Special Force units were still being created.

One US SF unit formed towards the end of the war was the first black Airborne unit, the 555th Parachute Infantry Regiment – the Triple Nickels – which, much to the disgust of the troopers, was kept out of the war. The black troopers therefore took eagerly to another highly hazardous occupation, parachute fire fighting, an early example of how a Special Force skill can be turned to civilian use. The 555th was an elite unit in the then-segregated US Army and one of its officers, Lieutenant-Colonel Bradley Biggs describes how their parachute expertise was eventually used: 'Through December 1944 and January 1945, the Triple Nickels continued to jump, and grew to a strength of over 400 keen, battle-ready officers and men. During that same period a deadly action was taking place on the battlefields of Belgium – the Battle of the Bulge, the massive German counter-attack in the Ardennes that began on 16 December 1944. It lasted more than a month and, before the Germans were turned around, the American Army had suffered some 77,000 casualties, many of them in the 82nd and 101st Airborne at Bastogne.

'Eventually, the Triple Nickels would grow to more than 1,300 fit for duty, 600 in jump training at Fort Benning, and 1,900 on the morning report rosters, but, for now, the smaller number had some advantages. It enabled us to concentrate on intensive individual and small-unit training. Riflemen, machine-gunners and mortar men had sharpened their aim to perfection. Training in judo and other forms of hand-to-hand combat were intensified. They had time and opportunity to become superb combat soldiers.

'We were ready to take on anybody, but suddenly, midway through out rigorous combat training, our destiny changed. It seemed unlikely that any more paratroopers would be needed, and in late April 1945 we received new orders. The Triple Nickels became airborne fighters. It was in this field that our new training programme began on 22 May. It was a three-week programme which included demolition training, tree climbing and techniques for descent if we landed in a tree, handling firefighting equipment, jumping into pocket-sized drop zones studded with rocks and tree stumps, survival in wooded areas, and extensive first-aid training for injuries – particularly broken bones. We learned to do the opposite of many things we learned and used in normal jumps – like deliberately landing in trees instead of avoiding them.

'We would jump with full gear, including fifty feet of nylon rope for use in lowering ourselves when we landed in a tree. Our steel helmets were replaced with football helmets with wire-mesh face protectors. Covering our jumpsuits or standard army fatigues, we wore the Air Corps fleece-lined flying jacket and trousers. Gloves were standard equipment but not worn when jumping; bare hands manipulate shroud lines better.

'In February 1946 we were attached to the 82nd Airborne Division but we retained our own authority to discipline and manage our personnel matters. Further attachment was made to the 504th Airborne Infantry Regiment, then commanded by a colonel whose name will go down in history as the originator of "search and destroy missions" in Vietnam, General William C. Westmoreland.'

So the war ended, with Special Forces larger, better equipped, more widely accepted and much changed from the way they had started out in 1940. What did not change, at least to any marked degree, was the character of the men themselves. The attrition of war had thinned the ranks of the original Special Force soldiers but by 1945 they had established a tradition that endured long after their passing and inspires Special Forces today. The officers led from the front, the men maintained the advance and there was always room at the front for a fighting man. That was how it had started in the dark days after Dunkirk and that was the way it was when the Second World War ended.

M16 A2 rifle with M203 grenade-launcher

CHAPTER THREE

Terrain, Training, Technology, Tactics

I'll have you learn to sleep upon the ground,
March in your armour through the watery fens,
Sustain the scorching heat and freezing cold,
Hunger and thirst, right adjuncts of the war,
And, after this, to scale a castle wall,
Besiege a fort, to undermine a town,
and make whole cities caper in the air!

Christopher Marlowe, Tamburlaine

Special Forces are not called into existence to provide excitement
for the wilder spirits or to employ those soldiers unsuited to
regular warfare. They are created because they are needed, either
to fulfil a particular task or to tackle a particular problem. It is therefore
necessary to understand which situations call for the employment of
Special Force units and how such units are trained.

All Special Force units share common bonds and the most obvious
of these is the character and quality of the men, who are all volunteers.
The Special Force role is usually peripheral to the principle task, battle
or campaign and frequently consists of easing the path of the regular
forces, though SF units can – on occasion – take on the conventional
infantry role. One excellent example of a Special Force task related to
a larger effort is the 'Pedestal' operation in 1942. Malta was starving,
out of fuel and ammunition, and the Royal Navy was trying to force a
vital fourteen-vessel convoy through the Mediterranean from Gibraltar.

This convoy was certain to suffer heavy air attacks, so the SAS, LRDG and every other irregular unit in the Middle East was sent behind the Axis lines to attack enemy airfields. Every bomber they could destroy on the ground was one less available to attack the ships bringing petrol and ammunition to the beleaguered fortress of Malta, and it is partly due to their efforts that three vessels with their vital supplies finally got through – all the rest were sunk. This sort of action – harassing the enemy and so reducing his ability to attack – was a feature of SF activity throughout the Second World War and has been used in most of the campaigns since.

Raiding is one of the prime Special Force tasks, but the principal actions of the Falklands War of 1982, at Goose Green, Two Sisters and Mount Longdon, were 'heavy infantry' affairs where SOF units were used in the normal infantry role, though the campaign began with an amphibious landing. The battle for the Falkland Islands was largely fought and won by SOF troops from the Parachute Regiment and the Royal Marine Commandos, and it was their fitness, training and ability to 'stick it' that brought eventual victory over the much larger Argentine forces. This diversity of roles needs clarifying, in order that the case for employing SF troops is clearly understood.

The first step is to define a unique Special Force role. This is difficult because Special Forces of one sort or another have been employed in a wide variety of situations over the last fifty years. The very name 'Special' might seem to indicate that there are no situations where the use of Special Forces could be ruled out, but this is not the case. Special Force units have their limitations, and the military histories are full of instances where Commando and raiding units have been committed to tasks for which they were totally unsuited and where, as a result of unsuitable deployment, the outcome was not favourable. Sending a small, lightly equipped Commando unit to tackle a task best suited to a well-equipped and heavily armed infantry battalion is a recipe for disaster.

The general use of Special Forces seems to fall into five broad areas: reconnaissance, raiding, deep penetration, initial assault and support for resistance movements. These five areas of SF activity called into existence units like the Long-Range Desert Group and the SBS (intelligence gathering and reconnaissance), the SAS, the USMC Raiders (raiding, reconnaissance), the Chindits and Merrill's Marauders, the LRRPs and Force Recon (deep penetration behind the enemy lines) and the Royal Marine Commandos, the Parachute Divisions and the United States Marine Corps (amphibious and airborne assault), SOE and OSS (support for resistance movements). Other Special Force units, like those of Israel and Argentina, specialize almost exclusively in small-scale raiding and reconnaissance work.

Whatever their particular speciality, most SF units would regard many of these tasks as fitting somewhere in their professional remit and train to carry them out. The SAS, for example, list raiding and recce among their tasks, but have often worked closely with indigenous people and local resistance movements, as in the Oman and Borneo. The same was true for US Green Beret units in Vietnam, where their principal task, certainly in 1961–5, was the setting up of local defence forces – CIDG (Civilian Irregular Defense Groups) – to regain the initiative in the countryside and hold off Vietcong incursions into the native villages, rather than engage the Vietcong themselves.

Certain conditions or situations call for the deployment of Special Force talents and these conditions can be identified under the general headings of terrain, training, technology and tactics, though these must often be considered in combination; the state of the terrain might call for troops with special training, the task might require the employment of troops familiar with special technology.

The ground over which he fights, the terrain, has always been important to the soldier. Historically, certain types of ground have been regarded as hostile. Jungles, mountains, arid desert, Arctic tundra, the great plains, rugged sea coasts, all fall into the hostile category and were avoided by conventional armies whenever possible. However, as warfare spread across the world, armies began to use unlikely or inhospitable terrain to outflank or surprise their enemies. Special Forces soon discovered that terrain which might prove impassable for regular forces provided SF units with an undefended route around the opposing flanks and behind the enemy lines. The SAS and the LRDG used the wastes of the Western Desert and tracks across the supposedly impassable Qattara Depression to reach and attack Axis airfields in North Africa in 1942–3. Cliff assault became a Commando and Ranger speciality and was used by the US Rangers to scale the Pointe du Hoc on D-Day, and by the Royal Marines in operations after the war.

In the 1960s the heat, humidity and rugged mountain country of the Radfan in South Arabia did not deter the men of 45 Commando, 3 Para and the SAS from attacking tribal dissidents raiding the Dhala road. This was terrible terrain and the officer in command of this operation undertook it only after he had been assured of support from either 'a Royal Marine Commando or a Parachute battalion' – troops fit enough to move and fight in such conditions. During the Malayan Emergency of the 1950s the Communist bandits used the cover of the jungle to great effect until the training provided at the British Far East Jungle Warfare School in Jahore began to teach British soldiers how to live in the jungle, often for weeks at a time, and root the terrorists out.

The majority of troops employed in Malaya were not from SF units. Most of the British troops employed in the jungles of Malaya were in conventional infantry battalions trained in jungle warfare, and they did sterling work. However, the Commandos and the SAS (Malaya Scouts) were among the first British units to understand that the way to beat the terrorist was to adapt to the jungle, to go in and stay in, until living there was natural and the difficulties of the terrain were reduced by experience. That said, the most successful troops deployed by the British in Malaya were the men of the Gurkha battalions, who are said to be the finest infantry in the world and are certainly very special soldiers, superbly trained and highly motivated – as all special soldiers have to be.

Adapting to any terrain requires a combination of mental and physical toughness, a certain amount of training in the necessary survival techniques, and possibly some special equipment – from skis to mosquito nets – which will enable the soldier to live and fight in an inhospitable setting. The answer to all these needs is training.

Before a soldier can be trained he must first volunteer. Indeed, volunteering is one of the marks of the modern Special Service soldier, and has been from the early days. Fred Musson was serving with a tank regiment in Britain in 1940 when a Commando recruiting team visited his camp and called for volunteers: 'A chosen few were selected for what was then called "Special Service" and told to expect vigorous training in order to reach peak fitness. We would have to become skilled in all arms, including the use of explosives. In addition to our normal army pay we received an extra 6s 8d [33p] per day as a lodging allowance for living in "civvy digs", out of barracks, and were given addresses of family houses and told to go off on our own and find somewhere to live; that was the first lesson in self-reliance. The cost of this had to be paid by each man from the extra pay we received; a week's full board in those days was £1 10s [£1.50]. We were ordered to parade the following morning at 0800 hours on the sea front and were told we were to be 2 Troop of No. 5 Commando. We were a mixed lot, incorporating men from all regiments of the British Army, and some had recently returned from service on the North-West Frontier of India fighting the Pathans.

'The Commando was organized to six "fighting troops" and a head-quarters troop and we were issued with new weapons, some of American origin. Thompson submachine-guns, Garand rifles, .45 Colt pistols and the Fairburn-Sykes fighting knife, as well as British weapons like the .303 Lee Enfield rifle and the Bren light machine-gun. In the early days most of our training was done in Scotland, in the Loch Fyne and Lochailort areas, later moving to coastal areas around England. Each day we did speed-marches, carrying all our weapons and ammunition, about fifty pounds, perhaps more, covering five miles in fifty minutes and then on up. This meant a jog of 100 yards, then a walk of 200 yards. After many weeks of this training we could do fifteen miles in full kit in less than 3 hours and still be fit for combat.'

Ted Kelly was eighteen years old in 1942 when the word 'Commando' first came to his notice: 'I saw a newsreel in the cinema about a raid on Norway, and so when Lieutenant-Colonel Newman visited our unit on a recruiting drive, I could hardly believe my good fortune. He was the officer who led No. 2 Commando on the St Nazaire Raid and won the Victoria Cross there. Volunteers were interviewed like job applicants and it was a condition of acceptance that any non-commissioned rank held must be surrendered. Everyone started equal and the surrender of one stripe seemed a small price to pay for the opportunity to join this venture.

'Before long I was on my way to Achnacarry Castle for six weeks of very rugged training. Our Sergeant-Instructor was a veteran soldier, a tough, wiry Scot, as hard as nails but totally lacking any suggestion of brutality or malice. We were to be his lads for the duration of the course and we were not expected to fail. The course was hard, unremitting toil. We learned a great deal about weapons, mountain climbing, unarmed combat, using boats, fieldcraft and demolition work. We sweated over assault courses, with leaps of twenty feet off high structures, crossed precarious rope bridges and rode rope 'death-slides', all against the clock. We learned to speed-march, a fiendish activity which was to become a permanent feature of our lives. Marching in fighting kit, running and walking, covering seven miles in the hour.

'Our skills and powers of endurance were periodically tested on night exercises which included wallowing in mud, crossing rivers and scaling heights in mock battles in which the "enemy" used live ammunition to keep our heads down. I can remember returning to the hut muddy, soaking wet and taking my boots off to find my socks soaked with blood where blisters had burst and the skin had rubbed raw. No one had any difficulty in sleeping when given the opportunity, we were stretched to the limit. The important thing was never to give in. The disgrace of being sent back to our own regiment as unsuitable was not to be contemplated. So somehow, from somewhere within us, we found another breath, another ounce of effort and will. Only later did we come to understand that that was what it was all about anyway.'

All exercises at Achnacarry used live ammunition and over forty soldiers were killed there while under training between 1942 and 1944.

Victor Stevenson served with 5 Commando in 3 Commando Brigade, and found himself in the Burmese jungle: 'It was a matter of great pride then to be a "Commando", although, alas, the word has been appropriated by the media in the last few decades to describe half the murderous brigands of the world. What sticks in my mind are the things that made South-East Asia so different from other theatres of war: solid jungle, mosquitoes and leeches – the first cut you to pieces and the other two ate you alive. Everyone had malaria, dysentery and rotten jungle sores. I suppose we must have complained among ourselves at the time, but I can't remember doing so; these were just the occupational hazards of everyone caught up at the sharp end in Burma, quite apart from the doings of the Japanese.

'What I do remember most of all is that wherever we were – in the UK, in one or another of the South Coast resorts – we were billeted with landladies and their daughters, now with a living-out allowance that earned us the envy, if not active malice, of other units in the area. Being in a Commando was the best of all ... I remember it as a kind of landscape with figures ... chaps who you'd happily spend the rest of your days with, however many or few that there were left.'

Cecil Blanch found life in 12 Commando very different from that in normal Army units: 'There was no pettifogging or unnecessary discipline. It was made plain from the start that self-discipline was the order of the day and it had to be of the highest standard. One was expected to be well turned out always, to maintain our personal arms in perfect condition, keep out of trouble and be on parade whenever and wherever ordered – and it worked. We were not the "thugs" some made us out to be. Training was designed to achieve peak physical fitness, self-reliance and expert weapon handling. Route marches of up to thirty miles were undertaken on a regular basis and there was much emphasis on movement by night over open country. Sometimes we would be out for two or three days at a time, frequently in bitterly cold weather and soaking wet, yet I do not recall us suffering any ill effects from this.'

Ray Hanson, of the US 168th Infantry Regiment, was recruited into the Rangers in the summer of 1942: 'I think it was in July or August that they asked for US soldiers to train with the British Commandos. We were sent to Scotland, to Dundee, and there were about 300 of us and we lived in private homes picked out for us by the British Army, not in barracks. Our Commanding Officer was Lieutenant Mark Martin and we had nine men in the squad with a British training officer, who was very tall and fit and known to us as 'The Greyhound.'

'We trained on the river and up by Inverness and all over Scotland, and one night we boarded a ship and headed out to sea and they told us the next stop was North Africa – that was Operation Torch – and after some days at sea we met up with a big troop convoy from the States. On the night of 8 November we landed somewhere east of Algiers to take a fort manned by the Vichy French and we got to the side of the fort on our stomachs before the machine guns opened up and Lieutenant Martin said, "Let's go." My buddy Walter was the first on the wall and he was killed instantly, but we took it. The next day Walter was buried with a young English lad in a cemetery I think was French.

'After a few days we moved to the airport at Bône [now 'Annaba] and then we went about thirty miles down the coast in landing craft, well behind the enemy lines, and had to hold a bridge there until the British 36 Brigade came up to relieve us. We were there a few days and then the Germans came out of the hills with tanks and infantry and we couldn't hold our position and were getting out when the British troops [from 1 and 6 Commandos] helped us out. I still have the pay book and the overseas cap that was issued to us by Commando Group.'

Volunteering, selection, hard training, self-discipline, *esprit de corps* – these provide the foundations of a Special Service soldier. The sentiments expressed by these first Commandos will strike an echo in Special Force soldiers of every period and nation, and in their accounts there is no hint of self-regard, 'gung-ho' attitudes or, to put it bluntly, bullshit. Many of them had already seen a good bit of war, so the thought that wearing a green beret turned them into heroes never entered their heads. The unique element of Special Forces was summed up in the Second World War by an experienced Commando officer, who told his men, 'Given time, any infantry unit can do what we do; the point is that only Commandos can do it in the time available.' The requirements of any Special Force operation are usually more complicated, but the officer had a point. The real skill of special forces is the ability to do the job in the time available. The secret lies in knowing the extreme limits of the possible, and the way to know that is by training and testing.

Quite early in their training SF soldiers realize that they can do far more than they think they can do – if the will to press on is there. One of the objects of their training is to bring that fact out. 'It's all in the heart and the mind' was one of the first precepts taught at the Achnacarry Commando School, and it remains the basis of Special Force training to this day. But it does not follow that every man who volunteers for SF training is ideally suited to SF work.

While the requirements vary from unit to unit there are certain common elements in Special Force selection. The recruiters are looking for men with maturity and plenty of common sense but a sense of humour and a willingness to 'have a go and stick at it' are also essential. The volunteer should be able to fit well into a small group but be equally willing to work on his own for long spells. Intelligence is useful, for the volunteer must be able to grasp the elements of a task quickly but be able to adapt when the situation changes. The modern SF soldier must also be capable of absorbing a high level of technical information and have the ability to operate complicated equipment.

None of the above requires a great level of physical fitness or strength. Though both are useful, both can be acquired and the popular image of the Special Force soldier as a kind of military athlete is hardly correct. Physical fitness is still useful, because a man who is physically fit will function better and become tired more slowly than someone who is not in good condition. It is not a major requirement, though anyone who contemplates volunteering for Special Force training would be well advised to get fit, or fitter, before that training commences.

'We are not looking for muscle bosuns,' said an instructor at the Royal Marine Commando School at Lympstone in Devon in 1996, 'but if a bloke hasn't had the common sense to get his act together before he joins you wonder if he has the right sort of attitude. If he has the right attitude, we will get him through. I would rather have a man who ran until he dropped than one who looked around for a nice soft patch of grass before he keeled over. Basically, anyone can do it if they have the right attitude.' The 'right attitude' means a willingness to accept the rigours of SF training and learn from the experience. It means sticking at the marching, enduring the weather and the weight of the pack without complaint. It means being willing and able always to do that little bit more, to summon up from somewhere the ability to continue until the task is completed. Special Force soldiering requires a lot of that elusive quality called 'character' and one aim of the training is to bring that character out.

Lieutenant Bob Butt of the Australian Commandos did part of his training in England with the Royal Marines in the 1960s: 'I found that my six months wandering the world prior to arriving in Britain had taken a toll of my fitness and I had to work hard to keep up with the younger Pommie bastards. These soldiers – sorry, Marines – were in very good physical shape and spent part of every day on hard physical training. I spent time with the SBS at Poole on a Swimmer Canoeist Course, fourteen weeks in mid-winter, which meant sub-zero temperatures, being eternally cold and wet, sleepless nights, tiredness, fog, rain, hard work, exhaustion. It was the coldest and hardest three months of my life but I would not have missed it. I found a determined, aggressive and proud group of fighting men with a history of achievement like very few in the world today.'

Special Force training can be intensive. The Israeli Naval Commandos endure a course that can involve scuba training, parachute jumps, sharp shooting and target practice, unarmed and hand-to-hand combat, medical training, rappelling (abseiling) and cliff climbing, terrorist and hostage-rescue situations, intelligence gathering and much more. The length of training varies but the basic course is usually at least two months. Argentina started training Commando units in 1964 and the initial course lasted just thirty days. In 1967 this course, basically a weapons-training and fitness course similar to that given to the US Rangers and handled by instructors at the Cordoba Infantry Depot, was altered to give more attention to the counter-guerrilla role. In 1968 the Commando Course was reformed to combine Ranger training with counter-terrorist work and lasted six weeks. Those who passed the basic course were then often sent abroad to other SF schools, like the US Jungle Training School in Panama.

During the 1970s Argentina was in the grip of political repression and the Commandos took a full part in this distasteful activity, sustaining their first casualties in an ambush in 1974. In 1978 they were tasked to provide anti-terrorist protection for players and spectators at the World Cup Football Tournament – a strange role for a Commando unit. An umbrella organization, Halcon 8, was formed to co-ordinate security tasks at the World Cup, and remains the control and command centre for all Argentine SF activity to this day. The two Argentine Commando companies committed to the Falklands/Malvinas War of 1982 did well in small-scale actions but were largely outclassed by their better-trained and more highly motivated British opponents. The Argentine Commando companies are still an integral part of the Argentine Army and their basic course, which now lasts three months, is rated as one of the most demanding in the world.

Most Special Force units have some form of pre-recruit training where a volunteer can sample the life and see what he is up against. Meanwhile the instructors will take a look at him. If both sides are happy, the recruit is accepted for further training. If not, the volunteer can return to his parent unit, with no hard feelings and no sense of failure; SF soldiering is not for everyone.

Special Force training has changed over the years, from that which sought to eliminate the unfit or unsuitable to that which tries to assist a suitable volunteer to complete the course and join his chosen unit. The fall-out rate is still very high, averaging around 80 per cent in most Special Force units, but there is still only one sanction for failure and only one punishment for a failure to try – the RTU, Return to Unit. Those who do not measure up for any reason are simply told to pack their kit and leave. In the decades since Special Force units were first organized as fighting forces, the RTU has been the only form of punishment, and a highly effective one.

In the United States the training endured by recruits to the USMC has become legendary, as Jerry Wininger recalls: 'In 1962 the Marine Corps Recruit Depot at San Diego, California was a real shock for any teenager. We arrived after a night flight at 0300 hours and by daylight we were getting our first boot haircut and started training. We trained hard and realized that the training and discipline was for our own good. The DIs could be tough. I heard of one DI who put a recruit in a wall locker and pushed it down a hill. Another DI put a recruit in a wall locker, squirted some lighter fluid into the vent holes in the bottom and lit it. The recruit did some dancing but was not harmed. Horror stories abounded in Boot Training but I never heard of a recruit who was physically hurt and no recruit ever said, "I want out." I would rather a man fell apart in Boot Training than in combat and risk the lives of good Marines.'

Special Force training has always been tough. It aims to weed out those who cannot cope with the life while teaching the soldier all he needs to know. Most of the volunteers will have had some experience of service life or even been in combat, but this may be their first experience of incessant training since their time as a recruit.

In most armies the recruit starts service life with about three months of basic training. During this time he gets fit, learns to use a range of infantry weapons and the basics of fieldcraft and gets a grounding in the other elements of military life: drill, turnout, regimental history and tradition, the role of his squad, section, platoon, company and battalion in the military set-up. After initial training some men join their battalions, others go on to specialist training as signallers, gunners, cooks, drivers, a few may depart for officer school, and a few will be discharged. It is only after this that the Special Force volunteer, by now a fairly experienced soldier, starts his SF training.

A good example of Special Force training is that provided by the British 22nd SAS Regiment, which is generally recognized as one of the finest Special Force units in the world. The SAS soldier is not a superman or a trained assassin. He is a highly trained specialist, and the object of his selection and the continuous training which follows is to fit the man for the task. SAS recruits are drawn from the ranks of the regular Army, and volunteers will probably have served about three years with their parent unit before being considered for the SAS. This means that the SAS volunteer tends to be older, more experienced and more mature than the soldiers commonly found in other infantry regiments. The NCOs and men join for an initial period of three years, which is usually extended, but the officers tend to join the SAS for three years and then return to their parent unit. This last rule has had the effect of spreading former SAS men throughout the Army and providing the Regiment with friends in high places; indeed service in the SAS has come to form part of the necessary qualifications for higher command. Lieutenant-General Sir Michael Rose, who commanded the UN Forces in Bosnia, and Lieutenant-General Peter de la Billière, who commanded British forces in the 1991 Gulf War, are both former SAS officers.

On joining the Regiment all volunteers take a drop in rank and pay. Training begins with a rigorous selection process, in the wet, wild and windy country of the Black Mountains and the Brecon Beacons in South Wales. This process starts with a ten-day map-reading, marching and fitness programme. The packs are made heavier by the day and the period ends with a forty-mile cross-mountain march carrying platoon weapons, the march to be completed in twenty hours or less. By the end of this first ten-day period the number of volunteers has shrunk considerably.

One feature of this training was the so-called 'sickener factor', designed to add mental stress to physical effort. At the end of a long march the men might be required to crawl through a tunnel full of rotting sheep entrails, or have a truck pull up alongside and offer them a lift: any man who even looked like accepting was instantly RTU'd. Another method of seeking out the faint-hearted was to tell them at the end of a march that the real finish was still five miles away. Anyone cursing or groaning at this news was also sent back to his unit. But in the SAS today, as in other Special Force units, the instructors aim to get the men through the course rather than turn them away.

Much of this training is carried out alone or in small groups. Those who complete the first ten days then go on to a fourteen-week, all-arms infantry-training course, partly to hone infantry skills to the high SAS requirements and partly because many SAS recruits come from the technical arms, the Royal Engineers or Signals, and are less familiar with the infantry role. During this period the volunteers also learn to use some of the special SAS equipment and to handle explosives. They then go on a demolition course, as well as sampling some intensive training in CQB – Close-Quarter Battle. That done, they must all complete the standard Army parachute course of eight jumps, followed by a survival course. The small number who complete the full course are then 'badged', accepted into the Regiment and entitled to wear the much prized sand-coloured beret and the 'Who Dares, Wins' cap badge. This is only the start of their training, which really never stops.

Once accepted into the Regiment the SAS soldier has to specialize. The SAS is organized on a 'unit of four' principle: the soldier will train for a role in one of the four specialist troops that make up every SAS squadron. The Boat Troop contains underwater swimmers, canoeists and small-boat experts; the Mountain Troop contains climbers and experts in Alpine and Arctic warfare; the Mobility Troop uses specially equipped, machine-gun-armed Land Rovers and the desert vehicles used in the Gulf War; and the Free-Fall Troop contains the high-altitude parachutists. This specialization means that the SAS can fill any Special Force 'terrain' requirement. Every troop also contains individual specialists, radio men, first-aid and medical orderlies, snipers, signallers trained in sending and receiving high-speed Morse and a number of linguists. The SAS have always been keen on that 'hearts and minds' activity, so useful behind the enemy lines, and the Regiment contains men who speak most European languages, plus Arabic, Mandarin Chinese and Malay.

Finally, all SAS men receive training in CRW (Counter-Revolutionary Warfare) and anti-terrorist tactics. The Regiment keeps one squadron on standby for CRW work, ready to go into action anywhere in the world, and this standby squadron provided the men who broke the Iranian Embassy siege in London in 1980. SAS training is so thorough that it is closely copied by other SF units like the US Delta Force, and in 1996 the German Army asked the British SAS to undertake the training of their newly formed Kommando Spezialkraft (KSK) unit, which is tasked with behind-the-lines operations and hostage rescues outside Germany. This training will take place at Pontrilas on the Welsh Marches, close to the present SAS base at Hereford, and will follow standard SAS procedures.

The toughest Special Force training and selection process in the world is probably that endured by the US Navy SEALs. The process begins with a two-week Indoctrination Phase, involving large amounts of swimming, running and other forms of physical exercise. Those who complete this phase move on to Phase One, which lasts seven weeks and is devoted to weeding out those who are not up to the mental and physical strains of SEAL work. This phase requires instant obedience to orders, more swimming, running and assault courses, with the core of the training concentrated around Motivation or 'Hell Week', in the middle of the phase, when the men spend seven days of gruelling, non-stop training, with less than eight hours' sleep, and that in short stages of fifteen minutes or less. The pressure is increased by the fact that the completion of any task is left to the motivation of an ever-more weary student, without any assistance from the training staff. Live ammunition and explosive charges are also used extensively, an added danger to tired men.

Those who complete Phase One and wish to continue move on to Phase Two, learning the techniques of beach reconnaissance and land warfare. This includes recon work, patrolling, ambushing, rappelling from helicopters, submarine exit and underwater entry, sniping skills and demolition work. The phase terminates with a three-week exercise during which all the skills learned so far are called into use.

The next phase, Phase Three, concentrates on scuba and diving skills, working at sea and with submarines, but the physical side is not neglected. Students are expected to complete runs of up to fourteen miles and open-ocean swims of up to six miles and by this stage some 30–80 per cent of students will have dropped out. On graduation, the entire course is sent to the Airborne School at Fort Benning in Georgia to take the Army parachute course. On completion of all these phases, the initial training is over, but the student is still on probation. He is then attached to a UDT or SEAL team for a period of six months and only after that, if his colleagues and officers are satisfied with his skills and attitude, is he fully accepted as a trained SEAL. SAS and SEALs are two of the most highly trained and specialized SF units in the world, but most military organizations now contain a trained Special Force element.

A view of the extension of Special Force warfare into conventional military activity comes from Lieutenant-Colonel Landon Thorne III of the US Marines: 'Not to be left out, the other service components have gotten into the SOF act by creating their own niche capabilities. The US Navy has its SEALSs, whose forebears were UDT frogmen. The US Air Force created its Air Commandos to support US Army Rangers in the attacking and holding of defined airfields and it also has its Special Operating Squadrons, which contain the Black Bird gunships, AC130s loaded with Gatling guns. The AC130s are excellent quick fixes to a special op going sour – they pump a lot of lead and give you a curtain to run away behind.

'While our SOF organizations have their own organic structures within their service components, the Special Operator community has its own governing United Command, SOCOM, which manages the SOF systems and assets. SOF units are assigned to their respective theaters by SOCOM. The theater allocation of SOF is further broken down by allocation to the Unified Command which has specific theater responsibility and the SOCs (Special Operations Capable units), once allocated, are operationally directed by sub-unified command head-quarters within the Unified Command; ie. when I was assigned to SOCCENT [Special Operations Command, Central Command], I was a special operator assigned to the SOC serving US Central Command (USCENTCOM) – the wonderful people who brought you Operation Desert Storm and General Norman Schwarzkopf.

'But nothing in the foregoing has addressed the big question, i.e. what *makes* a special soldier? In my humble opinion, there are some folks [who] are just instinctive warriors. Combine that instinct with the pioneering spirit – the legacy of the Green Mountain Boys, Teddy Roosevelt, the Indian fighters, the Knights of the Round Table, what-ever – and the titillating rush of a little (or a lot) of danger, and you get the special soldier. Maybe he (and possibly now she) is someone who just wants to be different, for whom the commonplace, the safe and the banal is simply not enough. Someone who wants to look back at their life and believe that they did something to change the course of history.

'The SF calls a category of its operations DAs – Direct Actions – and maybe therein lies the clue. Forget all the complications of bureaucratic soldiering, just point us at the bad guys and let 'er rip. Those of us who are the breed know one another ... a few words of conversation and the "duffers" are separated from the long-ball hitters. It doesn't take a ton of words from a Special soldier's mouth to let another Special soldier know that they are warrior kin.'

The increasing use of technology has provided a great boost to Special Force units and Special Force activity, in both the range of opportunities it presents for targets and the means it offers for carrying the war to the enemy. A great many technological advances, originally designed for civilian use, have drifted into the hands of SF units, and Special Forces have also developed their own technology. Night sights, helicopters, parachutes, including the free-fall and steerable variety, submarines, both full-sized and midget, scuba gear, explosives, even hanggliders, have been used for SF purposes in recent campaigns.

This rapid acceptance and adoption of new equipment has not meant any decline in other, older methods or equipment. Some technologies are very old indeed, like the small crossbows carried by specialists of the French Foreign Legion for the silent elimination of sentries. Canoes, small boats and a varied range of landing craft are still employed, and the bulk of Special Force soldiers still go to war on their feet, but if some new device is need the SF soldier will soon seek it out.

The use of technology is not new. The Second World War saw the introduction of units based on the use of what were then the latest inventions, such as the parachute, the midget submarine, the 'human torpedo', the glider and, as the war ended, the helicopter. After the war the helicopter came into increasing use by Special Forces as a means of dropping small compact groups behind the enemy lines without the scattering inevitable with parachute operations. SOF units saw the helicopter as a 'force enhancer', especially in rugged terrain where the standard military yardstick is that a battalion with helicopters is worth a brigade without them. Helicopters were first used in the assault role by 45 Commando, Royal Marines at Suez in 1956, and ten years later the helicopter-equipped US Airmobile Division made a great impact on the war in Vietnam.

Special Force soldiers are at the cutting edge of war and have always been on the lookout for new and better ways of getting at the enemy. David Stirling, founder of the SAS, was one of the first to appreciate the possibilities of the jeep for desert warfare, and modern SF units were quick to take up the long-wheelbase, four-wheel-drive Land Rover and the US Hummer, which was widely used in the Gulf War, has a good weapons and cargo capacity and a range of 350 miles without refuelling. The Hummer seems to be infinitely adaptable, with fifteen versions in current use with the US Army.

Special Force units have proved equally quick to adapt other technical advances, military or civilian, to SF use. Surveillance equipment, derived from the kind used by security firms to watch offices and car parks, has been adapted by the SAS for counter-terrorist work, where the use of small radios and miniature cameras has proved increasingly useful in surveying a terrorist hideout before the assault. Sports parachutes and free-fall techniques of sky-diving clubs have been used for HILO (high-exit, low-opening) parachute operations, enabling SAS troopers to exit their aircraft miles from the target, and 'fly' silently for miles over hostile territory before deploying their parachutes and descending on the enemy position.

The Special Force soldier has to be open-minded in matters of equipment, for the question he has constantly to consider is 'What do we need to do the job – in time and with the minimum cost in lives?' Climbing equipment, popular with the Big Wall rock-climbers of Yosemite, has come in useful for such tasks as abseiling off the roof of the Iranian Embassy in 1980. Small boats, especially rubber dinghies like the Zodiac and the Ridged Raider assault craft used by the Royal Marine Commandos, were also developed from civilian craft, and proved ideal for landing troops on cliffs, rocky shores or wave-swept beaches. Modern technology has also been used to develop Sub-Skimmer craft, submersible landing craft, which can approach a beach under water slowly and silently, but escape back to sea again on the surface at over 25 knots.

Useful as these methods and devices are, Special Forces are military units and their main requirements for specialized modern technology have been in the field of weaponry. The rifle is the standard Special Force weapon, largely because of its range and hitting power, with the US M16 popular among Western forces and the AK47 Kalashnikov the chosen weapon of Eastern-bloc forces and in much of the Third World. Weapons like the German Heckler & Koch submachine-gun are popular for they are compact, light and offer a high rate of fire, but the H&K does not have the range required for all types of fighting. Silencers have also been developed which can be used on these high-velocity weapons without sacrificing accuracy or rate of fire.

Other popular rifles are the French FA-MAS rifle, the German G3SG sniper rifle, which fires the NATO 7.62mm cartridge and has an effective range of 600 yards, and the tripod-mounted Heckler & Koch PSG1, which was developed for police use but rapidly taken up by Western

Europe's Special Force and anti-terrorist units, not least because it has a laser 'red dot' sight, which makes for pinpoint accuracy in skilled hands. Not all weapons become internationally accepted and most nations stick to their own standard arms. The Israelis swear by their Galil assault rifle, while the Italians employ the excellent range of firearms produced by the Beretta company, and the Americans prefer the products of their own armaments companies. The SAS on the other hand employ a wide range of weapons, including the Heckler & Koch, US Winchester shotguns and the M16, as well as British weapons.

Special Forces have always been interested in sniping skills and many now equip their sniper units with the Parker-Hale 85 rifle, which comes with a bipod and can be fitted with various nightsights and optical magnifying scopes. The US Army have developed a sniping rifle, the 7.62 calibre M21, though this is really little more than the standard M14 rifle manufactured to tighter specification. Ammunition has become more standardized, with the 9mm calibre predominating, largely because it is widely available and many modern weapons systems are chambered for 9mm ammunition. Since modern weapons have a high cyclatic rate of fire – up to 1,000 rounds a minute is not uncommon – large amounts of ammunition have to be carried and it must therefore be light. In Vietnam US troopers carried up to 600 rounds of M16 ammunition, but M16 ammunition is light and the weight was bearable.

Special ammunition has also been developed for use in hostage-rescue operations where a heavy bullet with a low-charge propellant is the favoured cartridge. Such ammunition has the advantage that it will knock down and incapacitate the target without passing through the body to kill or injure an innocent hostage or penetrate the vulnerable skin of a pressurized aircraft. Armour-piercing rounds are used to stop cars, to penetrate body armour or fire through doors protected by armour plate.

Pistols are useful weapons for the Special Force soldier. In most armies officers and NCOs carry a pistol or revolver as a personal weapon simply because it leaves their hand free to handle maps and radios, but SF soldiers use these weapons in combat and are highly skilled in their use. The Browning Hi-power 9mm pistol is popular, as is the Heckler & Koch 9mm P9S, which was developed as a police weapon but is now the standard handgun with GSG9, the German anti-terrorist unit.

Shotguns are generally regarded as a sporting weapon or for police use, but they have been adopted by many Special Force units, for use at night or in close combat. Military shotguns are shorter than the sporting variety and carry a heavier cartridge, with the 12 gauge buckshot cartridge being especially popular. The SAS have adopted the Winchester pump-action shotgun, and equipped it with special rounds, including a solid-shot round that can take off door hinges or blast a lock clear of the woodwork.

Rocket launchers are another item in the SF armoury, weapons that have a high impact-to-weight ratio and deliver a considerable punch with a very small charge. The Soviet RPG (Rocket Propelled Grenade) No. 7 can be found all over the Third World and is possessed by most terrorist groups, including the IRA. The British Army uses the one-shot, disposable LAW 80, which can penetrate most tank armour and has an effective range of some 300 yards.

Technology has also expanded the range of targets. Oilfields, airfields, power stations, command and computer centres and military head-quarters, TV and radio transmitters, railways, bridges, aircraft, both military and civilian, provide an ever wider range of targets for Special Force attack. Armies and civil powers use a great deal of technology and can no longer function without it, but the reliance on such equipment makes them vulnerable to the well-placed bomb or the sudden raid.

Special equipment in current use includes plastic explosive, shaped charges, stun-grenades, 'flash bangs' for aircraft entry and terrorist assaults, the Wilkinson fighting knife, carried by most SAS troopers, a wide range of infra-red night and telescopic sights, Nautiraid folding canoes, Rigid Raider assault craft and Zodiac dinghies with silent-running engines. Special Forces also employ a range of aircraft, fixed wing and rotary, military and civilian, for entry and extraction, plus specially adapted mini-submarines and various forms of scuba gear and parachutes.

Much of this equipment is still on the secret list, but the world of the Special Force soldier is increasingly technological, and more devices are being developed for SF use all the time, continuing a trend that began in the early days of the Second World War.

The tactics employed by the Special Force soldier depend on one essential element: surprise. If the enemy can be surprised, taken off-guard or otherwise outwitted, then any discrepancy in numbers between the SF unit and the enemy can be largely discounted. Surprise is an essential element in most military plans but it is a hard one to achieve. A commander can usually work out what the enemy commander will do simply by putting himself in the enemy commander's position and considering his options, which are usually limited by terrain, weather or logistical considerations. The Special Force soldier has to surprise the enemy by taking an action which the enemy commander has not yet considered or rejected as one beyond the bounds of possibility.

The German–Palestinian terrorists and the Ugandan soldiers holding the Air France passengers hostage at Entebbe in 1976 (see Chapter Eleven) cannot in their wildest nightmares have thought that the Israelis would send paratroopers flying halfway across Africa to assault their positions. This was an operation of great daring, but the most daring part of it was the sheer audacity – or chutzpah – which enabled the Israelis even to consider it.

The 'Greatest Raid of All', the British Commando attack on the giant repair dock at St Nazaire in 1942 is another example of such enterprise and, as at Entebbe, it worked. The British force was detected and challenged as the destroyer HMS *Campbeltown* and her supporting launches ploughed upriver towards their target, but the Germans could not grasp that this actually was a British raiding force; such an assault was impossible, or so they thought. As a result they hesitated, and by the time they opened fire on the ships it was too late to prevent the *Campbeltown* ramming the dock gates with her cargo of high explosives. These are two classic examples of the use of surprise, attained by attempting and pulling off the seemingly impossible. If you have highly trained, resolute troops, commanded by men with imagination and daring, it can be done. The SAS motto 'Who Dares, Wins' is well chosen.

Surprise can also be achieved by attacking the enemy from some unexpected quarter or across terrain which he considers impassable. The cliff-assault skills of the Royal Marines Mountain and Arctic Warfare Cadre, a unit that serves as the 3rd Commando Brigade Patrol Troop, or of the US Rangers are an example of Special Force expertise deployed to take advantage of 'unsuitable' terrain. Colonel Rudder and his Rangers scaling the cliffs of the Pointe du Hoc in Normandy on D-Day, with the use of ropes established by rocket-fired grapnels, is a demonstration of this method.

Surprise can also be obtained by using Special Force technology, simple or highly technical. The Australian canoeists of the Rimau raid, who twice paddled into Singapore harbour to sink Japanese shipping, are a good example of a force using surprise and simple technology, while David Stirling brought the art of obtaining surprise a stage further when he led the 'Great Jeep Raid' on Sidi Haneish airfield in 1942. The

SAS had been attacking German airfields for months and the defenders were now alert for small parties of saboteurs. Stirling raised the stakes by sweeping out of the desert in eighteen heavily-armed jeeps, swamping the defences by the sheer weight of their fire. That is another Special Force tactic, taking a method of attack one stage further, adding new twists, to keep the enemy off-balance and maintain the advantage of surprise. On the Great Jeep Raid Stirling achieved this twice, by taking his men back to the airfield to destroy a few more aircraft in a second attack that night before the Germans had recovered from the first one. If the first attack had been a surprise, the idea of putting in another attack within hours of the first was a work of genius.

Subterfuge is another useful tactic, another way of keeping the enemy off-balance. In 1952, when Captain Kitson discovered that he could dress up like a Mau Mau terrorist and prowl the forests of Kenya with little risk of detection (see Chapter Six), he placed a new weapon in the hands of the British counter-insurgency forces. Kitson's 'pseudo-gangs', led by Kenya Regiment officers disguised as Africans, were able to penetrate and surprise the Mau Mau gangs and this led to many ambushes and useful captures.

An extension of the 'pseudo-gang' is the use of 'turned' terrorists, when a captured terrorist is persuaded to lead patrols against his former comrades. This tactic was widely used by the British in Malaya and by the Americans in Vietnam. It springs from the Special Force 'hearts and minds' tactic – a tactic which is not only sympathetic but sensible and highly effective. Those British SAS and American Green Beret soldiers who spent time learning local languages and customs, building schools, playing with the children, respecting the old and treating the sick, kept the local people on their side, and this paid good dividends in any subsequent fighting.

The main SF tactic has been summed up in the phrase 'Hit 'em hard, hit 'em fast – and get away to hit 'em again.' US Special Forces in Vietnam used that tactic again and again against the Vietcong and the Army of North Vietnam. They would attack a Vietcong position or defend their landing ground until all surprise was gone; then, when the enemy began to muster a force sufficient to overwhelm them, they would summon up helicopters to extract them. Fighter-bombers were then called in to attack the enemy gathering for the assault, and so the SF soldiers combined a good use of fighting craft with the impact of the latest military technology. Unfortunately, the Vietcong used much the same tactics against conventional US forces, fighting only when and where they wanted to fight, breaking off the action when the build-up of air and artillery support on the US side started to cause them casualties.

'Getting the hell out of it', or the 'Shoot and Scoot' policy used by the SAS in Borneo, breaking off the action when the enemy thinks he has you pinned, is another SF tactic. Special Forces are not designed for sustained combat, though as the British 1st Parachute Division showed at Arnhem and 41 (Independent) Commando, Royal Marines, showed in the retreat from Chosin in the Korean War they can fight for days if they have to. The tactics that Special Force units usually employ are dictated by their role, working in small groups, behind the lines or anywhere they are not expected to be. For as long as they employ tactics which ensure the element of surprise, they will be successful.

'Ten Commandments for Special Warfare' were drawn up by a US Navy SEAL, Richard Marcinko, in 1970:

1. I am the War Lord and the wrathful god of Combat and I will always lead you from the front.
2. I will treat you all alike – and like shit.
3. Thou shalt do nothing I shall not do first.
4. I shall punish thy bodies for the more thou sweatest in training, the less thou bleedest in combat.
5. Verily, if thou hurteth in thy efforts and suffer pain, thou art Doing It Right.
6. Thou hast not to like it – thou hast just to do it.
7. Thou shalt keep it simple, stupid.
8. Thou shalt never assume anything, thou wilt check it out.
9. Verily thou art not paid for thy methods but for thy results and thou will kill thy enemy before he killeth you, and by any means available.
10. Thou shalt bear in mind the Ultimate Commandment: There are no rules; thou shalt win at any price.

This chapter has outlined some of the rules that govern the use and deployment of Special Forces but, as Richard Marcinko says, there are no rules or at least there is no fixed centre in the SF world. Special Force soldiering is in a constant state of flux, the men and units constantly reacting to changes in warfare, by making changes in their role, in order to meet new challenges. But there are still a few core elements, some features that do not change, and these are summed up by John Grebby, now living in Ontario, Canada, when recalling his service with both the Parachute Regiment and the Royal Marine Commandos in the 1950s: 'Compared with soldiering in the 1990s, the services in the 1950s were in a different world. Comparisons can be unfair, but I believe that British forces are better trained today. Perhaps the discipline is not what it was, for in the 1950s service life was very strict, living conditions were very primitive and training was hard. Discipline was so strict that sometimes you got into trouble regardless of whether you actually did something wrong. This was especially so at Aldershot, or when the Parachute Battalions were stationed at home. Once we were moved overseas the "Toms" stopped grumbling and enjoyed their training in IS [Internal Security] duties and the Battalion became a well-oiled, efficient machine.

'Most of our middle and junior officers and NCOs were Second World War veterans and most of them were good as they had battle experience. Our living conditions in Talavera Barracks in Aldershot really were primitive. Light, heat, washing and bathing facilities were minimal, food was pretty awful and our equipment was all a hangover from the Second World War. We still had the Lee Enfield Mark IV rifle, the Bren-gun, the Vickers medium machine-gun and the 3-inch mortar in the battalion. The only new equipment was the 3.5-inch rocket launcher (anti-tank), and the Anti-Tank Platoon had the American 106mm gun mounted on a Land Rover or a tripod on the ground. Nor were we at all well paid. My pay on a three-year enlistment was £7 or £8 a week, but this eventually went up to £9 a week, plus £2 2s (£2.20p) a week parachuting pay, when I signed on for nine years. Despite our low pay and poor living conditions, my Parachute Battalion, the 2nd – 2 Para – was a fine unit to serve in.

'I was proud to serve in both the Royal Marines and the Parachute Regiment. The Royal Marines turnout and drill is very smart, more so than in the Parachute Regiment. This is not to say the Paras could not be well turned out, but the Marines' dress lends itself to efficient and quick drill movements. Generally the Marines were smarter on parade. The Royal Marines' regimental history was rammed home harder than the Paras', and they had to know it. In basic training with both regiments we had to know regimental history, but the Marines' history spans more than three centuries, back to 1664. The Paras' history starts with the Tragino Aqueduct Operation in Southern Italy on 10 February 1941. That apart, the men are the same. But the roles are different.

'The Marines excelled in cliff assault, and of course beach assault from LCIs, LSTs (landing craft – infantry; landing ship – tanks) and so on was their speciality. Only once in my seven years with the Paras did I get unarmed combat instruction, and that lasted only thirty minutes. The Marines trained at this much more. The uniqueness of the Parachute Regiment lies in their team spirit and willingness to slog it out to the end, no matter what. There were no special parachutes for officers, nor special exit doors in the aircraft for WOs [warrant officers] and sergeants. Everybody took the same risks.

'You don't have to be a Tarzan nor have an A-level education to be a parachutist, but it is very demanding for a short period of time during the jump. You have about forty-five seconds to check canopy, untwist if necessary, steer away from other parachutists, release your kit bag with all your ammo, weapons etc. in it, assess the drift, steer yourself and prepare for a landing without hitting someone or something. If you collide with another parachutist it can spell disaster, resulting in the collapse of your parachute. Then you drop to earth like a stone and hope that your reserve 'chute saves you. I remember the Recruit Company Commander, Major W. R. Corbould, saying, on our basic training completion, before we went to RAF Station Abingdon to do our parachute training, "Parachuting is only a means of transportation," and he told us that we shouldn't forget our infantry training. He was right, but parachuting drove us to our limits, physically and mentally. That's what made us excellent infantry soldiers.

'All members, regardless of rank, wore the same cap badge and red beret, officers as well, even including the Colonel-in-Chief. It builds team spirit and unit pride. Team spirit is drilled into you from day one, much more so than in the Marines. If your buddy is in difficulties, help him, don't grumble or ask questions. Just do it, to keep the Platoon, Company or Battalion functioning.

'One didn't have to be tough to be in either the Marines or the Paras, although it probably helped. What was required was some get-up-and-go and the ability to keep going to the end. The RM Commando School at Bickleigh was hard enough, but I later found some of the endurance marches even more demanding in the Paras. In Recruit Company a ten-mile road walk and run in full battle gear with a rifle in two hours was considered a minimum goal to achieve. In the battalions you were expected to exceed this, especially overseas in the more trying climatic conditions of Cyprus, Jordan and Borneo.

'The Royal Marines perform more varied tasks than the Paras, despite the fact that both train in the infantry role. The Marines perform these tasks very well and, to sum up, I think that the Royal Marines and the Parachute Regiment are very fine institutions and I am proud to have served in them.'

These thoughts of a post-Second World War soldier are echoed by Lieutenant-Colonel Johnny Cooper, MBE, DCM, who was one of David Stirling's first SAS recruits in 1941 and stayed close to SAS operations until he retired in 1979: 'Looking back on my close association with the SAS Regiment I consider it to have been more like a club or family, with no great emphasis on the physical toughness that is so often attributed to it today. We were carrying out David Stirling's initial insistence that small patrols of three men could do enormous damage on an enemy owing to their ability to penetrate behind the lines, and we certainly proved that in the early days. This was coupled with our ability to change our methods and keep the enemy guessing.'

The hard training of Special Force troops has one other purpose: to create *esprit de corps*. This spirit, unit pride, can last a lifetime. Nearly fifty years after he served with 41 (Independent) Commando in Korea, Arthur Derby of the Royal Marines still feels proud of his unit: '41 was a happy unit. We had some terrible times but we had it good too because of the blokes who served in it. They were just a great bunch of guys, and have never been equalled. I served in other places and in other Commandos, but 41 was special.' Creating that kind of feeling is part of the training process. The training is tough, not just to weed out the unsuited, but also to bind those who survive it into a composite whole, made up of men who know that the others have endured all that they have endured and come out of it with their heads up and their sense of humour intact. Over time, decades or centuries, this creates another feeling, that the whole is more than just the sum of the parts, that a reputation has been created which must be maintained.

No one has ever summed this feeling up better than William Manchester, the distinguished American author and biographer. Manchester served as a sergeant in the United States Marine Corps in the Second World War and was wounded at Okinawa. Honours and compliments have showered upon William Manchester since 1945, but at heart he remains a United States Marine, and he sums up what that means to him like this:

> There is a seed: unit pride. It is planted in every man during training and it grows to be tougher than he is. He may want it gone, but he can't shuck it. He may jeer at all heroes as 'Gung ho', and call the Sergeant 'Daddy-oh', but still the thing stays inside him and when he finds himself on the line, he's got it and it him. He may never have heard the Marine Band, may not even know where Tripoli is, or who the Montezumans were. Still he'll jump up and go when Daddy-oh pumps his arm for the assault, because someone once told him it was better to die than let the Marine Corps down, and he believed it then, and part of him always will.

Parachute Regiment badge

CHAPTER FOUR

The Post-War World 1945–1950

It has fallen to my lot to tell you, the Commandos,
who have fought with such distinction in Norway
and the islands of the north, in France, in Belgium,
in Holland, and in Germany, in Africa and Egypt,
in Crete and Syria, in Sicily and Italy, on the shores
and islands of the Adriatic, and in the jungles of
the Arakan and Burma ... it is, I repeat, with great
regret that I must tell you today, that you are to
be disbanded.

General Robert Laycock, speech to 1 Commando
Brigade, 25 October 1945

The Second World War ended on 15 August 1945 and the disbandment of the Western armies began almost at once. Some Special Force units, like Popski's Private Army, had been disbanded when the Germans surrendered in May, and other units were so worn down by years of warfare or so committed to the European theatre that they were not sent to the Far East after VE (Victory in Europe) Day and were ready for disbandment when the war ended.

Those Army Commando soldiers addressed by Brigadier Laycock had all been demobilized or returned to their parent units by the end of 1946. The two SAS Regiments, which had done so well in the late war, were disbanded by the end of 1945, as was the SRS (Special Raiding Squadron) and the wartime SBS. The modern SBS has more in common with the wartime COPP and the RM Boom Patrol than the seaborne raiders of the Aegean and the Adriatic. For a while it looked as if all the Special Force units created during the war had no role to play in the smaller peacetime armies, but some units did survive, though in a much reduced form.

Thanks to the intervention of Lord Louis Mountbatten, wartime Chief of Combined Operations, the Royal Marine Commandos escaped disbandment, though the eight Commandos raised in the war shrank to just three, 40, 42 and 45 Commando. These units regrouped in Hong Kong in 1945 and formed the 3rd Commando Brigade, Royal Marines, to which was attached a small SBS unit, also from the Royal Marines, for use in amphibious reconnaissance. The Royal Marines Special Boat Squadron is the amphibious equivalent of the SAS, but while it operates in much the same manner, in four-man teams, it specializes in beach recce for Commando landings, in submarine-launched raids by canoe or frogman parties and in attacks on shipping in the frogman role, using scuba equipment.

The Commando School left Achnacarry and was established for a while at Towyn in North Wales before coming under Royal Marine control and moving to Bickleigh in Devon as the CSRM (Commando School, Royal Marines), where all those destined for Royal Marine Commando units went through a six-week course. The purely volunteer aspect had gone, for most Royal Marine recruits were sent to Bickleigh, but the course retained what one post-war Marine described as 'all the usual torments' – assault courses, speed-marches, live firing exercises, the death slide across a rock-strewn river, a two-mile scramble course over the hills, cliff-assault training on Jennicliff in Plymouth Sound, a great deal of battle PT, and a gruelling final exercise.

The Cliff Assault Wing of the CSRM was based at Land's End in Cornwall, where it taught Royal Marine climbers the art of rock climbing by day and night after landing from small boats, often in gale-force conditions. With the commitment of 45 Commando Group to the Northern Front of NATO, the Cliff Assault Wing became the Mountain and Arctic Warfare Cadre, which trained Mountain Leaders – MLs – in climbing, Arctic warfare, including skiing and survival, sniping, raiding and irregular warfare. In peacetime the Cadre had a training function, but in times of war it became the Recce Platoon for the Commando Brigade, operating under the orders of the Brigade Commander. So, thanks to Lord Louis and the Royal Marines, the Commando tradition survived in the British armed forces.

The US Rangers were not so lucky. The six Ranger battalions survived for a while, but were then disbanded, though Ranger training continued in a small way at infantry depots like Fort Benning. The USMC Raider Battalions also disappeared, as did the OSS, though this clandestine organization soon reappeared as the Central Intelligence Agency, which ran spies in the countries behind the Iron Curtain.

When the war ended, most of the soldiers were very anxious to get out of uniform and back to civilian life. Armies are expensive, and the national governments, especially in the West, were keen to bring the boys home and reduce their military expenditure. Besides, with the invention of the atomic bomb world war seemed to have become unthinkable, and the United Nations, which met for the first time in San Francisco in April 1945, was charged with settling international disputes peacefully and so 'freeing future generations from the scourge of war'.

This pious hope was not to be realized. The Communist powers had no intention of giving up any of the territory taken during the war, and every intention of exploiting post-war tensions in order to seize more. The bombs of Hiroshima and Nagasaki may have prevented world war, but war has many forms and the form that appeared swiftly after 1945 was irregular warfare, subversion and terrorism. In these wars lessons were learned that would affect Special Force operations in the decades ahead. The first lesson was that irregular warfare, unlike conventional warfare, is not a simple matter of right or wrong, finding the enemy and bringing him to battle. In irregular warfare the issues are not clear-cut, objectives are confused, and all manner of factors, not least politics and propaganda, have to be taken into account when planning and executing a military campaign.

These factors were not grasped in the immediate aftermath of war. The disbandment of the armies continued even as guerrilla warfare sputtered on in the Balkans, in Greece, and especially in the Middle and Far East, largely in those territories which had formed part of the British, French and Dutch colonial empires. Even the Americans, who liberated the Philippines from the Japanese, were soon involved in a very vicious war with a strong force of local Communist guerrillas, the Huks.

An American colony since the end of the nineteenth century, the Philippines has never been the most tranquil of countries. The Japanese Occupation and the fight to regain the islands in 1944–5 had destroyed large parts of the capital, Manila, and left hundreds of thousands of Filipinos destitute, diseased or starving. Like many other people the Filipinos had fought for a safer world and a better life, not a reimposition of pre-war colonial conditions. Among the changes they sought in 1945 was land reform and the establishment of democratic political institutions. Terrible living conditions and little sign of the much needed reforms provided a breeding ground for Communist insurrection and gave a ready-made cause to the Huks, a local guerrilla force which had just finished fighting the Japanese.

During the war in the Philippines, as in Western Europe and Malaya, the Communists had provided the core of national resistance to the invaders. Their guerrilla force, the 20,000-strong Hukbo ng Bayan so Hapon – or Huks – the People's Army Against the Japanese, had waged war against the Japanese, and had the equipment, training and experience to continue the struggle against the 'imperialists' – the United States and the Filipino landowners – when the war ended.

The Philippines covers a vast area. The country is made up of over 7,000 islands, large and small, many of them cloaked in jungle, each an ideal place for irregular warfare. The Japanese were forced to maintain large anti-guerrilla forces in the Philippines and when the war ended the Huks naturally wanted a large say in the post-colonial government set up by the United States. The Huks did not at once take up the armed struggle, as the Communists were then doing in Greece, partly because the United States had large forces in the Philippines, partly because the Party was split between the all-out Moscow-line Communists and the slightly more democratic local socialists. Before long however, the Communist Huks decided to use force and take over. They mounted a terrorist campaign in the national elections of April 1946, which only resulted in their total exclusion from the elected Chamber and government. However, when the new government threw out the Land Reform Bill the Filipino peasants had been hoping for, the Huks saw their chance, dug up the weapons they had buried after the war and took to the hills.

The war against the Huks was to last more than twenty-five years, and the Filipino government often came within a whisker of losing it. In that war lessons were offered to the democratic powers – especially the United States – that they stubbornly refused to learn. The main lesson is that military force alone is not enough to stamp out a guerrilla war. There also has to be a political element, an alternative political solution to the one offered by the enemy.

The Filipino government did not offer this. Terrorism by the Huks was met with counter-terrorism from the government forces, corruption was widespread, the crucial land-reform issue was neglected, and the Huks were presented with a ready-made, popular cause. As a result, the uprising thrived. The Filipino military and their American advisers had no clear idea how to fight an irregular war and large areas of country were left under the control of the Huks, safe bases from which they could mount and maintain a campaign of terror and ambush in the country and the cities. The Filipino government responded to their attacks with heavy-handed tactics, cordon-and-search operations and the aerial bombing of suspected Huk bases, which all too often were innocent peasant villages.

These attacks only increased support for the Huks, who by 1948 had some 12,000 trained and well-equipped fighters in the field. The one government initiative that seemed to have some effect in curbing Huk activity was a special force, Force X, a pseudo-Huk company, which roamed Huk territory and lured many guerrillas to their death. Lacking any political solution that might lead to peace, the Huk war went on and the embers are still warm today, nearly fifty years after the Huks first took up arms, with no political end to the struggle in sight. Other post-war, anti-Communist struggles, if shorter, were equally or even more violent.

The Communist uprising in Greece, which culminated in the Greek Civil War of 1945–9, began even before the Second World War ended. The Germans evacuated Greece in October 1944, and an Allied force, 25,000 strong, called III Corps, composed of British paratroops from the 2nd Independent Parachute Brigade, plus Commandos from 2 Commando Brigade, was sent in. The first troops of this force, the 4th Parachute Battalion, dropped on to Megara airfield, east of Athens, on 12 October 1944 and was swiftly confronted by a large force of Greek Communist guerrillas, ELAS.

ELAS forces, numbering some 40,000 men, had fought the Germans in the war and now had every intention of taking over the country and stamping out any return to Western-style democracy. They had the power to do this, and enjoyed both political support from Moscow and military aid from Communist partisans in Yugoslavia and Albania. By the time the British Airborne arrived, the ELAS forces already controlled 80 per cent of Greek territory and were equipped with a range of modern weapons. The British forces had been sent in by Winston Churchill to ensure the installation of a stable, Western-oriented government, established by democratic elections, but ELAS had no intention of letting these elections take place. Civil war broke out in

December 1944, and eventually the Greek government asked the British for direct military assistance.

In a few weeks III Corps, reinforced by a British division flown in from Italy, had driven ELAS into the mountains. During the early part of this campaign the 2nd Parachute Brigade were engaged in fighting ELAS in the streets of Athens, and the fighting was severe; the 6th Battalion lost 130 men killed or wounded from a total battalion strength of 528 all ranks before the battalion was withdrawn in February 1945. As one paratrooper remarked, 'We had a lot of men killed in Greece, most of them shot by Greeks, people that we thought we had come to rescue from the Germans. A lot of the ELAS fighters were brainwashed kids, but they can pull a trigger just like anyone else.'

The British Army left Greece in February 1945 and an all-out civil war began between the National Greek Army and ELAS. This war soon became a vicious struggle, setting village against village, family against family. In an attempt to wipe out ELAS support in the countryside the National Army became involved in 'cleaning up' operations, in which a Greek Cypriot officer, Colonel George Grivas, had his first taste of guerrilla warfare. These 'cleaning up' operations often bore down heavily on villagers who had no connection with the Communists, and the rough behaviour of the Greek Army against those even suspected of Communist or liberal leanings drove many Greek peasants into the ELAS ranks.

The first year and a half of the Civil War in Greece caused terrible suffering. Greeks suspected of being sympathetic to the Communists were murdered or driven from their homes to starve and die in the hills. Thousands of children were abducted by ELAS and sent into Albania to be reared as Communists, and hundreds of Greeks suspected of pro-Western connections were tortured and murdered by the Greek Communists. Terror begot terror; outside forces from Communist Albania and Yugoslavia were soon meddling in the brew and the Greek government seemed incapable of containing the Communist threat.

The US government had not approved of the British sending their parachute battalions to help the Greek Nationalist forces in 1944–5, an action which seemed to the US to smack of British 'imperialism'. But, soon after the British left, the US government found it necessary to send in a group of advisers, the Joint United States Military Advisory and Planning Group – or JUSMAPG. JUSMAPG arrived in early 1948, headed by General James Van Fleet, an experienced officer who had commanded an army corps in North-West Europe during the war. This Planning Group was supported by a quantity of arms, 8,000 trucks and a large number of mules, all of which enabled the Nationalist forces to resume the offensive against the ELAS. This military action was supported by political action from the Greek government, not least the public execution by firing squad of more than sixty captured Communist guerrillas, who were shot to death in an Athens square.

It took another year of hard fighting and much bloodshed, but by the spring of 1949 the Greek government was beginning to get on top of the problem. One of its most successful actions was the removal of large sections of the rural population from their mountain villages into safe areas, where they were free of Communist pressure and unable to supply the Communist bands with food and information. The Greek Civil War finally ended in October 1949 with victory for the Royalist forces, after Marshal Tito, the Communist leader of Yugoslavia, had ordered the border closed to ELAS troops.

The Americans of JUSMAPG drew the wrong conclusions from this victory. They returned home convinced that *conventional* forces could beat guerrillas if they were on the ground in sufficient numbers and given adequate air and logistical support.

The pattern of repression, terrorism and counter-terrorism seen in the Philippines and Greece was to be repeated in other countries during the coming decades. The troubles in Greece and the Philippines introduced the Western military to a new and unwelcome kind of warfare – guerrilla warfare – with which they were seemingly unable to cope. In the Second World War the British and Americans had formed many irregular units, all charged either with conducting guerrilla warfare or with supporting partisan activity directed against the Axis powers. Now the British and American military were faced with guerrilla forces – often the same guerrilla forces – waging a terrorist war against *them*, and had no more idea of how to deal with such forces than the Germans and Japanese had a few years previously.

The lessons were there to be learned, but much time would pass and many lives would be lost before linking political action to counter-terrorist action was seen as providing the twin prongs of anti-guerrilla activity. The alternative was simply to pack up and leave, a course adopted by the British in Palestine in 1948, where a number of SOF units, the Royal Marine Commandos and the Parachute Regiment, got their first unwelcome taste of terrorism.

The British 6th Airborne Division, of Normandy and Rhine Crossing fame, was sent to Palestine at the end of 1945 to take part in the campaign which aimed to maintain order at the end of the British

Mandate. The Royal Marines arrived a few weeks later and both units were soon involved in IS – Internal Security – duties fighting both Arab and Jewish terrorists – a pig-in-the-middle situation which had deep political roots. The British had been handed the League of Nations Mandate for Palestine in 1922, after the end of the Great War. Following the Balfour Declaration of 1917, which accepted the notion that a 'National home for the Jewish people' should be created in the former Turkish state of Palestine, the British were charged with creating this home in Palestine, but with the Mandate came a host of problems they were quite unable to solve. The two peoples, Jews and Palestinians, were unwilling to live together and their animosity increased as more Jewish settlers arrived before, during and especially after the Second World War. No power on earth could make the Jews and Arabs live peaceably together, for each felt that the land they fought over belonged to them and them alone.

The terrorist campaigns mounted by the Jews and the Arabs between 1945 and 1948 had the aims of harming each other as much as possible and getting the British to leave. The Jews proved particularly adept at irregular warfare – and terrorism – blowing up the King David Hotel in Jerusalem with great loss of life, destroying railway lines and oil refineries, attacking police and Army patrols, raiding arms dumps and, in one horrific incident, kidnapping and hanging two British Army sergeants, in reprisal for the execution by the British of a Jewish terrorist. Peter Faggetter served in Palestine with the Parachute Regiment: 'The roads of Palestine took a steady toll of British soldiers, in ambushes or from mining. At Tel Letwinski, one of our three tonners was mined just down the road and thirteen of our chaps were wounded, three seriously, and our guard posts were a nightmare, especially when the unit was out on some cordon-and-search.'

Haganah, which was later to form the Jewish Army, took only a small part in these terror attacks, which were usually the work of the Stern Gang, a terrorist group that had been attacking British soldiers and Palestinian civilians since the Second World War. On 25 April 1946 the Stern Gang attacked a group of unarmed British soldiers on a bathing beach and killed seven of them in cold blood. Ian Wilson, an Engineer Officer, had to deal with a number of such incidents: 'A number of Jews had served in Special Operations groups during the war and were therefore very good at mining and booby traps. In June 1946 they blew up all the bridges over the river Jordan, and in October that year attacked the railway stations. We just managed to get a group of soldiers out of the station at Haifa East before that blew up and the officer in charge was killed by another booby trap in May 1947. New devices were being tried out on us all the time and by the time we left eight sapper officers had been killed trying to disarm them.'

Colonel Robin McGarel Groves, who served with 42 Commando in Palestine, remembers some other aspects of the Palestine problem: 'Our main problem, and I am sure one which affected all the British forces in the Haifa enclave at the end of the Mandate, was the security of our weapons. There was a thriving black market in weaponry, with prices ranging from £20 for a pistol to about £20,000 for a Comet tank, a fabulous sum in those days, when a Marine earned about 5 shillings [20p] a day. Two Comet tanks, complete with Army drivers, went over to Haganah when they were being driven to the docks from Ramat David by the airfield in Haifa. These two tanks were reported in action with various Israeli units during the war which followed our departure, until both were destroyed by fire from British 17-pounder guns which the Arabs had acquired by equally dubious means.'

The end of the British Mandate in Palestine in 1948 ushered in the first Arab–Israeli War and several decades of Arab terrorism against the West. It also led to the creation of two Israeli Special Warfare and counter-terrorism organizatons, Shin Bet and the Mossad, both of which came to stand in the first rank of anti-terrorist formations, having cut their teeth with terrorist operations against the British at the end of the Mandate. The main Israeli force in 1948 was the Haganah or Underground National Army, originally raised to protect Jewish settlements but quite capable of offensive actions. An early supporter of Haganah was Orde Wingate, commander of the wartime Chindits, who had formed his Special Night Squads in Palestine before the war to help the Jewish settlers combat Arab terrorism. An offshoot of Haganah was Palmach, the Spearhead Groups, regular soldiers used for sabotage operations, first against the long-suffering British Tommies and then against the Arabs.

The fighting and riot problems faced by the British Army at the end of the Mandate did have one unexpected benefit in future colonial campaigns. Their actions in Palestine were under the constant and critical eye of the world's media, not least the very hostile US media, and, although television had yet to appear on the streets, it was very important that British troops should not provide the media with hostile photo-opportunities. Denis Edwards, of the Parachute Regiment, experienced this last problem at first hand: 'After the Stern Gang blew up the King David Hotel in Jerusalem, every Tom in the battalion was trucked into the city for a cordon-and-search. I was on the roof of a building, poking my bayonet into a pile of rubbish, when the landing door behind me was flung open. I spun round, expecting to see an armed terrorist and found myself facing a young woman. Then there was the explosion of a flash gun and before I could stop them the woman and the photographer had dashed off down the stairs. It must have been a good photo showing a brutal British soldier pointing his bayonet at the belly of a very pregnant, but remarkably agile, Jewish woman.'

The need to enlist the support of the general public led to the development of 'hearts and minds' activity, in which the passive part consists in causing as little trouble to the innocent and uncommitted as possible, and the active part consists of taking all possible steps to help the general population, by offering medical assistance and help in public service, building schools and roads, giving parties for the children. In this 'hearts and minds' activity the British Army soon built up a considerable expertise, but they also learned to be extremely wary of the press.

In such 'hearts and minds' activity, Special Forces were to prove increasingly important. The normal actions of an anti-terrorist campaign – those roadblocks, cordon-and-search operations and curfews – inevitably disrupted civilian life and gave offence to people who had no involvement in terrorist activity. The use of small Special Force units, acting on information supplied by the police or intelligence sources, proved more effective, and far less disruptive, to normal civilian life.

The last British troops to leave Palestine were 40 Commando, Royal Marines, who went to the Far East and eventually to fight the Communist insurrection in Malaya, while the 6th Airborne Division returned to Aldershot and disbandment, the remnants becoming the 16th Independent Parachute Brigade in 1949.

While these independence struggles began to rack Europe and the Mediterranean, more Special Force units were fading into history, and not only the units vanished. Many of the men who had created the style and dash which had carried the Special Force units through the dark days of war were dead, often killed in the last few months of the war, like William Derby of the US Rangers or Anders Lassen of the SBS. After the war ended, David Stirling and Paddy Mayne left the Army; Paddy Mayne, who won four DSOs in the war and never settled down in peacetime, was killed in a car crash a few years later. Some men stayed on in the Army. David Lloyd Owen of the LRDG returned to command a regular infantry battalion and rose to the rank of major-general. Brigadier Peter Young of 3 Commando and 3 Commando Brigade went back to the Bedfordshire and Hertfordshire Regiment, transferred to the Arab Legion and eventually became head of the Department of Military History at the Royal Military College, Sandhurst. The same thing happened in the United States: the men either returned to civilian life or went back to duty with conventional units. The war was over and – as the old joke had it – the time had come to get back to real soldiering.

There was, however, a long-term benefit in this dispersal of the wartime Special Force soldiers. The men who had served in these many and varied units had seen what such units could do and the soldiers now spread throughout the armies all did their bit towards keeping that ideal alive in the post-war years. Indeed, some units survived to provide the basis for Special Force units in the newly liberated countries.

The Belgian Troop of No. 10 (Inter-Allied) Commando, together with some volunteers from the Belgian Squadron of the SAS, became the nucleus of the post-war Belgian Para-Commando Regiment. The French also established parachute regiments, in their regular Army and within the Foreign Legion, units which would fight in the bitter campaigns of Indo-China and Algeria. Other Allied nations also retained elements of their wartime Special Force capacity. The Royal Netherlands Marine Corps was swiftly reformed and became closely linked in the post-war years with the Royal Marine Commandos.

Among the nations of the British Empire, those taking the road to independence soon came to need armies and these armies often contained a Special Force element. In 1944, for example, the British raised a parachute division in India. With the partition of the country into India and Pakistan in 1947, that Division, the 44th (Indian) Parachute Division, became split between the two new nations and the separated formations actually fought each other in subsequent Indo-Pakistan wars. Another SOF formation which came into existence at this time was the Israeli Parachute Brigade, founded in May 1948, within weeks of the declaration of the State of Israel, and in the middle of the first Arab–Israeli War.

Canada had raised a parachute battalion in 1942, which landed in Normandy in 1944 as part of 6th Airborne, and this unit was retained after the war, forming up with the Canadian element of the 1st Special Service Force, the famous 'Devil's Brigade'. This combined unit was also retained for a while until it became absorbed into the Canadian Airborne Regiment, a para-commando formation.

The US Special Force units were either reduced to cadre strength or disbanded. The OSS was deactivated in 1946 and part of it was gradually transformed, as we have seen, into the CIA, which was set up in 1947. The Ranger battalions were disbanded, though elements of Ranger training continued at Fort Bragg and Fort Benning. The US airborne divisions were run down, with only the 82nd and 101st Divisions remaining as the main US parachute forces into the post-war years. The US Marines had become national heroes, thanks to their fighting ability during the Pacific campaign against the Japanese. Even so, their Special Force capability was dropped and the Raider Battalions disbanded.

The general picture is that the end of the Second World War saw a great reduction in the size and number of Special Force and SOF units. Most senior officers and the military powers-that-be had never been really at ease with irregular units and few tears were shed in the various Defence Ministries at the news of their disbandment. It was only when it gradually became clear that 'hot war' had been replaced by 'cold war', the forty-year confrontation between the democratic and Communist powers, and that the biggest potential danger came not from a nuclear holocaust, but from Communist-managed insurrection, that the SF concept began to revive. The revival began slowly and in different places and aimed to cater for some differing situations, but, within a few years of disappearing from Army Lists everywhere, the Special Forces were on their way back.

Because of their involvement in the struggle to retain their empires, the European nations retained a small SF or SOF capacity. The United States virtually abandoned all Special Force activity at the end of the war but a small active rump continued in the guise of Psychological Warfare, which was broadly concerned with propaganda and mis-information, both ways of spreading it and ways of countering it. All other forms of Special Operations activity, especially that concerned with the behind-the-lines or clandestine warfare, were seen as part of 'Psy-Ops Warfare' and given a very low priority. But, as the Communist threat to Western Europe became stronger, with the problems with Soviet Russia over Berlin and Yugoslav Communist attempts to retain the Adriatic port of Trieste, interest in special warfare began to revive.

Drawing on the experience of working with resistance groups in the Second World War especially, the US saw the need to create guerrilla units in Western Europe to fight the Communist powers if they ever crossed the Elbe. The chief instigator of this new special-warfare capability was Colonel Aaron Bank, an American OSS officer who had fought with the French Maquis in the Second World War as part of a Jedburgh team, parachuted in to assist local resistance groups. After the OSS had been disbanded in October 1946, Banks was reassigned to the Psychological Warfare branch where he was most unhappy. The secret tasks of clandestine warfare seemed to be drifting away from the military commanders in their newly built Pentagon in Washington towards Langley, the home of the CIA in Virginia.

Colonel Banks saw another need. He wanted to create a force not unlike the Jedburgh teams, a force that could stay on in Western Europe even after a Soviet invasion, to organize and train local resistance movements and lead the fight against the invader. President Truman, who had quickly come to realize that the wartime 'Big Three' alliance of the United States, Russia and Great Britain could not last, became interested in Banks' idea and together with another former Special Forces officer, Colonel Russell Vlockman, Banks was permitted to proceed with the creation of a Special Force unit.

This task did not prove easy. A large number of bureaucratic obstacles were strewn in their path by people in the Pentagon, and the project was frequently on the brink of collapse, but Bank and Vlockman believed in the SF concept and persisted in getting it together. The first post-war US Special Force unit, the 10th Special Forces Group, was eventually set up and posted to Bad Tolz in Bavaria. This force was charged with exploring the mountains of southern Germany and Austria, finding sites for guerrilla bases, establishing dumps of weapons and explosives, and assisting the newly established German and Austrian Armies in clandestine and behind-the-lines operations should the need arise. In view of the subsequent US Special Force involvement in the Far East and Latin America, it is interesting that their first deployment was in Western Europe, but in the late 1940s and early 1950s that was where the main threat from Communist subversion and destabilization seemed to lie. The task of the 10th SF Group was not to engage in irregular warfare directly, but to set up and train local resistance groups.

Communist 'destabilization' of the democratic nations was to form part of what another US President, Dwight Eisenhower, was to define as the 'Domino Theory'. According to the Domino Theory, one country after another would fall into Communist hands, as subversive forces inside each country undermined the existing government. Having risen to power on the back of civil insurrection, the local Communist Party would call for help from the Communist country across the nearest frontier and, having used that help to crush any democratic opposition, move its country forever into the Communist sphere of influence.

The Domino Theory did not achieve reality, even in the Far East, but it seemed a very credible scenario in Western Europe in the late 1940s. France and Italy were both politically unstable, with governments falling after a few months in power and large, well-organized and well-armed Communist Parties active in the streets and itching to take over. In Italy there was the additional problem of Yugoslavia, hovering at Trieste on the Italian frontier, ready and willing to assist the large Italian Communist Party to seize power. It was against this perceived threat, and all that might spring from it, that the 10th Special Force Group was activated and sent to Bad Tolz. Matters were also beginning to stir in the slim ranks of those supporting the US Rangers.

In 1946, the US Secretary of Defense, noting that the Airborne Forces had no reconnaissance capability, proposed the establishment of Airborne Reconnaissance units. A feasibility study proposed an experimental unit of forty men, which would be used to test out methods of employing such units in the field. This unit needed a name and came to be called the Ranger Group when it was finally established in 1948, though its tasks and many of its personnel were drawn from the old OSS.

The Ranger Group expanded. Within a year it had a strength of some 250 officers and men, and this growth in numbers went along with an extension of its role. This developed from straight 'recon' (what the British called 'recce') to include raiding, sabotage, propaganda, spying, contact and support for indigenous guerrilla forces, and escape and evasion. This was a wide brief for a small unit and it soon became clear that the Ranger Group would need to be divided and its tasks allocated to specially trained units. The clandestine side, especially that involving work with indigenous forces and local guerrilla groups, went to the US Special Force Green Beret units, which can therefore trace their origins, at least in part, to the wartime OSS. Unfortunately, the experimental phase was not permitted to continue and the Ranger Group was deactivated in 1949.

But the special-warfare concept would not go away. Clearly, there was a need for some form of special-warfare capability in the Western armies, if only to resist the growing threat of Soviet subversion. What was less clear was the form such a capability should take, but some examples were soon to be found across the Iron Curtain where the Warsaw Pact countries were actively training Special Force units. The Soviet and Eastern bloc (Warsaw Pact) nations all had SF units, most notably the Soviet Spetznaz (Special Designation) units, which were tasked with deep penetration, sabotage, raiding, assassinations, air and seaborne recce and intelligence gathering. Spetznaz units, descendants of those Cossack units which had harried the Wehrmacht in the Second World War, became an integral part of the Soviet order-of-battle with units attached to all Soviet armies and 'fronts' (army groups). Other SOF units, marines, paratroopers, assault infantry and counter-terrorist units, existed in all the other East European countries, ranging in size from the 400-strong Hungarian Airborne Battalion to the 25,000 Spetznaz troops deployed by the Soviet Union.

The Special Force learning curve in the 1945–50 post-war period was very slight. The lesson being taught to Western politicians and military leaders was that the world had changed and become not so much a battleground for armies as a proving ground for ideas and ideologies. Western leaders had yet to learn that the only way to fight an idea is with a better idea, and Communism was an attractive philosophy in the post-war period, at least in those countries where its full rigours had not been experienced. Just to begin with the Communists had credibility. They had fought hard against the Nazis, and the Soviet Union, having sustained the most grievous losses in the Great Patriotic War of 1941–5, had taken full credit for the eventual victory, even though for the first two years of the Second World War Soviet Russia had been an ally of Nazi Germany. The establishment and maintenance of democracy demands a sophisticated electorate, and this element was hard to find anywhere in the Third World; nor was it functioning well in a Western Europe still struggling with the after-effects of war.

Special Force and SOF units were involved in many of the post-war liberation struggles and would eventually be involved in clandestine and counter-terrorist operations on both sides of the political divide in Eastern and Western Europe, but their use in full-scale war only began again in 1950, when the United States, Great Britain and many other Western nations became involved in the Korean conflict. In that war the US Rangers and the British Commandos, together with the United States Marine Corps and some small SF units, took on tasks which were to bridge the gap between the Second World War and the dangerous world of the late twentieth century.

When the Korean War broke out most of the SF units raised in the Second World War had become part of history, and those that had survived were a shadow of their former selves. Nevertheless, where they were called upon in their specialist role, at Inchon and Chosin, these SOF units, especially the United States Marine Corps and the Royal Marines Commandos, proved how useful their special skills and fighting spirit could be. Since the Communists invaded South Korea in 1950, the survival of Special Forces has never been in doubt.

US Marine Corps badge

CHAPTER FIVE

Behind the Lines in Korea 1950–1953

> On the question of aggression by the North, there
> can be no doubt that their ultimate aim is to
> overrun the South ... as to their methods of
> achieving their objective, short of starting World
> War III, I think they will prepare the country from
> within rather than resort to open aggression.
>
> *Major J. Ferguson Innes, British War Office,*
> *December 1949*

Major Ferguson Innes' prediction was only half right. The
Communist North Koreans certainly intended to absorb the
South, but the situation in the South was not suitable for
the usual Communist tactic of destabilizing a nation from within.
South Korea (formally the Republic of Korea) was firmly in the grip of
President Syngman Rhee, a man who did not tolerate even the mildest
form of dissent, and in such a situation more direct methods were
necessary. Six months after Major Ferguson Innes made his assessment,
and without any formal declaration of war, North Korean tanks flowed
over the 38th Parallel and the three-year Korean War began.

News of the invasion came swiftly to the notice of the 1st Marine
Division of the United States Marine Corps, in which Lieutenant
Morton Silver USN was a medical officer: 'The 1st Marine Division at
Camp Pendleton was slated to parade in full-dress uniform on 25 June

1950, to give the civilians and the press a chance to see where their money goes. It was going to be a beautiful picnic but at dawn on Sunday 25 June the North Koreans invaded the South. It took a very short time for the news to affect the Marine Corps. At 1 p.m. that same Sunday, the 1st Marine Division paraded in review at Camp Pendleton, but in full battle gear. All troops carried rifles and full field packs, gone were the ceremonial swords and finery. Overnight we converted from a peaceful parade to a demonstration of Marine readiness. The cameramen had a field day and the Marine Corps had its image fortified.'

The Korean War was the first all-out confrontation between the Western democracies and the Communist powers. Like many post-Second World War problems, it arose from an issue created at the end of that war when Korea, an ally of the Japanese during that conflict, had been invaded by both the Americans and the Russians, the former from the south, the latter from the north. It had then been partitioned along the 38th Parallel, into an American-dominated, pro-Western South and a Communist-dominated North.

The two superpowers then set about organizing their half of the divided nation on separate lines, supporting local leaders who were, in effect, their surrogates. The North Korean Communist leader was a youthful Communist, Kim Il Sung; the leader in the South, President Syngman Rhee, was seventy-five years old when the Korean War broke out in 1950. Neither paid any great heed to democracy or civil rights. In the years between 1945 and 1950 the UN had made various attempts to unify the country, but no agreement could be found between the two national leaders and their backers in Moscow, Peking and Washington. Syngman Rhee was ruthless in dealing with any opposition to his rule, suppressing liberal sentiment in South Korea wherever it was in evidence. The United States found itself defending the bad against the worse, but Korea lay close to Japan, then the centre of US military power in the Far East, and the defence of South Korea was considered vital to US strategic interests.

Tension relaxed slightly when the Red Army withdrew from the North in 1948, though the Soviets left behind a well-equipped and well-trained North Korean Army. The US Army retained a small military presence of one or two divisions in the South, as well as training teams and advisers who worked with the South Korean forces. The problems between North and South appeared to be mainly political, and all sides, notably the United Nations, urged Rhee and Kim Il Sung to find some solution that would resolve their differences and unite the country. In 1949 a Coalition Conference, attended by Rhee's rivals and Kim Il

Sung's supporters, met in Pyongyang, the North Korean capital, and declared the creation of a People's Democratic Republic, embracing North and South Korea.

This was rejected by Rhee, and a series of border clashes and incursions into the South followed. Growing tension between the two nations led to the intervention of the UN which in May 1950 obtained a declaration from Kim Il Sung that all North Korea wanted was a peaceful reunification of the country. Four weeks later, on 25 June 1950, the North Korean Army advanced across the southern frontier and took the South Koreans and their US allies completely by surprise. The Southern armies reeled back before this onslaught and urgent reinforcements were called for. These did not at first include SF or SOF forces.

Special Force units faced considerable problems in Korea, not least those of climate, terrain and concealment. To take the last first, Caucasian SF troops were at a disadvantage when working among Asiatics; they were immediately identifiable and this limited their scope for behind-the-lines operations. There was no established resistance or opposition movement to the Communist domination of the North, and no basis existed for building up and supporting local resistance groups there or in the invaded South.

Climate and terrain presented more severe problems. Korea is a peninsula, over 600 miles in length and some 125 to 200 miles wide. To the north, across the Yalu River, lies Chinese Manchuria, which covered much of the North Korean border but for a ten-mile gap which led directly into Soviet Russia. The North Korean forces therefore had a secure supply route from both Soviet Russia and Communist China and the assurance of prompt military assistance should their situation become precarious. The Korean terrain is mountainous, with a large range in the north and north-east where the summits run up to over 15,000 feet. The seasonal weather tends to be extreme, for while spring and autumn are fairly pleasant, the summers are hot and humid and the winters vicious, with temperatures often falling to well below zero and relentless piercing winds reaching speeds of over 70 m.p.h. By any standards, Korea was a hard country to fight in.

These factors would have inhibited Special Force penetration north of the 38th Parallel, even had such forces existed. A further complication was that the Commanding General in Korea was General Douglas MacArthur, victor of the South Pacific campaign in the Second World War and liberator of the Philippines, but a man who was no supporter of irregular warfare or of its devotees.

The North Korean invasion had been predicted by intelligence sources, but it still came as a great surprise to the West. Seoul, the South Korean capital, fell on 30 June, by which time the US President, Harry Truman, had ordered the US air and sea forces in the Pacific to give the Korean government every assistance. This move was supported by the British government, which ordered the Far East Fleet into Korean waters and began to ship troops to Korea. Other nations soon followed suit, until twenty-two nations had troops fighting in Korea. All of these were conventional forces and they brought the full range of tanks and guns, but such a growing array of enemies did not deter the North Koreans.

Nor did UN condemnation. On the day Seoul fell, the UN passed a resolution ordering the North Korean forces to withdraw. But supported by the Soviet Union, Communist China and other Communist satellites, the North Koreans ignored this resolution, and their advance continued. For the first three months of the war, they carried all before them. US units continued to arrive and were thrown into the fray, together with British and Commonwealth units from Canada, Australia and New Zealand in the 1st Commonwealth Division, but the retreat continued until the UN forces reached their last possible defence line around the southern port of Pusan. Here they held on and here the fight-back began, led by one of the great fighting divisions of the war, the 1st Marine Division of the United States Marine Corps. Morton Silver again: 'The Division shipped out for Japan, *en route* for Korea, and spent some weeks on manoeuvres. Our troops were put through their paces from dawn to dusk, and in the darkness of night, and finally HQ made up their collective minds. MacArthur's grand scheme was to bypass the North Koreans engaged at Pusan and land up the west coast at Inchon. After many weeks of acrimonious debate MacArthur managed to convince the Naval and Marine Commanders that the "operation" was feasible ... by using the 1st Marine Division. Now committed, the Corps perceived a supreme opportunity to add to its reputation and thwart Congressional efforts to emasculate the USMC.'

General MacArthur may have had little time for Special Forces but he was a great believer in amphibious warfare. The two coastlines of the Korean peninsula offered various opportunities for amphibious landings, a means by which the rugged mountain terrain, so suitable for defence, could be outflanked. Brooding over his maps, General MacArthur's eye fell on the port of Inchon, just south of the 38th Parallel and close to Seoul, the Southern capital. On 15 September 1950 he sent the 1st Marine Division ashore at Inchon and turned the tide of the Korean War.

Operation *Chromite*, the Inchon landings, began with several basic snags. The first was the lack of an alternative landing site, vital if any deception plan was to be set up. Inchon was the only possible spot for a landing, all other suitable places being either in North Korea or too close to the Pusan perimeter. The second snag was that Inchon is a major port, not an open beach, and the landing forces would be involved in street fighting from the moment they scrambled over the sea wall. The next snag was that the waters of Inchon are tidal, with a 33 foot tidal range, and the men making the initial landing would have to wait for support as the tide fell throughout the day, turning the landing area into a muddy quagmire. The next snag was that surprise was impossible; the invaders must first seize the island of Wolmi-do, in the Inchon approaches. Finally, Inchon was surrounded by hills, which commanded the harbour, the port and most of the town. MacArthur's staff contained officers who had landed troops on hostile beaches from Guadalcanal to Okinawa, via Saipan, Tarawa and Iwo Jima, men who knew all there was to know about 'amphibiosity', the art of putting armies ashore. They took General MacArthur's proposal away, examined it carefully and announced that a landing at Inchon was impossible.

MacArthur rejected their opinion. A glance at the map revealed the choices open to the UN armies: they could either batter their way North throughout the coming winter, across terrible terrain against an enemy whose ability to resist grew with every mile he fell back, or they could land *behind* the enemy lines at Inchon, and force the North Koreans to withdraw or be cut off.

No one pretended that the Inchon landing would be easy, but MacArthur saw that it had to be done. His advisers argued against this judgement, but he wore them down until one said, reluctantly, 'The best I can say is that a landing at Inchon is not impossible.' Since the landing looked impossible to any reasonable man, the enemy would not be expecting it and this, as MacArthur pointed out, was their greatest asset. He harangued his sceptical audience for nearly an hour, concluding with the comment that 'I never thought the day would come when the Navy would be unable to support the Army in its operations.' At that the Chief of Naval Operations rose briefly to assure him, 'General, the US Navy will get you to Inchon.'

A considerable fleet sailed to the Inchon landings, a force composed entirely of American ships filled and manned by American sailors, soldiers and Marines, but sailing ahead of this armada was a single

British frigate, HMS *Whitesands Bay*, carrying ten Royal Marine volunteers from the British Far East Fleet. Commanded by Captain E. D. G. Pounds RM and therefore known as Poundforce, this little unit had been formed for raiding duties at Camp McGill in Japan before joining a Ranger company of the US Army for training in American weapons. Now it was bound for Inchon, to take a look at the landing area.

On 13 September, two days before the US Marines hit the beach, the Royal Marines paddled ashore in small boats to check out the beach defences. This task – one shared with US Navy UDT teams – they carried out successfully, though one boat hit a reef and was holed on the way in and all were sprayed with machine-gun fire on the way out. Their report was sent to the landing force commander, and two days later the 1st Marine Division went ashore.

Morton Silver again: 'The harbour and port at Inchon presented an almost insoluble problem. Thirty-two-foot tides combined with fierce currents, small island channels and a quagmire of mud made the amphibious assault a potential disaster. The large LSTs (landing ship – tanks), carrying the heavy equipment, would have to go in on the high tide, unload under enemy guns, and be off the beach in three hours. The first assault troops would have to scale a high rocky sea wall to attain a beachhead, all under enemy fire. Finally, the time of the high tide, on the designated day of the assault, would necessitate a landing at about 5 p.m, leaving only two hours of daylight for the main assault. We would then have to hang on till the next tide.

'The first attack on the enemy positions began at about 6 a.m. on the 15th. The 5th Marines had to neutralize the island of Wolmi-do, that commanded the harbour entrance. There now was a hiatus of almost eight hours and aboard my ship we all were elated with the success of the initial assault, but the euphoria was soon tempered by the arrival of landing craft with severely wounded men aboard. Bullet wounds were relatively simple, whereas the shrapnel trauma was frightful. Torn metal fragments, twisted and ripped into razor-sharp shapes by explosive force, created indescribable havoc. The simple penetration of such a scrap of metal caused so much internal damage that, on one occasion, I stood six hours assisting the surgeons before they called it quits – to resume the same operation the next morning.'

A fleet of nearly 300 ships carried the US landing force to Inchon, many of them vessels of Second World War vintage. The main landings were preceded by a five-day bombardment of Wolmi-do Island and the initial assault was made by the 5th Marines, who carried the defences inside two hours. The rest of the landing force then had to wait while the tide rose again, though the pounding of the defenders by carrier aircraft and the guns of the US Fleet continued.

Morton Silver describes the landing and some of his duties: 'Late afternoon on the 15th, as the tide rushed in, LSTs rammed themselves on to the beaches and the bulk of the Division was put ashore at Inchon. The attack was a success, demonstrating the unique ability of the Corps, supported by the Navy, to overcome extraordinary obstacles. The harbour was a scene of mass confusion. LSTs, like beached whales, were lying canted on their sides, small boats were mired in the mud, every craft was high and dry with the main fleet of transports and warships at least a half-mile offshore. It looked as if someone had pulled the plug out of the tub.

'Now ashore, we were billeted in an old factory amid huge rusting hulks of machinery. The medical set-up was in an old loft where emergency surgery was performed on those wounded who could not be moved to the hospital ship offshore, or evacuated to Japan. I received a most unenviable lesson in surgery when I was ordered to assist a senior surgeon doing an amputation.

'As I remember it now, this young Marine, not yet out of his teens, was hit by a mortar shell. He received most of the blast between his legs but was still alive and conscious. The surgeon anaesthetized him by spinal injection as I awaited his instructions. Because there was a meagre supply of sterile material, the surgeon ordered me to begin debridement of the wound site, which was contaminated, and I cut through the torn uniform to reveal the traumatized area ... with the surgeon pointing at specific sites, I removed the destroyed tissues until the "healthy" areas were revealed. My job completed, the surgeon brusquely shoved me aside and went to work. He was an unfeeling bastard but maybe such demeanour sustained his sanity in the face of such horror. I moved to the head of the table to try and comfort the patient, who remained conscious throughout his surgical ordeal. "Doc," he asked, "is it true that the government will get me a special car so I can drive – even if you cut off my legs?"'

By midnight on 15 September two full regiments, the 1st and 5th Marines, were ashore, followed by men of the 7th Army Division and the 7th Marine Regiment, and then by men of the Republic of Korea Marines, who were tasked with mopping up in Inchon while the 1st Marine Division set out for Seoul. Their aim was to capture the South Korean capital by 25 September, three months to the day after the North Koreans invaded.

Seoul fell on the 23rd, after a swift US advance, supported by air strikes. Another SOF unit, the 3rd Battalion of the 187th Airborne Regiment, was now ashore and advancing on the north flank of the Marines, and the advance went well, aided by the fact that the UN troops in the Pusan perimeter had broken through the North Korean lines there and were coming north at some speed.

MacArthur's gamble at Inchon had paid off, but there was bitter street fighting in Seoul before the North Koreans were driven out. Many of the North Koreans then took to the mountains, where they began to prey on UN and South Korean convoys in a form of guerrilla war. The main North Korean Army made its retreat over the 38th Parallel and was back in the North by the end of September, when General MacArthur went back in triumph to Japan. The reverses of the early days could be forgotten, the North Koreans had been licked, South Korea was again secure and the Communist powers all over the world had been taught that aggression did not pay. Unfortunately, that lesson had not been learned by the Communist Chinese.

Morton Silver tells what happened to his Division: 'It was late September, and the North Koreans were being routed. MacArthur was triumphant and gave orders for the Marine Division to be deployed to the east coast of Korea. We were to re-embark at Inchon and sail around to land at Wonsan. The Eighth Army would be on the west and the X Corps, consisting primarily of the 1st Marine Division, would be on the east and together we were to grind the North Koreans into the dust.

Returning to Inchon, we marched down the road loaded with our gear and supplies. We were a motley crew but victors, bursting with pride and bravado. We were the greatest, but the grungiest. We never had showers, clean clothes, nor any of the luxuries available to the Army troops, for this was the fighting Marines. We left Inchon with no feelings of loss except for the material we had to leave on the docks. There were piles of gear, souvenirs, trucks, jeeps, weapons, clothing and, if memory does not fail me, even a tank. The Marines are the world's best scroungers. Anything not screwed down or guarded by a company of Army MPs is fair game to us. We steal – I mean liberate – anything that might have some value, but the time of reckoning comes with the shipboard loading. Nothing is allowed except that which is listed in the organizational tables. That tank – where the hell did we get that? One fact must be emphasized at this time. Taking, scrounging or stealing anything from a fellow Marine would bring immediate and severe punishment.

'After about nine days at sea, the Navy managed to sweep a narrow patch through the Wonsan minefield for our transports but because of the lost time at sea it became ludicrous for the Marines to indulge in a full-scale amphibious landing. The Army's success in pushing the North Koreans towards the 38th Parallel made the entire landing operation superfluous. Lined up in a row like ducklings, our ships entered the harbour single file, under the 16-inch guns of the battleship USS *Missouri*. What we could have used were a couple of minesweepers, not some damn iron gun-platform that served as an admiral's billet. We came ashore, wading through the water to the beach, to be greeted by an Army banner that read "Welcome, Bob Hope".'

There now evolved a plan to complete the destruction of the enemy army and secure the entire Korean peninsula, north to the Yalu river. General Walker's Eighth Army would move north of the 38th Parallel, keeping to the west coast. General Almond's X Corps would head up the east coast and the 1st Marine Division would hold the mountainous region in the centre, acting as an anvil against which the enemy forces would be pounded and destroyed. This entire plan assumed that the Chinese Communist regime would not come to the rescue of its client state, North Korea.

The victory at Inchon and the expulsion of the North Koreans from the South did not lead to a peace conference. MacArthur was therefore permitted to pursue the North Koreans across the parallel – 'provided', said his instruction, 'there has been no entry into North Korea by Soviet or Chinese Communist forces'. The fear now was of escalation, and escalation was coming.

MacArthur elected to repeat the formula that had brought victory at Inchon and Pusan. Part of his forces would pursue the North Korean Army towards the North Korean capital, Pyongyang. Meanwhile, the 1st Marine Division and the 7th Army Division would advance from Wonsan on the east coast and strike north, past the Chosin Reservoir and Yudam-ni, to cut off the retreating North Koreans from refuge in Manchuria. This was a risky task for a two-division force, even if 50 per cent of it was from the Marine Corps. It was made more risky by the onset of the North Korean winter and the growing possibility of Chinese intervention as the UN troops approached their frontier.

On 9 October the US Eighth Army crossed the 38th Parallel into North Korea and advanced on Pyongyang. On the 25th the 1st Marine Division landed at Wonsan and headed north, past Koto-ri and Hagaru and Yudam-ni, places that were to become famous in USMC history. At Hagaru the US Marines were joined by a small force of British troops, 41 (Independent) Commando, Royal Marines, a 300-strong Commando force, attached to the US Marines for raiding and recon duties.

In early August 1950 the British Admiralty had called for a small number of Royal Marine volunteers to provide the US 1st Marine Division with a raiding capacity. Part of the response was Poundforce, which did useful work at Inchon, but it was then decided that a larger unit would be required. The signal to 'Raise 41 Commando' was sent to Stonehouse Barracks in Plymouth, Devon, concluding with the words, 'now let us see what the Royal Marines can do'. The Corps selected Lieutenant-Colonel D. B. Drysdale, then commanding the Officers School, to command this force. Colonel Drysdale, who had served with 3 Commando Brigade in the Far East during the Second World War, tells what happened after that: 'I went over to the Mess and wrote out an order calling for volunteers. It was no good raiding the squads coming in from Commando School as they were already spoken for by the Commando Brigade, which was fighting the Communists in Malaya. I would have to hunt out those who were not otherwise employed or anxious for a bit of action. One of the first to come in was one of the best, Colour-Sergeant Jimmy "Sticks" Baines, a regular who had been a drummer in the Band and served in 45 Commando in the war. Jimmy was sent off to Japan to meet the Yanks and I started mustering the unit. It was designed as a small raiding unit, just 200 men, but this was later raised to 300 – all volunteers. As units go it was simply superb; the men did all I ever asked of them and did it with a smile – even when, as at Chosin, smiling was not all that easy.'

Among the first recruits to join 41 was Fred Heyhurst: 'I did not volunteer for anything, except seven years in the Corps, which I joined in 1949. I had done my recruit training and Commando course and then a heavy-weapons course and was on a ship, *en route* for Malaya and the Brigade, when we were ordered to muster for an announcement. At that muster an officer read out the names of about sixty or seventy Marines, including me, for a "unit" now being formed, "somewhere". That was all the "volunteering" I did for 41 Commando – but it was the best unit anyone could have joined.

'We left the ship at Singapore and I noticed that all the volunteers had specialist rates, signallers, heavy weapons, assault engineers, whatever. We were taken to RAF Changi and flown out to Japan. It took about three days to get there and we kept stopping at US bases where the food and hospitality was superb. We still had food rationing in Britain and the huge steaks we were offered at every meal would have fed a British family for a week. Then we got to Camp McGill in Japan, where we were met by "Sticks" Baines and he told us what was going on. That was where I learned I was in 41 Commando and bound for Korea.'

As 41 was to serve with the US Marines it was to be clad in US clothing and equipped with US arms and equipment, the British Marines retaining only their green Commando berets, which they wore in every action, declining steel helmets. The Commando assembled for the first time on 15 September, the day of the Inchon landing, and began a frantic training programme on US weapons and equipment. 'There was tremendous spirit, to learn all we needed to know and get on with the job,' says Fred Heyhurst. 'We would get the hang of one weapon and go straight on to another, whatever the time was.' Colonel Drysdale had asked for a month to put his unit into fighting trim, but the task was completed in two weeks and on 2 October men of 41 Commando embarked on the US submarine USS *Perch*, for raids on the Korean coast. The *Perch* was a conventional Second World War attack submarine, made suitable for raiding by the conversion of her torpedo-tube space into a troop-carrying area and the fitting of cannon and machine-guns to the outer casing. The USS *Perch* makes regular appearances in Special Force histories and was to serve again in the Vietnam War in support of the US Navy SEAL.

The force embarked in the *Perch* consisted of 125 Royal Marines commanded by Captain Dennis Aldridge RM, accompanied by men of a US UDT team who would recce the landing beach. The ten-man dinghies were towed close to the beach and Lieutenant Peter Thomas RM then swam ashore for a final check before the Commando landed. The main railways in Korea were routed down the coast and the task of 41 was to blow up as large a section of the line as time ashore permitted. Two tons of explosives were ferried ashore in rubber boats and into one of the railway tunnels, and when the charges were fired 'a vast orange burst of flame and a great roar' indicated that they had gone off. Fred Heyhurst was on this first Commando raid: 'We were ashore about eight hours, humping explosives up a pebble beach, and getting the charges laid. We were back on the sub by about midnight and when we got back on the *Perch* we were met by a US sailor who said, "Thank God you are back; the waiting has been hell," and gave us each a bottle of medicinal brandy, US ships being officially "dry".'

A hundred men of C and D Troops landed again next night to blow up another section of the line, and the Marines on the *Perch* continued to land and attack the railway until early November, by which time the UN forces had advanced well into North Korea and raiding operations were suspended. The 1st Marine Division were now at Hungnam as part of X (US) Corps, and Lieutenant-Colonel Drysdale took his Commando, all 235 of them, up to join them. By the time his force arrived at Koto-ri, the 1st Marine Division was in considerable trouble.

Morton Silver again: 'From Wonsan we moved north toward the mountains. Resistance was sporadic but at times fierce and I believe that the enemy sensed that they were being forced into a trap and that their backs were against the wall. We had no opportunity to bathe or change clothes. The troops had to contend with the dust, while we medics wore the dirt and the dried blood of the wounded. The skin of our hands was cracked, sore and begrimed, our faces were adorned with various stages of beard growth, like moss on a rock. We were not a pretty sight, in truth we were a sorry sight, but we still were a damn fine fighting machine.

'We moved north into the mountains and, subjected to the Siberian wind chills, we wore all the clothing we possessed. The men found it difficult to fight with the added burden of heavy parkas and Arctic footwear. The down sleeping bag was the most essential possession; all else was dispensable. To lose one's down sleeping bag would be tantamount to a death sentence. The weather had become a grim factor, exacerbating the medical condition of our wounded. I was thankful that there were few firefights as the regiment ground north to the Chosin reservoir.

'Flushed with our apparent success MacArthur was oblivious to the threat of a Chinese invasion. He directed operations from his office in Japan while the Marines' General Smith became more alarmed at the situation facing his regiments. GHQ in Japan discounted the report of Chinese troops, deeming them inaccurate and exaggerated. Besides, these Chinese were untrained volunteers from Manchuria and would prove no match for the US troops, and at most there were only 30,000 of them...

'Winter then arrived with a vengeance. Temperatures plummeted to zero or below. The frigid winds from Manchuria ate into our flesh and froze any parts of our anatomy exposed for even a few moments. We tried to erect warm-up tents but were frustrated by the rock-hard frozen ground. Wooden tent pegs were useless, so at times we would use bayonets as anchors. This particular night a jeep hauling a small trailer pulled up to the medical tent. There were two wounded Marines lying together in the trailer, frozen to the metal sides by their own blood, unable to move. We had to chop them free with an axe.

'It was 25 or 26 November when the 5th Marines swung east of the Chosin reservoir, to the hamlet of Yudam-ni. We had marched through the bitter cold, from the coastal plains at Hungnam, through the now abandoned or destroyed villages of Hamhung, Sudong, Koto-ri, Hagaru-ri and finally to Yudam-ni, located on a plateau 5,000 feet in the mountains. It was snowing lightly and we were tired.

'The 5th and 7th Regiment paused and regrouped at Yudam-ni. We were slated to begin our attack north to join the Army on the border, at the Yalu river, but dire reports were coming in that indicated something or other had "hit the fan". The Chinese were coming in – in force. The Eighth Army reeled under the unanticipated blow and cracked. Training and discipline disappeared in the heat of battle. The same occurred with the ROK [Republic of Korea] troops and the X Corps, and from the Yalu river on the east and west, protecting our flanks, the Army was now fleeing to the south.

'The 1st Marine Division, consisting of almost 15,000 men, was therefore pitted against ten divisions of Chinese troops – about 120,000 men, all intent on annihilating us. We were exposed and isolated to the enemy onslaught and to the frigidity of the Korean weather. Casualties were beginning to pile up, the wounded and the frozen. The wounded we stabilized; the frostbite cases we treated with inadequate methods. These men were out on the ridges, exposed to wind chills that were beyond measuring, and no way to get relief. We used Vaseline gauze to cover their ears, noses and fingers; my heart went out to them as we sent them back to their frigid hell. Finally, overwhelmed with the increasing number of casualties, it became necessary to evacuate some of our wounded. We sent one ambulance loaded with wounded men down the road, fourteen miles to the comparative safety of Hagaru-ri.

'It took but thirty minutes before the ambulance returned. The driver, a young Marine, grinned as he explained that the road was completely blocked by the Chinese and that we were cut off to the South.'

41 Commando were at Hungnam on the coast when the first Chinese attacks came in against the Marines at Hagaru and Yudam-ni. During the day they made their way up to Koto-ri, where they took up defensive positions around the base and linked up with the 1st Regimental Combat Team of the 1st Marines, a regiment commanded by a famous US Marine officer, Lieutenant-Colonel 'Chesty' Puller. Colonel Drysdale again: '"Chesty" Puller was a great fighting man who loved the Marine Corps and drank a lot of whisky. He told me that the Chinese had cut the road ahead in several places and our task was to open it. 41 was now about 300 strong, divided into three fighting troops [rifle troops] and a Heavy Weapons troop, plus HQ. The Marine Division

was all strung out up the road and into the mountains, and although the Division had taken Chinese prisoners we could not convince the powers-that-be at X [Army] Corps what was actually going on. Chesty Puller was as tough as old boots, and I liked him a lot; anyway, that night he called me over to his HQ and passed on orders from General Smith, the Divisional Commander. I was to take 41, a few tanks and an Army company and push, batter or otherwise make my way from Koto-ri to Hagaru-ri, and see if the road was open. If not, we were to open it ... so off we went.'

Task Force Drysdale consisted of 900 men in trucks, all 300 of 41, the balance from the US Army and the Marine Corps, supported by seventeen Marine and Army tanks. The distance they had to cover was not far, about ten miles, but it lay through narrow defiles and they could expect opposition every step of the way from swarms of Chinese infantry and the bitter North Korean winter. One of the Royal Marines making this advance was Arthur Derby, of S Troop, 41 Commando: 'The best word for it was chaotic. S Troop was the Heavy Weapons Troop and we had US 81mm mortars. We tried firing these before we set out but the ground was frozen hard and we were unable to bed in. We would drop a bomb down the barrel and the base-plate of the mortar would just bounce into the air. Anyway, we set off, with the fighting troops clearing the hills and S Troop staying with the convoy. It was a long slow day, with lots of firing from the hills. One bizarre scene I do remember is when we saw a bunch of Chinese in a field above the road and a Yank fired at them with tracer, marking them for the US Marine Corsairs that were flying air cover. The Chinese must have known what was coming for they ran about, from one side of this field to the other, total panic – and then the Corsairs came swooping down and napalmed them. They were just charred after that.'

The men stayed in the trucks as they left Koto-ri, clearing the hills ahead with machine-gun and mortar fire, but they soon had to dismount. In the words of Colonel Drysdale: 'The Chinese were first-class infantry soldiers – make no mistake about that. They knew all about use of cover and infiltration, and they worked close. Eventually I had to dismount my infantry and do a proper "advance to contact" with the tanks in support. 41 Commando would clear a hill, then the US Marines would pass through and clear the next one, then the Army company, then 41 again, and so on, with tank fire in support.

'You had to watch it and clear the hills as you went, but even so we were soon engaging enemy soldiers in ditches and fields and, besides, an "advance to contact" is very slow. Then I got a message from

1st Marine Divisional HQ saying that a breakthrough that day was imperative, so I called the men in, mounted them in trucks and we made a dash for it, the tanks in the lead, 41 directly behind and the rest in the rear, all under heavy fire from machine-guns and rifles in the hills above. It was also bloody cold – 30 degrees below or more. Water bottles kept inside your parka would freeze, engine oil froze unless you kept the engine running, rifle bolts froze – it was very chilly indeed.'

Heavily outnumbered and under fire from every side, Task Force Drysdale were in a critical condition, but the men fought on. In mid-afternoon the Chinese managed to cut the column in half, but each half fought its way forward, pressing on to Hagaru-ri. A Royal Marine officer, Ralph Parkinson-Cumine, was killed in the fighting by the road, as was 41 Commando's doctor, killed while treating a wounded man. Captain Dennis Aldridge was a troop commander with 41 on the advance to Hagaru-ri: 'We were under heavy attack from the start and the pressure increased after dark. I can still see Chinese swarming down to attack the road in the moonlight, if I shut my eyes, and we had no trouble killing them in quantity, there were so many. The USMC were splendid, but I think they were glad to have us there, not many by comparison but numbers are not everything, and the effect of having British Marines there, in green berets, did a lot of good for their morale.'

Fred Heyhurst was wounded in this part of the action: 'We had four 81mm mortars, which would have been useful, but as Arthur [Derby] has said, the ground was frozen solid, we could not bed the base-plates in. I got a machine-gun and went up with Colonel Drysdale and along we went, the trucks nose to tail. It was too cold to feel much but I turned to Buck Taylor and said, "I think I have been hit – in the leg." It turned out that I had, the bullet going straight through, so Buck gave me a shot of morphine. By then it was like the Wild West, with us as the wagon train and the Chinese as the Indians, yelling, blowing bugles, pouring in the fire. Anyway, we made it. I was on the last truck into the Hagaru perimeter, and a lot of men on foot came in later. Quite a lot did not make it though, and the wounded died in the cold.'

41's arrival is summed up tersely in the official US Marine account: 'To the slender garrison of Hagaru was added a tank company and 300 seasoned infantry.' A USMC sergeant put it another way: 'The British Marines were the only ones to make it and join up in condition and willing to fight.'

Arthur Derby also remembers the arrival at Hagaru: 'We got there well after dark and it was freezing. I got in through the perimeter about midnight and to my surprise the entire place was lit up like Blackpool, with great bulldozers churning about, arc lights blazing, engineers hard at it, trying to finish or extend the airstrip, all this mortaring and machine-gunning going on, and attacks coming in around the perimeter. The Chinese mostly attacked at night; during the daytime you did not hear or see much of them, maybe because of our air cover. We went out on patrols during the day, well outside the lines and saw nothing.'

It was necessary to hold Hagaru-ri, for fourteen miles ahead at Yudam-ni was an advance force of US Marines from the 5th and 7th Marines, who had to fight their way back before the Marine Division could withdraw to the coast. Morton Silver was at Yudam-ni, tending the wounded: 'The Chinese were probing our positions and we knew that come nightfall we would undergo a major assault. We comprised a living body, a wall of determined, interdependent troops who would not yield an inch unless wounded or dead – and we had no intention of dying in this refrigerated hell at Yudam-ni. We were ordered to make ready, every man with no exception, to repulse the Chinese hordes. We could actually see the Chinese as they snaked down the mountain passes, like army ants moving inexorably in our direction. To the bitter cold of the weather was added the chilling sight of the oncoming enemy.

'All that night the Chinese surged over us, human waves of men in cotton padded uniforms and thin rubber sandals, making one fanatical charge after another, before their courage and fear gave way to cold and exhaustion. They passed through us and beyond us, now milling about, uncertain and frightened. We answered their uncertainty with directed fire that ended their misery for ever. In the darkness I could not see the dreadful results of our response. Dawn revealed the night's carnage. We suffered many casualties but the problem of frostbite was the predominant concern. The minds and limbs of the men were affected to such a degree that it took Herculean efforts for them to fight but help now came from the skies.

'Through the low overcast came the Marine Corsair fighter-bomber, the old, faithful, prop-driven workhorses of the Marine Air Corps. Coming in as low as possible, mindful of the coloured panels that marked our positions, they began their grisly work. Under the command of the forward Air Controllers, they made continuous runs, rocketing, bombing and strafing the pockets of Chinese. To die is death by whatever means, but there was one method – napalm, jellied petrol – that struck terror in the hearts of all. Like an avenging angel, the Corsair flying perhaps 30 feet above us, unloads a metal canister that falls slowly, end over end, toward the targeted humans crouched in ambush alongside the road. Great gouts of flame erupt, leap skyward, piercing the black billowing smoke, as the napalm incinerates the foe. I duck down to avoid the hot blast of air and smoke as it rolls over us all. Nothing remains but the blackened earth and ashes, the residue of a human presence.'

Yudam-ni was not the only Marine position being attacked. The Chinese were also attacking Hagaru and Koto-ri, and these were seasoned fighters and brave men, skilled in infiltration, fierce in battle, not afraid to die. They usually attacked at night, sending in advanced patrols to draw Marine fire and then infiltrating round the machine-gun positions, before putting in a heavy infantry assault accompanied with bugle calls, shouting and plenty of mortar and machine-gun fire. It was necessary to maintain a tight perimeter to keep them out and manning the line in sub-zero weather proved a sore trial to the Marines, many of whom were soon smitten with frostbite.

Dennis Aldridge again: 'We had "warming tents", big marquees with stoves in, and a few men could go off and get their fingers defrosted before they got too cold to press a trigger. The Colonel also caused a bit of a stir with the Yanks when he ordered 41 to shave every day, not a fun thing to do in sub-zero weather, but I noticed after a day or two that the US Marines around us started shaving as well. Every night we had heavy attacks and one morning I counted the bodies outside our immediate perimeter and there were over 500 lying out there; some of them were wearing US equipment, parkas and so on, looted from our dead in the pass.'

The Marines at Hagaru and Koto-ri were still hanging on, fighting desperately, waiting for their comrades to pull back from Yudam-ni, and Morton Silver at Yudam-ni still remembers that march out: 'All unnecessary material was to be destroyed. We would now survive on daily air-drops for ammunition, food and fuel. We would leave the Chinese nothing but burning and blasted supplies. Rearguard companies were in position as the long column of trucks and jeeps assembled. Doctors and corpsmen were interspersed down the length of the column to be in position for maximum medical aid. Every vehicle carried casualties, in the truck body and cabs, dead lashed on to the hoods and fenders. The men were in agony but they were leaving Yudam-ni with their regiments. On the morning of 1 December we began the breakout. The 5th and 7th Regiments began to grind forward, attacking the surrounding Chinese. All who could walk, walked. All who could fight, fought.

'The forward units would engage the Chinese, smash them for the moment, and we would move ahead a few hundred yards. After a few such engagements those in the vanguard would be replaced by another company to repeat the attacks over and over again. The waiting and the increasing apprehension were debilitating, requiring constant sensibility and mindfulness on the part of the officers. They were in their glory: they did not fail us; this is what they were trained for; they were magnificent.

'Late afternoon, and we had progressed only a few miles. It was obvious that we were going to spend a God-awful night on the road. We were going to need some divine intervention to survive the night, and I was so tired. Light snow was falling, downy white snow. So inviting to the exhausted troops – to lie down and sleep in its soft embrace, and never to wake. It was quiet; it was bitter cold. It was hell on earth. The darkness was shattered, split open, as star shells lit up the road – slowly falling from the skies, exposing us to the enemy, now intent on delivering the final blow.

'The column had stopped. Up ahead the 3rd Battalion, 5th Marines, was struggling to clear the road. We stood among the trucks and waited. We took turns, holding on to the contoured exhaust pipes, warming our frozen hands on the engine's exhaust.

'Something had to be done or we might go mad. Standing in the frigid darkness, in the frozen mountains of Korea, among men hungry for food and warmth, I spoke of dining at the best restaurants in New York; I told of my culinary experiences, my likes and dislikes; I regaled the wounded with my pseudo-sophisticated taste for escargot, truffles, wild boar, etc. I went on and on until my brain went dry, but they wanted more. We put together meals that would warm the innards of a corpse; we argued the delights of wine and brandies – and the time passed, and the convoy began to move on to Hagaru-ri. The 3rd Battalion had burst through the roadblock after three bloody attempts.

'Shuffling on frozen feet and dragging their exhausted bodies, the men of the 5th and 7th Marine Regiments began streaming into Hagaru-ri. Word spread among the defenders of the town that the 5th and 7th Regiments were coming in. They lined the road and watched in silence as the rifle companies, the walking wounded, even the medics, slowly plodded in, heads held high, undefeated and proud as hell. It was 4 December when the last of the men from Yudam-ni entered the perimeter at Hagaru. Fourteen miles in four days – with our men, our equipment, our casualties and our dead.'

41 Commando were scouting forward from the perimeter when the

5th and 7th Marines came in from Yudam-ni, as Dennis Aldridge remembers: 'I will never forget it – seeing the US Marines march in from Yudam-ni. They had fought their way back, and they brought their equipment and their wounded, even their dead, stacked in the trucks. They had wounded in stretchers tied on to jeeps and dead men lashed to mudguards. They were frozen and frostbitten but every man carried a weapon. They had been marching and fighting for a week, in screaming winds and terrible cold and they were still ready to go on and fight. Magnificent isn't the word for it.'

Arthur Derby remembers another incident: 'I did not see the main body come in, but I remember being on guard on a corner and seeing two US Marines from Yudam-ni come up, one almost carrying the other. Anyway, this one finally fell down and his mate knelt beside him and said, "Come on, buddy, just around the corner there is hot coffee," and picked him up and they staggered on. When you are young you think that sort of thing is sentimental, hot coffee and all, but when you get a bit older you realize the comradeship that kept those two going. It makes you want to cry.'

The admiration 41 felt for the US Marines was reciprocated, as one US Marine recalls: 'May a poor, slogging US Marine say a word of thanks for a job well done? I was one of those who marched in from Yudam-ni and when we got to Hagaru I heard that the British had supplied us with a fighting force. Before that day we had laughed at the words "UN Forces"; the only other troops we had seen had been Chinese. I was delighted to meet the British and when they were around you did not need to look for a fight. Just look for the British Marines and they would be in it – and none of them wore a steel helmet, just one of those green berets.'

The force at Hagaru now had to fight its way back to Koto-ri and then, with the rest of the Division, to Hungnam and the sea. This march of the 'Chosin Few', the 1st Marine Division, became an epic of Marine history on both sides of the Atlantic. Chosin was, said *Time* magazine 'a battle unparalleled in US military history – an epic of great suffering and great valour'. The words 'retreat' or 'withdrawal' do not appear in the US Marine dictionary, so their next move was referred to as 'an advance to the sea', or 'an attack in a different direction'.

At dawn on 6 December 1950, the 1st Marine Division, now numbering some 10,000 men, with 41 Commando forming part of the rearguard, set out on their march to the sea. The weather was still below zero, the enemy active and increasing in number and the road hard, especially for men worn down with lack of sleep and days of living and fighting in severe cold. The advance was led by the 7th Marines, with the 5th Marines and 41 Commando in the rear; the sixty miles from Hagaru to the sea took this force three days and nights of almost constant fighting.

Dennis Aldridge again: 'The march out was grim. We were getting the usual sniping as we left and the Colonel sent out a patrol to push them back, thirty men with no support. We had to do it the hard way, on foot, but we had air support and that made all the difference. I hate napalm but, by God, it saved my life up there, and when we got to Hungnam I slept for twelve solid hours.'

The 7th Marines and 41 held the Hangaru perimeter until the rest of the Division was on its way down and then fell back steadily, putting in attack and counter-attack to keep the Chinese at bay. Chinese attacks went on throughout the night and the rearguard were soon cut off from the rest of the Division, arriving at Koto-ri well after dark. There they were met by Captain Pat Ovens and a party of Royal Marines who had been cut off on the way up and fought their way back to Koto-ri. This reinforcement was welcome because 41, though much reduced, was still full of fight. Reporting the arrival of the Division to X Corps HQ, Colonel Puller thought it important to mention that his garrison of 10,000 men now included 200 British Marines from 41 Commando.

Morton Silver pushed on with 41: 'I marched south out of Koto-ri with the Royal Marines, the survivors of Task Force Drysdale. Disdaining any and all motorized transport, they tramped down the frozen mountain road back to Hungnam, singing their bloody song while waiting in the frigid darkness for the column to blast through the roadblocks. The tune is "Oh Come All Ye Faithful" and there are only four words, "Why are we waiting?" I can still hear them singing that song.

'At the port I was approached by the British medical chief petty officer, with a request to examine his troops. Only on direct orders, the Britishers removed their shoes and socks to reveal frozen, gangrenous, blackened toes and feet – they had marched, crippled and in pain, fought, singing and swearing, down the road, from the Chosin to the sea. The US Marines were proud to have the Royal Marines fight alongside us in that hellish place called Chosin.'

The story of the 'Chosin Few' is an epic of the US Marine Corps, and the Royal Marines played only a small part in it. Even so, they proved that a small force can make a difference and the friendships forged between the two Corps on the frozen roads around Chosin have never been forgotten.

The 1st Marine Division fought its way down to the Hungnam perimeter and on to the waiting ships. As the ships pulled away, the engineers ashore were already blasting the port facilities and burning any stores that could not be removed. 41 Commando spent Christmas with the 1st Marine Division, and in the New Year were withdrawn to Japan. They were then attached to the Commonwealth Division and sent on another minor raid before occupying islands in Wonsan, from where they continued to raid the North Korean coast, in craft ranging from canoes to LCAs (landing craft – assault). Finally, in December 1951, 41 Commando was withdrawn to England before being disbanded the following February, though not before the Unit Colours had been adorned with the ribbon of a US Presidential Citation for exemplary conduct in the field, a decoration rarely given to a non-American unit.

The 1st Marine Division stayed on in Korea but there were no more amphibious operations and the Division served as line infantry. In this they demonstrated the wide-ranging effectiveness of SOF troops, for not only can the SOF fulfil a special role, as in the amphibious attack at Inchon, and display great discipline and fighting ability against odds, as at Chosin, they can also take their place in the front line, like a conventional infantry force. It is this versatility, plus the thorough training given to the men, that makes SOF units so combat-effective.

Sergeant Charles Owen, Second World War veteran, was with the 1st Marine Division in Korea: 'The fighting was fierce, either when the enemy were infiltrating or coming on hard. In Korea the Chinese fired their artillery in mass as the Russian Army do. They placed the artillery hub to hub. Shells would fall like rain. After a barrage you would wonder why you were not killed. This would be followed by an infantry attack. In Korea we were not given the supplies and air support we had in the Second World War. Most of the troops had some good training before joining the infantry units but the best replacements were the volunteers sent from the rear units. They would be highly motivated and eager to learn. They would be sent to you until the replacements from USA arrived. They did not want to return to the rear units after the replacements arrived, they would beg to stay with the front-line units.'

The Korean peninsula was not suited to small-unit warfare, and conventional warfare, of a very bitter kind, came to dominate the war in Korea from the middle of 1951, but there were some Special Force operations. Lionel J. Hebert of Massachusetts was in Korea with Special Forces from April 1951 to June 1952: 'My outfit was an intelligence-gathering organization, 8240 Army Unit, Far East Command, Liaison Detachment, Korea. We were a part of CCRAK, which was the Combined Command for Reconnaissance Activities, Korea. We were further broken down into smaller units and were organized into Tactical Liaison Operations, or TLOs.

'The TLOs were comprised of one officer and three NCOs, three to four interpreters, ten agents from North Korea and various support personnel, all Korean. Our complete teams had around thirty-five to forty people and our mission was to infiltrate (by ground) the enemy positions and seek out enemy movements, troop locations, identify strength, locate supply routes and ammo points, train movements, and seek out the location of armoured units and so on. This mission was accomplished by using the agents we had recruited and trained. The agents had lived in North Korea prior to the war and knew the areas. Each agent was sent in with a mission. We would select areas and then take our agents through the lines and drop them off in no-man's land. When they had completed their mission they would surrender to friendly forces and we would pick them up, debrief them and pass on intelligence information to relevant units along the line.

'We received help from the 3rd US Infantry Division with items like food, ammo etc. We operated through all the units along the Imjin river; the British Commonwealth Division, Greeks, Filipinos and so on. I read somewhere that the winter of 51/52 was the coldest on record in Korea. I'm originally from New England and we have some real cold winters there, but never as cold as that Korean winter, and I applaud all those brave young men of all the units who survived the cold. Withdrawal under pressure is no sin, to be in disarray is only human, especially when the pressure is coming from thousands of angry, well-trained Chinese soldiers, whom I learned to develop a healthy respect for.

'In December 1951, one of the agents, two interpreters and I went on an ambush patrol. The patrol was made up of fifty men drawn from units of the 15th Infantry Regiment, 3rd Division. My agent led us to a location where a Chinese patrol had been observed for three days. We set up the ambush and captured four Chinese who were young, cold, and as scared as we were.

'In November 1951, my CO, Lieutenant Gile and I were visiting the Commonwealth Division. We visited the Intelligence Officer and were developing a plan to use our agents to screen the front of the Division.

It was late afternoon and we went to the Mess and shared a hot stew with a British buddy. All I can say about the stew is that it was hot. That evening the Commonwealth Division was hit with a pretty serious attack from the Chinese. During the battle a call came in from one of the outposts saying that a group was heading towards our location. The CO responded, "Well done, lad, let them come through and in the morning we'll close the net and pick them up". I don't know who the CO was but I've never forgotten that line and I've repeated it many times. He was cool under fire and in the morning, sure enough, they picked up a few disoriented Chinamen.

'I can recall that attack as though it was yesterday; total casualties were seven British killed, eighty-seven wounded, forty-four missing. I was proud to be a part of that battle and will never forget those brave men.'

The Korean War began just as the US Army were reconsidering the position of their deactivated Ranger battalions, and the outbreak of the war – and the poor showing of the conventional divisions confronting the initial North Korean onslaught – gave added impetus to the move to reactivate the Rangers. The task was given to Colonel John G. Van Houten on the day of the Inchon landing, 15 September 1950. Colonel Van Houten was sent to Fort Benning in Georgia, given two weeks to muster volunteers for Ranger training and ordered to produce a Ranger Force inside six weeks. A call went out for volunteers for 'hazardous duty in the Far East', and the volunteers flooded in. A great many came from the 82nd Airborne Division and from soldiers who had served in the 1st Special Service Force or the OSS, but quite a few had never seen SF service, including a group of black paratroopers, a rare sight in the still segregated US Army. These men completed their Ranger training with great success and were formed into the first black Ranger unit.

There was no intention of reforming the Ranger battalions of the Second World War. The concept evolved for Korea was to improve the soldering and fighting skills of the Army at large and provide each infantry division with a 112-man Ranger Company, specifically for recon duties. Four Ranger companies were raised and on 17 December 1950 the 1st Ranger Infantry Company (Airborne) arrived in Korea and was attached to the 2nd Infantry Division. Two more companies followed, the 2nd going to the 7th Infantry Division, the 4th to Eighth Army HQ, from where it was deployed to the 1st Cavalry Division, an armoured formation. The 3rd Ranger Company stayed on at Fort Benning to assist in the training of another four Ranger Companies.

The Ranger Companies in Korea were soon in combat, including countless patrol actions and an airborne assault on Munsan-Ni. In general, though, the Rangers were not used in their proper role, but were employed as reinforcements for any battalion that needed help. The 1st Company, for example, fought with the 2nd Division at Chi-pyong-ni in February, when strong Chinese forces put in a strong thrust against X Corps, but this battle did not go well. The Rangers leading the attack experienced almost as much fire from American units as from the attacking Chinese and many Rangers were killed or wounded in fruitless counter-attacks.

Two months later the Rangers were used again in an attempt to seize and blow the sluice doors of the Hwachon Dam, which overlooked the positions of IX Corps. Fourteen Rangers were killed or wounded on this operation without result, and in July 1951, less than a year after they had been reactivated, orders reached Colonel Van Houten at Fort Benning, ordering him to cease training Ranger Companies as those in the field were to be stood down.

In spite of strong protests from Colonel Van Houten and many regimental commanders who had seen the Rangers in combat or had them under command in Korea, this order was put into effect in November 1951. Many of the Rangers were then transferred to the 187th Regimental Combat Team, the paratroop formation which had done good work after Inchon. This winding down of the Ranger force was a disappointment, but the Ranger concept had been given another airing and many of those who served in the Ranger Companies in Korea would find that experience useful when the Vietnam War broke out ten years later. Besides, their performance in Korea had already attracted the attention of higher command in the USA.

In October 1951, a few weeks after the Ranger units were deactivated, General Lawton Collins, the US Army Chief of Staff, directed that Ranger training should be kept in being and extended to all infantry units of the Army. A Ranger Department was established and a Ranger training course organized for US infantry units, with the aim of having at least one Ranger-qualified officer in every rifle company and one Ranger-trained NCO in every rifle platoon.

Another Special Force unit, Army Unit 8086, was formed to supply North Korean, anti-Communist partisans now fighting in the rear of the Chinese and North Korean Armies. AU8086 was led by Colonel John McGee, who had commanded guerrillas in the Philippines in the Second World War. This force was formed in July 1951 and soon mustered some 7,000 men, all but sixty of them Korean. Led by American

officers, AU8086 carried out a number of coastal raids and deep-penetration patrols before being deactivated in 1953. By the end of the war
there were over 20,000 US-trained and -led Korean guerrillas engaged
in operations against the North, organized into battalions and commanded by another US officer, Lieutenant-Colonel Jay Vanderpool.

The difficulties of conducting Special Force operations in Korea have
already been pointed out. After the landing at Inchon and the battles
around Chosin, the Korean War became a conventional war, with an
established front line and few opportunities for irregular warfare other
than along the coast. However, some clandestine operations did take
place, many organized by officers of the newly formed CIA. The CIA
attempted to recruit and train agents for insertion into North Korea,
but the men were not well chosen and the North Koreans were too
vigilant for this 'secret agent' activity to prosper.

A slightly more hopeful enterprise was undertaken by a British
officer, Major Ellery 'Bill' Anderson MC of the Royal Ulster Rifles, a
Second World War paratrooper and a former SAS officer. With some
encouragement from Eighth Army HQ, Anderson assembled a small
force of Korean volunteers and put them through some rigorous training, including exercises in escape and evasion, and a parachute course.
In April 1951, he and six of his men parachuted behind the North
Korean lines and blew up a railway tunnel near Wonsan. Then matters
went awry. Their coastal pick-up failed to arrive and they were forced to
evade the enemy for three days until they were extracted by helicopter,
though not before two of their number had been captured.

The next operation went seriously wrong from the start. Their
landing was spotted and North Korean patrols were soon hunting
for them. Resupply also failed and when Anderson was extracted by
helicopter and returned to base to sort matters out, his men in the field
lost contact. Three days later the raiders were attacked and overrun.
Four of the team, two Koreans and two American Rangers, eventually
made their way back to the UN lines and reported to Anderson, but
the rest were never seen again. Anderson put forward various schemes
for other raids but none received official approval, though Anderson
himself received a bar to his Military Cross and the US Legion of Merit
before he was posted back to Britain. The Korean War ended on 27 July
1953, when armistice terms were agreed at Panmunjom. Korea remains
partitioned and both sides maintain large armies in a state of readiness.
But, though border clashes occur frequently, South Korea remains
intact.

The fighting in the Korean War did not see much participation by

Special Force troops but it did reveal that even conventional forces needed a raiding and reconnaissance capacity. Hence the attachment of 41 Commando to the 1st Marine Division and the rapid raising of Ranger Companies for attachment to US Army divisions. These forces were not always used correctly or in their designated role, but they filled a void and kept the Special Force concept alive.

SOF forces, represented by the 1st Marine Division and 41 Commando, did all and more than could be expected of them, landing at Inchon and Wonsan, fighting in the line from 1951 to 1953 and enduring the 'advance in a different direction' from Hagaru to the sea. Following the Korean War, the US Army reassessed the need for recon and Special Force troops and by 1960 the US Army had developed an SF capacity. The Korean War provided an opportunity for some Special Force units to show what they could do but for the next few years the focus of SF and SOF activity must turn to the campaigns fought by the imperial powers, especially France and Great Britain, as their empires came to an end in various corners of the world.

Wessex helicopter

CHAPTER SIX
Colonial Wars 1950–1960

> We give express charge that, in our marches
> through the country, there be nothing compelled
> from the villages, nothing taken but paid for, none
> upbraided or abused . . . for when lenity and cruelty
> play for a kingdom, the gentler gamester is the
> surest winner.

> *William Shakespeare,* Henry V, *Act III, scene vi*

Warfare in the 1950s and early 1960s was marked by a succession of colonial campaigns, some of considerable size, in the countries then ruled by the imperial powers, Britain, France, Portugal, Belgium and Holland. There were massacres of European settlers in Indonesia, the Belgian Congo and Angola. The French fought full-scale wars in Algeria and Indo-China, a territory made up of Laos, Cambodia and Vietnam, and a dozen smaller struggles took place in the colonies and protectorates of the old British Empire. These struggles for colonial independence were fought with varying degrees of ferocity but all ended, eventually, in the withdrawal of the imperial powers. Few of these conflicts involved Special Forces to any great degree, but SOF troops were regularly employed in these colonial campaigns, notably by France and Great Britain.

The most marked difference between the campaigns fought by the French and the British was that while the French wars in Indo-China and Algeria cost many thousands of lives and were all-out struggles involving land, air and sea forces, those fought by the British were far more low-key and often amounted to little more than anti-terrorist campaigns, though many lives were lost and much property was destroyed before the campaigns were brought to a conclusion. Nevertheless, these small, 'colonial' campaigns are of interest to the Special Force story for they demonstrate how SF and SOF troops should be used in small-scale wars.

The main reason for the relative lack of bloodshed in the British colonies, when compared to that which flowed in the French, Dutch, Portuguese and Belgian colonies was that the British Empire was not built to endure and the local people had been prepared for independence, if only to a limited extent. The intention of successive British governments since the middle years of the nineteenth century, and certainly since the Indian Mutiny of 1857–8, had been to advance the colonies to independence through a process of regional or provincial control, where local politicians could get experience of democratic government, leading on to internal self-government, Dominion status within the Commonwealth and eventual independence.

In the greater part of the British Empire, this is exactly what happened. The major countries within the Empire – Canada, Australia, South Africa and New Zealand – were fully independent by the 1930s and India was to follow as soon as the fundamental problems between the Muslims and Hindu communities could be sorted out. Independence came to India and Pakistan in 1947 and forty of the fifty-three nations that at the time of writing make up the Commonwealth achieved independence from Britain by 1960–1, without any major trouble at all.

Some countries did pose problems. When these could not be resolved by discussion or when, as in Malaya or Cyprus, one of the parties to the independence movement attempted to seize control of the colony or dominate the issue by force, the British Army was summoned for public order duties usually described as 'actions in aid of the civil power'. Most of these problems arose from the handing over of power at the end of imperial rule, rather than from any British desire to retain control.

While the British Empire endured, local differences were suppressed and the people could intermingle in safety. When the imperial grasp began to slip, ancient feuds and ethnic hatreds re-emerged, a problem compounded by the fact that with the competing communities now living together, civil disorder, riots and bloodshed were extremely hard to prevent. The main task of the British Army in this period was to keep the disputing communities apart while the politicians found a formula that would grant the independence which the majority – or at least their political leaders – craved without abandoning the minority to post-independence persecution. That this last objective was not always achieved was not the fault of the soldiers.

The first example of a colonial struggle came in Malaya, in the immediate aftermath of the Second World War. Here the British Army cut its teeth in guerrilla warfare against a skilled, experienced and ruthless Communist enemy and, in a ten-year jungle struggle, fought him to a standstill. In Malaya, the Army learned the value of 'hearts and minds', of keeping the civil population on your side, in spite of propaganda and carefully engineered provocation – quite apart from enduring attacks and ambushes and taking a steady stream of casualties in the jungle.

A great many soldiers of the British Army served in these colonial struggles, in Malaya, Kenya, Cyprus, Aden and Borneo, but the attention here must be on the SF and SOF troops, the Royal Marines of 3 Commando Brigade, and the soldiers of the Parachute Regiment and the Special Air Service Regiment – though the contribution of the line infantry and the doughty Gurkhas of the 17th Gurka Division, who fought with great skill and distinction in Malaya and later in the Borneo Confrontation with Indonesia, must be acknowledged. The Gurkhas were an 'elite force' rather than a Special Force, but their worth in irregular warfare is indicated by their kill-rate in Malaya. The SAS killed 108 Communist terrorists, the Royal Marine Commandos 221, the Gurkhas over 3,000.

The Malayan 'Emergency', as the British called it, lasted for twelve years, from 1948 to 1960, and had its origins in Special Force activity dating back to the Second World War. During that struggle a force of Chinese guerrillas, the Malayan People's Anti-Japanese Army or MPAJA, led by a dedicated Communist, Chin Peng, kept up the fight against the Japanese troops, a struggle in which they were armed, trained and supplied with weapons by British officers of Force 136, the Far Eastern arm of SOE.

When the war ended, the MPAJA Communists expected to seize power in Malaya, but swiftly encountered a couple of snags. The first obstacle to a Chinese Communist take-over of Malaya was that the majority of the population were Malay and the Malays had no intention of seeing their country fall into the hands of the large Chinese minority. The second snag was that the returning British, while declaring that they intended to grant independence and leave Malaya, also declared that they would not do so until the country was politically stable and democratically run. If that meant fighting their former allies, the MPAJA Communist Terrorists – or CTs – so be it. The Communists renamed their fighting force the MRABA (the Malayan Races Anti-British Army), withdrew to the jungle and started a terrorist war.

The Malayan campaign saw the rebirth of one of the most famous wartime units when the SAS Regiment was reformed in 1950, at Kota Tingi near Jahore, named the Malaya Scouts and sent into the jungle to fight the bandits. The Malaya Scouts were raised by Major Mike Calvert, a Chindit officer who had commanded SAS soldiers in the last months of the war. Calvert raised his new unit from the ranks of the Hong Kong garrison, intending to use it for deep-penetration patrols into the depths of the jungle, where the CTs had established their training camps. In 1951 Calvert's troopers were joined by men from the UK Territorial SAS Regiment, the 21st SAS, and shortly afterwards the Malaya Scouts were reformed as the 22nd SAS Regiment. The two big contributions of the SAS to the jungle war were the development of 'hearts and minds' activity, offering food and running medical-aid programmes among the Sakai tribes in the jungle, and the practice of parachuting into the jungle canopy, a skill that was not without risk.

Bill Sculthorpe, of Oakville, Canada, served in Malaya with the Parachute Regiment Squadron, 22nd SAS, from 1955 to 1957 and remembers SAS life at that time: 'At the end of 1954 the War Office announced that a seventy-five-man contingent of volunteers from the Parachute Regiment would join the desperately under-strength 22nd SAS, which was heavily involved in the Malayan conflict. Needless to add, the volunteer application list was over-subscribed.

'The "Independent Squadron, the Parachute Regiment" was commanded by Major Dudley Coventry, a brilliant officer with a distinguished, though non-conformist, military record. The Squadron was transported by RAF Hastings aircraft from Lynham to Singapore, at that time the longest distance any Army unit had been transported by air. Accommodated in Selangor Barracks, close to the FARELF [Far East Land Forces] Parachute Training School, the Squadron underwent training in techniques developed for parachuting into dense jungle. These included a Bergen rucksack on the chest (no reserve parachute), and a 200-foot length of webbing strapped to the leg which was used to abseil down to terra firma. This very hairy practice of "tree jumping" relied on the parachute canopy being caught in the trees but often it did not – with disastrous consequences. Eventually, non-operational "tree-jumping" was discontinued due to high casualties. A further innovation learned at this time was jumping from S55 Whirlwind helicopters, which were just making an appearance.

'From Changi the Squadron moved to the Jungle Warfare School at Kota Tingi in Malaya. British and Australian instructors taught basic jungle tactics with assistance from a company of Gurkhas. This course ended with the Squadron's first operation off the east coast of Southern Malaya. Landing from Navy MTBs, the Squadron stormed ashore into flat, dense, sea-swamped jungle. Unfortunately, nobody had considered the water supply (never usually a problem in jungle). Here the water was salty, so we lived on coconut milk, a miserable experience. Finally to SAS HQ in Kuala Lumpur and a new designation, "Para Sqn 22 SAS Regt", followed by a further four weeks' operational training in SAS deep jungle-penetration techniques with personnel taking intensive courses on signalling, medical work, etc. The Squadron now became fully operational, comprising four troops of one officer and fifteen ORs [Other Ranks], HQ Troop OC and seven ORs (a SQMS and four ORs in SAS base). Unfortunately, injuries and sickness would often reduce manpower by up to 20 per cent, meaning heavier workloads for those still operational.

'The sharp end of SAS operations was arduous and dangerous work. An operation would be for up to three months with resupply by parachute every fourteen days, security permitting. Fresh meat and bread would be dropped and consumed the same day before the beasties got it. It was not unusual for supply 'chutes to "whistle in" – plummet to earth without fully opening or become hung up in the trees or be otherwise inaccessible. These would invariably be the ones with the mail or rum ration aboard.

'One of the attractions to this type of soldiering was the accumulation of pay while on operations. At the end of an op, after a couple of days' debriefing, medical tests and the obligatory lecture from the medical officer on the perils of passion, the Squadron would be despatched on seven days' leave. With pockets full of hard-earned money, the deprivations of three months could be rectified in grand style in Singapore or Penang.

'The SAS had a rest and retraining camp on the island of Blakang Mati, in an idyllic beach-front setting. Light training until noon when the SQMS would open the beer bar (credit available, proceeds to Squadron funds) and the remainder of the day would be spent on various sporting activities or simply lounging around regaining lost weight. This ten-day sojourn would culminate in a Squadron barbecue with nurses, Wrens, Waafs, etc., invited to the fun, frolic and inevitable punch-up.

'Ten to fourteen days before the next Op would be spent on more rigorous training, back at Base HQ. On completion of their two-year tour and a notable contribution to the success of SAS operations in Malaya, the Para Squadron was disbanded, but a large proportion of personnel transferred to the SAS and returned to Malaya.'

Tree jumping was employed in a number of SAS operations, including the hunt for Ah Hoi, the 'Baby-Killer', in 1958. Ah Hoi's method of spreading terror was to pick out a pregnant woman and cut her open before the eyes of terrified villagers. Ah Hoi had to be caught and executed, and the task was given to D Squadron 22nd SAS, who parachuted thirty-seven men into the Telok Anson swamps of Selangor, where Ah Hoi was believed to be in hiding. The jump went reasonably well but one man broke his back and had to be evacuated by helicopter before Lieutenant Harry Thompson led the rest of his men into the swamp after Ah Hoi.

It took nearly two weeks to hunt him down, days and nights spent deep in the swamps, sometimes in water up to their necks, always subjected to attacks from leeches and swarms of mosquitoes. It was a week before the soldiers even had their first contact when Sergeant Sandilands' section ran into a CT sentry whom they killed before rushing Ah Hoi's camp, only to find that the CTs had gone. The swamp was then surrounded by regular troops while the SAS continued to patrol inside the cordon. After more days of patrolling Ah Hoi was flushed out and surrendered, the rest of his group giving up some days later, worn out by the relentless harassment of the SAS. The British SAS in Malaya were joined by men from the Australian, Fijian and New Zealand SAS, all of which were formed or reformed in the late 1950s or early 1960s.

The Malayan Emergency also saw the brief rebirth of Force 136, recreated as Ferret Force, the recruiting of Iban warriors in Borneo, who were attached to the British and Gurkha battalions in Malaya and used to track CTs in the jungle, and the setting up of the first Jungle Warfare School. This was to be the prototype for other such schools, including the one set up in Panama for the training of US Special Forces, and US SF units bound for Vietnam trained at this School in the 1960s. The School also trained many Indonesian officers and NCOs in jungle warfare, only to meet these same soldiers in battle during the Indonesian confrontation of the 1960s. 'They were good soldiers, and obviously well trained,' says Brigadier Christopher Bullock, who served in Borneo

Australian commandos on parachute training.

Zodiac Inflatables Company, 1st Commando Regt, training in Broken Bay, Sydney.

ABOVE PFC Charles Owens and his platoon holding captured Japanese
flags during battle for Pelelieu, September 1944. 'A' Coy, 1st Marine Division,
United States Marine Corps.

LEFT Canoe recovery to submarine, Australian
commandos. 1 Commando Company and HMAS *Ovens*.

LEFT Lt Morton Silver USN, with the 1st Marine Division in Korea, 1950.

BELOW Marines of 41 (Independent) Commando destroy an enemy supply line in North Korea, April 1951.

A wounded Communist bandit is held captive in Malaya, 1955.

SAS patrol in Malaya. Peter de la Billière is second from left.

LEFT Mau Mau dead after an ambush, Kenya, 1954.

RIGHT A Commando patrol in the Kyrenia Mountains of Cyprus, 1955.

LEFT Patrol of 'Z' Troop, 45 Commando, Lapithos, Cyprus, 1955.

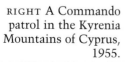

Helicopters of 45 Commando
landing by De Lesseps' statue,
Suez, 1956.

Commando Brigade sniper, Port
Said, Suez, 1956.

ABOVE Soldiers of 42 Commando advance across the Radfan, Aden, 1962.

RIGHT Parachute soldiers on patrol in Aden town, 1965.

with the 2/2nd Gurkhas, 'but fortunately not as good as us.'

The Malayan Emergency and the Borneo Confrontation which followed spurred the Australian Army to introduce Special Force units, the first of which was raised in 1954 by Major W. H. 'Mac' Grant, who had served with the 3rd Royal Australian Regiment in Korea: 'I had been with the 1st Commonwealth Division in Korea and then been Second-in-Command of the Commonwealth Battle School at Hardamoura in Japan. This had a British CO and a training programme which I still rate as the best infantry training I ever saw. This was a perfect grounding for my next job, raising 1 Commando Company in Sydney. At this time Australia had a National Service Training Scheme by which all men were called up for seventy days' military training and then for three years in the CMF, the Citizens' Military Force, now called the Army Reserve, like the British Territorial Army or the Royal Marines Reserve. The members of the first Commando Company were all from the CMF, and they volunteered in droves. The unit was finally formed in July 1955 with a strength of 150 troopers, and we eventually had a company in Sydney and another in Melbourne.

'We worked on basic infantry training to start with, lots of weapon training, including night firing, fitness training and, of course, speed-marching, which was not terribly popular. We got into the Commando habit of telling the troops where to parade and they had to get there, wherever it was, by themselves and that worked like a charm, and that remained the routine while I was in England, on a programme with the Royal Marine Commandos. While I was away two Royal Marines, Sergeant McDermott of 42 Commando and Sergeant Len Holmes of the SBS, came out and were attached to the Sydney and Melbourne Commando Companies as instructors. The first small-scale amphibious raiding course was started using folboats [folding canoes] of the type used for the Rimau raids.

'By the time I returned in May 1956 we were at Gan Gan camp near Nelson Bay, where we did a lot of assault landings, with explosive charges in the sea and on the beach and Brens firing tracer into the headlands. The locals loved it, but it made a helluva lot of noise and you would never get away with it today. We also established a scramble course and did some fully loaded cross-country marches of up to twenty miles, and a parachute course was added to the curriculum about this time, and we also formed up with the 4th Submarine Squadron, Royal Navy, for infiltration and landing exercises from their subs.

'We started awarding green berets to those who had successfully completed our course and the first fifty-six men passed out in September

1956. In the following year, 1957, we added diving to our range of skills, using scuba sets borrowed from the Royal Australian Navy, put on more amphibious raiding exercises and affiliated to Commando units of the Royal Marines, with 2 Commando Company affiliating with 45 Commando RM. In 1958 we were able to play a part in the founding of the Australian SAS Regiment. This was raised and commanded by Major Len Isles, a personal friend of mine, and after our annual camp at Gan Gan a number of 1 Commando personnel stayed behind to train the first SAS recruits – and so Special Force units came to the Australian Army.'

Major Grant stayed with the Australian Commando Companies until 1959 and, apart from service on attachment with the Royal Marines, also joined the British SAS Regiment in Malaya during the Emergency. He retired from the Army in 1977 with the rank of brigadier and is now Honorary Colonel and Patron of the 1st Commando Regiment.

Malaya is the place where the British drew up some rules for the effective conduct of an anti-guerrilla or anti-terrorist campaign. To be successful such a campaign must combine political and military action in a common approach to the situation. These rules rebut any thoughts that the answer to terrorism is counter-terrorism, as some counter-terrorism 'experts' allege. Counter-terrorism, fighting the enemy with the enemy's methods, is not only wrong, it is usually illegal and eventually destroys military morale. It is also completely ineffective. There is no finer way to turn a bystander or a non-combatant into an active enemy than by denying him justice, ill-treating his wife, murdering his student son or daughter and burning his crops. All the British experience in a dozen anti-terrorist campaigns indicates that the less the civil population are hassled by the police and Army, the more support they will give to the security forces.

The rules vary from place to place but the first rule, as we have seen more than once before, is that there must ultimately be a political solution to the problem that underpins the terrorist campaign. That solution must enjoy the support of a majority of the local population. The next rule is that this solution must be on offer throughout the confrontation and must be understood to be on offer, in unequivocal terms, by the bulk of the population. This calls for good communications, a sound grasp of propaganda and counter-propaganda techniques, and clear political direction. Unless that is supplied, the troops are fighting a pointless war in a political vacuum, and any victories won in the jungle or jebel are lost around the conference table.

The final rule – again – is that the war must be fought with minimum impact on the civilian – or uncommitted – portion of the population. In this the British Army had the inestimable help of the regimental system, with which to control the soldiers and prevent bad conduct. A British regiment is best regarded as a family, with an internal code of conduct and rules of behaviour that supplement and transcend anything in the Army Discipline Act. That some British soldiers did, from time to time, get out of order and ill-treat members of the civilian population cannot be denied, but such incidents were rare, without any official sanction and swiftly suppressed. They also brought down on the perpetrator the strong disapproval of his comrades. There are no Vietnam My Lai massacres of innocent civilians in the post-colonial history of the British Army and the popular theory advanced at the time by the CIA that 'when you have them by the balls, their hearts and minds will follow' has no practical validity; the support and friendship of the local people is vital.

To maintain unit discipline during a guerrilla war or a terrorist campaign is not easy, for one aim of the terrorist – or 'freedom fighter' – is to involve the civilian population in the 'armed struggle', deny the existence of a peaceful political solution and put the security forces in a bad light before the world media. The problem for the troops is that the usual tactics employed in fighting a counter-terrorist war – curfews, roadblocks, patrols and cordon-and-search operations – inevitably bear down on the civilian population. Unless counter-insurgency operations are conducted with skill, tact and understanding, they have the effect of alienating large sections of the population. It is at this point that Special Forces can be most useful. The essence of SF activity has been summed up as 'the use of the stiletto instead of the bludgeon'. SF units, if supplied with good intelligence, should be able to target the enemy forces and take them out with minimum impact on the local population. Special Forces were among the first to realize and apply the principles of 'hearts and minds', a phrase first employed by General Sir Gerald Templer, a fighting general who was High Commissioner in Malaya at the height of the Emergency. The solution to the terrorist problem, he said, 'lies not in pouring more British troops into the jungle but in the hearts and minds of the Malayan people'.

Templer's comment summed up a principle that already existed and was being widely applied, but 'hearts and minds' activity was backed with military action which gave the terrorists no rest and steadily eroded the support and supplies they obtained from the civilian population. The village people were removed from the jungle fringe where they were supplying the terrorists and placed in protective camps, camps equipped with schools and roads and clinics, far better than their kampongs. Local politicians were encouraged to participate in local government, while national politicians were given an ever-larger share of political power. The war against the CTs went on in the jungle, with increasing success as the troops learned to live and fight in that rugged terrain, and carry the war to the enemy. The British also maintained good relations with the Thai government, so although the CTs maintained safe bases across the Thai border in the north, they were never able to develop these in a way that seriously affected the struggle inside Malaya.

Malaya became independent in 1957, after which some of the SAS squadrons departed to fresh fields in the Arabian Gulf. It was still necessary to provide military aid to the new nation in order to combat the two or three thousand Communist guerrillas still roaming the jungle and, by rotating their squadrons, the SAS managed to keep their jungle fighting skills well honed until they were once again required. This opportunity came in Borneo between 1962 and 1966.

The Borneo 'Confrontation' with Indonesia was a war in two parts, the quickly quelled Brunei revolt of December 1962 and the three-year border war with Indonesia that followed. By 1962 Malaya had been independent for five years, but the British still had a military base in Singapore. The leader of Malaya, Tunku Abdul Rahman, now wished to federate his country with Singapore but he also wanted to reduce the number of Chinese in the proposed Federation of Malaysia and to include in this new grouping the British colonies of Sarawak and Sabah and the British Protectorate of Brunei. This idea was welcomed by the British but not by the Sultan of Brunei, who had no wish to lose his kingdom or share his vast oil revenues – the Sultan of Brunei is the richest man in the world – with the government of Malaysia.

The proposed Federation was also unwelcome to the Kendayan people of Brunei, who are of Indonesian stock, and in December 1962 they rebelled and seized the oil town of Serai and a number of European hostages in the river town of Limbang, capital of the Fifth Division of Sarawak. The British immediately dispatched troops from Singapore, including L Company, 42 Commando, commanded by Captain Jeremy Moore MC (the officer who was to command the ground forces in the Falklands War of 1982): 'I joined 42 in Singapore in 1962, on HMS *Bulwark*, off Muscat, then we went to Aden and up to Dhala for a while, then we went on a visit to Hong Kong. It was there that the Commando changed from Troops to Companies. My QMS [Quartermaster-Sergeant] – Company Sergeant-Major now – was Cyril Scoins, a fine man. On 9 December, a Sunday, I was in my room at Simbang, doing my Christmas cards, when a Marine came in and said the Colonel would like to see me. I went to his room and he told me about the Brunei trouble and asked me, "How quickly can you move the Company?"

'We got to Brunei airport in the evening of the 10th. L Company were about eighty-seven strong, and we were joined by a section of Vickers medium machine-guns (two guns). There was a lot of confusion but the Gurkhas had already retaken Brunei Town from the rebels. Next day, Brigadier Pat Patterson, commanding the 99th Gurkha Brigade, arrived and said to me, "I want you to think about Limbang and prepare for the arrival of the rest of the Commando – and find some transport."

'There was not much information about Limbang. I knew it was a town in Sarawak, that there were half a dozen or so British hostages held there and an unknown number of rebels. A police launch went up there – most movement in Borneo is by river – and got fired on. I got an air photograph of Limbang, not a good one but enough to identify the main buildings, the police station, the hospital and so on. Then our CO arrived, so I handed the task over to him, but later that day he told me to take L Company to Limbang and do the job.

'I went down to the waterfront and met the Senior Naval Officer, Lieutenant-Commander Jeremy Black, who had two minesweepers under command. We had also found some sampans and a couple of great flat craft called Z-Lighters. We decided to go through the "leads" up to Limbang in the Z-Lighters ... one of them had two yellow bulldozers on board, which came with us; we didn't have time to get them off. Jeremy Black came too, and the local Captain of Marine of Brunei Town, a man called Mouton, came to help us find the way. Now we knew there were quite a few rebels there, and a few hostages, so I didn't want to make a slow, grinding advance through the town which could put the hostages at risk, and I decided to go directly for the police station, which I thought might well be the rebel HQ. We had my Recce Group, Company HQ and a troop of Marines in my craft in front and the main company HQ, the MMGs and another troop and a half on the rear craft.

'We made good time up the leads into the Limbang river and lay up for a sleep before setting off again, aiming to arrive at first light. We came to the town quite suddenly when we rounded a bend in the river.

All the lights were on but they all went out abruptly, so we thought we had been spotted – in fact they were putting out the lights because dawn was breaking.

'When they finally did see us the place exploded; it was exactly like an ant-heap, with people running everywhere. Our "I" Sergeant – who ran the Intelligence section – hailed the town through a loudhailer, and told them the rebellion had failed, to lay down their arms, and so on. This news was greeted with a hail of shot, so we drove our landing craft straight at the bank, opposite the police station, with the second craft with the Vickers firing in support ... the enemy had light machine-guns, lots of rifles and shotguns, so the fire was heavy and a number of people were hit, including the helmsman of the leading craft – lots of bullets were coming aboard and splinters were flying about – something hit me in the middle of the back, hard enough to knock me down, and I thought, "Good grief, Moore, you seem to have been hit!", but I put my hand up to feel my back and there was no blood, so I thought, "Get up, man – there's a battle to be fought." My Second-in-Command was hit on the other craft, so CSM Cyril Scoins took over and asked the naval officer to "Move the craft over, please Sir, so I can give fire support." The naval officer shook his head and said, "Sergeant-Major, Nelson would have XXXXX loved you." But he moved the craft over and we got good support.

'The two sections ashore were doing everything perfectly – observing, firing, checking magazines, moving position, all the things we had practised so many times – it's very exciting to see the blokes doing it just right. You could pick the moment when the Corporal said "Go!" One of them told me later that he hated my guts in training, when I had them doing these drills day after day, "... but I understand what it was all for in about two-thirds of a second as soon as we came under fire".

'My craft had drifted off the bank – the helmsman had been hit and the naval officer in charge was busy firing a rifle. I wanted to put my third section ashore, so the officer took the helm and put us back again, but we were now about a hundred yards further upstream. Sergeant MacFarlane took his men over the bow to clear the shoreline down from there to the police station and we then found that we couldn't get the craft off again, so I went ashore. The main deck was by now pretty chaotic, with lots of packs and cartridge case littered about, and a couple of bodies. I went up the road past the hospital where Dick Morris, the Resident, and his wife were held hostages. Sergeant MacFarlane and two of his Marines were killed here, at very close range.

'Dick Morris told us there were about 300 rebels in the town and where the other hostages were kept . . . they included a young American from the Peace Corps. We had some resistance from the bazaar, and after Cyril Scoins landed the other two troops, we set out to do a bit of street clearing. The two troop subalterns hadn't done this, so we taught them on the job – a real live firing exercise. One colossal Marine fell through the roof of one house and plummeted all the way down, through various floors to the ground floor, landing in a heap beside a bath containing an entire Chinese family, all of them peering at him worriedly over the rim . . . the Company performed extremely well and I was very proud of them.'

This swift reaction, and others like it throughout the country, caused the Brunei revolt to collapse, but General Sir Walter Walker, commanding the 17th Gurkha Division and the officer in charge of the Brunei operation, was convinced that Indonesia was behind this revolt and that more trouble would follow. In this General Walker was quite correct. The main engagements of the 'Confrontation' took place in the jungles of Borneo, along the vague frontier with Kalimantan, the Indonesian part of the island, and by February 1963 SAS troopers, Gurkhas and the Royal Marine Commandos were patrolling the 900 miles of swamp, jungle and mountain that divided Indonesian Kalimantan from the Borneo states of the Malaysian Federation.

The word 'confrontation' may give rise to the idea that this campaign was more a matter of belligerent statements than actual fighting, but this is far from the case. The British, Malayan and Gurkha forces were frequently under attack and often outnumbered by well-trained regular units of the Indonesian Army. To the people at the sharp end, the Confrontation frequently resembled a war, and winning this war demanded good intelligence and the use of helicopters. Helicopters, which now play such an important part in modern warfare, were a major weapon – a force enhancer – in the rugged Borneo terrain. In that dense uncharted jungle it might take a patrol two days to cover ground which a Wessex helicopter could cover in as many minutes. Knowing where to place the troops demanded good intelligence, and gathering such intelligence became a prime Special Force function.

22 SAS were tasked with surveillance along the border and with the training and support of the Dyak and Iban Border Scouts, many of them former head-hunters, who had been engaged by the British to 'watch and warn' against Indonesian incursions. This border surveillance was not without risk, as Sergeant Lillico and his SAS patrol discovered in February 1965. They were moving along a track towards an Indonesian

post which their Scouts had spotted the previous day. This post appeared to be empty, but as the leading trooper approached it he spotted an Indonesian soldier in the jungle to his flank. In the exchange of fire the SAS trooper was hit in the thigh and fell into a clump of bamboo on top of yet another Indonesian soldier, whom he shot and killed. The SAS had walked into an ambush.

The Indonesians now engaged the SAS from well-concealed positions. Sergeant Lillico was wounded in the first exchange and lay out on the track, unable to move, but he returned the enemy fire while the others in the patrol took cover and began to work their way around the ambush site. The leading trooper was unable to walk, but he hopped back to join Lillico, who ordered him to find the rest of the patrol and bring it forward while Lillico opened fire in the direction of the enemy positions. Shortly after this the Indonesians withdrew, thinking that SAS reinforcements would soon be surrounding their positions. The remainder of the SAS patrol decided to withdraw to the nearest infantry post and returned next day to search the area for their wounded colleagues. The injured trooper was found on the morning of the following day, having dragged himself halfway back to the infantry post before he was found by the search party. Sergeant Lillico was winched out by helicopter later that day, thirty-six hours after he had been injured in that first fierce exchange of fire.

The average size of an SAS patrol was four men and they were often matched against Indonesian companies of 100 men, all well-trained troops who would fight hard when contacted and lay ambushes to trap their pursuers if forced to retreat. This led to the development of an SAS 'Shoot and Scoot' policy, where after making a contact and a brief exchange of fire, the SAS would break off the engagement, radio for reinforcements, often Gurkhas, and then dog the enemy's footsteps until they could be brought to battle.

'Confrontation' incidents were not always small affairs involving a handful of combatants. On one occasion a large force of at least 150 well-trained Indonesian soldiers, backed by two further regular Army companies, mounted a night attack on the jungle fort of Plaman Mapu on the Sarawak front, a position held by B Company, 2nd Battalion, the Parachute Regiment. When the attack came in, most of B Company were out on patrol and it was left to those remaining in camp, twenty-seven recently arrived young soldiers, to hold the position, fighting hand to hand against heavy odds, on a dark and rainswept night, with whatever weapons they could snatch up. The Company Sergeant-Major, 'Patch' Williams, was blinded in one eye during the battle, but he so inspired the men that, when dawn broke and the Indonesians drew off, over thirty Indonesian casualties were counted, against British losses of two killed and eight wounded.

The Indonesian Confrontation even saw the award of a Victoria Cross, to Gurkha Rifleman Rambadahur Limbu, who won his medal in the course of a day-long battle well inside the Kalimantan frontier in the course of a top-secret Claret operation, one of a series of deep-penetration raids which the British mounted well behind the Indonesian lines, to carry the war to the enemy and destroy his bases. The Indonesian Confrontation finally ended in August 1966 when the new ruler of Indonesia, General Suharto, recognized the Federation of Malaysia.

Every colonial campaign added to the stock of counter-terrorist techniques in the British Army, and British troops became very skilled in fighting and winning these small-scale wars. The quality of an SF or SOF unit depends on the ability of its NCOs, and this constant round of colonial campaigns – 'Corporals' Wars' in military jargon – where the weight of responsibility falls on the lower ranks was a great testing and training ground for Britain's NCOs and junior officers. In these campaigns they learned the value of constant practice, learned how to survive and fight in inhospitable environments, learned to navigate and patrol by day and night and how to use their weapons. Most of all they learned how to work with local troops and respect the local people. Not the least of these useful campaigns was the one in East Africa against the Mau Mau terrorists of the Kikuyu tribe, which took place in Kenya from 1952 and 1956.

The colonial situation in Kenya differed from that in India or Malaya. In those countries British expatriates went out to work or serve in the local administration, but returned home to Britain at the end of their service or on retirement. In Kenya, however, there was a large minority of British and South African settlers, some 30,000 in number, who were born there or who had chosen to make their homes in Kenya and had no intention either of leaving or of handing power over to the African majority, who under the leadership of Jomo Kenyatta were now demanding independence.

Kenyatta was a canny and sophisticated African politician and a member of the Kikuyu tribe. In addition to forming a political party, KAU, the Kenya African Union, he also set up a clandestine terrorist organization called Mau Mau. When independence was not granted with acceptable speed and the settlers seemed disposed to fight it every inch of the way, Kenyatta turned Mau Mau loose on the settlers and those Africans who favoured a democratic solution. The Mau Mau campaign was remarkably bloody, and caused great loss of life, especially among the Africans, who suffered greatly at the hands of the Mau Mau gangs. Only thirty-two white settlers were killed, though those who died were often slaughtered with great brutality, slashed to pieces while in their beds, or surprised and massacred during dinner by terrorist gangs let into their houses by servants.

The security forces, British and Kenyan, African and European lost some 600 men, while more than 1,800 loyal Africans were murdered, including more than eighty hacked to pieces at the Liri Massacre in 1952, when a Mau Mau gang surrounded a village, set the huts alight and slashed the men, women and children to pieces with pangas as they ran from the flames. In the course of the struggle, 10,000 Mau Mau were killed, mostly in patrol actions in the forests around Mount Kenya and the Kikuyu Reserve, where the Mau Mau rebellion was concentrated.

The soldiers who did most of the patrolling and killing during the Mau Mau time were either African troops of the King's African Rifles, locally raised regular battalions commanded by British officers and African NCOs, British infantry battalions flown out from the UK or men of the Kenya Regiment, a locally raised territorial force made up of white settlers and their sons. There was no Special Force involvement, but the campaign has to feature in any SF history because Kenya was where a young British officer, Captain Frank Kitson of the Rifle Brigade, formulated some useful theories about counter-insurgency warfare and how to fight it.

Kitson went to Kenya in a liaison capacity in August 1953. His task was to collect and analyse information gathered by the police and Army in two Kenya districts and attempt to supply the security forces with useful 'contact' intelligence which would enable Army patrols to find the Mau Mau gangs. He soon discovered that there was very little actual 'contact' information available and if he wanted any he would have to find it himself. Kitson then sat down and thought hard about the sort of information the troops needed and the sort of information currently available and how to put the two together.

The main source of intelligence was the police, and the police had a great deal of 'background' information on the various Mau Mau gangs. They had information on their strength and membership, on their leaders, on the home villages of at least some of the members, and about their previous employment before they took to the jungle. This information was regarded as useless by the Army, which wanted 'contact' information, the sort which would enable the troops to find the enemy in the jungle or anticipate their attacks. Kitson thought that 'background' information, if put together with the information gathered by the Army on patrol and spiced with common sense, should enable an intelligent officer to make a good, calculated guess about where a gang was operating, where they obtained supplies and where they might strike next.

Kitson also believed that the more one could learn about a terrorist the easier it would be to predict what he would do next. He therefore set out to learn everything he could about the main gang leaders: tribe, family, schooling, character, interests, previous raids and close confidants. Gradually a picture began to emerge and, as more information came in, so it became easier to collect, as one detail led to another. This process, the intelligence–military function, of turning 'background' information into 'contact' information was to be used by Kitson in Malaya and by British troops in many counter-insurgency campaigns since.

To increase their intelligence-gathering capacity, Kitson and his field assistants, mostly young NCOs of the Kenya Regiment, started interrogating captured terrorists. During this phase Kitson developed his techniques and came up with two more innovations. The first was a technique for 'turning' captured terrorists and getting them to inform or actually fight against their former colleagues. For this Kitson evolved a four-part strategy that was to prove highly effective. This began with a two-part 'carrot and stick' approach. In this the captured terrorist would be told the options. If the terrorist co-operated he would be treated well, charges would be dropped, eventual liberty became a strong possibility; that was the first part, the carrot. Otherwise the prison cell or the gallows awaited; that was the second part, the stick.

Another man might have left if there, recruiting the willing and hanging the obdurate, but Kitson realized that the terrorist had to feel good about changing sides and be convinced that this was the right and proper thing to do – otherwise his new loyalty would always be suspect. Instilling that conviction was the third step. The fourth step, which aimed to give the surrendered terrorist increased confidence, was that once accepted into the counter-terrorist fold he was to be treated with complete trust, allowed the freedom to move about, even to carry weapons.

The use of 'contact' intelligence and 'turned' terrorists soon began to take effect and the Army kill rate increased. Then Kitson made his next discovery. To aid concealment and lower the risk of alarming the Mau Mau gangs if they should be seen entering the forest, Kitson and his men took to disguising themselves as Mau Mau fighters. They realized that this could provide further benefits when they stumbled on a large gang which took them for genuine Mau Mau. Since many of Kitson's Kenya Regiment recruits spoke Swahili and Kikuyu fluently they were able to maintain the deception and slip away, their paler skins and greater height somehow passing unnoticed by the Mau Mau fighters. Kitson took this discovery one stage further and set up a force of 'pseudo-gangs', composed of Kenya Regiment volunteers, loyal Africans or turned terrorists, dressed and armed as Mau Mau, and sent these 'gangs' into the forests around the Kikuyu Reserve and Mount Kenya.

F. J. McCartney, who still lives in Kenya, worked with the pseudo-gangs: 'Kenya Regiment NCOs were posted to all the Central Province Districts, where they came under the control of a District Military Intelligence Officer (usually a British Army Officer) called 'Dimo' for short! There was no problem with uniforms as we wore civilian clothes. I was posted to Meru District on the slopes of Mount Kenya. Meru was not as badly affected by Mau Mau as the purely Kikuyu Districts were, and there were many loyalists throughout the Reserve and an active Home Guard centred on small, fortified posts. Because we were Swahili-speaking Ken Reg personnel, we were most useful in gathering information from captured Mau Mau gangsters, the Passive Wing, and surrenderees. This information was fed through the DMIO to Special Branch, and then to the Security Forces.

'On arrival in Meru in the back of a police truck with half a dozen new "two-year-wonder" policemen, I reported to my DMIO, Captain Geoff Dowse, and was told to book myself into the Pig & Whistle Hotel, where I spent my first night or two. I was very impressed by forested countryside, the crystal-clear trout streams, the tortuous roads and of course the interesting foothills leading up to snow-capped Mount Kenya.

'After a day or two Geoff Dowse told me I was to go on a patrol in the forest above Kiberichia. The senior officer on the patrol was Captain Bill Raynor and several Tribal Police and Home Guards accompanied us. The first night we slept in a cave and at first light moved out on to the moorlands. Very thick tufty grass interspersed with small groves of trees made the going fairly slow. At about midday a shot rang out from a nearby grove of trees, and we immediately took cover, and returned the fire. We had stumbled on a quite sizeable gang who let loose at us with whatever they had got in the way of firearms, while at the same time beating a hasty retreat. The Home Guard had a field day blasting away with their single-barrelled shotguns. The Mau Mau gang made good their escape without suffering any casualties, and surprisingly we did not suffer any self-inflicted casualties either.

'A search of the copse revealed a home-made gun factory with more than a dozen primitive home-made guns being recovered as well as a lot of meat, cooking utensils, a pair of field glasses, and most important of all a satchel containing the diary of "Generals" Ruku and Kaggia and the "Haraka No. 65 Battalion". This diary disclosed the names and "bush names" of just about every Mau Mau gangster in the northern part of the District, and was of great assistance subsequently as a "who's who" of the Meru Mau Mau. It also gave some insight into the day-to-day activities of this important gang. Over the next three years I was able to cross off the names of some 90 per cent of those listed as either killed, captured or surrendered.

'Soon after this episode I was posted to a station called Egoji, where the Mau Mau had committed a number of murders including that of a well-known African Agricultural Instructor. My companion there was John Benning. We were under canvas and conditions were fairly primitive. I had not been very long at Egoji when I was asked to go up to a station called Katheri in Upper Abothuguchi to hold the fort while Alan Paine, the DOKG, went on some compassionate leave. Alan had built up a sizeable Home Guard and Combat Unit, and had built for himself in the middle of the Home Guard Post a very pleasant bungalow of off-cuts, with a cement floor and corrugated-iron roof – and a bathroom!

'I spent my time on foot patrols into the forest and the Meru Tribal Reserve. At this time the Meru were living in their scattered homesteads. Later they were to be "villagized" so as to be under closer administration, and a mile-wide strip had been cleared of all cultivation and habitation bordering on the forest. Any suspected terrorist seen in this no-man's land was fair game. Captain Frank Kitson [later to be Lieutenant-General Sir Frank Kitson] had appeared on the scene, and had set up a training establishment at Kamiti in Kiambu District for field intelligence assistants with the purpose of initiating us into the intrigues of "pseudo-ganging".

'This proved to be a very effective weapon against the Mau Mau. The idea was to make up pseudo-gangs comprising ex-Mau Mau gangsters and loyalists with one or two members of the Kenya Regiment to provide firepower. All would be disguised in tatty, smelly clothing, with dreadlock wigs and blackened hands and faces added in the case of the Europeans. Then, given a good contact with a Mau Mau member, a meeting would be established with a Mau Mau gang. These would often take place in the labour lines of a local European farmer, and when as much information as possible had been obtained, and at a given signal, the shooting would start. Many important gangs and their leaders were eliminated in this way. So off I went to Kamiti to Captain Kitson to learn all about "pseudo-ganging" and on my return, fired with great enthusiasm, I arranged my gang.

'Our first attempt nearly ended in disaster. Our first contact, whose house we visited in the middle of the night, was obviously not Mau Mau inclined, from the shouts and ululations that emanated from within. Immediately the cry was picked up by the whole area, and Home Guards appeared on the scene. As we were togged out like Mau Mau terrorists, the only thing to do was beat a hasty retreat to the nearest stream to wash and make oneself look like a European again. Shotgun pellets were soon whizzing around, and we had quite a job establishing our identity. Luckily no one was hurt, and the Home Guard thought it quite a joke.

'We were not very successful with these tactics in Meru because we had a large percentage of loyalist Africans in the district. It became very risky operating where loyalists knew they had recourse to their own Home Guard if they had a visitation from a Mau Mau gang. "Pseudo-ganging" was far more successful in areas where the population was almost 100 per cent Mau Mau. We knew that Kikuyu-led gangs visited Meru, and we imagined that they trudged wearily over the high shoulders of Mount Kenya.

'Not a bit of it! I soon discovered that the gangs travelled along a string of labour lines, from one European farm to the next, obtaining food, milk, shelter and information as they progressed around the mountain through Nanyuki and Timau to Meru. Having received a tip-off I stationed myself with a handful of British troops at Lewa Downs fairly near the border with Meru. I was holding a Mau Mau suspect from whom we had extracted information that a Kikuyu-led gang was in the area and was in the habit of obtaining milk at a dairy on a nearby farm early every morning. This involved our very early departure in the morning from Lewa, and then a drive without any lights in the dark for a couple of miles. On one occasion I thought I had gone off the road as a telegraph post loomed up and I braked to avoid a large giraffe standing in the road!

'After three days of ambush without results, my "squaddies" were getting a bit bored and one morning as we trudged along I overheard them telling their NCO to approach me with a view to shooting the informer! I must say I was beginning to feel the same way. However, on the fourth morning, as we emerged from the bush near the dairy, there to everyone's complete surprise there was the gang drinking milk. I think they were less surprised than we were for our hurried pot-shots at their retreating rear ends only brought one gangster to the ground with a bullet through the ankle. He seemed fairly unconcerned about his plight and gave us a lot of useful information which led to the elimination of that gang when they got into the Imenti Forest some time later on. We picked up the usual paraphernalia with which these gangs travelled light – binoculars, rucksacks, diaries, dried meat, matches, cigarettes, tobacco (snuff), knives, simis (machetes) and discarded clothes and blankets, all very smelly!'

Kitson's pseudo-gangs proved highly effective. If the real gang was small enough to attack, the pseudo-gang was able to approach and spring a surprise ambush. If the real gang was too large, the 'pseudos' could break contact and slip away after gathering more useful intelligence. Before long, the pseudo-gangs were so confident of their ability to carry out these deceptions that Kitson himself was dressing up and going out on operations, even attending Mau Mau oathing ceremonies. In doing so he took considerable risks for had he been detected and captured his fate would have been grisly indeed. The pseudo-gang concept had the further advantage that after a few months the Mau Mau 'generals' in the forests became aware that something was going on and grew highly suspicious of other Mau Mau gangs. This helped to fragment the terrorist movement and led to a decline in attacks on settler farms, loyalist villages and cattle herds.

The Mau Mau campaign lasted until 1956, and effectively ended when the last Mau Mau general, Dedan Kamathi, was hunted down and shot. Jomo Kenyatta returned from exile and took up the democratic road to independence, which proved rather more effective than a terrorist campaign. Kenya became independent in December 1963 and Kenyatta was the first President.

Out of these colonial campaigns came a number of useful lessons for SOF deployment. Troops campaigning in the jungle have to be very fit, skilled with their weapons and good shots, for any target will be a fleeting one. They must be able to survive and fight in an inhospitable climate. Above all, they must be able to stay out in the jungle; short patrols which stayed close to the base camps rarely produced any results, but the longer the troops stayed in the field, the more effective and jungle-wise they became. Becoming 'jungle-wise' does not happen overnight. It takes time and constant practice and, since the Malayan Emergency and the Borneo Confrontation, SOF troops, from the SAS, the Parachute Regiment and the Royal Marines Commandos have returned regularly to the jungle to keep their hard-won skills alive.

These campaigns, in the jungles of Malaya or Borneo and in the forests of Kenya, ended with the granting of independence to successful, well-established states. Other places posed other problems, but few were as intractable as the problems of Cyprus.

Foreign Legion Para badge

CHAPTER SEVEN

Commando Attacks and Low-Intensity Operations 1955–1960

> Low-intensity operations cannot be won or contained by military power alone. They require the application of all elements of national power across the entire range of conditions which are the source of the conflict.
>
> *US Army Training and Doctrine Command,*
> *Special Forces*

The campaign against Mau Mau in Kenya was still going on in 1955 when a further revolt against British rule broke out on the Mediterranean island of Cyprus. As in Malaya and Kenya, Britain had few objections to granting independence to Cyprus, as long as some bases could be provided on the island to protect British interests in the Eastern Mediterranean, but there was one fact that made the granting of independence extremely difficult. This was the desire of the majority Greek community for *enosis*, or union with Greece, a desire that the minority Turkish community were solidly against.

Cyprus is a small, mountainous island lying fifty miles south of the Turkish mainland. The population in the mid-1950s was 70 per cent Greek and 30 per cent Turkish, and there lay the root of the problem.

The aim of the Greek majority was not merely independence; that was only the first step. Having got rid of the British the Greeks Cypriots then wanted *enosis*, and this proposal was anathema to both the Turkish Cypriots and the Turkish government, which had no intention of allowing the Greeks to obtain possession of a useful base just off Turkey's southern coast. The British, not for the first or last time in their post-colonial career, were caught in the middle of an intractable problem.

The situation was politically delicate and Cyprus became the first of what came to be called low-intensity operations, where the necessary military action needed the lightest possible touch. US military doctrine considers all guerrilla wars and other limited conflicts fought with irregular units as 'low-intensity' conflicts, though the results locally, as in El Salvador, can be devastating. These low-intensity operations, which require the ability to apply the necessary force without inhibiting the search for a long-term solution, have become a major part of Britain's military capability, as well as an SF speciality, but, as in Malaya or Kenya, the secret of military success in such circumstances lies in the ability to contain the violence until a political solution is obtained. In Cyprus a political solution was never on the table, as the two communities had no real intention of reaching a compromise.

Diplomatic moves towards a compromise having failed, the Greek Cypriots, under their leader Archbishop Makarios, opted to drive the British out by mounting a terrorist campaign conducted by a group called EOKA, led and trained by that Colonel George Grivas, who had been so active against the ELAS guerrillas during the Greek Civil War. The EOKA campaign began on 1 April 1955, when several bombs went off in Nicosia, the island capital. These caused little damage and no loss of life, but worse was to follow. A few weeks later another bomb killed a Greek bystander and injured a dozen Turks, which added inter-communal problems to the simmering brew.

Grivas had around 100 well-armed men organized in several gangs and throughout the summer of 1955 these gangs carried out a series of attacks on police stations and Army lorries. Public order was breaking down and Greek Cypriot students took to the streets, demanding *enosis* and attacking British government offices. The object of this activity was to provoke the British into some reaction that could be used against them at the UN, where the anti-colonial caucus of Third World powers and the USA was in full cry. Eventually the British were forced to respond, and more troops were sent to the island, among them 45 and 40 Commando, two units of the 3rd Commando Brigade, Royal Marines, which arrived in September from Malta. Among them was Marine Colin 'Sid' Ward of Z Troop, 45 Commando: 'We usually operated in sections, based in tented camps or police stations, patrolling out from there by day and night. At first we were in the Kyrenia Mountains, north of Nicosia, but later in the year, with winter coming on, we moved to the Troodos Mountains, 6,000 feet high and snow-covered in winter, where it got pretty cold. Our patrol section from Z Troop consisted of Marines Johnny Gerard, Joe Snow, Jock Steen, John Mac-Partlin, Pete Degnan and myself. There was a Jock Corporal who was very unfit, also a young officer, both names escape me.

'Our first location was at Paralimni, where the local police station had been raided by an armed gang. Our job was to patrol the area, as it was considered sympathetic to EOKA. We were called out one night as the local lighthouse keeper had reported being threatened by an armed gang. We had spent two hours walking to the nearest police station. Our section, together with the Troop Commander, Captain Michell, who was always to the fore, went to investigate. It was a horrendous drive across country by Land Rover, the vehicles kept catching their axles on rocks with us in the back hanging on for grim life. We finally arrived at the lighthouse. Obviously there was no sign of the gunmen – in fact Mitch thought it was a put-up job by the keeper as he was feeling lonely and was looking for some company.

'We were in daily radio contact with the Inniskilling Fusiliers in Famagusta. One night they called and said that Archbishop Makarios was on a tour of the area and could we set up as many roadblocks as possible. We stopped him at one of ours and he reminded me of the pictures of Rasputin; he had real evil eyes, in fact he looked an evil bastard altogether. He was probably in a foul temper by the time he had finished with all the roadblocks.

'From Paralimni we moved on location to Myrtou. Here we patrolled the Kyrenian range and manned Lapitos police station a section at a time. Two incidents stand out in my mind from our time there. The first was when half the section decided we would go to the local film show. We put on camouflaged smocks and carried Stens without butts and a couple of 9mm pistols. The film was *Pagan Love Song* and starred Howard Keel and Esther Williams. The first two reels were fine but when it came to the third reel we were in fits of laughter. It seems the projectionist had put the film in back-to-front and upside down. The locals just sat there wondering what the crazy Royals were laughing about.

'The second incident happened at the police station. We had all got our heads down but we had all by this time become very light sleepers. Anyway we were all pushing out the Zs when a shot rang out; we all leaped out of our pits, grabbed our weapons, slammed open the shutters, ready for action. I looked around; there were four very naked Marines wearing nothing but green berets and bandoliers and holding their weapons. I said weapons. Anyway, Johnny Gerard decided to take a look to see what was going on, so covered by the rest of us he disappeared into the night. As it turned out it was a false alarm, someone had let a round off in error. One of the Turkish Auxiliaries was sitting in that same place fiddling with his Greener shotgun, as was their wont, when it went off. Unfortunately for him, the station sergeant's motorcycle was parked at the end of the building with its front wheel protruding beyond the wall and our friend succeeded in blowing his front tyre off. His pay was stopped until he had paid for the tyre.

'We were involved in many riots and skirmishes in Lapitos. I remember when the Jocks withdrew from a set-to with the locals in Morphou as the Cypriots had put women and girls in the front ranks and then pelted the Jocks with bricks. They tried it with us in Lapitos a week later and got a nasty surprise: Royal was not adverse to a little hand-to-hand combat with the local females, who soon broke and ran. At the end of this little skirmish we were minus Marine Degnan. Where did we find him! Chatting up some Cypriot bird, trying to convince her that he was part-Greek; you know he had that Latin look about him. Another time we moved into Lapitos before sun-up; it was some National Day or something like that. So as not to let the locals know we were about, we took the precaution of cutting through the church bell ropes leaving just a few strands. We were in position by sun-up and one of the locals spotted us and decided to ring the bell, which they did by running up the wall of the bell tower and yanking the bell rope. You can imagine his surprise when he landed face down in the dust accompanied by roars of laughter from Royal.

'One of our last operations at Myrtou was a search and cordon. We did a two-hour lorry drive, then a few hours in LCAs [landing craft – assault] which landed on a beach. We were to proceed inland searching wells and buildings until we arrived at the village that had been cordoned off by an Army battalion. When we arrived at the cordon the pongoes [soldiers] were sitting around on chairs drinking tea. It turned out that the pongoes had let a young boy through the cordon and he had warned an EOKA gang not to come into the village as they planned. This came to light when a diary was found in some EOKA caves during a search.

'From Myrtou we moved to Platres in the Troodos Mountains. Here our time was taken up with patrols and searches. Two incidents stand out in my mind. One of our operational chores was to patrol the Kasusor pipeline. This pipeline supplied water to Episkopi and the other main bases near Limassol. It came out of the ground about a dozen or so times on its way down from the main water source. To patrol we had to wade through a stream that followed the pipeline. Not a very comfortable way to spend a night, soaking wet at 6,000 feet. To get to the pipeline we had to break one of the cardinal rules of patrolling in that we travelled out and back on the same route, since there was only one road from Platres down to Limassol.

'We knew we were going to get it sooner or later even though we varied our times. As the weather was cold we always travelled with the canvas top on the three tonner, and apart from the Bren-gunner we all got our heads down below the canvas sheltered by the metal sides of the lorry. Sure enough, one night we were fired upon; there were no casualties or damage, but after that we always travelled without the canvas top.

'The other incident took place on the Agros Road, which was hard-packed earth. One day a small patrol of REs [Royal Engineers] consisting of a Land Rover and Dingo scout car were going along the road; as they rounded a corner the driver of the Land Rover spotted some men on the bank overlooking the road. As he pointed them out to his passengers he was shot in the head. The Land Rover went out of control and rolled over the bank on the other side of the road. This information was gleaned from the crew of the Dingo, who turned up at a police station manned by E Troop, 45, and from the survivors picked up by E Troop later. A Major Coombes was involved in this; either he was in the patrol and later shot dead an EOKA gunman in an ambush or the REs were his men and he was credited with avenging the death of the driver.

'E Troop set an ambush on the crashed Land Rover that night and ended up shooting a suspected EOKA terrorist, although the locals said he was just looking for vehicle spare parts. Anyway the following day a patrol from Z Troop set out to link up with E Troop to search the area. We set off in two Humber Combats, met up with E Troop and returned to the ambush site. Three of us, myself included, were sent a couple of hundred yards up the road to set up a roadblock.

'We were getting in position when MacPartlin found a wire leading up to the bank at the side of the road. I was standing in the middle of the road at the time. On following the wire we found it was attached to a detonator complete with T handle. He followed and it was buried in the dirt road and where I was standing we dug down and found a bag of explosive powder and some sticks of dynamite. I went back to the trucks to let the rest know what we had found and they had found another similar mine. The two mines had been planted at each end of an area of road shaped like an elongated U. If they had gone off as planned anything between would have been cut off between the fields of fire from the slit trenches dug into the higher bank.

'It seems the ambushers had been surprised in the middle of setting up the ambush and had connected the wires on the detonator to the wrong terminals or had not had time to fire them. The thing was that we had driven over these two mines on our way to pick up E Troop and on the way back had parked one of the lorries over one. When we swept the area we caught an old local who was the equivalent of a Special Constable; he had a big metal and brass arm-band with his number on it. He was lucky he was not shot as the mist had come down and he was slow in answering the challenge to halt.

'The morning of Jock Macgee's ambush I was on the road with the 45 VIP Escort. We were taking the new C-in-C Cyprus on a familiarity trip round the Troodos and Platres area; we took him up to the top of Olympus. I can't remember his name but he was wearing the dark-green beret of the light infantry with, I think, a silver bugle badge. It was while on this trip we called into Troodos and I saw Jock Macgee. He said he was escorting a lorry load of explosives and we both said, "What a target for an ambush – no wonder we got the job of escorting it." We were on the Agros Road when the call came through and we immediately turned round and made our way back to the site of the ambush, but by the time we arrived it was all over.'

The campaign in Cyprus bridges the gap between rural terrorism, as practised in Malaya and Kenya, and the urban terrorism that was to plague Europe in the 1960s and 1970s. The terrorists struck mostly at civilians and even managed to place a bomb under the bed of the British Governor, Field Marshal Sir John Harding. Fortunately for Sir John, the bomber was not acquainted with the British passion for fresh air. Harding slept with the windows open and the temperature remained too low for the bomb to explode. Apart from bombing cinemas, post offices and public buildings the Cyprus campaign was fought out in the mountains, but there were plenty of student riots and shootings in the streets of the towns and villages between EOKA activists and British infantry patrols, and the number of troops in Cyprus far exceeded the number of terrorists. At one time Britain deployed eighteen battalions in Cyprus, to contain the activities of less than 200 EOKA terrorists.

The SOF units in Cyprus during this campaign included all three Royal Marine Commandos, Nos 40, 42 and 45, and units of the 16th Independent Parachute Brigade. These SOF troops were usually deployed in the Kyrenia and Troodos Mountains or in towns like Paphos and cities like Famagusta, though the plains and the cities were usually left to the conventional infantry battalions. Commando units were at a certain disadvantage here for the three Marine Commandos were still organized on the Second World War pattern and quite small, at about 600 men, mustering 40 per cent less than an Army infantry battalion. However, every man was a fighting man and the Commandos were well trained and skilled in small-scale patrolling, which lay at the heart of the Cyprus campaign. They were therefore able to dominate areas that had previously taken a full, 1,000-strong infantry battalion, and maintain control in their areas with a small number of men.

'Our village in the Kyrenia Mountains had been held by a company of the Middlesex Regiment before we arrived,' says an NCO of 45 Commando, 'and the local lads had given them a hard time, stoning lorries, rioting and generally acting up. There were only eight of us, under a sergeant, so we had a chat with the mayor and told him to spread the word that if anyone got it on with us we would blow his head off. We never had to do that, I'm happy to say, but we waded straight in when trouble started and if any local went looking for trouble he did not have to look far. The result was that after about a week we all got on very well. The lads were nice to the young kids, the mothers liked that, and the fathers and sons had to do what they were told. Is that what they mean by "hearts and minds"? Nobody told us. I've been back there since on holiday and all the locals – only Turks now, of course – made me very welcome.'

Bob Strickland was in Cyprus with the Parachute Gunners: 'I was born in 1937 and because National Service was compulsory for those who were eighteen years old I became eligible for service in 1955. I thought of a career in the regular Army, not least because the money was better. In those days the pay for National Servicemen was £1 8s od [£1.35] a week, but regulars' pay was £3 3s od [£3.15]. I did not want to go to Cyprus and was told that one way of getting out of it was to volunteer for the Royal Artillery Para Regiment. I volunteered, was accepted and like all Para volunteers went on the very hard selection course at Maida Barracks, Aldershot, and received my badge and wings on 3 May 1956 – the proudest day of my life.

'I joined the 33rd Parachute Field Regiment, Royal Artillery, at Lille Barracks in Aldershot, where we were equipped with 25-pounders. The 16th Independent Parachute Brigade was shipped out to – guess where? – Cyprus, in August 1956 in two aircraft-carriers, HMS *Theseus* and HMS *Bulwark*. I was on *Theseus* and the sea was so rough in the Mediterranean that we lost one man overboard but, miraculously, the carrier turned, stopped and picked the man up and we were back to full speed within the hour.

'We all knew from day one that our final objective was the Suez Canal, but the situation in Cyprus was very touchy and we had to be on our guard at all times. When travelling along roads in vehicles you avoided going over any rubbish, because it could contain a bomb. The other things that you avoided were people wearing clothes with large sleeves, and especially people who smoked. More often than not, these people would wait until a military vehicle was approaching before lighting up, and concealed in their sleeve was a bomb, and they were in fact lighting up a fuse. Then, with a flick of the wrist, you would have a bomb in the boot of your truck. It happened.'

These parachute artillery soldiers, like those in the conventional infantry battalions, were all employed on IS tasks throughout the years of the Cyprus struggle, before and after the 1956 Suez operation. Some less conventional units were created by the brighter spirits in 45 Commando and one of these was 45 Commando's Ski Patrol, created after a hutful of skis was discovered in the Commando base at Platres, a camp set 6,000 feet high in the Troodos Mountains, used before the troubles as a Combined Services sports resort.

One task of 45 Commando in the winter of 1955–6 was to store the dynamite needed for the asbestos mines at Amiandos and release only enough for that day's ration of explosions, to prevent the balance being used for bombs. Getting the explosives down the icy snowbound roads to Amiandos was a problem, and the Marines therefore created a ski patrol; the only snag was that none of the Marines could ski. 'Little considerations like that don't bother the Bootnecks,' says one veteran of the Ski Patrol. 'We called for volunteers and a smart young officer from the Blues, an exquisite young man who actually could ski, was called in to give us lessons. These were carried out on the steep-sloping, icy car park, and after about an hour, when three blokes had run under lorries or vanished screaming into the truck inspection pit, we decided to declare ourselves operational and just get on with it. The assault engineer officers used to work out if the amount of explosives called for was about right and we would put it in Bergen rucksacks and take it down. The style used was called the "Racing Snowplough" and we used to stop by falling over or running into trees. There was no great rush to carry the detonators, so we used to spin a coin to see who got the job. Skiing down a mountain with a load of fulminate of mercury detonators on your back, wondering if a sniper has a bead on the rucksack, is one way of growing grey quickly.'

Bryan Ricketts was an engineer NCO in Cyprus in 1958–9 and describes what the troops were up against during this time: 'As ever in a war of this type, the attackers held most of the cards: local knowledge, a friendly population and the "cause". The average soldier had none of these assets and had to rely on the odd scraps of intelligence which might come from informers, the questioning of prisoners and sheer guesswork. It was a classic no-win situation. Army troop movements were traced by the local population and the details passed to the terrorist organization almost minute by minute. They could always remain one jump ahead of the Army, although there were occasional successes.

'We learned stealthy methods of surrounding a village and closing the ring before anyone could break out. A convoy carrying a detachment of troops would drive quite openly towards the village to be searched, but instead of stopping to unload they simply slowed down and allowed them to quietly drop over the tailboard. In this way it would appear that the column of vehicles was simply passing through. The convoy continued through the village and repeated the drill on the far side. Then the net would be tightened and any arms caches or terrorists within the ring of soldiers stood a good chance of being unearthed. On some of these occasions, if fighting broke out, the EOKA men battled very bravely and often fought to the death.'

The Cyprus campaign lasted from April 1955 until August 1960, when the island became a republic within the Commonwealth, with Archbishop Makarios as the first President. The island had the independence it could have had five years earlier, without all the deaths and violence, but *enosis*, their ultimate prize, still eludes the Greek Cypriots, four decades later.

Not all campaigns were long drawn out or capable of resolution by low-intensity operations. Now and again the heat was turned up, and the campaign in Cyprus was interrupted in the autumn of 1956 when the Parachute battalions and the Royal Marine Commandos were involved in a major operation of war, Operation Musketeer, the Port Said landings or Suez Operation, a campaign in which the Royal Marines Commandos made the first helicopter assault in history.

The British had been experimenting with helicopters for some years but had failed to solve the problems of using them in battle mainly because early military helicopters were unarmoured, unarmed and had a very limited carrying capacity, especially in humid climates or in the mountains. The two 'types' employed in the Port Said assault by 45 Commando were the Whirlwind, which could carry about six fully armed Marines, and the Sycamore, which could carry around four, the number depending on the weight of equipment, the weather and the altitude of the take-off zone.

The helicopters used at Port Said came from JEHU, the Joint Experimental Helicopter Unit, which had been formed at Middle Wallop in Wiltshire, now the home of the Army Air Corps. JEHU had been set up in 1955 to examine the uses of the helicopter in the operational role and this was their first chance to try out the helicopter in action. The JEHU pilots, though accustomed to land-based operations, had had only a few days of flying off HMS *Theseus*, cruising in the Solent, before being ordered to pick up the Royal Marine Commandos in Malta for the Suez landings of November 1956. The use of helicopters for a Commando assault had never been tested until 45 flew ashore at Port Said, and most of the Marines had never been in a helicopter before they left the carrier flight-deck off Port Said on the morning of 6 November 1956.

The background to this operation can be sketched in briefly. In 1954 the British came to an agreement with the Egyptian government by which the British withdrew from the Zone protecting the Suez Canal, on the understanding that the Canal would remain an Anglo-French possession at least until the lease expired in 1958, and that the British could return to their bases in the Canal Zone if those bases were needed to protect the Canal or if British interests in the Middle East were threatened. A few weeks after the British left, Colonel Nasser, the Egyptian President, nationalized the Suez Canal and tore up this agreement.

There followed several months of negotiation and prevarication while the UN and the US sought some solution short of war. Meanwhile the French had come to a secret agreement with the Israelis, by which Israel, which was already anticipating an Egyptian attack, would launch a pre-emptive strike across Sinai towards the Canal. The French, claiming that this attack put the Canal in jeopardy, would then intervene – effectively on the side of the Israelis, but ostensibly as a neutral –

and evict the Egyptians from the Canal Zone. Britain, though not initially consulted, eventually became involved in this plan and gave it full support.

As a result, on 1 November 1956, a considerable armada of British and French warships and transports sailed for Port Said at the northern end of the Suez Canal and on the 5th the landings began with an assault by the 3rd Battalion, the Parachute Regiment, on Gamil Airfield, a mile or so west of Port Said. As the British landed west of the Canal, so several battalions of French paratroopers from their 10th Parachute Division landed at Port Fuad on the east bank. The task of these parachute battalions was to hold the flanks of the invasion area until the amphibious force arrived and put the Marines ashore on the following day.

Operation Musketeer was a military success but a political disaster of the highest magnitude. The French and British paratroopers held their ground without undue difficulty until the 3rd Commando Brigade came ashore at Port Said and then advanced into the town, which fell by 1700 hours after some heavy street fighting involving the use of tanks and aircraft. That night, following threats from Moscow and Washington, the British and French called a ceasefire, even though their leading troops, the 2nd Battalion, the Parachute Regiment, had reached El Cap, more than twenty miles down the Canal.

Bob Strickland went to Suez with the Parachute Gunners: 'During our time in Cyprus, small detachments from the 33rd Para Field Regiment, Royal Artillery, were sent to Malta to train with the Royal Navy. These detachments were our OP [Observation Post] officers and their signallers etc. These OP officers are used by the RA [Royal Artillery] units in forward areas to locate and direct gunfire on to enemy targets. The idea was to send these groups in first, by parachute, to direct the naval gunfire support while the infantry were waiting for the 33rd Para Field guns to arrive by sea.

'Besides the British paratroopers on Cyprus, there were also many French paras made up of French Colonial Forces and French Foreign Legion parachute regiments. Just before 5 November 1956, a local press release announced that the 16th Independent Parachute Brigade, together with French paratroopers, was going to do a twenty-four-hour exercise. 3 Para were loaded into aircraft and the rest of us, 2 Para, with all the heavy equipment were loaded on to LSTs, as were the 33rd Para Field Regiment guns, together with their gun crews. It was not an exercise but the real thing; none of us returned to Cyprus; 3 Para went to parachute on El Gamil airfield in the early hours of 5 November and next day 2 Para and the Gunners were landed by landing craft at Port Said just behind the Marine Commandos.

'This was a very short battle, with the fighting over within a couple of days. This was because everyone but the French and British seemed to be against this operation, especially the USA. The furthest the 33rd Para Field Regiment penetrated along the Suez Canal was El Cap. We stayed here until we were withdrawn a few weeks later. We captured lots of Russian weapons, many still covered in the packing wax. A lot of these weapons were taken out to sea and dumped and I will always remember the Russian rifle with its flexible, hinged bayonet, thinking to myself that I would not like to be stabbed by one of those.'

The Suez operation did reveal two facts of lasting significance, one political, one military. Firstly, it signalled the end of British imperial aspirations; if Britain went to war again, it would be with the economic and political permission of the United States or as part of a US-commanded UN force. The second significant development was that the helicopter had been proved, in action, as a viable military machine, capable of carrying troops ashore and supporting them throughout the attack. The helicopters used at Suez were small, underpowered machines compared to those that would be used in Vietnam twelve years later, but a beginning had been made and helicopters were to play an increasing part in military operations from then on. They became especially popular with Special Forces.

JEHU had just six Whirlwinds and six Sycamores on HMS *Ocean* and ten Whirlwinds on board HMS *Theseus*, the two British fleet carriers of the Suez Task Force. These twenty-two aircraft had to carry ashore 429 men of 45 Commando plus all their ammunition, heavy weapons and stores. The first wave was sent in at 0610 hours and duly set off, the pilots with only a faint idea of where they were to land. The eventual LZ (landing zone) was by the statue of Ferdinand de Lesseps at the head of the Canal and all the men were ashore and in action in exactly one hour and twenty-five minutes, taking with them twenty-five tons of equipment, ammunition and stores. The helicopters also carried the wounded back to the ship and lost only two aircraft, both to engine failure, though more than one helicopter returned to *Ocean* or *Theseus* well dotted with bullet holes. The vast helicopter forces deployed by the United States in Vietnam twelve years later can trace their military history to this successful, small-scale British operation in 1956.

Another, long-established SF tradition was also maintained here – leading from the front. Sergeant Eric Blythe of 42 Commando recalls one rare meeting during the Suez assault: 'I was mortar troop sergeant in S Troop, 42, and my young brother Bert was in one of the fighting troops, P, I think it was, so I was anxious to get ashore, get the mortars bedded in and give them some support. Anyway, we did that, and I was up on a rooftop, trying to see where the bombs would fall, when I got a tug on the shoulder and a voice said, "Make way." I turned round and it was the Commandant General of the Corps, Lieutenant-General Campbell Hardy, armed with a rifle. He was a bloody good shot and started sniping at the enemy in the Navy House down the road. A bit after that I saw 45 Commando coming ashore in helicopters, bloody marvellous, and then, just when we had it in our hands, they called the whole thing off.'

Suez is usually regarded as the point at which the British Empire went into its final and terminal decline. The French had reached that point two and a half years previously in March 1954, when the pick of their armies, the Foreign Legion and the Colonial Paratroop Regiments, were defeated by the Communist Vietminh at the battle of Dien Bien Phu. This was no low-intensity operation either, but an all-out battle culminating in one of the great last stands in military history, largely conducted by one of the great SOF units, the parachute battalions of the French Foreign Legion.

The French Foreign Legion had started to form parachute units in 1948, when two parachute battalions were raised for service in Indo-China. This was something of a departure for the Foreign Legion, a force best known for its ability in dogged but controversial infantry fighting. The first Legion Parachute Company was raised in Hanoi in April 1948 and three battalions were formed near Sidi Bel Abbes, the Legion base in Algeria. These eventually became the 1st, 2nd and 3rd REP (Régiment Etranger de Parachutiste), the 1st and 2nd being combat battalions destined for Indo-China, the 3rd staying in Algeria to train and supply recruits.

The two combat battalions fought in all the major battles of the French Indo-China War and the 1st REP supplied one of the battalions which took the Dien Bien Phu position in Vietnam and fortified it in November 1953. The siege of Dien Bien Phu by General Giap and his 50,000-strong Vietminh Army from North Vietnam began on 13 March 1954 and lasted three months. One of the main French positions was overrun on the first day and by the end of March the Vietminh had overrun many of the defenders' positions and controlled the vital airstrip. The only way in was by parachute and on 9 April the 2nd Battalion of the Legion was dropped in to aid its comrades.

Other reinforcements followed, all parachuted in, mostly by night, but never enough to turn the scales. Most of the Legionaries who were parachuted into Dien Bien Phu were not paratroopers, and had never jumped before. In their first engagement, to recapture the strongpoint of 'Hugette 1', the 2nd REP lost 150 men out of the 380 committed. The remnants of the 1st and 2nd REP were grouped together into one slim *battalion de marche* on 25 April and were finally overwhelmed when the last outpost, Isabelle, fell to a human-wave assault by the Vietminh on 7 May.

The 1st REP lost 575 men out of the 635 who jumped into the valley of Dien Bien Phu in November 1953, and only fifty men of the 2nd REP returned from captivity in Vietnam. But both these battalions were reformed for the war in Algeria.

These colonial wars which marked out the end of the British and French Empires coincided with the rebirth of Special Force soldiering in the United States. Gradually, from the early 1960s, other countries recognized that the shape of military conflict was changing. Wars were becoming split into the short, violent kind, typified by the Six-Day War or the Yom Kippur War, between Israel and the Arabs, or conventional wars between evenly matched opponents, like Iraq and Iran, or long-drawn-out, low-intensity, anti-terrorist conflicts, of the type described in the last two chapters.

World war was not on the cards, mainly because of the fear that any major war could escalate towards a nuclear exchange, so the war between the great powers was fought at second hand, by surrogates. The empires established in the nineteenth century faded away, but post-colonial wars continued in Algeria, Angola and Mozambique, in Rhodesia (Zimbabwe), in the Persian Gulf and in Central America, where the United States backed one side and the Communists supported the other. These were places where SF soldiers were to make their mark in various ways, but nowhere were Special Forces employed so widely or for so long as by the United States in the twelve-year struggle for victory in South Vietnam.

82nd Airborne badge

CHAPTER EIGHT

Revolts and Renaissance 1960–1970

> Military action is called the ground of life or death.
> Therefore, measure the ground in terms of five
> things, and make comparisons; these five things
> are the way, the weather, the terrain, the lead-
> ership and the discipline.
>
> *Sun Tzu,* The Art of War, *1st Century* AD

Viewed with the benefits of hindsight, the 1960s were a very troubled decade and not just for the embattled colonial powers. The decade began with great optimism, certainly in the United States and Western Europe, but many parts of the world in the 1960s saw war and uncertainty, oppression, revolution and civil unrest. These were the years when the most bitter fighting of the Vietnam War took place, a conflict that was to cause dissension far outside the boundaries of the United States and South-East Asia.

The 1960s were transitional years, a decade marking the end of the old colonial empires, which had largely vanished by 1965, but establishing the equally worldwide Cold War between the Western powers and the Communist bloc, especially the United States and Soviet Russia. This Cold War frequently became unpleasantly hot for those serving on the countless minor battlefields where these two opposing ideologies came into direct conflict. The Cold War and the differences which underpinned it often fed 'urban terrorism' – another feature of the 1960s. This was the decade when a number of 'urban guerrillas' took their first steps in student politics or street violence, supporting grievances that they had not personally endured, striking against any form of authority in the name of some wider justice. There was also a failure to find a solution in the continuing Arab–Israeli conflict, and those who supported one side or another in this dispute were soon taking up arms or turning to terrorism.

More bloody events took place in Central Africa, where the event which opened the decade was the Belgian Congo crisis of 1960. This began on the day after the Congo obtained its independence from Belgium, when the Congolese militia, the Force Publique, mutinied and went on the rampage against the white population. There were massacres and mass rapes in many Congolese towns and terrible incidents, including a reversion to cannibalism, as the local Africans took revenge on their former colonial rulers, who had made no attempt to prepare the Congolese for the responsibilities of independence.

After some days of riot and murder, the Belgians flew their Para-Commando Regiment to Léopoldville, and the Belgians reoccupied their former colony until the situation could be brought under some sort of control. The Belgian Para-Commando Regiment, raised from the Belgian Troop of 10 (Inter-Allied) Commando and the Belgian troops of the SAS – and still bearing the SAS winged-dagger badge and 'Who Dares, Wins' motto – was a skilled, highly trained force of regular soldiers, and they swiftly brought peace to Léopoldville, though not to the surrounding countryside. Eventually, after a horrific death toll, the UN intervened and sent in troops, though one Irish battalion, part of the UN force, was also set upon by the Force Publique and took heavy casualties.

The war in the Congo was to rumble on for many years and attracted a large number of mercenary soldiers, black and white, who were formed into 'Commando units' under leaders like Colonel Mike Hoare, and played a decisive part in the subsequent fighting there, especially in the breakaway province of Katanga in 1962–3. The action of the Belgian Para-Commando Regiment at Léopoldville was a classic Special Forces operation in which decisive action allied to SF skills overcame a difficult situation and saved many innocent lives. Belgian and French SF and SOF forces were to intervene in Africa again and again in the coming decades, but never in such difficult circumstances.

As for the mercenary units that appeared in the Congo, their history can be swiftly told for they did not contain many Special Force soldiers and, though they often called their units 'Commandos', this owes more to the number of South Africans in their ranks than to the use of Commando tactics in their training and operations. Mercenaries were hired to fight in the Congo because the local military were incapable of controlling the violence following independence or had mutinied and were themselves a major source of civil insurrection. The mercenaries' paymaster was Moise Tshombe, pro-Western leader of the breakaway province of Katanga – now Shaba province in Zaire – a deadly enemy of the newly independent state's first President, Patrice Lumumba.

At first the mercenaries did well for a force that was never more than 500 strong, driving off the Force Publique, saving many white lives and putting Tshombe in a strong position in his claim for an independent Katanga. More mercenaries were recruited in Belgium, South Africa and Rhodesia (now Zimbabwe), and under leaders like Colonel Trinquier, a former officer in a French colonial parachute regiment, Jean Schramme, a Belgian mercenary, and Bob Denard, a former French Marine, they put down a revolt by the Baluba tribe, and killed Patrice Lumumba in Katanga in 1961. None of this made the mercenaries popular with the African leaders – who referred to Tshombe's recruits as 'white vermin' – or with the United Nations. Eventually UN troops were sent in and Katangese secession was ended in 1963.

A year later came another outbreak of trouble in the Congo and more work for mercenaries. This was the Simba revolt of 1964, a brutal affair involving gangs of well-armed young thugs, the Simbas, led by a local fanatic Pierre Mulele. The Simbas took over towns and districts and started massacring the whites and anyone else who stood in their way. To stamp them out, Moise Tshombe, now leader of the entire Congo, called on a South African, Mike Hoare, who raised a force of some 250 mercenaries, called it Five Commando and led it out against the Simbas. Five Commando drove the Simbas back with a massive use of firepower and speedily retook town after town. The Simba revolt was eventually crushed with the aid of yet another parachute drop on Stanleyville by the Belgian Para-Commando Regiment in November 1964, the parachutists landing just in time to prevent another massacre of the local whites by a mob of Simbas.

Hiring mercenaries was easier than getting rid of them. They continued to operate in the Congo, supporting various sides in the ongoing civil wars until the end of the decade when the new ruler, President Mobutu, a man who seized and retained power in that benighted country, finally drove them back to the town of Bukavu. There, surrounded by Congolese troops, the remnants of the mercenary units held out until they were evacuated from the new republic of Zaire by the UN in 1969.

Africa had not seen the last of mercenary forces. Mercenaries fought in the Biafran War in Nigeria, in Angola and in Rhodesia and took part in coups mounted against the elected governments in the Seychelles and the Comores. But none of these were true Special Force operations, and they are worth mentioning here only to refute the notion that inside every Special Force soldier is a mercenary waiting to be hired. In spite of many extravagant claims, very few mercenaries were actually former members of the SAS or the Parachute Regiment or any other SF or SOF unit. Those few who had served in such units had often been dismissed or discharged for bad conduct, and those mercenary units that served in Africa, even Five Commando, a unit which certainly did contain good soldiers, form no part of Special Force history.

The major event in Special Force history in the 1960s is the re-emergence of the United States Special Forces, a rebirth fostered by President John F. Kennedy, who came to office in 1960 convinced that one great task of his administration was to combat the growing threat of Communist-inspired insurgency in the Third World and curb the growing power of the Communist North in Vietnam. Whether this was a correct assessment of the situation is hard to judge, for the situation varied from country to country. Much of what Kennedy and his administration saw as 'Communist agitation' was no more than the reaction of a peasant people driven to fury or resistance by the brutality and injustice of autocratic, unelected governments. These governments spouted anti-Communist rhetoric in order to enlist American support and in this they were largely successful, at least in the short term.

The most notorious and most fatal US involvement was in South Vietnam, where the USA picked up the struggle abandoned by the French after Dien Bien Phu. One feature of the US anti-Communist campaign in Vietnam was the training and equipping of local police and security forces, including local Special Force units, who were supposed to take the lead in fighting Communist infiltration and insurgency without the need for direct US intervention. The spearhead of this involvement was teams of US 'advisers', usually drawn from the US Special Forces – the Green Berets.

When John F. Kennedy came to power in 1960 the United States already had several Special Force units, but their future did not seem too secure. The first was Colonel Aaron Banks' 10th Special Forces Group, raised in 1952, currently based in Bad Totz in Bavaria and charged with organizing guerrilla resistance in Europe in the event of a Soviet invasion. The second SF unit, the 77th Special Forces Group (Airborne), had been raised in 1953 and was based at Fort Bragg in North Carolina, home of the 82nd Airborne. Lastly there was the 1st Special Forces Group, raised in 1957 and based in Okinawa.

There were also a number of SOF units, some large and well established, like the United States Marines and the 82nd Airborne Division and some small like the US Navy UDT detachments. The United States had not yet become involved in counter-terrorist or insurgency warfare outside the Philippines, and the US Army lacked the training and equipment – and the attitude – necessary for counter-insurgency operations of the type then being fought by the British in Malaya, Cyprus and Aden which, though wars on a much smaller scale, could have provided useful lessons for the US military in Vietnam.

The US Army was a conventional force, trained and equipped to fight conventional wars, but President Kennedy soon realized that a conventional war was not the immediate threat. A far greater danger was the crumbling of the Western position in the unaligned countries of the Third World and in those places recently freed from colonial control, where disputes between rival parties struggling for power provided a fertile ground for Communist infiltration and insurgency. To combat this the President needed Special Forces and plenty of them, units capable of fighting low-intensity operations. Kennedy ordered an expansion of SF strength and their further deployment overseas. Shortly after encouraging the Green Beret expansion he was ordering the US Navy to develop its Special Force capacity with the creation of the US Navy SEAL, which were first activated in 1962.

This lack of SF or SOF troops had been underlined in the Korean War, but Kennedy visualized the main use of Special Forces in Cold War conflicts, especially in damping down public discontent or small-scale insurrection in some unstable ally before the Communists could take advantage of the situation. The problems of containing Cold War insurgency were analysed at the US Command and Staff College at Leavenworth, Kansas in 1961 when the dangers of the Soviet-inspired 'wars of liberation', then being waged against the French, British and Portuguese, were seen as potentially dangerous to American interests as well. The Command and Staff College drew up a fresh assessment of America's counter-insurgency forces and advised an expansion of Special Force capability, not least to counter the successful Communist campaign in Vietnam, which was well under way by 1960 and sucking in ever more American advisers. When Kennedy took office in 1960 there were nearly 800 US advisers in Vietnam and this number was soon to increase.

The Vietnam War is so pivotal in the post-war history of Special Forces that it deserves special treatment. This chapter will therefore record the rebirth of the main Special Forces units raised for Vietnam, especially the creation of the 5th Special Forces Group in September 1961, and its deployment to Vietnam. From that time on, until his assassination in November 1963, Kennedy took a personal interest in the Special Forces units. Indeed, US Special Forces attribute their headgear and popular title – the Green Berets – to a suggestion by Kennedy that green was the colour of his ancestral home, Ireland, and the right one for their berets, which discounts any link with the famous green beret of the British Commandos. Kennedy certainly authorized the wearing of the green beret by the Special Forces and ordered the establishment of the Special Warfare Centre at Fort Bragg, where SF units could be raised and trained. The first of these groups, the 5th Special Forces Group, 1st Special Forces, the unit that was to play such a major part in SF Vietnam operations, was activated at Fort Bragg on 21 September 1961.

The Soviet Union and Warsaw Pact countries were not slow to follow the US lead, where they were not already ahead of it. Russia has a long history of irregular warfare dating back at least to Napoleonic times and is a country well adapted to the employment of guerrilla forces – as the French of the Emperor Napoleon and the armies of Hitler's Germany found to their cost. The Soviets made good use of Cossack and partisan forces in the Second World War and kept some of these units in being after 1945, drafting them into the Soviet Army for use in the raiding role and for behind-the-lines operations in the Third World.

The Soviets soon introduced advisers and SF training teams into all those countries where they supplied weapons, like Egypt and Syria, but began to develop Special Forces in the modern pattern from 1962, notably with the creation of heliborne and parachute strike forces. Russian airborne and heliborne forces spearheaded the invasion of Czechoslovakia in 1968 and Spetznaz troops – Soviet Special Forces – were subsequently employed in both the operational and training role in places as far apart as Angola, Afghanistan and Cuba, anywhere the USSR regarded as falling within its sphere of influence. Spetznaz troops – *Spetzialnoje Naznachenic* – were first recruited from the Soviet parachute forces and remained under Soviet Army Command until the early 1960s, when they came under the control of the KGB and GRU, Soviet Military Intelligence. The Spetznaz then divided into two forms: KGB Spetznaz, comprised of small groups, often based in Soviet embassies and charged with internal protection and, if need be, local assassinations of local dissidents or political leaders; and GRU Spetznaz, the military or Special Force arm. It was a GRU Spetznaz unit in Czechoslovakia which seized Alexander Dubček in Prague in 1968 and sent him in chains to Moscow.

The GRU wing of the Spetznaz was used for military intelligence gathering in the field, and proved highly effective as an anti-guerrilla unit in Afghanistan. These GRU units were recruited from the Spetznaz Special Operations Brigades, of which there was one to every Soviet front, or army group. The task of these units if Cold War ever became hot was to target NATO bases and command centres and carry out behind-the-lines action against key NATO personnel and nuclear bases.

During the 1960s British SF and SOF forces were constantly in action, the sole exception being in 1968, the only year since the end of the Second World War when no British soldier was killed in action. The SAS were serving in the Oman, Dofar and the Aden Protectorate, and the Parachute Regiment and the Royal Marines Commandos were constantly employed in anti-terrorist wars, notably in Aden and Borneo and, at the end of the decade, in Northern Ireland. Britain's shrinking Empire was not matched by a shrinking of its global responsibilities, but the diminishing number of overseas bases forced the British into devising new methods of military deployment, specifically with the widespread introduction of the force-enhancing helicopter and, for the 3rd Commando Brigade, the introduction of the 'Commando Carrier' concept.

Two fleet carriers, HMS *Bulwark* and HMS *Centaur*, were converted to carry helicopters rather than fixed-wing aircraft and used to carry a fully equipped Royal Marine Commando. As the centre of a small amphibious task force, this Commando could stay at sea, in international waters, for months if necessary, and appear off any threatened shore to send the Marines in by landing craft and helicopter. The Marines from HMS *Bulwark* were used to defend Kuwait against Iraqi threats in 1961, and to suppress the mutiny of the Tanganyikan Army in 1964, at the request of President Nyerere, as well as being used for the rapid deployment of SAS, Marine and Gurkha troops during the Borneo Confrontation.

Let us now turn to some of the other SF units that were active at this time, notably in the Israeli Defence Forces, the IDF, an organization which has produced many fine SF units and set up many classic SF operations.

Israeli Special Forces can trace their origins back to that legendary soldier, Orde Wingate of the British Army, who, as already related, served in Palestine (as it then was) before the Second World War and became a passionate Zionist. The Arab and Jewish communities were already at each other's throats, and the local police force, the British Palestine Police, were unable to contain the violence or protect the outlying Jewish settlements. Wingate therefore set up small guerrilla units – the Special Night Squads – which defended the Jewish settlements and made raids on Arab camps. Wingate had no official mandate for this action, but the British authorities chose to turn a blind eye. Another clandestine force was the Jewish Ha' Stromer, the Watchmen, who were equally active in defensive and offensive operations against the Arabs during the British Mandate.

The British left Palestine in May 1948. The first Arab–Israeli War broke out within hours, ending after about a year in complete victory for the Israelis but with no prospect of a permanent peace. During that first struggle the Pal'mach, a Jewish unit not unlike the British SAS, did well in various engagements but was disbanded in 1949, the year in which Israel formed its first regular parachute battalion.

The next irregular unit to form was Unit 101, raised in 1953, and used to detect and combat Arab infiltrators from Egypt, Jordan and the Lebanon, crossing into Israel and attacking settlements and kibbutzim. Unit 101 soon abandoned that defensive task and took to raiding across the Jordan and Syrian borders and attacking guerrilla bases in the Arab countries, a task it performed to such effect that by mid-1954 Arab raids on Jewish kibbutzim had virtually ended, at least for a while. Israel then formed the Unit into a parachute brigade, called Unit 202, and went on to create three territorial units, to guard the national frontier.

This move was followed in 1957 by the creation of a highly placed SF unit, Sayaret Mat'kal, which operated under the orders of the Israeli General Staff and was used for intelligence and clandestine operations. By the 1960s Israel's armed forces had a large SF element, which included three parachute units, a force of naval Commandos for coastal raids, a reconnaissance force for the Sinai and a strike force for operations on the northern and eastern flanks of Israel – in other words, against terrorists based in Syria, Jordan and the Lebanon.

Since the founding of the State of Israel, the defence of the country had been affected by one simple, geographical fact: Israel is very small. This fact affects every aspect of its military strategy, for it lacks the depth of territory to absorb an all-out conventional attack. If threatened, the Israelis must attack first. Therefore, the assessment of impending danger and the evaluation of enemy forces close to their borders are constant concerns of the Israeli Staff, and the secret of successful assessments and accurate evaluations is good intelligence and regular reconnaissance, which are prime SF tasks. The Israeli intelligence services – Shin Bet and the Mossad – are rated among the best in the world, together with the KGB, the CIA and Britain's SIS, but the Israeli intelligence services are also seeking information which can and often has led to swift Israeli Special Force action.

Apart from the periodic danger of all-out attack and a war of annihilation, Israel and Israeli citizens at home and abroad are in constant danger of terrorist attack, and a large part of Israel's Special Force capability is devoted to countering the terrorist threat, notably by attacking terrorist bases and killing terrorist leaders. Drawn from a well-educated and intelligent population, Israel's SF troops are well equipped, superbly trained and highly motivated. Indeed, they have the ultimate motivation. On their success depends the very survival of the Jewish state.

During the Suez War of November 1956 the crucial blocking of the Mitla Pass through Sinai was carried out by the 890 Parachute Battalion, and this successful action was the main SOF battle of the war. The recce unit of this battalion, Sayaret T'zanhanim, was then employed in defending the frontiers of the state, where the men saw plenty of action leading up to the Six-Day War in 1967, the third round in the ongoing Arab–Israeli conflict. In that war Sayaret T'zanhanim, riding in a force of jeeps armed with anti-tank guns, in the traditional SAS fashion, took on a force of Egyptian tanks on the banks of the Suez Canal and destroyed them all. A year later a detachment of this unit mounted Operation Shock, a helicopter raid on the Egyptian power station in the Nile Valley, blew up the facility and withdrew without loss. These daring raids, this willingness to take on heavy odds and pull it off, owe a lot to chutzpah.

In March 1968 Israeli Special Forces mounted a major attack against a strong Palestine base at Karameh in Jordan. This attack, by tanks, infantry and aircraft, was supported by SF troops, who were taken by helicopter into the surrounding hills to cut off the Palestine forces from support and mop up as they started to withdraw. Nine months later, in

December 1968, another Arab country, the Lebanon, saw a further example of chutzpah when, in retaliation for permitting Beirut to be used as a base for PFLP (Popular Front for the Liberation of Palestine) guerrillas, Israeli SF swooped across the frontier in helicopters, took over Beirut International Airport on the edge of the city and destroyed a dozen Lebanese airliners on the ground.

Israel also maintains a strike force of Naval Commandos, Shayet 13, (Flotilla 13). This unit has existed in various forms since it was set up by the British in 1940 but first came to Israeli notice after an abortive raid on Alexandria during the Six-Day War of 1967 when a detachment of Flotilla 13 frogmen attempted to attack Egyptian warships with limpet mines. Detected by the Egyptians these men were forced to surrender and underwent brutal interrogation and torture before they were eventually exchanged for Egyptian prisoners. Another unit of Flotilla 13 carried out a highly successful raid on an Egyptian radar installation in 1969 and the force was used with great effect against Palestine guerrilla bases in the Lebanon.

Perhaps Flotilla 13's most famous raid was an attack on the Black September terrorist headquarters in Beirut on the night of 9–10 April 1973, when three high-ranking Black September terrorists were killed and the HQ destroyed by explosives. The Israelis have no hesitation in launching their SF troops on raids deep into 'enemy' territory or even into that of neutral or friendly powers if they feel that their national security is threatened, and their Special Forces, which enjoy ample opportunities for real action, are among the most professional in the world.

While the British Empire was fading quietly away, the French were engaged in a full-scale 'war of liberation' in Algeria, a war in which a number of SOF units but particularly those of the Foreign Legion, were actively engaged. After their return from Indo-China in 1955 three Legion parachute regiments were raised at Sidi Bel Abbes, the Legion HQ. On 1 September that year, the 1st and 3rd REP (Régiment Etrangers de Parachutiste) were established, followed three months later by the 2nd REP. All three were soon actively engaged in operations against the Algerian guerrillas of the ALN – the Army for National Liberation, the military arm of the FLN, the Front for National Liberation.

The paras worked closely with the *harkis*, Muslim irregulars who either wished the French to remain in Algeria or were former soldiers of the ALN. The Algerian War, which began in November 1954 and lasted until the early 1960s, was one of the most bitter of all the post-colonial wars, with a large number of atrocities committed on both sides and little or no quarter given to collaborators or the wounded. The French enjoyed some initial success and the ALN soon split into two forms, the ALN proper which drew supplies from across the Moroccan and Tunisian frontiers and operated in battalion strength, and the ten-to fifty-strong guerrilla bands, which lived in the *bled*, the rugged hinterland of Algeria, raiding villages, ambushing convoys or attacking French patrols.

This guerrilla war proved more successful, from the Algerian point of view, than any large-unit actions, for the guerrillas were able to tie down a large number of French troops and inflict a steady stream of casualties on the civilian population. In an attempt to cut the flow of arms into Algeria, the French built a long, mined and fully electrified fence, the Morice Line, along the Tunisian frontier and a similar though shorter one on the Moroccan side. These wired and mined barriers proved very effective and a large number of ALN units were detected and brought to battle while attempting to break through the barrier of the minefields. Most of the interior operations, however, were standard cordon-and-search operations, backed with the rapid deployment of helicopter or parachute units, often from the REP. These operations were highly successful 'cleansing' or 'search and destroy' missions.

Terrain has already been mentioned as one of the yardsticks for the deployment of SF troops and the Algerian terrain, fairly open though extremely rugged, did not offer the ALN much in the way of concealment. Once a guerrilla band had been detected, helicopter-borne forces would be flown in to contain them, followed at once by parachute or Legion infantry, who would then sweep through an area, searching every hilltop, cave and gully, killing anyone they came across. These operations, though successful, were not without loss, and the death toll among junior officers and NCOs was especially high. The 2nd REP lost 741 men killed in Algeria in return for killing or capturing some 4,200 ALN fighters. In one action, on the jebels of Beni Sbihi the 2nd REP killed or wounded more than 200 ALN fighters for the loss of just thirty-one Legionaries.

The Algerian war ended in March 1962, by which time the REPs were down to just one battalion, the 2nd REP, which like the other two was in danger of disbandment. In June 1962, however, the new commander of the 2nd REP, Lieutenant-Colonel Caillaud, came up with a new proposal, to transform the 2nd REP into a strike force, a para-commando regiment, on the lines of the Belgian unit that had recently done so well in the Congo.

Caillaud recognized that, although the French Empire was over, France retained overseas interests and might, from time to time, need to protect them. His vision of the 2nd REP was of a highly trained and multi-skilled intervention unit. His officers and men must be parachute-trained, used to canoes and small boats, and skilled in all weapons, unarmed combat, demolitions, patrolling, insurgency work, medicine, languages and long-range reconnaissance. When the Legion withdrew to France in 1967, Caillaud installed the 2nd REP at a base in Calvi, Corsica, and rigorous training became the order of the day. Within two years, in April 1969, the new 2nd REP had deployed to Chad in Central Africa, where the pro-French leader, President Tombalbaye, had problems with two separate rebel groups along the Sudanese and Saharan borders. The 2nd REP took up active patrolling against these groups and crushed these small rebellions before they could blossom into anything serious, for the loss of twenty-six Legionaries killed or wounded.

Other forces were also changing roles at this time. The Canadian Parachute Regiment, which had fought in Normandy and the Rhine as part of the British 6th Airborne Division, now became the Canadian Airborne Regiment, trained and equipped for intervention and low-intensity, anti-guerrilla operations. Since Canada, a normally peaceful and totally democratic state, was then riven by arguments between the Anglophone and Francophone sections of the population, this unit was not entirely designed for deployment abroad, but could have been used to treat Québécois terrorism if need be.

In 1960 the Australian SAS Regiment, formed in 1957 as a small company, was raised to regimental status and in 1964 became a regular unit in the Australian Army. This unit was first deployed to Borneo during the Confrontation with Indonesia, where it did sterling work with the British SAS, and later served with the US Green Berets in Vietnam. The New Zealand SS Squadron, first formed for Malay in 1954, was disbanded in 1957 but reformed in 1958. Elements of this force served in Borneo during the Confrontation and a troop of New Zealand SAS also served in Vietnam from 1968 to 1971, as part of the Australian SAS Squadron.

These developments provide a paradigm of what was happening in the SF during the 1960s. The role of the former imperial powers was being taken over by the United States and the exercise of the imperial role was already imposing changes on its military capability. Irregular warfare was replacing conventional warfare, partly for political reasons, but mainly because of the fear that conventional war could escalate into nuclear war. The broad picture is of a worldwide but small-scale revival in both Special Force and SOF units, but this general situation was to be completely overshadowed by the developments taking place in the US Army, where all considerations were gradually being consumed by the need to find a path to victory in the jungles of South Vietnam.

SEALs badge

CHAPTER NINE

The Green Berets in Vietnam 1961–1965

The multiple skills and individual motivation of
SF soldiers are exploited to the full in the combat
environment of the A Detachment in Vietcong-
dominated areas...

Commander, 5th Special Forces (Airborne),
Vietnam

Special Force units tend to have their defining moments, at least
in the public imagination. For the 22nd SAS Regiment it was the
ending of the Iranian Embassy siege in London in 1980. For the
Royal Marines of 3 Commando Brigade it was the 'great yomp', the
march across the Falkland Islands to victory in the hills around Port
Stanley in 1982. For 2 Para it was the Battle of Goose Green in the
same campaign, for the Belgian Para-Commandos the parachute drop
on Léopoldville in 1960. These were the moments when the public
woke up to the existence of these units and began to follow their
actions with interest. For the US Special Forces – the Green Berets –
their defining moment was more traumatic and longer lasting than any
of these. They came to public notice in the agonizing, ten-year time-
frame of the Vietnam War.

The Vietnam War was one of the most unusual wars in history. The scars of that conflict live on in the United States and South-East Asia, and will do so until the last veteran of that tragedy has gone to his honourable grave. Even then, the issues, the strategy and the tactics of the Vietnam War will continue to be discussed. It is a war that almost defies comparison; the closest parallel is provided by the Spanish Peninsular campaign waged by General Lord Wellington and the Spanish guerrillas against the Army of Napoleon Bonaparte between 1808 and 1814, when the combination of a small, superbly trained army of British and Portuguese regular soldiers and a multitude of Spanish irregulars halted, defeated and finally evicted a much larger force of French troops, led by generals who had won battles in every corner of the Continent.

Substitute the North Vietnamese Army (NVA) and the Vietcong for Wellington's Peninsular Army and the Spanish guerrillas, and the US and South Vietnam forces for the Napoleonic French, and a rough comparison exists. The lesson to be drawn is that, against a skilfully used combination of regular and guerrilla forces, the largest and best-equipped army will struggle in vain. The man commanding the NVA and the Vietcong in South Vietnam was General Giap, a schoolteacher-turned-soldier who had already defeated the French, a man who knew all there was to know about guerrilla warfare, a general who can be ranked among the Great Captains of military history. The USA tried to fight that war with mobility and firepower, but the lessons of history dictate that the Americans were bound to lose the war in Vietnam and in the end they lost it.

Every rule for winning an irregular war was broken in Vietnam. There was little or no public support for the war in the USA and what support there was fell away when the body-bags began to come home. President Johnson, whose political career was blighted by the war, is on record as saying, 'The weakest link in our armour is American public opinion.' This is probably true, but the war was fought without definite, achievable political aims, and was not even supported by the bulk of the Vietnamese people. Another chronic problem was that the war in the South could not be fought to a conclusion while the North enjoyed security from invasion and could train, supply and shelter NVA and Vietcong fighters north of the DMZ or Demilitarized Zone, the dividing line between North and South Vietnam laid down when the French left in 1955.

It was politically impossible for US troops to cross the DMZ and track the NVA to their bases, and bombing alone could not interdict NVA supply routes feeding rebellion in the South, routes like the famous Ho Chi Minh Trail through Laos, so the supply of men and arms to the Vietcong, and increasingly to the regular troops of the NVA operating in the South continued virtually unchecked throughout the war. Thus the two requirements for winning the war, a political objective and victory in the field, were both beyond America's grasp.

There were also plenty of mistakes in the way the war was fought, which will be touched on shortly. But, although the strategic problems outlined above played a part in these errors, they might have been reduced if the higher echelons of the US military and various political administrations in Washington had been able to grasp exactly what they were trying to achieve in Vietnam, and what they needed to do in order to achieve it. The first error was a political one, a failure to accept the nature of the war and supply the Southern Army with a reason to fight it. The USA tried for years to buttress the ARVN – the Army of the Republic of Vietnam – and get it to fight properly: but the motivation to fight and win was missing. Eventually the US had to become directly involved.

After 1965 the US military tried to fight a conventional war, with firepower and technology, spending billions of dollars in an attempt to wipe out a guerrilla army that refused to come and be killed. The armies of the North were led by General Giap, a soldier of genius, and his soldiers, both Vietcong and the NVA, were highly trained, very experienced and powerfully motivated. They had been fighting for years, against the Japanese, then the French, and then the South Vietnamese, before the Americans took over, and they knew their business. When they were deployed against the US soldiery, man to man, their greater experience often carried the day, a point made by that veteran US Marine Gunnery Sergeant, Charles H. Owens: 'One of the many mistakes in the Vietnam War was the one-year tour of duty. In one year a trooper has just begun to learn how to fight the enemy. In World War 2 you could not think of leaving combat before at least two years. I think the politicians should have turned the war over to the generals, like President Bush did during the Gulf War of 1991. I also believe that the Vietnam War was a just and honourable war and that those who spoke against it were just afraid of their own skins. I believe I must serve my country, if she is right or wrong.'

The Vietnam War was complicated, and unravelling the complications of fighting it would fill several books. It can be – and has been – maintained that the US Army did not lose the war, and in the sense that the US Army defeated the NVA whenever it could be brought to battle, that is quite true. The problem is that such defeats did not bring the North Vietnamese to the conference table or lead to any decline in the fighting ability of the NVA or its Vietcong allies, while the casualties inflicted on the US Army – more than 50,000 dead and nearly half a million wounded – plus the devastation wrought on the Vietnamese people, North and South, and brought into American homes nightly on the television news, caused great anguish among the public at home, an anguish all too often unfairly expressed in anger against the US Army and the returning soldier.

There is some truth in the military's belief that the war in South Vietnam was lost in the campuses and living rooms of the United States, but this is a simplification. Before discussing the role of SF and SOF forces in Vietnam, it is necessary to look at the causes of the war and the circumstances under which it was fought. That scrutiny will reveal the nature of the Vietnam War, and how almost every lesson for fighting such a war was ignored. The result was a shattering defeat, not on the battlefield but in the 'hearts and minds' of the American people, a defeat that left them very unwilling to risk such conflict again.

Most wars arise from issues left unsettled after, or created by, the previous conflict, and so it was in Vietnam. Vietnam was only one of the territories occupied by the French in Indo-China, the others being Cambodia and Laos. These last two also became the scene of vicious, post-colonial wars in the late 1940s, but not on the scale endured by Vietnam before the French were evicted by the Vietminh in 1955. After the French defeat at Dien Bien Phu in May 1954, their colonial possessions in Vietnam were divided into two republics, North Vietnam, which was Communist, and South Vietnam, which was ostensibly democratic but was actually a despotism headed by Premier Ngo Dinh Diem. However, as a fervent anti-Communist who could make the right kind of speeches, Diem enjoyed the support of the American President Dwight D. Eisenhower, who established a Military Assistance Group, Vietnam (MAGV) in Saigon in July 1954.

The partition of Vietnam was consistently opposed by Ho Chi Minh, the President of North Vietnam; and his supporters, the former Vietminh, continued to be active in the South, inspiring and supporting resistance to the Diem government. Ho Chi Minh was *the* hero of the anti-colonial struggle and far more of a Vietnam nationalist than the usual Third World, Communist stooge. Ho's principle demand was for country-wide elections, on the issue of a united country, an election which he would certainly win. Since this fact was well known to President Diem, he refused to permit open elections in the South, and the two Vietnams, the North supported by China and the Soviet Union, and the South by the USA, were soon at war. Here arose the first US error, a failure to understand the political root of the war. 'We thought we were fighting Communism,' said Robert McNamara, the US Secretary of Defense from 1961 to 1968, 'while in fact we were fighting nationalism.'

This fact underpinned the stout resistance to American arms put up by the forces from the North, the tenacious struggle of the Vietcong Communist guerrillas, and the half-hearted support of the Army of South Vietnam and the general population in the South. In South Vietnam, the government was corrupt and unpopular with the people. The South Vietnamese did not support it and the ARVN was reluctant to fight for it. The people in the North, on the other hand, were determined to resist foreign aggression and were relentless fighters in the field. One of the constant surprises for American soldiers in Vietnam was the difference between the lacklustre performance of the ARVN soldiers and the fanatical fighting ability of the Vietcong and the NVA. These were the same people; the difference was a matter of motivation.

The people of Vietnam were fed up with outside interference; they had experienced that from the French and the Japanese. They were also fed up with corruption, but that is all they got from the Diem regime and the regimes that followed Diem's murder – by his own generals – in 1963. Basically, the Vietnamese wanted to be left alone, to follow their own destiny and sort out their own affairs. It is moot whether such a course would have led to any long-term Communist control of the country.

American involvement arose from a conviction that Vietnam would be the next piece to fall to Communist expansion under Eisenhower's so-called Domino Theory. The Domino Theory stated that one country after another would fall under Communist control, until the whole world was under the sway of Moscow and Peking. President Eisenhower was determined to resist this expansion and chose South Vietnam as the place to make a stand. United States troops first became involved in Vietnam in 1954. The first Green Beret involvement came in June 1957 when the 1st Special Forces Group was activated in Okinawa and 'advisers' from this Group set up a Commando Training Centre – the MACV Recondo School for ARVN officers and NCOs at Nha Trang on the coast north of Saigon ('Recondo' was a combination of 'Reconnaissance' and 'Commando'). The trainees were to become the first members of the Vietnamese Special Force units.

Special Forces are a brotherhood and many of the US instructors at Nha Trang had previously attended a course at the British Jungle Warfare School in Malaya, as Sergeant-Major Ray Garofalo of the 5th Special Forces, Project Delta programme recalls: 'Early in the Vietnam War 5th Special Forces were sending people from Okinawa to the British School because, quite frankly, it was the best course of its kind in the world. The people there not only had a good working knowledge of the region, they understood its history, its politics and how best to approach counter-insurgency operations. They were also the most civilized Special Operations soldiers I have ever known ... certainly among the best. Our instructors in the field were SAS, from Britain, Australia or New Zealand. They worked on drills, 'stand to' at dawn and dusk and the layout of defensive positions whenever they stopped ... and if anyone entered those positions they opened fire ... there was a war going on in Malaya at this time, at least up on the frontier. They had also produced a *Jungle Warfare* handbook, which I took back with me to Vietnam. I had copies made and distributed them among my soldiers and it became our bible. We used to send six people at a time to the School at Kota Tingi and over a few years we had a cadre of men who could pass on what they had learned to our own Delta, Sigma and Omega programmes ... quite probably a few of our people owe their lives to what they learned from the British in Malaya.'

At this point, with the beginnings of SF involvement in Vietnam, two points have to be made clear. The first is that from 1955 until 1965 the war in Vietnam was a counter-insurgency war. Only with the deployment of large numbers of US troops from 1965 did the Vietnam War take on conventional form. The second point is that the involvement of US Special Forces was first seen as a commitment only in a training and advisory capacity. The Green Berets sent to Vietnam were supposed to *train and advise* their Vietnamese colleagues, not to take charge of irregular units and certainly not to lead offensive missions against the Vietcong. The United States intended to wage this war at one remove, but the South Vietnamese Army proved unable, and in some cases unwilling, to fight and win against their tough, highly motivated Vietcong opponents. Willy-nilly, the SF troopers had to take charge of patrols and defensive operations, and it was this circumstance that sucked the US Special Forces ever deeper into the quagmire.

Before going on to detail the actions of the Green Berets in Vietnam and the actions of the many other SF and SOF units that saw combat there, the rules of counter-insurgency warfare, a neglect of which governs all that follows, should be restated, appreciated and borne in mind throughout this chapter and the one which follows.

The first rule of counter-insurgency warfare, one observed by the British in Malaya, is that there must be a clear political objective. Otherwise the troops are fighting in a vacuum. Secondly, this objective must be known to, and supported by, the majority of the local population. Neither point applied to the South Vietnamese population and it applied even less to the people of the United States. Nor was this point lost on the higher echelons of the US military. Lieutenant-General Shoup, Commandant of the USMC and winner of the Medal of Honor at Tarawa in the Second World War Pacific campaign, a man not afraid of combat on or off the battlefield, stated after his retirement that 'The United States has no business in South Vietnam ... the whole country is not worth the life or limb of a single American soldier.'

Thirdly, the war must be containable and the enemy forced to fight on ground of the defenders' choosing. This rule was ignored in Vietnam and was politically unachievable; as has already been noted, the NVA could operate from secure bases in the North and the Vietcong could train and be supplied with weapons stockpiled there, safe from attack. Attempts to interdict the main Vietcong supply route down the Ho Chi Minh Trail from the air brought the USA fresh problems in Cambodia, and the 'Rolling Thunder' bombing campaign against NVA bases in the North brought no significant military gains in return for an unwelcome escalation in the war, international condemnation and a significant number of American aircrew delivered into long and severe captivity.

Fourthly, in fighting the war the democratic forces must not alienate the uncommitted civilian population. The war in Vietnam broke this rule in almost every possible way, from the very fact that it was fought to shore up an unpopular government to the inevitable result of using modern military might – and plenty of it – among a population of rural peasantry, in an attempt to suppress a skilled and dauntless enemy.

Giap followed the principles laid down in China a generation before by Mao Tse-tung, the doyen of guerrilla fighters. The rules were:

1. You must not take anything without permission.
2. You must not be disorderly.
3. You must learn and fall in with local customs.
4. You must live with the peasants and help them with their work.
5. You must make propaganda all the time.
6. You must attend open meetings and form study groups among the peasants.

The US military made various attempts to follow similar guidelines, and such 'hearts and minds' activity was a major function of the Green Berets and the US Marine CAP (Combined Action Program) teams, but this was not enough to spare the Vietnamese people from the horrors of all-out war.

The local people were fired on, bombed, napalmed, harassed by ARVN and US Army forces, saw their crops and animals destroyed, their forests maimed by chemical defoliants like Agent Orange – which allegedly had carcinogenic after-effects – their culture eroded, their wives and daughters becoming prostitutes. By the time the war ended nearly half a million Vietnamese women had taken to prostitution, having no other way to survive and support their children. The population of South Vietnam suffered terribly in the war and their sufferings were a major part of the reasons why the world at large, and the United States in particular, wished to end it.

Fifth, the defenders must control and win the propaganda battle. The rule here is a strict adherence to the truth, however painful the facts or limited the information. The propaganda battle, for the hearts and minds of people in South Vietnam and the United States, was always going to be difficult, given the 'liberal' or left-wing cast of the majority of the free-world media, but this problem was compounded by the inclination of US Army Public Relations personnel to put a gloss on the war that was not borne out either by the facts or by the experience of war correspondents assigned to cover the fighting. The briefings on the Vietnam military situation, given in Saigon at 1700 hours each day, were often so far from reality, in their claims of high body counts and victories in the field, that they were generally known as 'The Five O'Clock Follies'. The general impression was that the Vietcong and NVA were winning the war and that in the end victory would be theirs. This impression had a deleterious effect on the public and politicians in the USA, especially in their support for the troops in the field.

These hard facts should not obscure other facts; the Communist regime in North Vietnam was an expansionist, totalitarian dictatorship bent on controlling the long-suffering population in the South, who were denied the benefits of free speech and civil rights by their rulers in Saigon and coerced by Communist terrorism, brutality, summary execution and torture, to obey the wishes of the Vietcong and their North Vietnamese masters. The real victims of the Vietnamese War were the Vietnamese people and this fact is borne out by those tens of thousand of 'boat people' who risked everything and suffered greatly to escape from Vietnam when the war was over and the Communists took over.

This is the background to the war in Vietnam. To trace the campaigns of the Special Forces in that struggle we must now go back to 1961, when John F. Kennedy was starting his regrettably short term as President of the United States and discovering, as he moved into the White House, that a neat little war was raging in Indo-China, a war which was gradually sucking in more and more American troops.

Nine months after Kennedy took office in 1960, the 5th Special Forces Group, 1st Special Forces, was activated at Fort Bragg and charged with handling all SF missions in Vietnam. The number of SF personnel deployed in Vietnam had already risen to over 500, most of them engaged in training ARVN units in counter-insurgency and special operations. In September 1961 Kennedy ordered a further expansion of SF units and the setting up of the Special Warfare Centre at Fort Bragg.

The first result of this was the start of US efforts to broaden the base of Vietnamese action against the Vietcong, by sending SF troops to Vietnam tasked with developing counter-insurgency activity among the Montagnard mountain tribes, the Nung, the Ruarde and the Jarai, as part of what came to be known as the Civilian Irregular Defense Group (CIDG) programme. This Special Force task was supposed to operate at one remove from active combat. The US Special Force soldiers were to train, to advise and to assist in civil action programmes, not lead the Montagnards in combat operations. Indeed, they were not to do anything but supply cash and expertise, since all instructions were to be relayed to the Montagnards through ARVN officers and senior non-commissioned officers.

This worthy intention was blighted from the start by the dislike and distrust prevailing between the Montagnards and the Vietnamese. This was essentially a 'hearts and minds ... with teeth' operation, to enlist the support of the mountain tribes, who did not get on well with the coastal Vietnamese and were wide open to Communist indoctrination. The Montagnards, an unsophisticated tribal people very different from the Westernized Vietnamese, numbered about a million, spread over about thirty-three tribes, most of which lived in the Annamite mountains of Vietnam – the jungle-clad and strategically important Central Highlands. Since the tribal lands occupied much of the hinterland of South Vietnam, the support of the Montagnards was vital, but the entire concept of 'hearts and minds' was alien to the ARVN soldiers.

The Montagnards had always rejected attempts by the Vietnamese to control their lands or degrade their culture. For their part, the ARVN soldiers, like most Vietnamese, regarded the Montagnards as primitive savages and thought it beneath their military dignity to build bridges, roads and schools to assist them and keep them 'on side'. The Montagnard people were soon caught between the Communist Vietcong and the ARVN, and suffered terribly in the war; over 20,000 were killed and most of the tribespeople – one estimate says 85 per cent – were eventually driven from their mountain homes, after their fields, villages and livestock were destroyed in the fighting.

This mutual antagonism between the Montagnards and the ARVN culminated in a rising by the tribespeople in September 1964, in which some thirty ARVN soldiers were killed by Montagnard CIDG fighters. This rising was put down without difficulty or brutality by American SF soldiers working in the villages, but the US Special Forces faced an uphill struggle right from the start in Vietnam, even without the growing resistance to their efforts from the Vietcong. The very nature of their deployment was unusual. The US Special Forces had been raised to train and support guerrillas in an enemy country, not to fight them in a friendly one, yet that is what they had to do against the Vietcong in South Vietnam. The task of raising CIDG units and organizing a programme of public works was also a far cry from the public image in the USA and elsewhere, which saw Green Beret soldiers as simply highly trained killing machines.

The SF task, certainly from 1961 to 1964, was not to go out in small groups and kill the enemy, but to raise the confidence of the Montagnard people in the government of South Vietnam and get them to support it. To do this the Green Berets aimed to provide the villagers with the means and training to defend themselves and their villages from Vietcong attack. Ways of doing this were learned and refined at the first village to benefit from SF assistance, Buon Enao, in the Dar Lac province of South Vietnam, where US Special Force advisers moved in and worked alongside the villagers, sleeping in their huts, eating the same food, sharing the same dangers. The SF troopers found that the local people were much like the folks back home, and more than willing to fight off the Vietcong, if they felt that by doing so they were fighting for a better life for themselves and their children. When this project proved successful, and the local population became strongly anti-Vietcong, the CIDG programme expanded.

To get the Montagnard villagers 'on side' was vital. Without their support in the Central Highlands the war was lost and so a great deal of money, time and effort went into a programme of public works in the mountains, with the aim of ensuring their continued support. Since the ARVN was reluctant to help, this task fell to the Green Berets and later to the CAP (Civil Action Programmes) of the US Marine Corps. This involvement with the local people soon led, perhaps inevitably, to direct military action against the Vietcong by the various SF groups deployed in Montagnard territory. These groups, a combined force of SF troopers and CIDG volunteers, were eventually placed on a full war footing and supplied with kit, uniforms and heavy weapons.

The 5th Special Forces Group (Airborne) which headed up this development was organized with an HQ company and a signal company, plus three SF companies which were much like infantry battalion rifle companies but more heavily armed, and an aviation detachment. An SF company was commanded by a lieutenant-colonel, and divided into three elements. The administrative element, C, consisted of the HQ and the administration personnel. Detachment C commanded three Detachment Bs, each commanded by a major, who in turn controlled four A detachments, the cutting edge of the Green Berets in Vietnam and popularly known as the A Teams. Each A Team consisted of twelve men, each one a first-class, fully trained SF soldier, with individual specialist skills in scouting, sniping, recon, signalling and patrolling, as well as medical and language skills.

By the time SF troops were deployed in Vietnam the Vietcong dominated the Montagnard regions and soon began to resist the infiltration of Special Force troopers and their efforts to raise effective CIDG forces in the Montagnard villages. Nevertheless, by December 1963, the Green Berets had trained around 44,000 Montagnards in arms and minor tactics and organized them into village militias, while a further 18,000 Vietnamese had been trained and equipped as rapid-reaction forces – strike forces – which could move to assist any village under Vietcong attack.

The Vietcong were now meeting resistance to their Communist indoctrination from the Montagnard people, who had previously been either supportive or indifferent, and the ever-combative Vietcong therefore elected to strike directly at the SF–CIDG bases in the villages. These attacks always came in at night, and usually consisted of violent mortar and machine-gun fire followed by infiltration and infantry assault. These attacks were usually aided by Vietcong members who had joined the CIDG programme and were serving in the camp garrisons. Two small camps, at Polei Krong and Hiep Hoa, were attacked and overrun in 1964 and in July of that year a Vietcong battalion 700 strong attacked the SF camp at Nam Dong, which was defended by

Nung CIDG irregulars and a twelve-man A Team commanded by Captain Roger Donlon.

Accurate 82mm mortar fire falling on the camp at 0230 hours shattered the camp buildings and killed a number of men caught in the open, but the SF radio operator managed to send a message calling for reinforcements before the first of three Vietcong infantry assaults came in over the wire, the Vietcong having crawled up to the outer defences under the cover of uncut grass. By this time all the garrison were in their trenches and ready to fight back but, having overrun the perimeter wire, the Vietcong became involved in a firefight around an SF 81mm mortar pit. This pit was lost and retaken several times by Captain Donlon, who drove the enemy back with grenades, rescuing a wounded mortar-crew member and sustaining several wounds himself, actions for which he was later awarded the Medal of Honor.

The fighting at Nam Dong went on until dawn, when the arrival of reinforcements forced the Vietcong to draw off. This was a typical Vietcong action, a fierce attack which was broken off when the odds turned against the attackers. Any idea that the Vietcong would stay and fight against odds until destroyed was soon seen as faulty: the Vietcong fought only when and where they wanted to, and always kept the initiative.

These three night battles were just the first of many. The Green Berets were in action in Vietnam throughout the 1960s and were not finally withdrawn until 1971, but as the war escalated more Special Force units began to form, many of them staffed or trained by SF personnel. The original SF–CIDG forces concentrated on 'hearts and minds', but, not least because their ARVN colleagues seemed unwilling to do so, they soon also became involved in long-range recon units, used for hunting the Vietcong, and in the creation of other anti-Vietcong units. Among these were the Mobile Strike Forces – the MIKE Forces.

Gerald (Bob) Bunnell served with the US Special Forces in Vietnam from 1963 to 1971 and describes a MIKE Force action: 'I first arrived in Vietnam in 1965, and in early January 1968 I was in Nha Trang. As medics we were to report to the Group Surgeon's office, where I heard that the "Mike Force" had just lost a senior medic, killed in action. I went over and asked to talk to the Team Sergeant. Later I discovered I had passed an interview I didn't realize I was having and I had a new home – Detachment A-503, MIKE Force.

'This team had developed quite a reputation since being formed in 1965. One of their first major actions was deployment into the Special Forces Camp of A Shau as it was about to be overrun in March 1966.

A good friend that I still see periodically was one of the Americans to be deployed and his room mate on the MIKE Force was a tall guy from Oklahoma named Billy Hall, the dead senior medic. I found out several weeks later how Billy died. He had both his legs blown off by a mortar round. He refused evacuation and ordered the personnel to carry him into the medical bunker, where he accepted basic attention but continued to direct the treatment of the "Little People", as we affectionately called our Montagnards and Chinese Nungs. This he continued until he eventually bled to death, in spite of all efforts to save him.

'The first combat operation I went on in Vietnam and drew my first hostile fire was near a huge granite dome near the base of Nui Coto. My last combat operation on the MIKE Force was a battalion-size combat parachute assault, also near the base of Nui Coto, so the very last hostile fire I received on the MIKE Force was near the very dome where I had received my baptism of fire, over three years previously. Led by Captain Joe, we had entered this large, flat valley nearly twelve hours earlier on a routine patrol to locate the Vietcong. The valley was a beautiful, soft green, bordered on both sides by the darker green of hillside vegetation. The occasional cleared areas formed a patchwork of tall golden grass that swayed in the slight breeze as if swept by some invisible hand. Officially the valley was called the Dong Bo. Later, we would come to know it by our own name: Death Valley.

'Captain Joe wasn't supposed to be on this operation. He had received orders for transfer back to "The World" for two years of postgraduate study, followed by a three-year assignment as a geography instructor at West Point. "Five years with the wife and daughters!" he had shouted, so Captain Joe wasn't supposed to be here, but he had exercised his command position for one last go.

'Other patrols in this valley had been rather uneventful; either a sporadic sniper harassed us, or there was a brief hit-and-run firefight. This time was different. We had been trading fire off and on for nearly three hours, the intensity building. In addition to several slightly wounded patients, I had two critically wounded men to treat. We were trying to keep order among our Vietnamese soldiers and get our wounded back to camp when we reached a huge clearing. We Americans vehemently advised against entering this exposed area but the Vietnamese soldiers, on the verge of panic, pushed out toward the centre of the field, trying to escape the loud cracks and snapping thuds of the increasing gunfire.

'The clearing was the most direct route out of the valley and to safety, but it was completely bare and flat. The only cover of any type were the occasional large ant mounds. It was a deceiving cover, though, since the Vietcong forces were infiltrating around us through the tree line. "My God," I thought, "we're going to be surrounded." The cry "Medic!" came more often now. When anyone attempted to rise off his stomach and rush forward, the tree lines to our right, behind us and to our left erupted with heavy volumes of gunfire.

'During all this action I would catch glimpses of Captain Joe. His camouflaged flop hat shielded his eyes and the radio handpiece held tight to his ear as he called base camp for help. The next moment he would be gone from sight, lying flat on his stomach as another hail of fire swept the area. Then he was back up to his knees again, surveying the scene, shouting orders, trying to pull off a miracle. "Stay down flat!" he shouted to me. Now there were five of us, hugging one large ant mound. A Vietnamese sergeant on one side of me, and our interpreter on the other, had just received grazing gunshot wounds to the head. "Medic!" Captain Joe shouted. "I don't make house calls," I said.

'Then the round you never hear hits its mark. "I blew it," muttered Captain Joe as he slumped forward, his flop hat turning crimson red above both temples. I crawled over and began to treat him. They say I dragged him for some time, reaching the safety of the tree line at dark. I don't know. They say God doesn't listen to prayers of dying men. I don't know about that either. I do know that Captain Joe wasn't supposed to be there.'

Wars are a great catalyst for Special Forces, and dozens of SF units were created during the Vietnam War, each filling a niche in the US–ARVN order-of-battle, each an attempt to stamp on some element of the Vietcong or the NVA. Among these were the Kit Carson Scouts – North Vietnamese soldiers who, for pay or from conviction, had fled to the South and enlisted in the ARVN forces. There was the Lac Luong Dac Beit or LLDB, the Vietnamese Special Forces, and then there was the Apache Force, a unit composed of SF and CIDG irregulars tasked with training American units before they were fully committed to the battlefield, but frequently joining these battalions on their first missions.

The Eagle Scouts were another recce unit, attached to combat units for patrolling use before the LRRP units were formed by the newly arrived conventional divisions. There were other, more clandestine outfits, like Phoenix, which became involved in assassinations, and units sponsored or supported by the CIA, which was funding the 'other war' in Laos. There was even a programme called the Fighting Fathers, a group of militantly anti-Communist Catholic priests who were trained by the Green Berets and led their parishioners on patrols against the Vietcong.

The MIKE Forces and other CIDG offshoots were fully operational by 1964 and tasked with operations in Vietcong safe havens, or with attempting to cut the routes by which the Vietcong went to and from North Vietnam. By October 1964 the 5th Special Forces Group in Vietnam had expanded to over 1,200 men, located in some eighty CIDG camps and villages dotted about the rural areas, usually in areas dominated, at least after dark, by the Vietcong. This force controlled, at its peak, some 42,000 CIDG and PF (Popular Force) personnel, as well as 'advising' the LLDB, which, in theory anyway, were in charge of the CIDG companies.

Apart from the Green Berets, the US Navy SEALs were also active in South Vietnam at this time, partly engaged in beach recon, partly carrying out patrol and intelligence-gathering work in the swamps and creeks of the Mekong Delta around Saigon. SEAL Team One was despatched to Saigon in March 1962 and two members were detached to spend six months instructing Vietnamese Commandos in maritime operations. This was basically a frogman course, and sixty-two Vietnamese frogmen were trained and graduated by October of that year.

In 1963 an old war-horse returned to the scene when the troop-carrying submarine, the USS *Perch*, of Korean War fame, was reactivated and made ready for SEAL operations off Vietnam; and in April 1964 a new establishment, the Military Assistance Command, Vietnam – Studies and Observations Group, or MACV–SOG, took over responsibility for all clandestine operations, naval or military, in South Vietnam. SOG was a Joint Command organization covering Army, Air Force, Navy and Marine Corps operations, and was of some size; the HQ staff alone totalled some 2,000 personnel, deployed in three HQ sites in the I and II Corps areas. The SEALs arrived officially in Vietnam as part of the SOG team and reached a peak in 1968, when about 100 SEALs were deployed in the swamps and river deltas of South Vietnam or in raids along the coast of the North.

Most of them were attached to Force 116, a unit tasked with river patrols in the Mekong Delta area. SEAL missions had little to do with 'hearts and minds'; their task was to interdict all waterway supply routes from North Vietnam and Cambodia, by ambush, patrols, sabotage – the laying of mines – and raids on Vietcong bases. This work was not only dangerous – forty-three SEALs were killed in action –

but highly unpleasant, since the swamps were alive with leeches, mosquitoes and rats. The SEAL teams' normal operating areas were deep mud and tidal mangrove thickets in which they lived and operated, often for weeks at a time.

The SEAL teams were equipped with fast, Norwegian-built patrol craft known as 'Nasty' boats, used for coastal patrols and raiding work against Vietcong groups operating in the Mekong Delta. Most of this work, including raids on the North Vietnam coast, were made by Vietnamese Special Force troops, as the US SEALs were still supposed to be serving in an advisory capacity, but there is little doubt that SEAL personnel went along on these operations. Direct SEAL participation began in 1965, after the escalation of the war caused by the 'Gulf of Tonkin Incident'.

The build-up of US conventional forces was already under way by early 1965, when the command and control of CIDG forces passed from the ARVN to the direct control of the MACV under a process called Operation Switchback. MACV charged the CIDG forces and their SF advisers with contact patrols and above all with the collection of intelligence on Vietcong camps and strengths.

Training the Montagnards to do this work went on as the Switchback procedure continued and worked in step with another programme called Leaping Lena, which trained Vietnamese Special Force units and CIDG people in the techniques of long-range recon, a programme that evolved into Project Delta, which, in its final form, consisted of Recon Teams, charged with intelligence gathering on long-range patrols of up to two weeks or more, deep into Vietcong or NVA-held areas, backed by a Reaction Force which could rescue the Recon Team if it got into trouble or could be flown in by helicopter to back up the Recon element in attacking some likely target. The word 'Project' is confusing; basic-ally Project Delta was a small-sized Commando force, mustering at full strength some 600 men.

It will be seen from all this that for the first few years of the US involvement in Vietnam the Special Forces were largely engaged in forming and training the Vietnamese CIDG units. All that changed in 1965 when the main US build-up of conventional forces began, a move triggered by the Gulf of Tonkin Incident.

The background to the Gulf of Tonkin Incident is as follows. By mid-July 1965 the war in South Vietnam was not going well for the government and its American backers. The ARVN were showing no enthusiasm for the fight and although the US was continuing to supply arms and advisers the war was going to be lost and another country fall to the Communists unless something was done to increase the fighting power of the South Vietnamese forces. The President of the United States, Lyndon B. Johnson, wanted to commit US regular ground forces in large numbers, but the US Congress would not support either a declaration of war on North Vietnam or an open deployment of large numbers of American troops. A way had to be found round this snag and in August 1964 the North Vietnamese provided one.

The US destroyer *Maddox* was deployed in the Gulf of Tonkin, in international waters off the coast of North Vietnam, listening to radio signals between Hanoi and Vietcong units in the south. On 2 August 1964, the USS *Maddox* encountered a fleet of North Vietnamese junks and, fearing that they might be armed and attack his ship, the Captain, John J. Herrick, sounded 'General Quarters' and sent a signal for assistance to the US 7th Fleet. In the event, nothing happened that night, but on the following day, when the USS *Maddox* was just ten miles off the Red River delta, three North Vietnamese torpedo boats appeared and proceeded to chase the USS *Maddox* out to sea. The *Maddox* opened fire on her pursuers, and her call for assistance produced aircraft from the US carrier *Ticonderoga*, which attacked the North Vietnamese craft with cannon fire. In a twenty-minute skirmish, just one bullet struck the *Maddox*, and two North Vietnamese boats were sunk. This small, unimportant and unnecessary skirmish was all it took to expand the Vietnam War.

The US government chose to make much of the Tonkin Gulf Incident and sent more ships to the area. The *Maddox* closed the North Vietnam coast again and was allegedly subjected to a torpedo attack, though again without result. This last attack could not be verified – and may never have happened – but the US decided to retaliate against this 'aggression' and sent in bombers to attack the North Vietnam harbour at Haiphong, sinking more than twenty ships and setting the harbour oil tanks ablaze. US aircraft flew sixty-four missions against the North Vietnamese before they drew off, losing two aircraft to ground fire. One pilot who survived, Navy Lieutenant Everett Alvarez Jr, had the dubious honour of being the first US airman to be captured in North Vietnam and he spent the next eight years in a North Vietnamese prison.

Subsequent investigation tends to confirm that there was no second attack on the USS *Maddox*, but the incident was blown up by the military and the media and proved a godsend to the US administration. The North Vietnamese could be presented as aggressors, attacking US ships on the high seas, and a resolution was sent to Congress, proposing that the President be authorized to take 'all necessary measures to

prevent further aggression'. President Johnson said later that this resolution was 'like grandma's night-shirt . . . it covered everything'. More
to the point, it enabled him to escalate the war.

Like the original participation, the new escalation began slowly.
From August 1964, the South Vietnamese were encouraged to mount
Commando raids on the North Vietnam coast, and used US ships to get
there. The North Vietnamese were not cowed by the August bombing or
US warnings, and their participation in the Vietcong campaign
increased. In December 1964 the Vietcong swarmed into the village of
Binh Gia, a hamlet close to Saigon, and held it for eight hours before
fading away into the jungle. Five days later, when ARVN Rangers
supported by tanks came up to Binh Gia a major battle erupted after a
big Vietcong ambush, which ended with no fewer than seven ARVN
battalions being cut to pieces by the Vietcong; in this engagement five
US advisers were killed. On Christmas Eve 1964, a bomb in Brinks
Hotel in Saigon killed two US officers and badly injured fifty-eight
others – and so it went on, with the Vietcong – 'Charlie' to the US
soldiers (after 'Victor Charlie', the phonetic alphabet for VC) – striking
where and when they wished.

In February 1965, with no improvement in the military situation,
the US commenced bombing the North, and in March 1965 a Marine
Expeditionary Force came ashore, landing on beaches near Da Nang.
The first troops to land, and be greeted by charming Vietnamese girls
carrying necklaces of flowers, came from the 3rd Marine Regiment, 3rd
Marine Division, though the beach had been recce'd by a group of
frogmen from UDT 12, a SEAL unit. These first Marines were charged,
or so it was said, with the simple task of protecting of the Da Nang
airbase which was then under construction. Charles H. Owens, that
veteran Marine NCO, arrived a year later to fight in his third big war,
and by then all had changed: 'In 1962 I retired from the Marine Corps
after twenty years' service, but in 1966 the Corps asked me to return
to active duty for two years because of the Corps' involvement in the
Vietnam War . . . in the end I did two and a half more years.

'I was sent to join the 3rd Marine Division in Vietnam. We flew out
via Okinawa and then by commercial airline to Vietnam, which did
not give us time to acclimatize to the heat and humidity before we
arrived in Da Nang. By then it was big, and it gave us a false first
impression of Vietnam. Near the landing field the Air Force were living
in air-conditioned barracks and the food was good. Both food and living
conditions were to change as we moved north to join our units in the
3rd Marine Division at Phu Bai, near the city of Hue and then on to

Dong Ha. Anywhere north of Dong Ha you could get killed fast...'

From the moment the USMC landed at Da Nang the Vietnam War changed from a counter-insurgency conflict to an all-out war, using all the weaponry and technology in the US military's gift. The number of troops committed to the war in Vietnam rose inexorably, to top half a million in the end, but these troops were often one-year draftees and not all were ready to fight this war.

Even the SOF forces were forced to realize that the nature of this war was different to the war they had trained for, that the NVA and the Vietcong were not about to fight a 'conventional' war, that this war had no 'front', no 'safe areas' and no reliable shape. The Vietcong were everywhere and nowhere, and the NVA were coming south to back them up. If the Communists were to be beaten in Vietnam, the US Army would have to find new ways to do it and the answer, or part of the answer, was found in the hard years after 1965 in two new fighting units, the LRRPs and Force Recon.

Huey VH-1H helicopter

CHAPTER TEN

LRRPs, SEALs and Force Recon, Vietnam 1965–1973

No training, in any amount, could have prepared us for the actual trials and tribulations of combat; combat is its own finishing school. But we learned, slowly but surely.

Gary Linderer, L Company, Rangers, Vietnam,
1969

The war in Vietnam put extraordinary strain on all the units involved, but especially on the US Army's 'conventional' units, which began to arrive in quantity from 1965. These units – and their commanders – had been trained to act and think in terms of large-scale conventional warfare, against equally large and equally conventional Warsaw Pact and Chinese forces. The fighting they knew, understood and were good at was the kind of fighting they had faced in Europe during the Second World War and in Korea, where there was a definite front line, where tanks and artillery could be deployed in large numbers and where America's overwhelming firepower and hardware could be used with telling effect.

Unfortunately, the war in Vietnam was not like that at all. This was a guerrilla war, an irregular war, mainly fought by infantry, in mountainous, jungle or swampy terrain, places where tanks and trucks were useless – and reliance on the helicopter total – a war conducted among a peasant population who suffered mightily in the conflict. All these factors created problems. In addition most of the US soldiers serving in Vietnam were draftees, sent to Vietnam for a one-year tour, young men with no wish to soldier at all and who counted off the days 'in-country', until they could return to 'The World'. They had received three or four months' recruit training, but were in no way prepared or trained for a guerrilla war in the jungle.

No one is to blame for this lack of preparation; there simply was not enough time to put these draftees through further training and still deploy them in the field before their time was up. Nevertheless, this gave the enemy a great advantage. The North Vietnamese and Vietcong fighters were veterans, fighting in terrain they knew well, and with methods they had perfected against the French. This was a war in which the enemy could be anywhere and was usually where he was least expected. The great demand, therefore, was to know where the enemy was and how he might be fought. That called for first-class intelligence and that meant reconnaissance (or recon), but the US divisions which flooded into Vietnam from 1965 had very little recon capacity.

The conventional divisions and their regimental components had very little training in reconnaissance work and initially saw little need for it. Their commanders, from General William C. Westmoreland down, believed that if there were sufficient American troops on the ground to swamp the Vietcong, then the enemy could be brought to battle and destroyed by a series of vast regional sweeps, known as 'search and destroy' missions.

From 1965 the US military therefore divided the task of fighting the Vietcong and NVA into two parts. The US Army would carry out search-and-destroy missions of battalion or brigade size or larger, to find and pin down the enemy forces and bring on a battle in which the Vietcong–NVA would be destroyed. This is a classic US military doctrine, dating back to General Grant and his strategy following the Wilderness battles in the US Civil War, but the essence of this doctrine requires that the enemy is willing to stand and fight or be manoeuvred into a position where he is forced to do so.

While the US Army was thus engaged, the task of protecting the rural Vietnamese population would be left to the ARVN. As for the US Special Forces, they could now leave the CIDG programme to ARVN Special Force control and start interdicting the Vietcong supply lines, providing intelligence and carrying out raids, the sort of tasks they were trained for. This division of responsibilities seemed sensible, the plan was implemented, and there was only one snag: it didn't work.

The Vietcong and the NVA continued to fight when and where they chose and kept the initiative while the American infantry scoured the countryside and inflicted yet more distress on the hapless Vietnamese peasants. When the NVA or the Vietcong elected to fight it was on ground of their choosing, and while they took terrible losses, especially from aerial interdiction, bombing, strafing and napalm, they were willing to do this, knowing that the smaller casualties inflicted on the US forces would have a growing effect in the USA. The North Vietnamese were playing the long game and they made no secret of it. 'If the war lasts twenty years, so be it,' said Ho Chi Minh, 'and if we lose twenty soldiers for every American who dies, we will accept that … but I do not think the Americans will.'

It was soon apparent that footslogging alone would not contain the Vietcong and NVA. But the Americans had another weapon, the helicopter, which, it was believed, should give them the vital assets of mobility and quick reaction. The helicopter provided the US military with the means to rush reinforcements to any threatened group or area and pin the enemy down until air power, artillery and more US troops could be brought up to finish them off. Helicopters had come a long way since the Royal Marines had first flown ashore in them at Port Said in 1956, and the Americans were to deploy thousands of them in Vietnam. The Vietcong soon got the measure of the helicopter and began to shoot them down in large numbers, ambushing likely LZs and luring the helicopters into range of their heavy machine-guns. The Bell Huey helicopter became the symbol, the icon, of the Vietnam War but in the end, as in all guerrilla wars, it came down to the man on the ground, the infantryman, who could find the Vietcong cadres and beat them on their own ground.

As described in the previous chapter, the main activity of Green Beret units in 1961–5 was the creation of CIDG companies and the recovery of Vietcong-dominated areas from Communist control. As this task continued and succeeded, the CIDG companies were gradually taken over by the ARVN, and most CIDG companies were eventually transferred to the ARVN Rangers. The ARVN – with a vast amount of US financial and military input – built up a large SF and Ranger capability of varying effectiveness, but the war was still being lost. Hence the commitment of US forces, a commitment which continued with ever more troops being fed in, without a significant improvement in the military situation. This result had been foreseen by President Kennedy in 1961 when he rejected the first suggestion of a full-scale US troop commitment in Vietnam: 'The troops will march in, the bands will play, the crowds will cheer ... and in four days everyone will have forgotten. Then we will be told we have to send in still more troops. It is like taking a drink. The effect soon wears off and you have to take another.'

It was soon apparent that more troops alone was not the answer to the tactical problems the military faced in Vietnam. To make any sort of impact on the military situation it was necessary to find the right troops and the right tactics. Since the US could not invade the North and finish the war there, at least not without the grave risk of provoking a third world war, the only way to achieve victory was to cripple the Vietcong and NVA in the field by killing their men in quantity, until it was clear – even to Ho Chi Minh and General Giap – that they could not win; perhaps then Ho Chi Minh would come to the conference table and talk peace.

Vietnam was not a 'conventional' war, and the fact that it involved ships, aircraft of all types, tanks, artillery and the full range of modern weapons should not conceal that fact. The Vietcong and increasingly the NVA, which crossed the DMZ in ever-larger numbers from 1965, chose when and where to fight, and when they fought they were very good at it. They fought hard, they killed a lot of American soldiers and when the battle was turning against them they broke off the fight and disappeared. They also managed to limit the effects of US airpower by doing much of their fighting at night, with the result that 'The night belongs to Charlie' became an accepted convention among US forces in Vietnam.

The Communists also enjoyed the advantages of good intelligence, supplied by villagers, bar girls – and the Western media. And the Vietcong or NVA usually took the initiative in mounting attacks. If the war was to be won, or the North Vietnamese brought to the conference table, all that had to change, and the first step towards that change was an improvement in contact intelligence and recon. By the end of the war fifteen full-strength US divisions had fought in Vietnam and not one of them had arrived with a recon element. This shortage created an urgent need for recon patrols in the front-line battalions which the LRRP (Long-Range Recon Patrol) units were created to fill. LRRPs were small patrols of skilled soldiers tasked to scout well ahead of their units, deep into Vietcong- or NVA-held territory, locate the enemy and provide their regimental and battalion commanders with contact information. It was not a task for the unskilled or the faint-hearted.

In an ideal world this information might have been provided by the

CIDG units or by Vietnamese SF soldiers attached to US battalions, as the Iban and Dyak trackers aided the British battalions fighting in Malaya and in Borneo. This indeed happened, on a small scale, with the attachment of CIDG companies to American units in 1964–5 in the Leaping Lena programme, but the integration of US and Vietnamese abilities did not happen to any useful degree. It may be that the sheer scale and violence of the Vietnam struggle was against such integration, but the most likely cause is that the US military – often with good reason – had no faith in Vietnamese abilities, were reluctant to trust them with the vital recon and scouting role and failed to understand the use to which CIDG units could be put if properly handled. They elected to raise their own recon units and the chief result of that decision was to create two of the hardest-fighting Special Force formations of the Vietnam War: the Army LRRPs, or 'Lurps', and, for the USMC divisions, Force Recon.

The LRRPs were Ranger-style formations and most Lurps became Rangers as the war ended. Ranger training had continued in the US Army in the years after the Korean War and a Ranger Course had been set up at Fort Benning, where the old Ranger skills – map and compass work, night patrolling, marksmanship, small-unit actions, amphibious, mountain and jungle training, plus a great deal of physical and endurance activity – were forced into volunteers during a gruelling eight-week course. The Ranger patch became a valued addition to any uniform, and any officer worth his salt and with an eye on promotion wanted the successful completion of the Ranger Course marked on his records.

As a result, knowledge of Ranger tactics and techniques was widespread in the units that went to Vietnam, but no actual Ranger units existed. Therefore, through sheer necessity, the front-line units created the Lurps. The task of the LRRPs was partly to gather intelligence and partly to carry out raids and ambushes, but mainly to sniff out the ground for future operations by their parent unit. In this they differed from the usual patrols sent out by all US and ARVN units, for the conventional infantry patrol stayed within range of artillery support or did not stray far from a firebase. The LRRPs and Force Recon patrols were very much out on their own, and relied for relief or assistance on airpower or the ubiquitous helicopter, which they used for the insertion or extraction of their patrols.

There was no central command structure for the LRRPs but a standard SAS-style team formation soon evolved at local level, and some units, like the 1st Cavalry Division, raised LRRP companies soon after they arrived in Vietnam in 1965. LRRP Companies were attached to divisions for patrol and intelligence-gathering purposes – in military jargon they were 'Divisional Troops' – and the basic LRRP patrol was a six-man team, led by a team leader who would usually be a junior officer or senior NCO, each patrol containing a range of specialists, including snipers and radio men, and a Montagnard scout.

The Green Berets, which might have supplied long-range recon, were fully employed with the CIDG programme and coping with an increasing number of attacks on their jungle bases and MIKE Force camps, but the first recognizable LRRP unit – though not so designated – was an SF unit, Detachment B-52 Project Delta, raised in May 1964 by the direct order of General Westmoreland, the US Commander in Vietnam, and commanded by a Special Forces officer, Major Charlie Beckwith.

Beckwith had spent a year with the British SAS, even managing to serve with them in Malaya at the end of the Emergency, and had returned to the USA bursting with enthusiasm for the SAS concept and determined to create an American unit on SAS lines. Beckwith found Project Delta in some disarray when he arrived at the end of 1964, so he sacked a number of people and started again, organizing the unit into twelve teams, made up from about 100 SF soldiers and over a thousand Vietnamese personnel. Another Delta innovation were the 'Road-runner' teams, which had the particular task of finding and ambushing Vietcong and NVA supply trails. Beckwith also led Delta to help defend the SF camp at Plei Me when that was attacked by a large Vietcong force and commanded several long-range patrol missions, before he was hit by machine-gun fire and seriously wounded. He was evacuated to the USA where he spent months in hospital. His wounding put a stop to any immediate development of the SAS concept in the US Army, but a start had been made and we shall hear of Beckwith again. The next unit, Project Omega, was similar to Delta, as was Project Gamma; all these 'Projects' were battalion-sized units, of 600 to 1,000 men, a mixture of US and Vietnamese personnel, tasked with long-range patrolling.

Australian Special Forces also served in Vietnam, among them Captain Mike Wells of the then 1st Royal New South Wales Regiment (Commando), who arrived in Vietnam in May 1966 and went to Baria, Phuoc Tuy province, as an Operations Adviser: 'In November 1966 we put in a couple of quick operations inside a couple of weeks and got ourselves a good band of Vietcong. I went out on every operation and had a few close calls and I got quite adept at leaving my jeep rather quickly. The first one covered two days and I managed to con twenty-eight APC [armoured personnel carriers] from Task Force to work with us, as the mobility we gained from using them enabled us to cover a much wider area with plenty of firepower on hand. The first day we struck nothing so I suggested a change to just east of Long Tan and I had the FAC [Forward Air Controller] up, guiding the APC along the tracks. He spotted three Vietcong dodging into the bush so we dismounted the infantry and went in after them; we got that three plus another nine. After kicking the shit out of them one of the women led us to a base camp where we struck a few more, killing two and wounding one who escaped, so all told we killed two and captured fifteen. We then came back through Dat Do, south of Long Phuoc, where we rounded up another nine Vietcong and killed another. This was a rough bunch; even when we had them cold they kept punching with the ARVN soldiers.

'On the following Monday about 0220 hours a battalion of Vietcong hit a few of our outposts. At one stage the District Compound and six of our other outposts were being mortared. One of the outposts at Phuoc Hai was completely overrun. They had mortared and fired 57mm at it and then blown the wire and slung grenades around; out of twenty-five in the outpost only three got out without a scratch, sixteen were killed and six wounded. They certainly made a mess of the place, though from the blood trails and the guts and clothing we found I think the garrison hurt the Vietcong a fair bit too. We put in a lot of air and naval gunfire from a destroyer offshore and we must have killed quite a lot but as usual when we went in there were no bodies around – plenty of blood trails but no bodies, which was frustrating. If we could have seen some results it would have helped the Vietnamese morale. There is one thing for sure – everyone in that area knew what the green beret is and I feel sure for many reasons they were wary of it.'

The one exception to the conventional situation, where divisions arrived in-country without a recon capacity, was the US 173rd Airborne Brigade, which arrived in Vietnam in May 1965 but had started to prepare for jungle and irregular warfare while still based in Okinawa. The Commander of the 173rd, Major General Ellis Williamson, later said: 'We had only been in-country a few days when it became clear that small units could get out and bring back information far better than large search-and-destroy missions at battalion strength or above. We had already trained our men for small-unit operations, in strengths ranging from three men to a full company, sending them into the jungle on patrols lasting from a few days to a full month, supplying them in the field by parachute drop or helicopter.'

The 173rd formed small patrol units, called Delta Teams, five for each battalion, and these teams were soon at work, recce-ing areas of operation before the full Brigade moved in. The next Airborne unit to arrive, the 1st Brigade, 101st Airborne Division, followed a similar path, swiftly creating LRRP-style units, known in the Brigade as Hatchet Teams.

The 173rd Airborne Brigade, 'The Herd,' was the first US Army combat unit to be deployed in Vietnam, entering the field in May 1965 and taking under command a battalion of the Royal Australian Regiment and a battery of Royal New Zealand Artillery. The 173rd were also one of the few units to make a combat parachute jump in Vietnam, during Operation Junction City in 1967, and put up a tremendous fight against the NVA at the battle of Dak To in the same year. However, the combat effectiveness of this Brigade largely lay in the fact that the officers in command had anticipated the need for long-range recce before arriving 'in-country', and other units earmarked for Vietnam swiftly followed their example.

There is nothing remarkable in this need for deep reconnaissance; without some knowledge of what was going on out there, beyond the jungle tree line, the US units would be reduced to blundering around in the bush, hoping to stumble on the enemy, and losing both surprise and initiative, two vital ingredients in any military campaign. The only extraordinary thing is that after nearly five years' experience in Vietnam the US Army had not anticipated such a need when conventional forces were first committed. Fortunately, the units arriving realized the need and acted swiftly to deal with it, creating *ad hoc* intelligence-gathering and recce units – the LRRPs – that had no place in the standard US Division order-of-battle. General Westmoreland, the US Commander in Vietnam, sent the commanders of newly arrived units to the 173rd Brigade, to study the setting up of LRRP units and their employment in the field. Westmoreland also issued an order formally authorizing the formation of LRRP units in July 1966, and it is from that time that the LRRP story officially begins.

At the same time an official definition of LRRP units was added to the files: 'A Long-Range Patrol is a specially trained unit, organized and equipped for information gathering, and responsive to the requirements of the tactical commander. The LRP (or LRRP) units consist of specially trained personnel, capable of reconnaissance, surveillance and target acquisition within the despatching unit's area of interest.' Put simply, an LRRP unit went out deep into Vietcong-dominated territory, to find the enemy, report back on his numbers, position, direction of travel and possible intention, attack him if the situation was favourable and, if not, call in larger forces, including air strikes, to deal with him. This called for special men and special training, so a school, the Recondo School, was set up at Nha Trang in September 1965, where suitable candidates, US and Vietnamese, could be sent to learn the elements of recce – or, in US parlance, recon – tactics and to develop skills in small-unit activity. Graduates from the Recondo School were soon acting as instructors in the newly arrived units.

In April 1966 these US teams were joined by an Australian unit, the Australian SAS Squadron, and a forty-man team from the New Zealand SAS, which carried out similar recon tasks within the Australian Task Force area, where some 9,000 ANZAC troops were deployed by 1968. According to a report published in 1975 by the US Department of the Army:

The Australians and New Zealanders were popular with the Vietnamese people, and respected for their discipline and fine soldiering qualities. One reason for the success of the Australians in Vietnam was their experience in fighting guerrilla wars in Malay and Borneo and the fact that the small Australian and New Zealand armies had trained exclusively for the one kind of war they were likely to face – guerrilla war in the swamps and jungles of South-East Asia ... and furthermore this was an army composed entirely of volunteers.

By 1967 every US battalion had – or should have had – a LRRP platoon, and as these units spread throughout the Army so the number of their tasks increased. The Green Berets were also active, and this account, from James E. Butler, describes a behind-the-lines action in Laos typical of the combat experienced by many SF, LRRP and Force Recon units in South-East Asia: 'When the time came for me to join the service I opted for the infantry and volunteered for Airborne training, Ranger School (which I loved) and Special Forces training. I hated mass tactical jumps and large troop activities, I wanted to be in small, elite units. I was assigned to MACV-SOG from 1968 to 1971. I later returned to Vietnam on a classified mission in June of 1972 and left in November 1973. I then went to Special Ops Europe, where I was assigned to work with the British SAS.

'On 16 January 1971, Recce Team Python (I was Python) was inserted into Laos to ascertain whether an upcoming Laotian Incursion called

Lam Son 719 was compromised or not. We spent five days on the ground, dodging large enemy troop concentrations that seemed to be pulling back in a north-eastern direction. I was directed to try to pick up a POW. We were successful in getting an NVA sergeant, who I was later told confirmed that the massive attack into Laos had been compromised almost two weeks earlier. Unfortunately, on the extraction from Laos, I was wounded in the back of the head. (I would later receive my second Silver Star and third Purple Heart for this action.)

'After emergency medical treatment in Phu Bai's hospital, which was a story unto itself as my heavily armed indigenous Commandos refused to leave the operating room while the doctors and nurses were trying to work on me, I returned to duty. The indigenous Commandos that were on my team were different nationalities. They were Thai, Chinese, Laotian and Vietnamese. RT Python was the only ethnically integrated team at CCN. We had spent almost two years together and their presence in that hospital really scared the doctors and nurses.

'I was airlifted to Da Nang and debriefed by my headquarters at CCN. Due to the headaches I was having, my Commanding Officer decided that I should be sent to a larger hospital for other tests. I went to Camp Kue Hospital on Okinawa and my head was opened up again, cleaned of more shrapnel, and sewn back up. Before they could Medivac me back to the United States, I went down to the Marine Airbase at Futima and bullshitted myself a ride back to Da Nang. I wasn't ready to go home yet. Also, I still had thirty-eight stitches in my head. I reported into CCN Recon and was immediately operational, stitches and all.

'In early February 1971 the stage was set for a similar-type flanking move on Khe Sahn, the staging area for Lam Son 719, which was the invasion of Laos. But this time there was no Lang Vei Special Forces Camp to act as a buffer. Hence six small, six-man SOG recon teams would be inserted into the hills high above the AN Shau Valley. We had very sophisticated equipment including secure radios and specialized transponders to direct the entire 7th/13th Air Force in interdiction should the North Vietnamese try to attack the base camp at Khe Sahn from the rear. My team and RT Intruder, commanded by Captain Ron (Doc) Watson were the first two teams to be inserted.

'Doc's team went in first on the valley floor and was attempting to walk up to the heights that they would direct their ops from. The equipment that he carried was the normal equipment that a team would carry for a seven-day reconnaissance mission. My concept for this mission was quite a bit different than Doc's. I saw a static road-watch mission as a King of the Mountain mission. The nature of the mission took away our two greatest advantages, stealth and mobility. (These were the first and only static roadwatches that CCN ever participated in.) I wasn't walking anywhere and I arranged to have tons of equipment delivered to my position via additional choppers as soon as we secured our perimeter. Some of this equipment included four M60 machine-guns with 20,000 rounds of ammunition; fifty mines; twenty LAW rockets; a 60mm mortar and fifty rounds; over 200 rounds for the three M79 grenade launchers; 20 pounds of demolitions; powdered CS gas; over 100 M14 toe-poppers or small mines; sandbags; and a 292 radio antenna in order to remain in contact with Intruder and the other teams that were going to be inserted to the north of our positions over the next few days as well as the 7th/13th Air Force; this equipment was not common to a reconnaissance team. I prepared for the worst because this mission had all the earmarks of being my last stand.

'The approach to our LZ was "hot" (the choppers took fire) and that was just the beginning of our problems. The helicopters that took us in would not land because their maps showed that where we were getting out at was an old abandoned minefield. I knew that I had the only equipment which could link all the teams together and that there was already a team deployed, so we had to get down. I took an educated guess and jumped the 15 feet from the helicopter to the ground with all my equipment on and ran around in front of the helicopters, jumping up and down to show them that it was not mined. (I later described this as a Marine Corps Mine-Sweeping Technique.) The choppers landed and left and we began to set up our gear. We cleared the area of two NVA snipers/watchers and received our resupply helicopters, placed the additional equipment and began to dig in. Within forty-five minutes we monitored RT Intruder ambushing a large element of NVA and were able to direct Air assets to their position. This was the beginning of the nightmare.

'Due to the compromising of Intruder and the fact that they had not reached their primary base area, it was decided that they would be extracted and flown back to Phu Bai and reinserted the following morning. I monitored all of this and recommended that due to deteriorating weather conditions they be brought to my position. It was only a ten-minute ride, it would strengthen my position and, as I said, we were already under fire, so Doc and I jointly could co-ordinate the activities of the other teams. My recommendation was disregarded. Intruder would be extracted and taken all the way back to Phu Bai, a three-hour round-trip. The next problem was that when the choppers got to Intruder, the team was too high and all of the team members couldn't be extracted on "strings" in the first lift. (One of the methods that we had for getting out of heavily forested areas was via the use of "strings". Strings were 120-foot ropes attached to the floors of the helicopters via D rings and would be thrown down to the teams who would snap the ends of the strings into stabo rigs (like parachute harnesses) attached to our bodies. The strings would have a 30 per cent stretch factor depending on the weight of the individual at the end. The team members would remain suspended under the chopper until the choppers set down. It was not unusual for team members to be shot during extraction while hanging below the chopper.)

'Again my request was denied. Three members of Intruder would remain at the site of the ambush and wait for extraction at last light. Needless to say the last-light extraction was a disaster, the team members Lloyd, Watson and Hernandez were on the radio with me as they hung on 120-foot extraction strings below the chopper when the chopper fell out of the sky. Counting the aircraft crew, there were now eight down Americans and no hope of reaching them until the next morning. We had no idea as to whether they were living or dead.

'I set up a radio watch and co-ordinated the search effort to begin at first light next morning. As night fell, we also started observing large units of enemy troops moving up the valley floor on both sides of our position. (They were approximately 2,500 feet below us.) I immediately called Moonbeam and requested air support. They rounded up some Stinger gunships (C119s) but they aborted the mission when they realized that we were in Laos. Moonbeam scrambled up a Specter (AC130). This was the first time that Specter was used in a close-support role for troops in contact. Specter had four 20mm Vulcan cannons, two 40mm Balfour cannons and a side-mounted 105mm how-itzer. It was primarily used for truck and tank killing. I directed Specter's guns into orbit above the unsuspecting NVA. Believe me when I tell you that we turned out every light in the valley. The carnage was unbelievable. We could hear the screaming from the NVA troops for hours after Specter left station.

'At first light, RT Habu with Chuck Danzer, Cliff Newman and Jimmy Horton inserted on RT Intruder's LZ and started to follow the team's direction of march. They had an OV10 Bronco (Covey) over them for communications and directions. They reached the crash site at approximately 1.00 p.m. and began to collect the bodies. Unbelievably, Sammy Hernandez survived, due to his rope breaking when the heli-copter fell out of the sky. It was his survival radio that I had monitored the night before. He was recovered at RT Intruder's primary LZ.

'We were still under sporadic fire and heard metal hammering off to our south. We had three slightly wounded at this time. When I reported this, I was told that they would extract us later in the afternoon. I said no and gave them the same reason as before, they told me that they didn't need me because of the RT Covey team. At 4.00 p.m. Cliff Newman relayed to me that Covey had gone down. I relayed this immediately to Phu Bai and Captain Freddie "Lightning" Wunderlich and RT Moccasin was immediately sent to brightlite the Covey crew. The pilot was dead, as was José Fernandez, one of ours, the back seater. "Lightning" relayed to me that the forests were crawling with NVA. RT Habu would have to spend the night in a very dangerous position.

'At 9.30 p.m. we received a serious probe from the south-east. Fortunately I had seen this as one of the weaknesses of our position and had placed numerous booby traps, toe-poppers and claymore mines covering this approach. The NVA got to within 50 metres of our position before they encountered our defensive devices. We never had to fire our individual weapons and hence never gave away our exact positions. The moans of the NVA wounded in this attack lasted for hours.

'At 10.30 p.m. we again noticed large elements of enemy troops moving up the valley and again contacted Moonbeam, who again sent. us a Specter aircraft. Due to the intermittent cloud cover, Specter had problems locking on to our infra-red strobes and our transponders. I decided to mark the NVA positions by firing directly down on them using M60 machine-guns firing tracers and 60mm mortars firing white phosphorus rounds. These rounds acted as marking rounds for the Specter aircraft and once it got on station the carnage to the NVA troops was unbelievable.

'At 12.30 a.m. we began to take fire from at least two crew-served weapons, best guess was that it was a 90mm recoilless rifle. The fragmentation of these rounds hit our radio antenna and shredded the small US flag that I had put on it. A second Specter was able to lock on the weapons and fire directly into their positions. As all of this was going on a large enemy force was again attacking our positions. The fighting was close. I had the Specter who killed the guns firing within 50 yards of our position (we used infra-red strobes and laser transponders to mark our positions). I had them walk the rounds to within 10 yards of our position. The fighting was hand-to-hand at times as we tried to maintain our perimeter. Two more Specters joined the fray. They were hosing down the troops that the NVA were trying to slip by us while we were occupied by the attack. This went on until 3.30 a.m. and there seemed to be a lull in the action. We now had six wounded, including an American who was smashed in the face by the hot barrel of an AK47. The fighting was that close.

'I checked out the team, shored up some positions, redistributed certain weapons and ammunition, made radio checks with the outside and requested a flight of A1-Es for first light. The drone of another Specter high over our heads was a very comforting feeling. They told me that they would remain with us for the remainder of the night. At this point, I had been up and in actual combat for over forty hours. I was exhausted and took one of the issued Green Hornets (dexemil) in order to stay awake and alert. (This was the one and only time that I took it.) At 5.30 a.m. we received a minor probe from in front of my position from the east. I felt all along that this was the route that the NVA would take in attacking our positions. We repulsed them with LAW and M79 rounds.

'At 6.30 a.m., RT Habu called and said that they had spent an uneventful night and were preparing to break their night defensive position, recover the bodies of the Americans and get out of there. At 6.45 a.m., though, we received a distress call from Habu. They were being hit and hit hard. Danzer, the team leader, had his radio blown right off his back, and Cliff Newman was calling for help on his survival radio. RT Python was their only point of communication.

'At 6.50 a.m., the flight of A1-Es that I had ordered up buzzed RT Python's position. I told them what was happening to RT Habu and gave them the direction and the guard frequencies that Habu was using. They released immediately and flew to Habu's position loaded for bear. Cliff Newman expertly directed them in and literally called for rocket strikes within 10 yards of his position. (One of the indigenous Commandos was wounded by the rocket fire, it was that close.) All of this firepower was not enough, the enemy was decimating Habu. There seemed to be no way out. Danzer was fighting wounded, Jimmy Horton had his right leg practically blown off, and through it all Cliff Newman was cool as a cucumber directing the airstrikes closer and closer to his position. When all seemed lost, Cliff (6 foot 4 of muscle) grabbed Jimmy Horton, threw him over his shoulder, and directed the team to follow. He jumped off the back side of a cliff 50 feet to the jungle below. The rest of Habu followed. At this point I lost contact with RT Habu because at 7.42 a.m. Python got hit by a very large element coming up the east slope. The NVA persisted in their efforts to annihilate Python. Heedless of orbiting Allied aircraft, they launched a massive assault at

0830 in a final attempt to overrun the team's position.

'Taking heavy casualties, they still managed to fight their way uphill to the RT's entrenched position, seemingly oblivious to the overhead air armada. Using B40 rockets and automatic weapons, the NVA began to swarm over the perimeter, firing directly into the team's position. Air assets on station expended all their ordnance in an attempt to save the RT. Using miniguns, rockets, white phosphorus bombs and CBU32 clusters, they wiped out the enemy on the salient and all the NVA along the eastern perimeter. An hour later, at 1038, Python – still under heavy enemy fire – consented to extraction. They had been in continuous close contact with the enemy for more than seventy-two hours.

'In the after-action and debriefings which followed, RT Python was officially credited with killing forty-two NVA during this operation, as well as playing a crucial role in directing air assets which resulted in an additional estimated 350 NVA killed by air.'

As the above account indicates, apart from guts and fighting ability, LRRP patrolling often involved using sophisticated electronic equipment. Sophisticated training was therefore called for and a large number of LRRPs, if they had not previously done so, completed an Airborne course, in-country or at Fort Bragg, or attended a Ranger Course or a Jungle Course in Malaya or at the US Jungle Training School in Panama. In 1967 a National Guard (Territorial) LRRP unit was formed, Company D of the Indiana 151st Infantry. The LRRPs were also established in the Army order-of-battle with the 75th Infantry Regiment selected as their parent unit. So the LRRPs came to be part of the long and honourable tradition of the US Rangers.

The US Army was not alone in discovering a need for recon. The first large SOF unit to arrive in Vietnam was from the 3rd Division of the USMC. US Marine Ed Wyn Nicholls served two tours in Vietnam and recalls his efforts to get there: 'I quit school in January of 1955 and enlisted as a private in the United States Marine Corps. I graduated from Boot Camp in early June of 1955 after four months of training, and served my time before leaving to join the Los Angeles Police Department, where I served five years as a police officer. In 1962 I had heard on the news that a Marine Helicopter Squadron was ordered to somewhere called Vietnam. I recalled the old days in the Corps and the traditional saying, "The Marines have landed and the situation is well in hand." As time went on, I didn't recall any news that things were "well in hand" in Vietnam. It just sounded as though more Marines were landing, and that went on and on.

'I was longing to go back to where I belonged, to "The Corps," so on 17 September 1964 I rejoined the United States Marine Corps. The Marines didn't normally ask you where you wanted to go or what you wanted to do. They didn't in 1964, but I told them I wanted to go to Vietnam and fight the Vietcong. Naturally after that they sent me to Camp Pendelton and then I got a thirty-day Mess Duty at Camp Del Mar. After that ordeal, I was transferred to the Base Legal Section as a court orderly. When I arrived at the Legal Section I immediately put in for a transfer to Vietnam. As a result, I got transferred to the Marine Barracks, Whidbey Island, Washington State, as a gate guard!

'I immediately put in a transfer request for Vietnam and finally – happy as a pig in shit – I got my orders for the 'Nam. Now it is 1965 and already the people wearing round glasses and smoking them cigarettes with twisted ends, sang a lot about our guys killing babies, burning and pillaging, etc. I thought they'd grow up some day. We now know they grew up to be lawyers.

'The process of getting to a war is not simple. You just don't get there from Washington State. You go on a little leave. Then you go to Camp Pendelton's famous Staging Battalion. From there to an airport, to an airport, to another airport, then to Japan, Okinawa, Guam or Wake, or somewhere else. When you land in Okinawa they take away all your worldly possessions and put it where it is most likely to rot. Then back on a plane for Da Nang.

'On 27 June 1965, I arrived in Viet Nam "in-country" at last, in a stinking, foul-looking, steaming place called Da Nang. Dust, the smell of human excrement, graveyard death, and raggedy-ass children every-where. This certainly wasn't what I had expected. Culture shock didn't creep up on me, it zapped me with a belaying pin! When you first arrive they issue warlike things: helmets, cartridge belts, canteens, packs, suspender straps and a bunch of other garbage, plus a well-used M14 rifle. Some of these items hadn't been cleaned very well. There were stains on some of the stuff. We knew what the stains were but we didn't say much. There was still dried blood on my M14, which had seeped into the well on the butt plate.

'Everything was fast. We heard something about "The Night belongs to the 'Cong." We new guys were separated and sent to various units and I went to 3/3 [3rd Battalion, 3rd Marine Regiment], south of Chu Lai, to help protect an airfield.

'My arrival at 3/3 HQ is still a mass of confused impressions. I believe I was in shock, like major culture and physical shock. This was dispelled as I was assigned to Kilo Company of 3/3. A short skinny sweating piece of grizzle brought me to my senses. He was the ferocious "Ray Gun" Whitten, a Marine Gunnery Sergeant. Gy-Sgt Whitten was of "The Old Corps" of Marines. All the Marines were apparitions. No meat on their bones, just muscle, wire-taut muscle. Their eyes never rested. Their head and eyes darted everywhere – "with the thousand-yard stare" – looking but not seeing, and that was how I arrived in Vietnam.'

Eventually two full USMC divisions, the 1st and 3rd, served in Vietnam, along with a number of USMC brigades and these units soon recognized the need for long-range recon. The Marine Corps had experience with the Raider battalions of the Second World War and duly formed its own recce unit, now famous in USMC history as the Marine Force Reconnaissance Companies, Force Recon.

Force Recon has been described as 'an elite without an elite'. Operating like the LRRPs, in four- to six-man teams, they had the same tasks, long-range patrolling, intelligence gathering and close combat. A statistic produced after the war claims that Force Recon killed thirty-four Vietcong or NVA soldier for every Force Recon Marine killed; the Corps average was eight Vietcong for every Marine killed. The main use – and usefulness – of Force Recon lay in the edge they gave to the conventional Marine units by providing them with up-to-date and accurate contact intelligence. Ninety-five per cent of Marine–Vietcong contacts followed Force Recon information, a fact pointed out after the war by Lieutenant-General G. Davis, who had commanded the 3rd Marine Division in Vietnam: 'Our most reliable intelligence came from small four- to six-man Marine patrols. As many as forty of these patrols were kept in being in our area of operations and they provided a rapid and accurate means of checking out enemy activity. As a result we knew with some precision where the enemy was, what he was doing and, just as important, where he was not.'

The USMC had been experimenting with small-unit patrols for at least ten years before the Corps was committed to Vietnam. A Reconnaissance Platoon, of one officer and twenty-four enlisted men, most of them sergeants, was formed in 1955, all the members being volunteers, of considerable physical fitness and possessed, in the words of their first commander Colonel Rydalch, of 'initiative, self-reliance and interest in the Marine Corps'. This Recon Platoon received a vast amount of specialized training, including the Ranger course and parachute jumps at the Army Airborne School at Fort Benning, Georgia.

Two years of training and a fine performance on exercises convinced the Corps that the Recce Platoon had a place in the USMC order-of-battle and the platoon was raised to company level. A second company was raised and trained, and it was attached to the Corps at Force – or theatre – level: the First Force Recon Company went to the Pacific, the Second Force Recon Company to the Atlantic.

The Recon Companies were organized into three platoons, Parachute Recon, Amphibious Recon and Parachute Pathfinders. Their task was to provide any landing division with deep-patrol intelligence at distances up to 100 miles from the beachhead. The Force also took up beach recce, using that veteran Special Forces submarine, the USS *Perch*, already in service with the US Navy SEALs, and, like the SEALs, Force Recon Marines were soon adept at the various 'locking-in and locking-out' techniques required to leave and re-enter the submarine while it was submerged and moving.

All this was designed to complement and enhance the main purpose of the Corps, amphibious warfare, but the skills, training and experience gathered by these Recon Companies came in very useful when the Corps found itself committed to the mountain and jungle war in Vietnam. However, if this war was to be different from any other war the Marines had fought in, at least they entered the war zone in the traditional way.

The first elements of the US Marine Corps waded ashore near Da Nang on 8 March 1965, the beach and landing area having previously been checked out and cleared by a squad from Force Recon and some Navy SEALs. A further recce near Chu Lai three weeks later was less easy; the Recon team were fired on as they came ashore and when they returned the next day the team was ambushed by a Vietcong platoon dug in behind the beach. Three Recon Marines were killed before the squad could be extracted, and with those deaths the Force Recon war in Vietnam began.

Force Recon started its career in Vietnam with one great advantage and one small disadvantage. The advantage was that they had ready-formed companies, skilled in long-range patrolling and information gathering. The disadvantage was that the Marine commanders, like the Army commanders, had as yet no real grasp of the complexities of the Vietnam War, and only a sketchy idea of how to use Force Recon. In the words of Lieutenant-Colonel Roy Van Cleve, of the 3rd Recon Battalion: 'Recon was used for any mission that came up. If you had no one else to do it, whatever it was, give it to Recon. So we got some raider-type missions and we got some infantry assault-type missions.'

One little-known fact of Marine activity in Vietnam was 'hearts and minds', a task undertaken in USMC areas by the Combined Action Platoons – CAP. Steve Richmond was a Marine first-lieutenant with CAP in South Vietnam: 'When military experts gather to discuss the efficacy of different aspects of strategy and military doctrine, they often reminisce about "expert" or "elite" units that have carried out textbook operations using extraordinary tactics. But there is one hybrid group that in all probability would not figure prominently in any such conversation, and my particular fighting force may garner no mention at all.

'This unique formation of United States Marines was the antithesis of a highly trained "special" or "elite" military unit. However, it was made up of Marines, and for almost seven years they were quite probably the most consistently successful combat unit in South Vietnam. Most people, including some very knowledgeable military historians, have never heard of this outfit – the Combined Action Force.

'The concept behind Combined Action was simple; take a Marine rifle squad, mix it with a platoon of Vietnamese Popular Force soldiers (known as PFs, a local village militia), and permanently station the resulting Combined Action Platoon (CAP) in the village from whence the indigenous members of the PF were drawn. The object was to help the men of the village learn basic individual combat techniques and small-unit tactics by fighting at their side; defending "their" village and its people from the unbelievable variety of government brigands and bandits, local Viet Cong (VC) cadre, and the various VC, North Vietnamese Army (NVA), Army of the Republic of Vietnam (ARVN) who could be harsh on the local people. We lived in the hamlets; no wire, no bunkers, no trenches or fighting holes, and no signs that read "Off Limits – Do Not Enter" in Vietnamese. CAP Marines were often invited to sleep and eat, to live, in the villagers' homes. They stood guard and helped with the work of the village during the day, and every night they patrolled and set ambushes. Combined Action Platoons, and their Marines, became part of the fabric of life in villages spread from the Batangan Peninsula north to the DMZ.

'Marines assigned to command and administer the programme fought an ongoing bureaucratic battle to keep the infrastructure and operation of the Combined Action Force as simple as its tactical concept, but they were tied to the military–political mess that characterized the war in South Vietnam. Understanding the operations of the CAF and the CAPs gives a general perception of the Byzantine complexity and Machiavellian fratricide practised at all levels of the civil–military government of South Vietnam. One also might begin to understand why much of the US effort in Vietnam was useless at best. Politically the country was divided into provinces, the provinces into districts, the districts into villages and those into hamlets. Large cities like Saigon, Hue and Da Nang were separate entities.

'Located at each seat of government was a military headquarters. These were divided into four geographic Areas of Operation (AOs), each the responsibility of one of four numbered Corps (I, II, III and IV), I Corps (or "Eye Corps") being the northernmost, up by the so-called Demilitarized Zone between North and South Vietnam, then II Corps, then III, and finally IV Corps, around the Mekong Delta in the south.

'There was a US advisory staff at each military headquarters and every level of government down to the district, sometimes down to the village. These "advisers" fell into four broad and often interlocking categories (most often they were falling over each other): Regular Military, Civil Government, Military Intelligence and the "spooks" (primarily the CIA), but there were a bewildering variety of organizations, sometimes with MACV-SOG (Military Assistance Command Vietnam – Special Observation Group) thrown in. The Marines of Combined Action didn't work for any of them.

'The CAPs didn't belong to the regular Marine Corps combat effort in-country either. That effort was directed by the III Marine Amphibious Force (known as "Three MAF"). Headquartered in Da Nang, it operated almost exclusively in the northern half of I Corps, from Chu Lai to the DMZ. A Marine lieutenant-general commanded III MAF. He had the 1st and 3rd Marine Divisions, a couple of "special landing forces", the oversized 3rd Marine Air Wing, a Force Service Regiment or two and other assorted cats and dogs (Force Recon, Radio Battalion, etc.).

'He also had the Combined Action Force, a Marine organization that existed only in Vietnam, could not move or manoeuvre (the CAPs were anchored to their villages), did not work for or with any of his other units, operated in autonomous zones tied to the political infrastructure, and generally made things difficult for any US or Vietnamese operation that came in contact with them.

'I didn't know what a CAP was when I was offered the opportunity to transfer from the 7th Marines to Combined Action. I was a fairly experienced first-lieutenant, a "mustang" (officer commissioned from the ranks) well into my second year in "the bush", and had just returned to the regiment from my second stay in hospital. Before standing up when I should have stayed prone, I had served as a platoon commander, company executive officer and company commander. Because I was junior the possibility of being given command of another rifle company was a matter of pure luck, the first change having arisen due to combat losses. So when the CO offered me a chance to interview for a company command in the Combined Action Force I said yes. Only then did I ask, "What the hell is a Combined Action Force?"

'I quickly found myself in an orientation course held at the CAF Headquarters in Da Nang. The CAF tried to get only combat-experienced Marines in the CAPs, but anyone who has been around a war knows that one thing the infantry is always short of is people. Of the eight Marines that were in that week-long course with me, only a young buck sergeant and I had any time in-country and I was the only one with any real bush time. The other six were FNGs (Anglo-Saxon euphemism for an individual starting his initial combat tour), and two of those were "boots" (a Marine who was starting his first tour straight out of recruit training, that is, Boot Camp).

'Orientation consisted of the usual semi-hysterical information about the enemy, his weapons, capabilities and the like. They also introduced the uninitiated to the daily life of a Vietnamese peasant, and there was a brief (very brief) primer on the language. They spent almost a full day on local customs and religions, but the information I was most interested in was where I was going, who I would be working with and how I would operate. That formed the basis for the majority of the course.

'At full strength the CAF operated in the four northernmost provinces of I Corps. Each provincial capital had a Combined Action Group (CAG) headquartered in, or near, the city. Next to the DMZ, in Quang Tri Province, 4th CAG had its headquarters on Highway One just south of the city of Quang Tri. Next south, the old imperial city of Hue was the capital of Tinh Thua Thien. 3rd CAG operated in this province. Tinh Quang Nam stretched from the Hai Van Pass overlooking Da Nang Bay, south, to just below the capital city of Hoi An. 2nd CAG had a compound about three miles west of the city near the Korean Marine fortress in Dien Ban District.

'Before I joined the CAF, 1st CAG had operated in and around Chu Lai and the Batangan Peninsula. But the Americal Division of the US Army had taken over that part of the country and they had very pointedly invited the CAPs to leave. So 1st CAG had been disestablished. There is an interesting sidelight to this. The village of Son My was very close to a CAP village in 1st CAG's old area of operation. One of the hamlets in Son My was a little place called My Lai. A platoon lead by a Lieutenant Calley from the 11th Infantry Brigade of the Americal Division practised its own kind of "people-to-people" programme there one afternoon when they massacred a large number of women and children.

'Each CAG controlled a varied number of Combined Action Companies (CACO, since "Cac" has an unpleasantly scatological connotation in written Vietnamese), each of which operated in one of the districts of that province. The CACOs generally had their CPs [Command Posts] co-located with the military headquarters of the district. Each CACO supported a diverse number of CAPs located in various villages spread around the district. If all this sounds complicated, well – it was more complicated than it sounds.

'When I arrived at the CAF for orientation they had given me a shower to use, new shaving gear and a new set of utilities. These are precious commodities to an experienced grunt, especially new socks and trousers (water and new clothes, two other things the infantry is always short of when they're being shot at on a regular basis). So when I saddled up to head north I carefully "packed" my new clothes, took off my rank insignia (surviving as an officer in the bush required you not to advertise who you were with conspicuous pieces of shiny metal – the movies have this one cliché right), picked up the "boots" semi-wearing all of their new gear and went over to the air terminal at Da Nang Air Force Base, where Teeny Weeny Air Lines (non-standard nomenclature for a Marine C130 squadron) hung out.

'Quang Tri had changed some, since the last time I had been there as a brand new second-lieutenant with the 26th Marines. The biggest change was that the Army had taken over completely. The combat base was now run by a US Army MP battalion and Charlie Med (Navy Hospital) was now an Army Evac Hospital. We flagged down the first Marine vehicle we saw and asked for a ride to the CAG. It turned out that the ¾ ton was a CAG vehicle, so we were standing in front of the Administration (S-1) hootch in no time. After meeting the CAG CO, I was taken in tow by the Operations Officer (S-3) for a lesson in how to operate as the CO of a Combined Action Company.'

Working in small groups in territory dominated by the Vietcong the CAPs took heavy casualties, but almost 60 per cent of the Marines who served in CAPs volunteered to extend their tours and stay on in 'their' villages, working with the local people, sharing the dangers. This was 'hearts and minds' at its most dangerous level, but the CAP Marines took to the job with gusto and soon developed great affection and respect for their Vietnamese charges.

The war in Vietnam intensified after 1965, and the Special Forces were in the thick of it. The Green Beret–CIDG camps at Au Shau and Lang Vei were the scene of fierce battles in May 1967, when the Vietcong attacked with infantry *and tanks*, and at Con Thien and Bo Dop were also attacked by strong Vietcong–NVA forces. Project Delta teams were successful in locating large Vietcong and NVA concentrations, which led to search-and-destroy operations like Operation Attleboro', and the CIDG–Project-Sigma-initiated Operation Blackjack 41. Operation Crazy Horse, in May 1966, the first major action fought by the 1st Air Cavalry Division – a helicopter formation – was initiated by intelligence information provided by a CIDG–SF patrol. All over Vietnam, the Special Force and SOF units were proving their worth.

The main actions of the war, like the seventy-seven-day siege of the US Marines in Khe Sahn, an NVA attempt at a rerun of their Dien Bien Phu success of 1954, and the Tet offensive of 1968, when Vietcong guerrillas struck in every town in South Vietnam, even invading the US Embassy compound in Saigon, and making a one-week stand against the US Marines in Hue, tend to obscure the fact that SF, LRRP, SEAL and Force Recon operations were going on all the time, attempting to stem the rising tide of NVA regular-unit incursions and Vietcong attacks.

A few examples drawn from each type of Special Force unit must suffice to tell the story of this time, starting with the attack on the SF A Team base at Con Thien on 8 May 1967. The camp was held by Green Berets and Vietnamese Special Forces, with a US Marine battalion close by, and the attack was no small-scale Vietcong raid. The attackers came from two battalions of the 812 NVA Regiment, with sappers attached, and their assault was supported with artillery, rocket fire, mortars and flame-throwers. The attack began at 0210 hours and within fifty minutes the NVA had penetrated the perimeter wire and were throwing grenades into the command bunker and the surrounding weapon pits. The SF troopers held on, repelling all attacks, until the NVA brought up a flame-thrower and began to burn out the infantry bunkers. The HQ personnel then withdrew to the Sea Bees (CB – Construction Battalion) bunker, and carried on the fight from there. Fighting was also taking place all around the perimeter of the US Marine battalion, which had to be resupplied with ammunition, sent over in armoured Amtrac personnel carriers. By 0400 hours the situation was under control, but the fighting continued all over the camp area, and it was not until dawn at around 0700 hours that the NVA pulled out. In that fierce five-hour fight more than 200 NVA were killed; US losses included 44 Marines killed, and 110 wounded, 14 CIDG killed and 4 US Special Forces soldiers wounded.

The SEALs were still fighting their small, bitter war in the swamps of the Mekong Delta. In July 1968 a SEAL unit attempted to raid a Mekong village in order to capture a well-known Vietcong commander. This patrol was led by SEAL Frank Bomar, a giant of a man, 6 foot 4 inches tall. Bomar's team was ambushed as it approached the village, one of their Vietnamese guides being severely injured. Frank Bomar picked up the wounded man, and ran for over 200 yards through heavy gunfire, taking the man to safety outside the ambush. He then returned to the fray, led a counter-attack to drive off the enemy and went rampaging on into the village, where the Vietcong commander and eight of his men were shot down. For this action Frank Bomar was awarded the Silver Star, though his Team believed that his conduct justified the award of the Medal of Honor.

For an account of Ranger operations there is Ben Dunham's account of the 75th Infantry's Team Alabama in the Dragon Valley in October 1969: 'The Dragon Valley was an area where playing hide and seek with the Vietcong–NVA was difficult even on a good day. No Team had lasted more than three hours on the ground in the part where we were headed, which was a comforting thought but we cammie'd up – put on our face paint – and got our gear together.

'We were inserted by helicopter and the insertion went without a hitch. I then gave the order to move to an OP in a bomb crater near the top of the mountain and as the sounds of the chopper faded we could hear the jungle coming to life ... we were alone now, with nothing around except us and the enemy. As we moved it was hard to avoid leaving a trail in the wet grass and I had to know if the dinks were on to us, so I got Steve "Crabs" Crabtree to lay a warning wire, a vine laid across the trail at chest height attached to a can with a pebble in it; not much of a warning perhaps, but better than nothing.

'We established our OP on top of the mountain and laid out claymore mines on any likely approaches – then we settled in for our three-day wait before extraction. Before long we started spotting dinks moving about on the slopes below and I decided that we would move down and take a prisoner just before we were extracted. We had already sighted more than fifty Vietcong–NVA in the first hour, some no more than 500 yards from our position. We had to find out the reason for this activity and a prisoner was the best way to get it.

'On the second day we moved about 600 yards down the mountain and came out on to a wide trail under the jungle canopy, wide enough for small trucks. We found bunkers and hooches, one containing five male Vietnamese and two females and another containing ten males, six females and a large dog. There was too much activity in the area for us to remain any longer; we were obviously in the middle of a large base complex and it was only a matter of time before they spotted us – and then we would be in the shit. On the other hand, most of the Vietcong were not armed, so there was still the chance of a snatch, which I decided to go for next day.

'We had moved back to the OP when it happened. Fish, who was on security at our base position, called out to Crabs, "Dinks!" [Vietnamese soldiers] and Wright put an HE [high-explosive] round in his M79 grenade launcher. Then Fisher said again, "Crabs, there are dinks behind you." Crabs thought this was a joke until Wright fired his M79 right over his head. An enemy soldier was trying to loosen the can from the vine we had laid out on arrival and the little noise he made had caught Crabs' ear. Crabs rolled over, picked up his M60 machine-gun and opened up, nailing the dink holding the can. A second dink, NVA, then opened up from behind a nearby tree, but Crabs brought the M60 round and really shredded the trunk and the NVA behind it.

'Pogo and I were in the forward OP observing the dinks in the valley when all this started. Snatching up our gear, we headed back to camp at the dead run. By the time we got there the shooting had stopped, but clearly we had to go. I turned to Pogo and told him to get a sitrep [situation report] back to base and ask for an immediate extraction. I then went to look at the contact area, but Crabs and I had not gone more than fifteen yards when we came under fire.

'At this point I knew we were screwed. We were cut off from the LZ and had no place to go without running into more of the bad guys. However, we had one chance, to get to the patrol base where there was a clear area and get out on a ladder extraction. So far there seemed to be only a small enemy recon group on the mountain and now they knew there were "men with painted faces" up there, I guessed the NVA leader would go to ground and send for reinforcements before coming on again. We therefore moved to the OP and reached it just as the extraction birds arrived overhead. I called for a McGuire-rig extraction and told Pogo, Wright and Dane to go on the first lift, while Crabs and I moved back to the patrol base. On the way we saw lots of legs running about in the undergrowth, which was not a good sign. They were maybe fifteen yards from our position.

'We then got support from the Cobra helicopters, who put down rockets all around us, giving Charlie something to think about. The slick pilot was not keen on hovering while we got lifted out on the McGuire, and neither were we, so I asked him to hover in and try it that way. This was tricky because of the steep slope; when he put a skid down there was a good chance his rotor blade would hit the side of the mountain. But he came in anyway and Crabs fired cover, with the rotor spinning around just a foot or so from his head.

'The crew chief on the chopper helped the first couple of guys on board and it was a beautiful thing to see the way the pilot handled that helicopter, compensating for the added weight as we swarmed on board; he had made up his mind to pick us up or die in the attempt. We finally had everyone on board and with us all yelling "Go, go, go!" the pilot turned the heavily ladened Huey down the mountain and shot off into the valley trying to get up flying speed ... and then the Cobras moved in to finish the business with rockets. So we got back. I don't remember who bought the first round of drinks and I sure as hell don't remember who bought the last. All I do know is that Team Alabama spent thirty hours in the Dragon Valley, a record that was never bested.'

Reconnaissance and intelligence gathering remained the first priority, as the following Force Recon account, concerning Team Recline, makes clear. Team Recline, a six-man unit commanded by USMC First-Lieutenant Richard E. Miller had been tasked with capturing an enemy prisoner and bringing him back for interrogation. Duly inserted by helicopter, they found the Landing Zone deserted but seamed with well-used trails and surrounded by carefully prepared slit trenches. The Team took cover in some thick undergrowth and soon discovered that the area was swarming with NVA regulars.

In their first twenty-four hours the Team noted more than 150 NVA moving about their position, but they remained undetected, though any plans to seize a prisoner had to be abandoned. Instead they decided to stay in the area for a further four days, to gather intelligence about the enemy and fix up a bomber strike for after they left. An OP on a nearby trail counted 120 NVA passing by on the second day and then came the bad news: when the time came for the Team to be extracted there were no helicopters available. The mission was extended by another day and on that day another 139 NVA were counted on trails around the LZ. Lieutenant Miller and his men were now beginning to recognize some of the NVA soldiers and realized that they were hiding in an area occupied by at least a full NVA battalion.

Team Recline had not eaten for three days, but a heavy rainstorm enabled them to pull back a little and have a meal before moving to the helicopter-extraction point. As the original LZ had clearly been prepared for a helicopter ambush, Miller pulled his men back to an area of bomb craters, passing undetected through the NVA base area on the way. The helicopter duly arrived and the Marines were pulled out by ladder at 0600 hours after five days concealed inside an enemy battalion area. An hour after they left, a concentration of B52 bombers blew the NVA area to pieces.

'Ladder' extraction was a common, if somewhat alarming, method of pulling SF troops out of the jungle, if the helicopter could not land. The ladder was of the kind used for caving or mountaineering, composed of flexible steel cables and kept rolled up in the troop compartment of the extracting helicopter when not in use. For an extraction the helicopter Crew Chief would let out the ladder as the chopper hovered or made a slow pass over the extraction point and the team below would hook on to the ladder rungs using metal snap-on 'carabiner' hooks. The helicopter would then lift away, the men dangling below like a bunch of grapes, stopping at some distance from the LZ to let the troops climb aboard. Men could be cut and bruised during a ladder extraction, but it was better than being left behind, to the uncertain mercy of the NVA soldiers or the Vietcong.

For an LRRP operation there is Gary Linderer's account from his time in F Company LRRPs, 101st Airborne, describing a day's work on 3 November 1968: 'We received a warning order for a four-day mission into the rocket belt around Nui Ke Mountain. Our task was to locate the NVA rockets that had been hitting our camp and Hue in the past week and destroy them, calling in artillery or Tac-Air to strafe the ground. The insertion went according to plan and we landed on an abandoned firebase on Nui Ke. The chopper pilot elected to overfly the actual metal plates of the chopper pad and hover to get us out, and that saved our lives. We got out and discovered a USAF 200lb bomb, fused and buried, nose up, under the chopper pad.

'We eased off the firebase at about 0900 hours and began a cautious sweep down the mountain, working from boulder to boulder, taking advantage of every scrap of cover. We had moved out into the open but were anxious to get back into cover when we heard the toop ... toop ... toop of mortars going up their tubes. I shot a glance at the rest of the team, raised my fist to signal danger, and we dispersed among the boulders.

'The first salvo landed in front of us, the second one behind. They had us bracketed, but Zo found the mortar position and called in our 105mm from Firebase Brick; within minutes shells were coming in, with Zo calling back corrections. Secondary explosions erupted below us, and Zo looked back with a big grin on his face. Then I saw several enemy soldiers, NVA, moving uphill towards the old firebase. I yelled this information at Zo and he told me to take the rest and get back to the top. We won the race to the crest and took up defensive positions while waiting for Zo and the radio man, who soon came panting up the hill. We were spread pretty thin, just six of us to defend an area that could have contained a company.

'Then we heard the heavy pounding of a Huey rotor and looked up to see the CO's Command and Control helicopter orbiting overhead. He radioed that he had four Cobra gunships on station, ready to work the area over as soon as we called off the artillery. Zo called in a cease firing to the guns and the Cobras began to quarter the ground. Just as the last Cobra expended its armament I saw three green-clad NVA break cover just ahead of the exploding rockets and run up a ridge just below me. They were about a hundred yards away when my first two shots took the first one in the back, tumbling him head over heels. I popped off three more quick aimed shots at the next man, punching him spreadeagled into the jungle. The last one disappeared before I could draw a bead on him.

'The Cobras left but the CO radioed that Phantom F4 fighter-bombers were on the way and for us to keep our heads down. I saw the first one coming in from the east, over the Perfume River, and he dropped his 200 pounder and as he climbed steeply out of the valley I could see right into the cockpit, to the pilot and his rear seat. At the second run the Phantoms got some good secondary explosions from out of the valley, but it was now around 1630 and the TL (Team Leader), Zo, decided that we had had enough fun and spent enough of Uncle Sam's money. We had to wait for extraction as another team had been comprised and needed to go first, but after about half an hour, when the NVA were starting to probe up at us again, a single chopper came in. We told it to stay away from the booby-trapped heli-pad, which was destroyed by artillery fire soon after we left, and he hovered down to pick us up, making a tight turn to take us back to Camp Eagle. No sooner had we landed than the word came down that we had to go back into that valley that night...'

Escape and evasion was another SF task, and since the US government was rightly concerned about the growing number of US servicemen held in NVA prison camps, in November 1970 sixty SF volunteers under Colonel Arthur Simons mounted Operation Kingpin, against the NVA prison camp at Son Tay, just outside Hanoi. The volunteers trained and rehearsed for this operation in Florida, and after three months of planning the raid went in on the night of 21 November. The camp at Son Tay had held a large number of prisoners but these had been moved before the raid, so the prison compound was empty when the US helicopters landed and disgorged their troops. A number of the raiders landed in the wrong compound, but they killed a number of NVA guards before withdrawing without loss. As a result of this raid, the North Vietnamese brought all their prisoners together at a prison in Hanoi – later called the Hanoi Hilton – where conditions, though hardly comfortable, were much better than they had been in the scattered, outlying camps.

Another offshoot of SF activity in Vietnam was the Phoenix programme. This was designed to root out the Vietcong intelligence and operational infrastructure inside the towns and villages of South Vietnam, by finding the Vietcong activists and killing them. The operational or execution arm of the Phoenix programme was the PRU Counter-Terror Units, composed of Vietnamese mercenaries, thugs who would kill anyone if the price was right. Most of the PRU were criminals, and they took on the work partly to get out of prison and partly because they were paid a bounty for each killing. It is also alleged that they took an active part in the interrogation and torture of prisoners.

It was clearly necessary to destroy the Vietcong networks in the South, but the Phoenix–PRU operation was a very blunt instrument indeed. It is probable that a large number of completely innocent people suffered imprisonment, torture or death at their hands and the number of people murdered – or executed without trial, which comes to the same thing – has been variously estimated at between 6,000 and 25,000. But it is fair to add that after the war was over the Vietcong stated that the Phoenix–PRU programme severely damaged their intelligence-gathering capability in the South.

As the US began to withdraw from the war in 1969, handing over the fighting to the ARVN, the various SF and SOF units began to pull out. The Tet offensive of January 1968 may have been a military failure, costing the NVA and Vietcong far more than it gained, but the fact that they had been able to mount such a nationwide offensive at all, with half a million US troops in the country, convinced the US that the Vietnam War could not be won. That being so, the only option was to make what terms they could, and pull out. The new US President, Richard Nixon, began negotiations with the North Vietnamese in Paris, and by May 1969 these had reached the point where the US withdrawal could begin.

The 3rd Marine Division withdrew to Okinawa in November 1969, by which time the 3rd Force Recon Company had already been stood down, the men extracted from their positions in March 1969. The 5th Special Forces Group began to wind up its operations and withdrew to Nha Trang in January 1971, leaving Vietnam for good in March of that year. The SEALs stayed on another year, finally leaving towards the end of 1972, by which time the bulk of the US forces had left and the North Vietnamese Army was advancing inexorably on Saigon, driving the ARVN before it.

The war did not end when the US Army pulled out. The last US troops left Vietnam in March 1973, but the fighting went on for another two years until, on 30 April 1975, the NVA entered Saigon. The day before they arrived, with the last ARVN units holding out on the fringes of the city, the staff of the US Embassy were lifted off the roof of the Embassy by helicopter and flown out to the waiting carriers. The war had lasted over ten years and cost millions of lives, including those of more than 50,000 Americans. Many of those soldiers who went home during and after the war remain bitter about the treatment they received from the American public.

Master-Sergeant Charles Owen, already a veteran of the Second World War and Korea, returned to the USA from Vietnam and met a very different reception at the end of his third big war: 'This is one part of my Marine Corps time I do not like to talk about because of the American people's lack of support. This really hurt me and the rest of the troops when this happened. When I was a Marine, this was my country, right or wrong.' Curiously enough, those former US servicemen who have returned to Vietnam years after the end of the war report a warm welcome from the local population. Arus Whillhite, a former CAP Marine, returned to Vietnam with a group of his fellows in 1989. 'Once they found out we were Americans and not Russians the Vietnamese made us tremendously welcome. I went back to my village, Nuoc Ngot – Hotel 4 in the old days – but there were few signs that we were ever there, though I met people who I remembered and who remembered me. I met Ho, who was about thirteen then, and her family cooked chow for us. She says she remembers the night we were overrun and can remember "VC! VC! Fire in the hole! Incoming!" – phrases like that. I just wish I had gotten half the welcome back in the States that I got on my return to Vietnam.'

Tom Harvey, another CAP Marine, who organized this return visit, recalls a conversation he had with a colleague on the return trip, Phil Ovelman: 'We were driving back into Hue and it was growing dark. My mind flashed back twenty years, for this was the time of day when we would be moving out into our night positions and setting up our ambushes. I mention this to Phil and the same sensation overcomes both of us, driven by the terrain, the weather, the vegetation, the people, all the same. Then comes a twinge of anxiety, a sense of duty and a feeling of relief that it is all over and we don't have to do it again, and I remarked to Phil that the welcome we experienced that day in Ba Lang made up for the one we never got when we returned to the USA after the war.'

'Yes,' Phil replied. 'I wonder what it would have been like had we won.'

GSG9 (German anti-terrorist unit) badge

CHAPTER ELEVEN

Terrorism and Counter-Terrorism
1970–1997

The purpose of terrorism is to terrorize.

Vladimir Ilyich Lenin, 1917

Terrorism has to be defined. One man's terrorist is another man's freedom fighter, which is why neutral terms like 'guerrilla' or 'irregular' have been frequently employed in this book. A terrorist may be defined as 'Someone who ignores or defies the democratic, electoral process or the wishes of the majority and inflicts death or injury on innocent parties in order to impose his beliefs or politics on the general population.'

That definition, if hardly succinct, will cover most of the terrorist situations current at the end of the twentieth century. When there is no democratic process available, there may be no choice but to take up arms, but even then terrorism is not usually the only option available. To give an example, the Palestinians have been at war with the State of Israel for the last fifty years, until the peace process began in 1995. If they had restricted the 'armed struggle' to attacks on the Israeli Army or along Israel's borders they could have claimed a certain amount of support, for their aspirations for a Palestine state have a legitimate basis. But when they began hijacking aircraft, planting bombs in foreign capitals and murdering innocents in an attempt to bring attention to their grievances, they rightly attracted nothing but odium and contempt.

In the decades from 1970 the words 'Palestinian' and 'terrorist' were almost synonymous, but terrorism is now a worldwide phenomenon. To fight this scourge Special Forces in many countries are now studying anti-terrorist techniques or forming anti-terrorist sections. The British SAS Regiment's Counter-Revolutionary Warfare (CRW) role and the US Delta Force teams, trained in hostage rescue, are two examples of this, and terrorism is featured in this book because anti-terrorism activity has become a Special Force task.

Twentieth-century terrorism comes in various forms. Nationalist terrorism is practised by the Provisional Irish Republican Army (PIRA) in Northern Ireland, by ETA, the Basque terrorists in Spain, and possibly by some of the US 'militias'. Urban terrorism is, or was, practised by subversive groups like the Japanese Red Army, Germany's Baader–Meinhof gang, the Italian Red Brigades, Action Direct in France, Hamas inside Israel and their imitators or successors throughout the world. Then there is 'international terrorism,' which may be defined as nationalist terrorism outside the national territory, as practised or supported by the 'terrorist states', countries like Iran, Iraq and Libya, who use terrorism as an instrument of policy and employ international terrorist groups like Black September or individuals like Abu Nidal or the now imprisoned Carlos, the 'Jackal', to carry out their attacks.

At a conservative estimate there are over 800 terrorist organizations at large in the world at the end of the twentieth century, with the Palestinians alone mustering eighteen separate groups, although at the time of writing most of these have suspended their operations. The total number appears to be growing and so too does the number of people killed in terrorist attacks. In the fifteen years from 1970 to 1985, terrorist attacks claimed in excess of 40,000 victims and the pace has not slackened since. The IRA alone have killed more than 3,200 people and maimed over 100,000 in Northern Ireland since their terrorist campaign began in 1969, and their violence continues.

Many of these terrorist organizations are loosely linked with one another, in that they will share weapons, training and expertise with other terrorist groups, regardless of political affiliation. 'International terrorism' as a concept may belong to the world of James Bond, but the 'internationalization' of terrorism is well under way and the Special Force units – military, police or paramilitary – have to be ready and willing to confront it with force. But terrorism also has a political dimension.

International terrorism could not function without the cash and assistance provided by the terrorist states. In mid-1996, for example, a group of Islamic terrorists planned to blow up twelve Western airliners in different parts of the world on the same day. Each attack would have involved at least three people, who would board these aircraft at different points, assemble the bomb in the aircraft lavatory, hide it under their seats and get off before it exploded. The cost, in air tickets alone, would have exceeded US$100,000, and this sort of money is not easily found. The terrorist teams would also have needed passports and some form of cover, in order to move about without detection. Clearly, this proposed attack was backed and funded by one of the 'rogue' states, probably Iran or Syria. It was thwarted when the ringleaders were arrested in New York, but no doubt something similar will be attempted again.

For the members of these groups, like the terrorists who serve in ETA and the IRA, terrorism has become a way of life. For others it is a cause, a profession, even a kind of distinction. To quote the words of Mehmet Ali Agca, who shot and wounded Pope John Paul II in 1980, 'The only thing that matters is to be an international terrorist.' Ali Agca was a member of the Turkish Grey Wolves, but he had been trained for the attack on the Pope at Palestinian camps in the Lebanon, and his attack, while widely deplored, still drew favourable comment in some quarters. In the 1960s and 1970s some parts of the liberal establishment, especially in the USA or France, thought it chic to have a terrorist or two on their guest lists. Che Guevara was a student icon, his poster displayed in many a campus dorm, and in the 1970s the Black Panthers were often seen gracing Manhattan cocktail parties.

The response to the challenge of terrorism has been both slow and piecemeal. A number of countries, notably Britain and Germany, maintain standing anti-terrorist units, the British with their standby CRW Squadron of the SAS and the Germans with the paramilitary GSG9, two units which have worked together and which are ready to go into action as soon as a terrorist incident is reported. This practice is not yet common and most countries, while having army or police units trained in the anti-terrorist role, use them for other purposes as well and are usually taken by surprise when the terrorist strikes. This, indeed, is one of the terrorist's chief assets; he – or quite often she – chooses where, when and at whom to strike and, as has been demonstrated time and again in the preceding chapters of this book, the unit with the initiative, and the advantage of surprise, is a long way down the road to victory.

Victory, however, is not in the terrorists' gift. Terrorism does not usually pay any worthwhile political dividend. Many groups, like the

Royal Marines of
42 Commando
on river patrol in
Borneo, 1962.

A jungle patrol
in Sarawak,
Borneo, 1965.

'Hearts and Minds': Royal Marines Commandos distribute clothing in Kuching, Borneo, 1962.

British jungle fort on the Kalimantan frontier in Borneo, 1964.

Ready for Recon: Kenn
Miller, M60 Gunner,
101st Airborne LLRPs,
Vietnam.

'Terrible Team 10', 101st
LLRPs, Vietnam, 1968.

LEFT A soldier takes a patrol break, Vietnam, 1967.

BELOW 81mm mortar in action, 101st Airborne, Vietnam.

ABOVE Air Cavalry Huey
Helicopters, Vietnam.

LEFT Hearts and Minds:
river patrol, Vietnam.

INSET Commando observation post, Divis Street flats, Belfast, 1969.

BELOW Briefing photos for street patrols, Belfast, 1969.

'For putting out burning
Marines', Belfast, 1969.

Argentine Commando Company parade, Falklands War, 1982.

2 Para move on Stanley, Falklands War, 1982

Kikuyu in Kenya with Mau Mau, or the Greek Cypriots with EOKA, tried terrorism without success, were beaten in battle by the British Army – whatever their revisionist historians may claim today – but eventually got all or part of what they wanted through the democratic process. Only in Aden, where the political will failed, did terrorism pay a dividend, but that was in a place which the British had no wish to retain. The IRA campaign in Ulster will never produce a united Ireland unless the Protestant majority in the North vote for it, and ETA has got all it is going to get from the government in Madrid. But still the struggle continues.

One notable fact about terrorism is that it rarely appears in totalitarian countries. Terrorism was not a feature of resistance activity in Nazi Germany, the Soviet Union or the states of Eastern Europe after the Second World War, but it grew and flourished for a while in the democratic states, Western Germany, France, Italy, Belgium and the United Kingdom, from the end of the 1960s. The main reason for an absence of terrorism in totalitarian states is that the governments there would not tolerate it and, having no free press or an electorate to worry about, were able to take severe measures to suppress dissent or eliminate dissidents, usually before they took up arms. Detention, internment without trial in labour camps, torture and murder were all employed against dissidents in places as far apart as Romania and Nicaragua. Throw in Argentina, Indonesia, Brazil, Chile, El Salvador ... the list of countries where 'suppressing terrorism' is an excuse for stamping out legitimate political dissent is a long one.

This is one of the dangers of terrorism, even in democracies. Terrorism and counter-terrorist activity are both potentially corrupting. Eventually, if terrorism looks like succeeding, the states and governments it threatens will act ruthlessly to suppress it, but the laws they pass and the steps they take to achieve that end may then be employed to crush dissent of any kind. France, for example, suffered a loss of civil rights and the spread of illegal action, including the use of torture by the French security service, the DST, during the OAS terrorist campaign in the 1960s. In the years since, the French have not hesitated to take extreme measures against anyone they see as a threat, even sending their operatives to sink a Greenpeace ship in a New Zealand harbour, an action which resulted in the death of a Greenpeace worker, because the French government did not want activists interfering with its nuclear test site on the Muraroa atoll.

Britain has also been accused of using extreme interrogation measures, falling just short of torture, in Northern Ireland, and the loss of civilian life in the course of counter-terrorist actions is always a possibility. Another danger in taking extreme counter-terrorist actions is that they give the terrorists or their supporters a reason to claim that all talk of democracy is claptrap, that the established order they fight against is every bit as bad as they say and that the press and government have no moral grounds for disparaging violent actions taken in the course of the 'armed struggle'. All this forms a background to the fight against terrorism, which has been going on for thirty years and shows no signs of abating.

Post-war terrorism began in the late 1960s, and the 1970s opened with a spectacular act of terrorism by the PFLP – the Popular Front for the Liberation of Palestine. In September 1970 the PFLP hijacked three Western airliners, forced the crew to fly them to Dawson's Field, an airstrip in Jordan, and, having released the passengers and assembled the world's media to view the outcome, blew them up. Aircraft hijacking, already popular in the Americas, where a number of aircraft had been hijacked and flown to Cuba, promptly spread to the Middle East and became far more violent.

It took some years to find the answer to aircraft hijacking, but while airport security increased, to the irritation of most travellers but without deterring the terrorists to any marked degree, the eventual introduction of 'skymarshals', armed, plainclothed policemen or Special Service troops, on aircraft did at least raise the price of aircraft terrorism and deter the terrorists from the bland assumption that aircraft hijacking was an occupation without risks. Even so, hijacking has continued and aircraft terrorism has been given a new twist with such acts as the bombing of Pan Am Flight 103 over Lockerbie in December 1988. This atrocity has been laid at the door of the Libyans, but no one has yet been arrested for the attack.

A most horrific and spectacular terrorist action took place during the Olympic Games in Munich in 1972, when Palestine terrorists from the Black September group broke into the Olympic Village and took most of the Israeli athletic team hostage. Two Israeli athletes were killed in the Village and another nine, together with the terrorists, were killed when an attempt to release them was bungled by the German police at Munich Airport as the terrorists and their hostages were about to leave. This incident, and several less dramatic ones, finally convinced the various Western powers that standing forces should be created, equipped and trained to tackle such incidents, for cobbling together a reaction force when the terrorist incident was actually in progress left too much to chance and – as at Munich – could lead to disaster. Most of the Palestinian terrorists who planned and executed the Munich affair were eventually hunted down and killed by the Israeli Secret Service, the Mossad, but this operation was flawed when the Mossad hit the wrong man and killed a totally innocent Norwegian citizen.

In Britain, the SAS were given the anti-terrorist role and began to keep one squadron on standby at their base in Hereford, ready to intervene in a terrorist incident as soon as the request for assistance came in. This task was rotated through the various squadrons so that the entire SAS Regiment knew the routine. All the soldiers were intensively rehearsed in such actions as entering a hijacked aircraft – every civil aircraft type in service was examined – and a fast method of entry developed. Another development was the construction of the 'Killing House', a full-sized replica of a modern home but with movable walls. In the Killing House the actual layout of a besieged building can be replicated so that the troopers can rehearse their moves before assaulting the building. The Regiment is also equipped with a wide range of surveillance equipment, which is used to pinpoint the exact position of the terrorists inside a building, and the assault teams carry a number of weapons and special equipment to break down doors and confuse the terrorists as they move in for the kill.

Prior intelligence is the key to most successful anti-terrorist actions. The SAS Regiment has inspected and obtained layout plans for places in the UK – and most probably abroad – that are likely targets for terrorist activity: the Houses of Parliament, Buckingham Palace and other Royal homes, the BBC Television Centre, radio stations, all the UK airports, and British embassies and consular offices overseas. Here, as in all other forms of Special Force activity, preparation, anticipation and a good supply of up-to-date information and intelligence are seen as vital.

The British had good reason to examine their counter-terrorist facilities, for the post-colonial campaigns and the constant threat of the IRA since 1970 have given them ample experience and plenty of practice in anti-terrorist work. Other nations swiftly followed the British path, with varying methods and different results, some using elements of their Special Forces, others employing development of established police units on the lines of the US police department SWAT (Special Weapons and Tactics) teams. The French and Germans formed para-military police units for the anti-terrorist role, the French forming the GIGN (Group d'Intervention Gendarmerie Nationale), and the Germans the Grenzesshutzgruppe 9 (GSG9, Counter Terrorist). The

GSG9 cut its teeth on the Baader–Meinhof terrorist campaign and works closely with the Israelis, the British SAS and the US Delta Force.

Delta Force is so secret that even its existence is denied; inquiries at the Defense Department in Washington elicit the curt reply, 'Delta is an airline, sir.' But Delta, a creation of Colonel Charlie Beckwith, that Green Beret officer encountered in Vietnam, does exist, as one of three CT (Counter-Terrorist) groups maintained by the federal government. Delta recruits from the Ranger and SF units of the US Army and is based at Fort Bragg, where it is said to maintain some 2,500 effectives operating under the direct orders of the Defense Department. Delta's main function is hostage rescue and, having had a terrible time while attempting to rescue the diplomats held hostage in the American Embassy in Teheran in 1980, has since honed its techniques considerably and proved highly effective in rescuing American businessmen held captive in Somalia during Operation Restore Hope.

Canada first chose the police option with the Royal Canadian Mounted Police SERT (Special Emergency Response Team), as a counter-terrorist unit. This was disbanded in 1993 but it still appears in the list of Canada's para-military units. Few details are available and the size, location and role of this unit can only be guessed at. The belief is that the unit is commanded by a lieutenant-colonel, musters some 200 men chosen from all three services, and has been deployed in Bosnia. Australia has the APS (Australian Protective Service), which guards the Prime Minister, ambassadors and VIPs and the AFPC-TU (Australian Federal Police Counter-Terrorist Unit), of which no details at all are available. There is also the Australian SAS Regiment, which served in Vietnam and, as part of its role, now trains for counter-terrorist duties.

The use of SF troops for counter-terrorist action is an interesting development and one which will repay close inspection. Part of the reason Special Forces have pushed for this paramilitary role undoubtedly lies in the need to stay in being as a fighting force when no other enemy is available. The British SAS has survived countless Defence Expenditure Reviews by continually finding and exploiting new roles, and the SAS commanders clearly identified terrorism as a new field for the SAS in the 1970s when it began to train its men in anti-terrorist techniques, besides supplying men, skilled in small arms, as embassy guards. The SAS also trains guards for foreign potentates and has established a sound reputation for anti-terrorist action, though this involvement in what might otherwise be a police function has not been conducted without some adverse publicity, not least in SAS actions against the Provisional IRA.

The Irish police, the Gardai, has a Special Branch and can call on the Irish Army Ranger unit. Israel has half a dozen Sayaret units and the highly secret – and very lethal – operatives of the Mossad and Shin Bet, two of the best intelligence services in the world. Italy has its 'Leatherheads', the NOCS (Nucleo Operativo Centrale di Sicurezza), a counter-terrorist unit, and the GIS (Gruppo di Intervento Speciale) for hostage rescue. The Netherlands has the BBE, which is like the German GSG9, as has South Africa with its rather unfortunately named SAPS, while Spain's Guardia Civil maintains the GEOS (Grupos Especiales de Operaciones), which acts against ETA in the Basque country. So it now goes in most other states, democratic or dictatorial. Terrorism is a thriving business and the nation states have raised forces to combat it. The lead in counter-terrorism has been taken by Israel – the security on El Al flights is legendary among travellers – and no counter-terrorist operation has ever been conducted with such daring as the Entebbe hostage rescue of 1976.

The story of Entebbe began on 29 June 1976, when an Air France jet, *en route* from Israel to Paris, was hijacked shortly after leaving Athens by a group of Palestinians from the PFLP and Germans from the Baader–Meinhof group, led by two Germans, Wilfried Boese, and his female companion, Gabrielle Tiedemann. The Captain was ordered to fly to Benghazi, where the aircraft was refuelled, and it then flew to a previously arranged destination, the civil airport at Entebbe in Uganda.

Uganda, formerly a British colony, was ruled in 1976 by a former Uganda Army NCO, Idi Amin, now self-promoted to Field-Marshal Doctor President Idi Amin Dada VC, Conqueror of the British Empire. Amin was at Entebbe to greet the terrorists when they arrived, and with him were several more terrorists. Troops of the Ugandan Army were deployed to assist these terrorists in guarding the hostages, who were taken into the main airport building to await the outcome of this affair. The terrorists demanded that fifty-three Palestine terrorists held in Israel should be released by 1 July. Failure to comply would result in all the passengers being shot, and as a step to that end the Jewish passengers were separated from the rest. It is to the undying credit of the Air France Captain and his crew that they protested against this action and insisted on being held with their Jewish passengers. In spite of pleas from all around the world, President Idi Amin refused to intervene and sent a battalion of his troops to secure the airfield against the threat of Israeli attack.

The rest of the world was either stunned by this hijacking or willing to play for time, but the Israeli government had long since established a rule for such incidents, often called the Eleventh Commandment – 'Thou shalt not give in to terrorism' – and ordered the Army to prepare plans for an immediate rescue mission. The task was taken on by the Israeli Chief of Staff, General Gur, and entrusted to 100 men of the 35th Parachute Brigade and the Golani Infantry led by Lieutenant-Colonel Jonathan Netanyahu, known to his men as 'Yonni' – the elder brother of the current Israeli prime minister, Binyamin Netanyahu.

The difficulties of mounting this operation were daunting. Entebbe lies 2,500 miles from Tel Aviv, across the airspace of several hostile states, time was short and, even if the force could fly to Uganda, how were they to get back? Gradually, all the planning difficulties were resolved. The Israelis had built the airport terminal at Entebbe, so plans of the building were available. The Kenya government agreed to allow the Israeli aircraft to refuel and the terrorists, confident of success, had extended their execution deadline by three days, to 3 July. The Israelis prepared a full-scale layout of Entebbe at one of their military airfields, where Yonni and his men rehearsed the attack again and again, and, with eight hours before the expiry of the deadline, four Hercules aircraft took off from Israel and laid course for Entebbe.

These aircraft touched down at Entebbe in the dark, at one minute past midnight on the morning of 4 July 1976. The first taxied directly to the control tower and disgorged a group of paratroopers, who seized the tower without firing a shot. They also unloaded a Mercedes saloon and three Land-Rovers which, laden with men, now made directly for the airport terminal. Amin had got into the habit of visiting the terminal in his own Mercedes and it was thought, in the event correctly, that the terrorists would be soothed by the familiar sight of Amin's approaching Mercedes if they came out to see what was happening.

The attack went in as planned. The Ugandan troops, surprised and confused, put up little resistance as the main group of Israeli paratroopers stormed the terminal building. Another group of paratroopers attacked and destroyed all the Ugandan Air Force jets to prevent them taking off in pursuit, while a third party ambushed the entrance road in case other elements of the Ugandan Army tried to intervene.

This sudden eruption of Israeli troops, bursting into the terminal out of the night, unnerved Wilfried Boese, who first rushed to shoot at his hostages and then turned back to fire at the paratroopers. He was shot down and killed, as was Gabrielle Tiedemann, who had been very anxious to kill some of the Jewish hostages even before the expiry of the deadline. Two of the Palestinian terrorists were also killed in the firing, as were three hostages. Several hostages were slightly wounded, but within minutes the fighting was over and the hostages were being rushed out and bundled into the waiting aircraft. It was at this moment that Colonel Yonni, supervising the evacuation of the hostages, was shot dead by a Ugandan sniper. At 0045 the aircraft took off with the hostages to refuel in Nairobi, and by 0054 the Entebbe operation, a textbook example of hostage rescue, was over. In just fifty-three minutes the Israelis had captured Entebbe airport and rescued 103 hostages, all for the loss of one man.

There was an aftermath. An elderly woman passenger, Mrs Dora Bloch, had been taken ill on 3 July and transferred to a hospital in Uganda. Enraged at the attack, in which more than twenty Ugandan soldiers had been killed, Amin had this sick old lady taken from the hospital and murdered. There was also a furious debate at the UN in which many countries, formerly reluctant to condemn the actions of Amin, rushed to condemn the rescue-attack in Uganda by the Israeli paratroopers. The rest of the world cheered, and the Special Forces community took particular notice when it transpired that the Israelis had been accompanied on the raid by Colonel Ulrich Wegener, commander of the German GSG9.

GSG9 may have found this experience useful a year later, in October 1977, when yet another German–Palestine group carried out another hijack, seizing a Lufthansa jet *en route* from Palma, Mallorca, to Frankfurt and ordering the pilot, Jürgen Schumann, to fly to Rome. The aircraft then flew to Larnaca in Cyprus and then to Beirut, but by then the word had spread. The aircraft was refused permission to land and the runway was blocked. The same thing happened at Bahrain in the Gulf and the aircraft was very short of fuel when it was finally allowed to land at Dubai. There it sat while the terrorists, who had no apparent political demands, announced their intention of blowing it up, complete with crew and passengers. However, later that day, having been refuelled, the aircraft took off and flew to Aden. By now, unknown to the hijackers, men of GSG9 and some British SAS soldiers were in hot pursuit.

On the Lufthansa jet were a crew of five and more than eighty passengers, many of them elderly and all now in great distress. There were four hijackers, two men and two women, all of them from the Red Army Faction, a spin-off from the Baader–Meinhof gang, though their leader, who called himself 'Captain Mahmoud', was subsequently identified as a notorious 'international terrorist', Zohiar Yussef. At Aden, Yussef murdered the Lufthansa pilot, Captain Jürgen Schumann, ordering the pilot to kneel in the open doorway of the aircraft before shooting him in the head. The pilot's body was then thrown out on to the tarmac and the co-pilot, Jürgen Victor, was ordered to take off and fly the aircraft to Mogadishu in Somalia.

Playing for time, the German authorities contacted Yussef and offered to release some terrorists held in German prisons if the hostages were released unharmed. Yussef then agreed to delay destroying the jet, whereupon an aircraft slipped into Mogadishu carrying a thirty-strong GSG9 team, led by Ulrich Wegener and accompanied by two members of the British SAS.

At Mogadishu, negotiations with the hijackers continued, led now by Jürgen Wischnewski, a West German Minister of State. His appearance on the scene convinced Yussef that the Germans were serious about releasing the terrorists and he agreed to stay his hand, though demanding that the eleven terrorists in Germany should be released at once and flown to Mogadishu. By now GSG9 had reviewed the situation, and at 0205 that night the assault squad went in.

The tactics of the rescue were both simple and effective. To divert the hijackers' attention a fire was lit ahead of the aircraft, some distance down the runway. The terrorists duly crowded into the cockpit to see what was going on and, while they were there, a team of GSG9 and the two SAS men climbed on to the wings of the aircraft and blew off the emergency exit doors.

The terrorists rushed back from the cockpit to be greeted with a volley of 'flash bang' stun grenades – high-powered thunderflashes – which shocked and blinded the terrorists as the rescuers swarmed aboard, screaming 'Lie down!' to the passengers. Yussef tossed two grenades into the passenger compartment, which exploded harmlessly under some empty seats. He was then shot dead, as was the second male terrorist and one of the women. The second woman terrorist, Suhaila Seyah, dressed in a tee-shirt adorned with a picture of Che Guevara, was wounded and captured. Three hostages were slightly wounded, but all survived.

Like Entebbe, Mogadishu was a classic counter-terrorist operation but, unlike Mogadishu, this was not an *ad hoc* operation, mounted in a hurry by first-class troops and succeeding because of its daring and surprise. The GSG9 team at Mogadishu had been carefully trained for just such an operation, they had all the right equipment, some of it obtained from the SAS, and they were well led by a man who had practical, recent experience of such operations. This is the sort of team that performs such operations well, using constantly practised routines.

The Mogadishu hijack caused a great deal of alarm in the Western world. In Washington, where SF Colonel Charlie Beckwith had been struggling for years to get his SAS-style Delta Force project accepted, the Mogadishu affair threw the need for such a force into sharp focus. Objections subsided, funds became available and Beckwith was ordered to get his force trained and ready for counter-terrorist action with the greatest possible speed. Beckwith therefore had the Delta Force ready for action when the first call came. This was on 4 November 1979 when, following the overthrow of the Shah, an Iranian mob burst into the American Embassy in Teheran and seized the American Ambassador and more than fifty members of his staff, holding them hostage and demanding apologies for American imperialism and an end to US support for Israel – though their main aim was to humiliate the American President, Jimmy Carter, and demonstrate America's impotence in the face of Islamic fundamentalism.

There is an international agreement, the Vienna Convention, by which nations are obliged to protect foreign embassies in their territory, but the new government of Iran blithely ignored that undertaking. Obtaining the release of the hostages became a matter of considerable importance to the Carter administration and, when the ayatollahs ruling Iran flatly refused to act against the 'students' and Revolutionary Guards holding the American diplomats prisoner, Delta Force was ordered into action.

Operation Eagle Claw, the rescue of the American hostages in Teheran, presented far more difficulties than the Entebbe rescue, with which it is often unfavourably compared. To begin with, the US Embassy lies in the centre of Teheran and hundreds of miles from the sea, where the US Fleet was waiting. Just getting into Teheran undetected was the first and major difficulty, compounded by the fact that the hostages had been dispersed and were not all at the Embassy or in one place. A parachute drop might let the rescuers in, provided their aircraft were not detected, but there was no way of getting them out again.

The only possible way to get in and out was by helicopter and, after two agents had been planted in Teheran to handle the ground arrangements, this is the option Beckwith proposed and the Pentagon accepted. It was still, at best, a very difficult operation and Beckwith did not conceal the fact that releasing the hostages and getting them to safety was a very long shot indeed.

The basic plan was that Delta Force would fly to the Oman, a British protectorate at the foot of the Persian Gulf, while eight Navy helicopters would be embarked on the USS *Nimitz*, a carrier stationed in the Gulf which would take position off the Iranian coast. When all was ready Delta Force, in six Hercules transports, three carrying troops, three carrying helicopter fuel, would fly to a base – codenamed Desert One – about 300 miles south-east of Teheran. There they would be joined by at least six helicopters from *Nimitz*, the minimum number of helicopters judged necessary to carry off the hostages and the Delta rescue team. The helicopters would arrive exactly thirty minutes after Delta and, having refuelled, would fly the Force to a spot near Teheran where the helicopters would wait until the team returned with the hostages.

Delta would then enter the city, carried in trucks hired by the agents already in the city, overcome Iranian resistance at the Embassy and at the Foreign Ministry, where the rest of the hostages were being held, and fight off any opposition until the helicopters could be called in to take the hostages and the Delta team away. While all this was going on, a Ranger force, embarked in C141 Stairlifter transport jets flown in from the Oman, would land and seize the Iranian airbase at Manzarieh, forty miles south of Teheran. The hostages would be taken there by helicopter and flown out in the C141s, covered by fighter aircraft from the Sixth Fleet.

It is not hard to imagine the difficulties of this operation and the slim chance of success. The time-scale alone made this mission hazardous; at Entebbe the rescuers had been on the ground less than one hour. In Iran they would have to stay on the ground for around a day and a half, and the chances of detection were clearly very high. Beckwith was well aware of this, but having fought for years to get Delta established, he could hardly turn down the first offer of a mission from his President.

The first part of the mission, the airlift of Delta Force to Desert One, went well. All the aircraft landed safely and the nearby road was blocked. Then came the first hitch, when a busload of Iranians ran into the roadblock. The passengers were detained but then a petrol tanker appeared. The driver, seeing the aircraft and the US troops, attempted to speed away, but the tanker was fired on and burst into flames. Surprise had already been lost and there was still no sign of the eight Navy helicopters. One had already had to land in the desert and been abandoned and the rest then ran into a sandstorm. Then another helicopter lost its navigation aids and turned back to the *Nimitz*. Only six, the very minimum needed for the rescue, actually arrived at Desert One, getting there an hour and a half late.

The helicopters were refuelling when Beckwith was told that one was suffering from leaking hydraulics and could not be used. This forced an agonizing decision on Beckwith: six helicopters was the minimum needed and, with only five available, the mission was off. Beckwith, fuming, had no option but to cancel it and order a withdrawal. This decision was relayed to Washington and pressure was immediately brought to bear on Beckwith to proceed with five aircraft. Beckwith knew that this meant leaving twenty men behind in the desert and promptly refused. Hardly had he done so when the matter was put beyond all doubt. As one helicopter was taking off its rotor touched one of the refuelling Hercules and both aircraft exploded. Eight men were killed in the fire that engulfed both aircraft, and as the sky around Desert One was lit up with petrol flames and exploding ammunition, Delta and the helicopter crews embarked on the remaining Hercules and flew back to Oman. Operation Eagle Claw had been a disaster.

When dawn broke next day and the Iranians found the abandoned helicopters, the charred bodies and the wreckage of the burning aircraft, their triumph was vocal and America's humiliation complete. Clearly some mistakes had been made, but most of what happened was purely accidental. The margin for success might have been greater if more helicopters had been sent, but the fact remains that the Eagle Claw operation was never viable. The distances were too great, the delays too long, the probability of detection too high. Above all, this was an *ad hoc* force, put together for the task, not a well-trained, fully equipped and totally integrated unit.

The powers-that-be in Washington clearly expected too much from Delta and had to learn – or relearn – and go on learning, that Special Forces cannot do everything. It was also clear that the integration of the helicopters and Delta needed tightening, and if Delta was to use helicopters in any future mission, then they needed their own, Delta-trained and Delta-integrated helicopter and transport unit on permanent standby, like the helicopter unit which forms part of the SAS and GSG9. These deficiencies have since been remedied. In 1997 Delta's order-of-battle includes an Aviation Platoon, with its own fleet of helicopters, painted in civilian colours, and this integrated force is highly effective.

The Byzantine complexity of the situation in Iran lay behind the Iranian Embassy hostage siege in London in May 1980, broken by the British SAS less than ten days after Delta's disaster at Desert One. The seizure of the Embassy was a symptom of the unstable situation in Iran and other countries of the Middle East and an indication of how that instability can cause problems in the West. The Embassy at No. 16 Prince's Gate, a fashionable part of London near Hyde Park, was seized on the morning of 30 April by six heavily armed men, who claimed to be members of the Democratic Revolutionary Movement for the Liberation of Arabistan. This was a Marxist organization, based in Libya, which had supported the Iranian revolution which overthrew the Shah, hoping that the revolution would lead to the independence of Arabistan, a provincial region of Iran. However, when they discovered that the Ayatollah Khomeini and his clique were little better than the Shah, the DRMLA rose against him. Nearly 100 DMRLA members were now enduring severe interrogation in Teheran jails, and the terrorists who seized the Embassy were demanding their release.

The different attitudes to the two Embassy incidents is interesting. When the American Embassy in Teheran was seized, the Iranian government refused to intervene and clearly enjoyed America's discomfiture. When their Embassy in London was seized the Iranians promptly invoked the Vienna Convention and demanded that the British do something about it. The British, bound by international diplomatic protocol, promptly hastened to comply. Apart from the Embassy staff, the Embassy contained four captive Britons, including a policeman, and although three of the staff managed to escape soon after the Embassy was seized, and two more were released the following day, negotiations to end the siege did not go well. Two days after it began, nerves in the Embassy were beginning to fray and three days later, on Monday 5 May, the leader of the terrorists, a man called Oan, shot one of the Embassy staff and had his body dumped on the doorstep. At that point the Metropolitan Police, who had been conducting the siege under the direction of the Home Office, called for the services of the SAS.

The SAS had been on the scene from the start and their CRW troop was already in London, standing by at a nearby barracks. The Embassy had been kept under close surveillance from the start and, having interrogated the released hostages, the SAS already knew the layout of the building and the probable location of the captives and their guards. The SAS plan called for an assault by twelve men, in three teams. Two teams would abseil from the roof, one at the back and one at the front, and break in through the windows on the ground and first floor. The third team would cross from the balcony at No. 15 and assault the windows on the second floor. Once inside, the terrorists were to be subdued with 'flash bangs' and then eliminated.

The attack went in at 1930 hours, before the amazed eyes of the TV camera crews who had taken up position opposite the Embassy days before and had to be prevented from immediately transmitting pictures of black-clad SAS men, swooping down on ropes from the roof. The terrorists were distracted from the television screens by a phone call from the police and then, with a crash of glass and a roar of grenades and machine-gun fire, the SAS broke in. The terrorists turned their guns on the hostages but had only wounded a few before they were shot down.

The SAS swept through the Embassy, clearing room after room, shooting any terrorist they came across. One escaped death by pretending to be a member of the Embassy staff, and the staff protected him until the attack was over, when his identity was revealed. But all the rest of the terrorists were killed. The entire action took just ten minutes and when the police led the hostages from the building, the SAS were already on their way back to Hereford. This is the anti-terrorist operation that put the SAS on the map, and the Regiment is widely regarded as second to none among counter-terrorist forces.

Americans were the popular target for terrorist attack in the 1970s and 1980s, and the next major incident took place in 1982 when an urban terrorist group, the Italian Red Brigades, kidnapped the NATO Commander in Italy, General James L. Dozier, and held him captive for six weeks. The Red Brigades were a Marxist–Leninist, anarchic, anti-democracy group of 'urban terrorists', mostly students and scions of the rich, who waged war against the capitalist system, American imperialism and any other target that came into their heads. Many European countries seethed with student unrest in the 1960s and 1970s, much of it ostensibly fuelled by antagonism over American involvement in the Vietnam War, though many of the more extreme elements took up revolutionary politics and terrorism because it infuriated their parents, inflated their egos, attracted attention and – be it admitted – was fun.

More sinister elements soon took advantage of this youthful enthusiasm, especially in the former Fascist states of Italy and Germany, where the Baader–Meinhof gang and the Red Brigades soon became a real menace. These groups and their supporters in society, politics and the media made many high-toned claims, that they existed to represent the oppressed, to right wrongs, to obtain justice or to establish a more decent society, but this was claptrap. Baader–Meinhof, the Red Brigades and the rest were just terrorists and nothing more, self-deluding anarchists, revelling in murder, torture and destruction. They were also extremely successful, at least for a while.

In 1978 the Red Brigades kidnapped a former Prime Minister of Italy, Aldo Moro, and held him for nearly two months while the police and security forces tore Italy apart looking for him. The Red Brigades then murdered Signor Moro and told the police where to find the body. They went on to murder factory managers and policemen, university professors, judges and politicians, to rob banks and destroy factories, to kneecap the senior personnel of large companies, or anyone who took their fancy. Most of these crimes went unpunished. By 1980 it was estimated that there were some 500 active Red Brigade terrorists in Italy, with another 10,000 supporters in high society and the universities supplying them with money, information or hiding places. Such an organization presented a real challenge to the state, but the Italian authorities seemed powerless to curb its activities. Over time however, the Italians had got organized and were ready to act when General Dozier disappeared.

Dozier was snatched from his apartment in Verona and taken to a student flat in the university city of Padua. There he was kept chained to a bed and blindfolded, while his ears were covered with earphones through which his captives played him pop music – a din which Dozier later claimed was the most gruelling aspect of his captivity. His captors announced that he would be brought before a 'people's court' at which he would have to face 'proletarian justice' for his 'crimes' in the Vietnam War, where he had served as a tank commander. Dozier's life was clearly in danger and there was no time to be lost if he was to be found alive.

Dozier's kidnapping ignited the full force of the Italian state and a massive sweep was launched against the Red Brigades. The gloves finally came off and tough action soon produced results. Student flats and offices were raided, hundreds of suspects were arrested and those interrogated began to talk. Before long the Italian counter-terrorist unit, NOCS, the 'Leatherheads', so called from the leather helmets they wore in action, had a pretty good idea of where Dozier was being held. The trail finally led to a small flat in the Via Pindemonte in Padua.

The Leatherheads decided to assault the apartment at midday, when the terrorists were not likely to be on the alert. From about ten in the morning, young, slim and scruffy members of the NOCS began to filter into the Via Pindemonte, and at 1130 hours the street was cleared. A ten-man squad then entered the target building, and stormed up the stairs to the apartment on the second floor. There were five Red Brigade terrorists guarding Dozier, but the one outside the door was quickly seized and knocked senseless. The snatch team then burst through the door, just in time to stop a second terrorist shooting the chained-up General Dozier. This man was beaten to the floor and the last three terrorists hurriedly surrendered.

The rescue of General Dozier proved a turning point in the fight against the Red Brigades. The terrorists had failed and in the process many of them had talked and betrayed their comrades. The Red Brigades organization began to unravel and, as more information came in, NOCS began to score more successes. With many of their activists in prison and others in exile the Red Brigades collapsed. Italy still suffers from urban terrorism but, for the moment at least, the worst excesses appear to be over.

Italy – or rather an Italian ship – was to provide our last example of terrorist and counter-terrorist action when, in October 1985, six Palestine terrorists seized the Italian cruise ship *Achille Lauro* in the Mediterranean. The terrorists demanded the release of fifty Palestine terrorists held in Israeli jails and threatened to kill all eighty passengers on board, starting with the Jews and going on to the Americans, unless this demand was met. After abusing and frightening the elderly passengers for a couple of days the terrorists finally shot dead a sixty-nine-year-old American, Leon Klinghoffer, who was handicapped and confined to a wheelchair. His body was tipped over the side.

Israel does not deal with terrorists, and when the *Achille Lauro* reached Egypt, the hijackers gave up and went ashore, surrendering to the Egyptian authorities, who came on board to comfort the hostages. The terrorists were not held for long and their release was attributed to the presence in Egypt of Abdul Abbas, an official of the PLO, who was suspected by the Americans of masterminding the entire *Achille Lauro* operation. The US government, furious at the murder of Klinghoffer, wanted Abbas and the other terrorists caught and brought to trial, but it was informed by the Egyptians that the Palestinians had already left the country. However, CIA operatives in Egypt had been keeping tabs on the situation. The CIA informed Washington that the terrorists were still in Egypt but were expected to fly out shortly on a scheduled flight for a destination in Algeria. The Americans therefore decided to intercept the aircraft.

This task was handed to the USS *Saratoga*, a carrier in the US Sixth Fleet. She closed the Egyptian coast and when the terrorists – now tailed by the CIA – boarded their Egyptair flight for Algiers, the *Saratoga* launched a flight of Tomcat fighters and a Prowler electronic warfare interceptor. The terrorists were just settling down to a mid-air celebration dinner in the first-class cabin when four US Tomcat fighters appeared off the wingtips of the airliner and ordered it to follow them to Italy.

There was considerable panic on board the Egyptian airliner. The pilot tried to radio Cairo for instructions, but the Prowler had jammed the radio. The aircraft then headed for the US airbase at Sigonella in Sicily, only for further problems to arise. The Italian air traffic controllers, appraised of the situation, refused the US aircraft and their Egyptian captive permission to land. All the makings of a major diplomatic incident were now in place, but eventually the airliner was allowed to land and the passengers taken into custody by the Italian police. The US government wanted the four terrorists and Abbas tried in Italy or extradited for trial in the United States for the murder of a US citizen, but the Italians were reluctant to comply, mainly for fear of Arab reprisals. Abbas was released on bail and escaped from Italy to Belgrade in a few days, but the others were eventually tried for the murder of Leon Klinghoffer and sentenced to long terms of imprisonment.

The outcome of the *Achille Lauro* affair was not entirely satisfactory, but it demonstrated the sophistication of US intelligence, the long arm of the US government and that government's resolve not to tolerate acts of violence against American citizens. Other governments will need to be equally resolute if the terrorist situation is to be kept under control, but these varied terrorist incidents do provide some lessons in how the terrorist menace might be reduced or combated.

First, there must be a firm resolve not to compromise or haggle with terrorists, whatever their demands. Terrorism must not pay and must be seen not to pay. Second, the price of terrorism must be raised. Terrorists must be hunted down, tried and imprisoned for long terms, and killed if they offer resistance. To this end democratic governments must raise, train, maintain and support highly skilled anti-terrorist teams. These teams must not only respond to terrorist incidents, they must anticipate them, which calls for the infiltration of terrorist groups, both their armed and political wings, and the planting of informers. Finally, terrorism must be deglamorized, and the full horror of terrorist incidents brought to public notice anywhere the terrorists enlist support. This may mean showing the full effect of an IRA bomb to the Irish-American lobby in the USA and displaying the result of Arab terrorist actions in Arab countries. Those countries which foster terrorism should also be penalized. The Vienna Convention by which embassies are free from interference by the host nation was not designed or intended to permit embassies to operate as bases for terrorists within the host nation or to use the 'diplomatic bag' – a term that can cover the contents of a truck or a container – to smuggle in arms or explosives.

Terrorist incidents have not ceased and are not likely to cease. New grievances are being created all the time and the people bearing those grievances seem inclined to seek redress by acts of terrorism. Various actions have been tried against the supporters of terrorism, but no solution has been found that will effectively discourage rogue states from funding terror groups or sponsoring terrorist attacks. Some deterrent must be found, and probably lies in raising the cost of terrorism to the host country by direct action, including the expulsion of its citizens from the victim country and trade sanctions, including the banning of all aircraft flights in or out of the terrorist state.

Sporadic terrorism will probably continue and no solution is yet in sight for Europe's longest-running anti-terrorist campaign, against the IRA in Northern Ireland, a campaign which began in 1969 and is still flourishing thirty years later. A large number of British SOF units and the SAS have long been closely involved and their experiences provide some example of modern terrorist tactics and anti-terrorist warfare within the boundaries of a democratic state.

SAS badge

CHAPTER TWELVE

SAS v. IRA 1969–1997

The hours are long and the amount of abuse you
have to take on patrol is terrible, and then you see
a mate go up under a 200-pounder ... and it can
get you mad, but the lads can take it, like they
always have and always will.

Colour-Sergeant Eric Blythe, 40 Commando,
Royal Marines, 1985

Britain's war against the IRA has been going on for some thirty years. That time-scale alone makes it one of the longest anti-terrorist wars in history, and this bitter period is but the latest stage in a struggle between two conflicting communities that has been going on since the end of the sixteenth century, when Elizabeth Tudor, Queen of England, decided to secure the back door to her Protestant kingdom by 'planting' English settlers in Catholic Ireland. Those who think that the current problems in Northern Ireland are of recent date are woefully ignorant of the facts.

The reign of Elizabeth Tudor saw constant war in Ireland, and Cromwell continued the 'planting' of Protestant settlers in the next century. Since the Antrim coast of Northern Ireland is only twelve miles from the coast of Scotland, many Protestant Scots crossed the water and settled in the province of Ulster, where they soon made up the majority of the population, as their descendants still do. In the nineteenth century steps were taken to give the Irish that independence they had long craved, but any solution was increasingly plagued by the problem of what to do about the Protestant population in the Six Counties of the North, who flatly refused to live in a Catholic-dominated Ireland. Protestant protests torpedoed various attempts at a settlement and the eventual solution was Partition, arrived at by the Anglo-Irish Treaty of 1920, which partitioned the island of Ireland into two unequal portions, the twenty-six counties of the Catholic south, now the Republic of Ireland, and the six-county province of Northern Ireland, which is part of the United Kingdom.

The Anglo-Irish Treaty was followed by a bitter civil war in southern Ireland, between the legitimate, elected government, which accepted the Treaty, and the IRA, the Irish Republican Army, which vehemently rejected both the Treaty and Partition. This first IRA rising was crushed by the Irish government, which tried and shot a considerable number of IRA men for treason and rebellion against the newly formed Irish state. From then on, with the support of its political wing, Sinn Fein, the IRA concentrated on driving the 'British', by which it means the British government, its officials, police and Army, out of the North, and a sporadic IRA terrorist campaign has been going on in the North and on the British mainland ever since.

That is a sketchy history, but a brief outline to the Troubles is necessary if the military campaign which has been going on since 1969 is to be seen in context. By the 1960s the IRA had changed. Many members had embraced a Marxist–socialist ideology and intended first to drive the British out of Ireland and then, on the basis of the political popularity gained by that victory, establish a Marxist state in the whole island of Ireland. In 1970, shortly after the current round of Troubles began, political divisions produced a split in the IRA ranks, with the Official IRA and Official Sinn Fein opting for a political settlement leading to a socialist Ireland, and the Provisional IRA – PIRA – taking the terrorist road. It is therefore with PIRA and those SF and SOF units that combat it in the North that this chapter is chiefly concerned.

The trouble that broke out in Northern Ireland in 1968–9 had a perfectly legitimate basis: civil rights. By gerrymandering the elections the Protestants – most of them members of the Orange Order (an organization of Protestant supporters of the Union with Great Britain) – had kept Catholic politicians from office, Catholic men and women out of jobs, Catholic children from a decent education, Catholic families from proper housing.

This disgraceful state of affairs had been allowed because the British government at Westminster had left the government of Northern Ireland to a locally elected parliament, Stormont, and the Stormont government was entirely composed of Protestants. In 1968 and 1969, unwilling to endure this discrimination any longer, the Catholics of Belfast, Londonderry and other cities of the North took to the streets in mass protests which were crushed with brutal and excessive force by the Royal Ulster Constabulary and, especially, by the mainly Protestant police reserve, the B Specials.

The police and Protestants had, however, forgotten one element in their current round of repression – the media. Newspapermen and television crews flocked to cover the riots in Northern Ireland and questions were soon being asked in Great Britain, by the public, the press and in Parliament, about the causes of these riots. The answers dragged from Northern Irish politicians disgusted the British people, as did the visible evidence of the tactics employed by the B Specials against the civil-rights protesters, which aroused widespread condemnation.

Clearly, the Catholics of Northern Ireland had endured a great wrong and these wrongs must be put right and the discrimination ended. Over the years since 1969, much has been done towards that end, not least with the abolition of the Stormont parliament and the implementation of laws to protect the Catholics from discrimination. What laws have not been able to do is end the hatred, brewed over centuries, between the Catholic and Protestant communities. These hatreds are exacerbated today by the actions of the IRA and those terrorist groups created by the Protestants, of which tit-for-tat sectarian killings are a typical feature. That such tribal hatreds can exist in a civilized, democratic, Western European country at the end of the ever-more-secular twentieth century seems so unlikely that many people, especially in the United States and Australia, have rejected that fundamental cause of the Troubles and laid the blame squarely at the door of the British, who, it is alleged, have invaded Ireland and are holding the Northern population in subjection with the British Army, against which the 'freedom fighters' of the IRA are maintaining a legitimate 'armed struggle'.

The current round of 'Troubles' in Ireland is, in fact, a vastly complicated affair with deep roots and a great many totally committed players. Integration with the Republic of Ireland can come whenever the majority of people in the North express the wish for it by a democratic vote, but since the Protestants in Ulster outnumber the Catholics two to one and show no sign of wishing for integration with the South, this solution is not currently on offer. The IRA campaign in Ulster has often spread to the British mainland and Continental Europe; it has cost more than 3,200 lives since 1969, and has resulted in the destruction of billions of pounds' worth of property for no valid reason or perceptible advantage.

The IRA campaign has the aim of so sickening the British government and the mainland population with an endless round of death, injury and violence that they will abandon the Northern Protestants and pull out. That this would immediately lead to a civil war in Ireland is not the IRA's problem; they *want* a civil war in Ireland and they intend to emerge from it victorious and establish their Marxist-oriented state.

So, with no likely political solution in sight, the struggle goes on. Among the British military regularly involved are SOF units like the Royal Marines Commandos and the Parachute Regiment, which undertake regular six-month tours in Northern Ireland. Their work in the Province is described by Marine Andrew Tubb of 45 Commando: 'We had been very well trained at a special camp in Britain where we could work out all the routines from patrolling to crowd control and riot drill. There were even Wrens dressed as housewives shrieking abuse at you and flinging bricks. Once there we went to Turf Lodge, a Catholic area. You get any amount of tasking, job after job and not much sleep for weeks on end. Later we took over from an Army battalion at Fort White Rock where the way out was down a narrow tunnel and one day, as we went out, we came under fire, by an automatic weapon, a semi-automatic and some single shots. The "brick" – that's four Marines – shot out of the tunnel, straight at them, and had pinpointed the firing point within one and a half minutes. I'll never forget that, the firing, no hesitation, straight at them.'

There has never been any real likelihood of a military solution to the Ulster problem but the British Army has been in the Province, acting as an 'aid to the civil power', since troops were first committed in 1969, some months after the first civil rights marches were brutally broken up by the Royal Ulster Constabulary B Specials. The B Specials were promptly disbanded, but this necessary move had an unwelcome side-effect. When the Catholic and Protestant mobs took to the streets and started 'ethnic cleansing' in their local areas, the Catholics burning Protestant homes, the Protestants attacking any Catholics living in their areas, the regular police force, the RUC, were unable to cope and British soldiers had to be deployed on the streets, and so the British Army came to Northern Ireland.

Those soldiers who went to Belfast and other Northern Ireland towns in 1969 recall that they were welcomed with open arms by the local population, Catholic and Protestant, invited into their homes and plied with plates of sandwiches and cups of tea. Lieutenant Ian Uzzell, of 41 Commando, remembers this early period: 'We were sent in to stop Protestant mobs attacking Catholic homes and the Catholics were very glad to see us. Our radios did not work too well in the narrow streets and among buildings so the best way to learn what was going on was to knock on a door and go in to see what was happening on the TV news, which was reporting the riots every night. It was also a bit disconcerting to be skulking along a street, avoiding bricks or sniper fire and have a hand come out of a door offering you a cup of tea or a sticky bun ... it did not last long, but it was nice while it lasted.'

One reason the friendship did not last was the resurgence of the IRA. When the Troubles first broke out those IRA terrorists based in Belfast or Derry promptly fled to the Irish Republic; a wall painting in the Catholic Bogside interpreted IRA as meaning 'I Ran Away'. But before long, re-equipped with weapons provided by their friends in the Republic, the IRA were back, ostensibly to defend Catholic areas from Protestant attack, actually to use these civil-rights disturbances for their own ends. One of their first commands was that there was to be no friendly contact with the 'Brits', and anyone caught smiling at a British soldier was marked for IRA attention.

'It was pretty sickening,' says Brigadier Joe Starling, an officer of the Parachute Regiment. 'The lads were well aware of "hearts and minds" and great efforts were made to befriend the Catholic community and show that we were totally impartial in this situation, but it did not work. I can recall when we set up a canoe camp on the River Bann for the kids on a nearby Catholic estate. They had never had such fun and the kids loved it, and so did the Toms, the soldiers; then the word came down from some IRA godfather and the kids smashed and burned the canoes and threw bricks at the soldiers. The word from PIRA was "Hate the Brits and be seen to do so." So what can you do? The kids get infected with this hatred and so the war goes on, generation after generation.'

There was rioting and sectarian fighting throughout 1968–9, with Catholics and Protestants battling in the streets, so the troops intervened and were promptly attacked by mobs from both sides. Then the IRA moved into the Catholic housing estates and established their rule of violence and intimidation, beating, kneecapping, tarring-and-feathering, torturing or killing anyone on those estates who dared to protest against their campaign. And so the long, bloody and now all too familiar Northern Ireland conflict began. There are usually about 15,000 British soldiers deployed in Ulster, and among this number are the men of the 22nd Special Air Service Regiment.

D Squadron of the Regiment arrived in Northern Ireland in August 1969, wearing uniform, and were quite openly based at Bessbrook Camp in South Armagh. One of their first actions was to hold a formal parade and wreath-laying at the grave of the wartime SAS leader, Lieutenant-Colonel Blair 'Paddy' Mayne, who had been killed in a motor accident after the war and is buried at Newtownards. That apart, the Squadron took part in routine patrol duties and road blocks, still in uniform. Major-General Julian Thompson who was in Northern Ireland at that time, commanding 40 Commando, remembers the SAS arriving. 'When they arrived they wore their own sand-coloured berets, but after a bit they took to going about in our green berets and when a Parachute battalion arrived they swapped to wearing red berets ... I think when a Highland battalion arrived they went about in bonnets, but otherwise it was a normal deployment and it was all very open and above board.'

The situation was relatively peaceful in Northern Ireland – a state the politicians were to refer to as 'an acceptable level of violence' – and the SAS Squadron was eventually withdrawn. The SAS returned to Northern Ireland in 1976 and have remained there ever since, apart from short deployments to Arabia during the Gulf War. But their role in the province has become increasingly obscure. The SAS returned to work in conjunction with the resident battalion at Bessbrook Camp, but they also began to go under cover. Before long they were operating in civilian clothes, patrolling in private cars and even crossing the southern border.

Soldiering in civilian clothes is not uncommon in Northern Ireland. It was – and is – highly inadvisable for a British soldier to go about on his own at all, and definitely dangerous to be alone and in uniform. Most of the soldiers deployed in the Province never leave their barracks at all during their four- to six-month tour of duty other than on patrol, for even going for a drink in the pub down the road is dangerous. A number of units took on patrolling IRA-infested districts like South Armagh in plain clothes, even equipping the outside of their cars with anti-personnel 'claymore' mines. These could be detonated and spray out a sweeping charge of shrapnel if the soldiers ran into one of the VCPs (Vehicle Check or Control Points) which the IRA had started setting up on the roads in South Armagh, an area that came to be known as the 'bandit country'.

As elsewhere, the first requirement for a successful fight against IRA terrorism was a reliable supply of relevant intelligence on the IRA gangs, or ASUs – their four-man Active Service Units, a polite term for murder squads. The main source of such intelligence should have been the Royal Ulster Constabulary Special Branch, but the RUC members had made themselves so unpopular with the Catholic community and were so well known on the Catholic housing estates that they produced very little usable information. It was therefore necessary to start again and recreate a good network of military intelligence gathering, based on reconnaissance and observation, two specializations of the SAS.

Other intelligence agencies also took a hand in the game. MI6 – the British Secret Intelligence Service, which operates overseas, began to track IRA personnel in the Republic, in Continental Europe and on fund- and arms-raising missions to the United States and Libya. MI5 – the Security Service, which operates within the UK – began to infiltrate Irish Nationalist groups on the British mainland, producing a great deal of contact information on IRA activity in London and other cities with large Irish populations.

The Army intelligence units also succeeded in finding and running a number of informers – 'touts' to the IRA commanders – most of whom were former or serving IRA men who, either for cash or from revulsion at the IRA's murderous activities, were willing to work against their former comrades. Designated the Military Reconnaissance Force, this last group were generally known as 'Freds'. Any 'tout' or 'Fred' captured by PIRA faced the certainty of brutal and prolonged torture, culminating with a bullet in the head. But though the operations of the 'Freds' are necessarily secret there appears to be no shortage of volunteers. The IRA, however vaunted their exploits may be in the United States, are vastly unpopular with all decent people in Ireland.

The risks remain high. People even suspected of 'touting' can suffer a similar fate of torture and murder, while the general Catholic population is kept on side, partly from conviction and belief in the Republican cause, partly because any outright show of opposition to the IRA can result in having one's kneecaps slowly pierced with a Black and Decker drill or, for a woman, having one's hair sheared off before being beaten, stripped naked, tied to a lamp-post in the street and covered with tar.

Such coercion cut down on the amount of intelligence the Army could gather, and normal anti-terrorist action – the stop-and-search or cordon-and-sweep routines, so often used in the colonial campaigns – here provoked riots, stone-throwing and unfortunate reports on the television news, adding to the alienation of the local population. Good intelligence offered the possibility that counter-terrorist activity could be targeted on those most directly involved in the IRA campaign and cut down on confrontations with the all-too-easily provoked activists on the Catholic estates.

The RUC strengthened their Special Branch and introduced armed Special Patrol Group units which roved about the back streets and lanes of the Province in cars, looking for trouble. One very useful – but very secret – Special Force element in this complicated brew was the 14th Intelligence Company, a group of police and army volunteers who work in plain clothes and were raised in 1974 by Lieutenant-Colonel Frank Kitson, an acknowledged expert in such covert, low-intensity warfare with experience of covert operations in Kenya and Malaya.

Not much is known about the 14th Intelligence Company, except that it was – and probably still is – composed of Army officers and NCOs, including women, who operate in plain clothes and take considerable risks. The Company numbers about 100 and acts as the operational arm of MI6 and MI5. Training for 14 Company is intensive and lasts six months, during which time the members immerse themselves totally in the life of the Province. They avoid military units, have no rank, never use their real names, buy their well-worn clothes in charity shops, and generally act on a cell-like, need-to-know basis. They drive unmarked cars, equipped with tracking devices and alarms, and armed with tear gas and stun grenades should they be caught or be at risk of detection.

None of this is unnecessary. Any 14 Company operative detected and taken by the IRA would be brutally interrogated and tortured to tell all he or she knows about the Company and those who serve in it. The vicious nature of the IRA campaign was underlined in May 1977 when an IRA ASU, operating from the Republic, entered Armagh and kidnapped a Guards officer, Captain Robert Nairac. Captain Nairac was serving in 14 Intelligence Company and was meeting a contact in a bar in South Armagh, alone and in plain clothes. He was attacked in the car park outside the pub, overwhelmed, taken across the Border into the Republic, tortured for information, and killed. His body has never been found.

About a third of the Company are women and they have proved

particularly expert in penetrating IRA cells. The Company has provided the information that led to the capture of a large number of IRA operatives in the Province and on the mainland, and the finding of many caches of arms and explosives, including the location of five tons of explosives in London in September 1996, a store intended for a devastating series of attacks on British cities. To acquire such information the Company personnel live in IRA-dominated areas, and carry out surveillance of IRA-friendly pubs and community centres. The IRA know they are there and would dearly love to lay hands on them.

This expansion of intelligence-gathering organizations did not at first greatly improve the quantity or quality of the information supplied to the security forces, and the security operation faltered. No one was happy with the state of intelligence gathering, but rather than improve the Special Branch of the RUC, each element in Northern Ireland – police, Army and secret service – set up their own intelligence-gathering networks, which led to unhealthy competition and a diffusion of effort. Intelligence gathering is also one of the principal roles of the SAS, which gathers intelligence by surveillance rather than by running informers, and their skills soon came into play. The SAS set up observation posts at crossing points on the border, and began keeping discreet watch on the homes of 'known players' and on tracks and roads surrounding Crossmaglen and other IRA strongholds. The Regiment had been at this task for some time before the British government finally announced, in January 1976, that elements of the SAS had been deployed in the Province.

This 1976 deployment was quite different from the open commitment of a full squadron in 1969. Only a dozen SAS troopers were involved at first and they worked with the regular battalions in a reconnaissance role. However, by the early spring of 1976, there was a full SAS squadron at Bessbrook Camp, sending out the usual SAS four-man patrols to quarter the countryside of South Armagh and tasked not just to observe the enemy but to act against them. Within a week of deployment this new policy was producing results.

On the night of 12 March 1976, an Army patrol claimed that they had picked up a drunken Irishman wandering about aimlessly just north of the Ulster Border. The soldiers took him to the police, who ran his details through the police computer and found that they had caught a major IRA 'player', Sean McKenna. McKenna was most unhappy about his arrest and had a strange tale to tell about how it had occurred. According to McKenna, he had been in bed in his house south of the Border when three masked men had entered the room, carried him off into South Armagh at pistol point, and handed him over to the soldiers. McKenna was tried in Belfast and sent to prison for twenty-five years, and his capture was tacitly credited to the SAS. The Irish government was not happy about British soldiers crossing the Republic's Border, but the fact that a known terrorist had been living openly in the Republic meant that no official complaint was made at the time. In fact most people, north and south of the Border, were highly amused.

A month later, in April 1976, the SAS killed their first IRA man, Patrick Cleary, another noted 'player', who had crossed the Border from the Republic to see his girlfriend in the North. The SAS had laid an ambush on the girl's house and when Cleary arrived he was promptly arrested, only to be shot when he attempted to escape. Sinn Fein and the IRA promptly claimed that Cleary had been murdered in cold blood.

All was going well, but a month later the SAS anti-terrorist activity went awry. On the evening of 5 May 1976, the Gardai – the Irish police – stopped a car a few hundred yards south of the Border. The men inside were armed, and, as more Gardai arrived, so did two more cars from north of the Border. The drivers and passengers of these cars were also armed, but offered no resistance when the Gardai arrested them. Matters then got very embarrassing when it transpired that the Gardai had picked up eight SAS soldiers, clearly intending to operate south of the Border.

The resulting publicity was considerable and very unfavourable to the British Army. The Irish government could not tolerate armed incursions across the Border, but the matter was tactfully handled. The SAS men were bailed and released, but returned later to be tried in Dublin and fined £100 each. Even so, the IRA and Sinn Fein, the IRA's political wing and no mean performers at publicity, were delighted at this evidence of British 'arrogance' and took full advantage of the incident.

British soldiers had to avoid trespassing in the Republic, but there was considerable resentment that, although the Irish government deplored the IRA campaign in the North, the IRA still enjoyed a safe haven in the Republic, where the British Army could not pursue them. Being able to pursue terrorists into their hiding-places is a prerequisite for success in guerrilla warfare, but this 'hot pursuit' requirement was and is denied to the British, who do not enjoy an adequate level of anti-terrorist support from the Irish authorities. The Gardai – who have had officers killed by the IRA – would usually follow up on contacts provided by the RUC but were slow to respond after a terrorist attack in the North; by the time they arrived on the Border the IRA gunmen had usually disappeared. The only real way to strike hard at the IRA was to put an ambush on a likely target and wait for an attack. It was this patient method which produced the next kill.

In January 1977 an SAS patrol spotted a parked car in a road close to the Border near the town of Crossmaglen, a terrorist hot spot in South Armagh. The car was still there next day, so a surveillance operation was mounted and maintained. Three nights later an armed man was seen approaching the car. When challenged by the hidden SAS men, he raised his weapon and was promptly shot down. He was clearly scouting the car before getting into it, for the SAS were fired upon by more IRA men further down the road and a heavy exchange of fire took place before the surviving IRA fled back across the Border.

Matters were going well, but the SAS activity also produced two incidents which illustrate the dangers of using Special Force troops in an undeclared, urban, guerrilla war, and brought the issue of SAS involvement in counter-terrorist work into question. The first occurred in June 1978, when three IRA men were ambushed and killed by the SAS while attempting to plant a bomb in a post office at Ballyskillen. A fourth IRA man ran off and escaped, but in the pursuit the SAS – or the RUC Special Patrol Group, who were also involved – killed William Hanna, who had no connection with the IRA and was simply walking home from a pub.

The Army Press Office put out a statement saying that the IRA had opened fire first and that Hanna had been killed in the crossfire. This statement was untrue. A police inquiry and the inquest revealed that the three IRA men, though clearly on a terrorist mission and carrying a bomb, had otherwise been unarmed, so there was no question of any 'crossfire'. It transpired that Hanna had simply been shot by mistake. Skilled, mature SAS soldiers are not supposed to make mistakes that result in the death of innocent passers-by, and the damage to the professional reputation of the SAS and the British Army caused by this tragic accident was exacerbated by the attempted cover-up.

Worse was to follow. In July 1977, John Boyle, a lad just sixteen years old, found a cache of IRA weapons near the family farm at Dunloy in County Antrim. The police were informed and a four-man SAS patrol took up position, ready to ambush those who came to claim the weapons. No one thought to tell the Boyle family of this ambush or order them to stay away from the ambush site and on the following day young John Boyle decided to see if the weapons were still there. They were still in the cache and, according to the inquest evidence, when he picked up one of the weapons for a closer inspection, two SAS marksmen promptly shot him dead. His father and brother, who came running up, were forced to the ground, arrested and taken to the police station in a helicopter.

Only then was the full extent of the tragedy discovered, but once again the Army attempted to avoid accusations of careless gunplay by making a number of false claims. The first claim was that John Boyle had pointed a loaded weapon at the patrol. This is unlikely; John Boyle had no idea that the patrol was there and he had no knowledge of firearms. The next claim was that a warning had been shouted to him and ignored; this too was soon refuted. The RUC eventually responded to growing public concern by arresting the two SAS men who had fired the shots. They were subsequently put on trial for murder but acquitted because the prosecution failed to establish that the men intended to kill, and proof of intent is crucial to any successful murder prosecution.

These incidents put the SAS in a bad light. British soldiers serving in Northern Ireland are bound by a set of instructions, the Rules of Engagement. In the delicate situation in Northern Ireland these rules are set out plainly on a yellow card, which every soldier has to carry, know by heart and apply. The SAS are soldiers in the British Army and therefore bound by Yellow Card rules; the essence of these rules is an insistence on minimum force. The troops are not to open fire unless fired at or unless they think beyond all or reasonable doubt that their lives are in danger. A warning should also be given before opening fire. It cannot be said that keeping to the Yellow Card rules is easy. If applied to the letter, they would make safe soldiering impossible, but they are designed to protect innocent citizens and bystanders against irresponsible shooting and are clearly necessary. They also reflect the fact that the IRA campaign is not a 'war', at least not as far as the British are concerned, and the soldiers sent to Northern Ireland are open to arrest and trial under the civil law if they are suspected of any crime.

The civil authorities must also interpret the Yellow Card rules sensibly, for rules that seem clear and easy to obey in a warm courtroom take on quite a different complexion to a tired young soldier when a car comes roaring through an ambush position in the middle of the night, or when a man looms up out of the rain carrying what appears to be a weapon. He who hesitates at such a moment could easily be killed, or see his comrades killed. Yellow Card rules have to be applied with reference to the situation, and when an error occurs the same criteria should apply to any subsequent inquiry. But there were grounds for serious disquiet over the John Boyle shooting. The SAS had been deployed to deal with the IRA effectively while reducing the impact of security operations on the civilian population. Now two, totally innocent, unarmed men had been shot dead and a further three far from innocent but still unarmed IRA men had also been killed, allegedly without the benefit of a warning.

These tragic incidents involving the SAS were to continue. In September 1977, James Taylor was shot dead by an SAS patrol when out with a shotgun for some rough shooting. Taylor had no connections with any paramilitary group, and this time the Army told the truth and apologized. Hardly had it done so when, in November 1977, another incident occurred, this time involving a 'known player', Patrick Duffy. Another IRA arms cache had been located at a house in Derry and was under surveillance by a four-man SAS team. Patrick Duffy entered the house and went to the cache only to be challenged and shot dead by the soldiers. Duffy was not armed and though questions were raised about why the four soldiers in the house did not simply arrest him, no action was taken to investigate the shooting.

However, following this affair, the SAS were withdrawn from ambush duties and returned to a more conventional surveillance role. In May 1980 the regiment suffered its first death in Northern Ireland when Captain Herbert Westacott, of G Squadron, was shot dead while commanding a party cordoning off a house in Belfast. Later that year a team of SAS caught four IRA men, including a very notorious 'player', Seamus McElwaine. These men were cornered, a warning was given and the IRA men elected to surrender.

During the spring and early summer of 1982 the SAS were engaged in the Falklands War, but they were back in the Province by the end of the year and in December 1982 they killed two armed IRA men after a stake-out of a weapons cache near Coalisland. In July 1983 two teams scored a major success after a tip-off about an IRA attack in County Tyrone, where the terrorists were intending to bomb a factory. Hearing of this plan, the SAS set up an ambush and prepared to wait, but they did not have to wait long. Soon after dark, two men were seen approaching the factory and, when they ran and failed to halt when challenged, they were fired on; one man was wounded and both were captured. Like the SAS, an IRA Active Service Unit tends to operate in groups of four and a search uncovered two more IRA men near by, who were also fired upon, one being captured and one killed.

The next SAS–IRA encounter had a less happy outcome. The factory ambush indicates that the SAS were now getting good contact information, either directly from 'touts' or via 14 Company. They therefore knew of a pending attempt to murder a member of the Ulster Defence Regiment, the local territorial unit, which takes an active part in security duties and is largely composed of Protestants, many of them former B Specials. The SAS set up an ambush near the man's home and the IRA killers duly arrived and were fired upon. Unfortunately, the only person killed was a civilian, Fred Jackson, who was visiting a timber yard just across the road from the ambush site when the soldiers opened fire. A bullet hit Jackson in the chest and killed him, and the IRA men escaped.

In December 1984 a second SAS man was killed in the Province during the course of a successful attempt to prevent an IRA ASU planting a culvert bomb under a road. Four IRA men in a van were stopped by three SAS men, but as two of the SAS approached the van, they were fired on by IRA men hidden in the hedges and Lance Corporal Alistair Slater of B Squadron was killed. In the gunfight that followed two IRA men died; one was shot in the action, and another drowned while attempting to swim a river and get back to the safety of the Republic. The two surviving IRA men got back across the Border, where they were arrested by the Gardai.

The next incident was not long in coming. Once again the IRA were attempting to murder a member of the Ulster Defence Regiment, a man who worked as an orderly at the Gransha hospital in Derry. In January 1985 the IRA intention was leaked to the police – probably from a 'Fred' or through 14 Company – and a team of police and SAS moved into the hospital grounds. The murder was entrusted to two experienced killers, Daniel Doherty and William Fleming, who entered the hospital grounds on a motorbike. According to evidence given at the subsequent inquest, the pair rode past a car containing SAS men, and the pillion passenger was seen to be holding a pistol. The driver therefore gave chase, rammed the motorcycle, and both men were thrown off. Fleming, the pillion passenger, was fired on by two SAS men, hit six times and killed. Doherty remounted and attempted to escape, but he too was shot and killed.

A month later, in February 1985, a roving group of five IRA killers were driving around Strabane, seeking to kill either a Protestant or an RUC man. Their presence became known, their car was directed into an SAS ambush and three of the IRA were killed in the firefight which followed. A fourth man, Declan Crossan, was captured later and the last one fled. Following this shooting, tales got about that the three men had been murdered, perhaps because the inquest revealed that the SAS had fired over 100 rounds into the three men during the ambush. Some local people claimed that at least one voice had been heard calling for mercy before the final burst of fire. The inquest failed to find evidence to support this claim and brought in a verdict of 'lawful killing'.

The rest of the year was quiet, at least for the SAS, but in February 1986 an arms cache was located in a farmyard near Londonderry and placed under surveillance. A man called Francis Bradley later entered the yard, was challenged by an SAS soldier and shot dead when he turned in response to the call. This caused further disquiet, for although it has been alleged that Bradley was collecting the arms for a terrorist group, he had no terrorist connections, was unarmed, had reacted normally to the challenge and been shot at close range no fewer than eight times.

These accounts should not lead anyone to suppose that soldiering in Northern Ireland was one round of danger and excitement. The main problem mentioned by the soldiers was boredom. Many soldiers served tour after tour in Northern Ireland without firing a shot or hearing an explosion. The old rule, that soldiering is 'long periods of intense boredom interspersed with short periods of intense terror' holds equally good in Ireland.

It took a great deal of hard, boring and routine work to get a contact, and at best the SAS were only making one every two or three months, with lots of time passing without any action at all, though the IRA continued to bomb, murder and kneecap their victims on an almost daily basis, both in Northern Ireland and, in a bid to attract more publicity, in the UK, where the HQ of the Parachute Regiment at Aldershot was bombed in February 1972, killing a regimental padre and two cleaning women. Special Force units have attracted a lot of IRA attention and Parachute or Commando units, which were highly effective in Northern Ireland and therefore deeply disliked, were often singled out for attack, especially after the Parachute Regiment shot thirteen people at the Bloody Sunday riots in Belfast in 1972. On their Northern Ireland tour in 1972, 40 Commando had three Marines killed and seventeen wounded by the IRA, but they captured over fifty terrorists. In 1975, 40 Commando caught ninety-one terrorists without loss to themselves, but in 1976 six Marines were injured in a mortar attack at Crossmaglen. On 27 August 1979, the day that the Queen's cousin Lord Mountbatten was murdered by a bomb in Mullaghmore

Bay, County Sligo while on holiday with his family, eighteen soldiers of 2 Para were killed by a car bomb at Warrenpoint in County Down. The Commandant General of the Royal Marines, Lieutenant-General Sir Steuart Pringle, lost a leg to an IRA car bomb outside his home in London in 1981. And so the fighting and killing has continued.

In May 1987, however, the IRA experienced a considerable setback when a large ASU was ambushed by the SAS in the village of Loughgall in North Armagh, where the IRA intended to bomb the police station using a massive bomb mounted in the bucket of a JCB excavator. The importance of good intelligence has been stressed frequently in this book, and it was good intelligence – probably supplied by 14 Company – that tipped off the RUC about the forthcoming attack. This information was passed on to the SAS, which was in position around the police station before the IRA appeared at about 7.15 on the evening of Friday 8 May. The IRA had stolen a Toyota van which, with five IRA men inside, was driven into the village. The JCB followed, with two armed IRA men riding on it and another driving. Three men jumped out of the van and opened fire on the police station as the JCB rammed the perimeter fence, and the two men got off to light the bomb fuse.

The IRA were greeted by a hail of fire from the hidden SAS men, which killed the three men riding on the JCB and the driver of the van. A great blast of explosive then almost demolished the police station and the JCB. Two more men were found dead inside the bullet-riddled van and another man was killed as he attempted to shelter under it. So the IRA had lost a good many key 'players' and the SAS had scored a notable victory. Then it all went wrong.

To maintain security no warning had been given to the villagers, and just before the attack two brothers, Oliver and Anthony Hughes, both garage mechanics, drove into the village. The men were wearing blue overalls, similar to those worn by the IRA, and when the firing started the two men decided to reverse up the road and out of trouble. The soldiers opened fire on their truck, killing Anthony and severely wounding Oliver. No challenge was given because the action had already commenced. The usual accusations of security force gunplay were made by Sinn Fein, but the shooting of the Hughes brothers was a complete accident.

The same cannot be said of the senseless and brutal IRA attack carried out in the centre of Enniskillen during the Remembrance Day Service of November 1987, when a bomb hidden in the War Memorial killed eleven people and injured a great many more. The pattern of killing continued up to the end of 1994 when a ceasefire was announced by PIRA, pending talks about the future of Northern Ireland, but that ceasefire, and the Peace Process talks which followed it, did not stop IRA beatings and killings in Northern Ireland, the murder of a Gardai officer in the Republic or the bombings at Manchester and at Canary Wharf in London in 1996.

As far as the Army and the SAS in particular are concerned, Northern Ireland has been a mixed blessing. Patrolling 'with a bullet up the spout' and learning to soldier when your life is at risk, however remote that risk might be, is a good way to give an army that extra little edge, but actions in 'aid of the civil power' should be undertaken only when all else has failed and will always carry the risk that soldiers will become involved in actions for which their training and temperament has left them less than well equipped.

Most of the soldiers, even those in SF and SOF units, are quite young and of junior rank, for terrorist wars are 'corporals' wars', and these young soldiers have to take on tasks that might be, or should really be, the responsibility of the police. One lesson that comes out of the Northern Ireland business is that soldiers should be committed to counter-terrorism tasks in an urban environment only in certain circumstances and as a last resort – a lesson underlined by what happened when an SAS unit went into action on the Rock of Gibraltar in March 1988.

The story of the 'Death on the Rock' affair, as it came to be called, an action which led to the death of three IRA terrorists – Sean Savage, Daniel McCann and a woman, Maraid Farrell – is both complicated and controversial, but all the facts have relevance and need to be considered. In the autumn of 1987 British intelligence – probably MI6 – located two 'known players', Savage and McCann, touring along the Costa del Sol in southern Spain. The pair stayed in the Costa del Sol, or made frequent visits to the area, throughout the winter of 1987–8, and, since the likely military target was the British garrison of Gibraltar, a close-surveillance team from MI5 flew to Gibraltar in early 1988 and drew up a list of possible IRA hits.

The most obvious was a regular weekly event, the Changing the Guard ceremony at the Governor's Palace by the resident British battalion. During this parade a military band and troops paraded through the streets to the Palace, watched by a large crowd of tourist and civilian spectators. Army ceremonial had provided the IRA with several bloody opportunities in recent years, notably the attack on the Household

Cavalry in Hyde Park in 1982, and all the signs were that another such outrage was being planned for Gibraltar.

It was known that the IRA had developed a remote-control, hand-held triggering device which could detonate a car bomb from a safe distance, and a car bomb seemed the most likely form of attack. On 4 March 1988 Maraid Farrell arrived in Malaga to join Savage and McCann, so it seemed likely that the attack would shortly take place. The Spanish police were willing to co-operate in the search for the car bomb and a sixteen-man team from the SAS, in plain clothes, had been flown to Gibraltar on 3 March to work with the police on the Rock. This was now a full-scale security operation and given the code name Operation Flavius. The commander of Flavius was the Gibraltar Police Commissioner, Joseph Canepa, and his orders were that the terrorists should be arrested and their arms and bombs made safe.

The pattern of the probable attack was quite familiar after twenty years of car bombs in Northern Ireland and London. The IRA would use two cars; one would enter the Rock and park somewhere on the route to the Palace used by the band and troops. This car would be completely clean of explosives, for its role was to occupy a space on the route so that the 'bomb car', arriving later, would have somewhere to park. The most likely spot for a bomb was in the plaza, where the troops and band assembled for the Guard Changing, so a close watch was kept on cars parking there.

Meanwhile, the Spanish police scoured hotels and car parks on the Costa del Sol searching for the IRA terrorists and the bomb car, but despite this, and despite close surveillance at the Gibraltar crossing, the bomb car was not located. The IRA were able to park a white Renault 5 in the plaza on Gibraltar and get back off the Rock without detection.

By the afternoon of Sunday 5 March, tension on the Rock was at its height. SAS troopers, in plain clothes but armed with Browning 9mm automatic pistols, were working eight-hour shifts in teams of four, and at about 1400 hours the police reported to Flavius HQ that Savage had been spotted at a car in the plaza, 'fiddling with something inside the car'. The assumption was that he had delivered the bomb car and was priming an explosive charge, ready for detonation by radio signal. A few minutes later another message reached Flavius HQ that Farrell and McCann had been spotted crossing the Border and were walking up into the town. The operation was now 'on' and the SAS went into action.

An explosive expert took a careful look at the car and reported that it probably contained a bomb. This was enough for Police Commissioner Joseph Canepa, who signed an order passing the operation into the hands of the SAS. This order was signed and timed at 1540 hours and the SAS then moved in on the three IRA terrorists, who were still under surveillance and walking back towards the Border.

By the Gibraltar airport runway, which crosses the road to the Border, Savage left the other two and started to walk back towards the town. By now four SAS troopers were within yards of the terrorists; two of them, identified at the inquest as Soldiers A and B, continued with McCann and Farrell. The other two, Soldiers C and D, followed Sean Savage back into the town. A few minutes later the SAS soldiers opened fire.

The shooting seems to have been triggered by a police siren, coming from a vehicle caught in heavy afternoon traffic while attempting to get to where the SAS men were going to arrest the IRA. The police driver switched on his siren in an attempt to clear a way, and McCann, looking round suddenly on hearing the noise, made 'eye contact' with Soldier A about thirty feet behind him. It seems that McCann realized that the police or the security forces were on to them, and Soldier A saw that he had been spotted. What happened then is harder to judge, but according to evidence given by the SAS men at the inquest McCann put his hand inside his jacket, as if to grab a pistol or trigger the firing device for the car bomb in the plaza. Taking no chances, Soldier A drew his pistol and fired one round into McCann. Then – again according to the evidence given at the inquest – seeing Maraid Farrell reach into her handbag, Soldier A fired a bullet into her. He then put another bullet into McCann. Soldier B had meanwhile drawn his pistol and he also fired a bullet into Farrell and another into McCann.

The shooting was heard by the third IRA terrorist, Sean Savage, who, again according to evidence given at the inquest, put his hand into his pocket. His followers, Soldiers C and D, then opened fire and shot him dead. At 1606 hours, just twenty-six minutes after being cleared for action, the SAS handed control of the incident back to Commissioner Joseph Canepa. A great tragedy had been prevented, and as far as the SAS were concerned the matter was closed.

The British press and public were at first delighted with the Gibraltar affair. The public saw that another IRA atrocity had been averted and three terrorists, intent on a cowardly mass murder, had got what was coming to them. Few tears were shed on the mainland for Farrell, McCann and Savage, and the first press comment was full of delight. Disquiet began on the following day when the Foreign Secretary got up in the House of Commons on Monday afternoon and, in the course of a statement on the Gibraltar affair, revealed that none of the terrorists had been armed or had a triggering device and that the car in the plaza did not contain a bomb.

This statement clashed with three previous statements beginning with the one issued at 1645 on Sunday afternoon, within an hour of the shootings, which stated that 'A suspected bomb has been found in Gibraltar and three suspects have been shot by civilian police.' At 2100 hours a further statement admitted that 'security forces' had been involved in the shooting and had 'dealt with a suspect bomb'. In addition, on the morning of Monday 7 March, the Armed Forces Minister in London said on a radio programme that a 'large bomb' had been found in Gibraltar and defused. This statement was incorrect. The bomb car – full of Semtex – was not located until the following day, Tuesday 8 March, hidden in a car-park at Marbella at the far end of the Costa del Sol. The effect of these conflicting statements was most unfortunate.

The press, which had at first hailed the Gibraltar shootings as a triumph, now changed their tone completely. The SAS and the government came in for a great deal of criticism, the first for the use of excessive force and the second for attempting a cover-up. Government efforts to suppress or disparage a TV programme, *Death on the Rock*, which was broadcast on 28 April and which went into the Gibraltar shootings in great detail, only served to increase public disquiet, and the affair rumbled on for months with the population deeply divided over whether the shootings were necessary or justified.

The fact that there were no explosives in the Gibraltar car is not relevant; the 'bomb car' did exist, in Marbella, full of Semtex explosive and ready to be moved into position in Gibraltar at some future time. There can be no reasonable doubt that the IRA fully intended to explode a car bomb in the crowded streets of Gibraltar and their activists clearly had to be stopped. The debate centres on whether they had to be killed.

These three IRA terrorists all had records and were indiscriminate killers. Had the terrorists succeeded in their plan scores of people would have been killed and maimed, the wrecked heart of Gibraltar littered with bodies and spattered with the blood and limbs of innocent victims, a scene familiar in many other British cities after an IRA attack, and those who whined about the shooting of Savage, Farrell and McCann would have rejoiced.

The main snag with the 'serve 'em right' argument is that the British government and its soldiers are supposed to maintain the moral high ground and act only with the full sanction of the law. But there is no evidence that a 'shoot to kill policy' was sanctioned by the British government in Gibraltar or anywhere else, and that accusation can be dismissed. That leaves only the circumstances of the actual shootings carried out by the SAS during Flavius.

The official version, the one accepted by the Gibraltar inquest in September 1988, is as given above and the result was a verdict of 'lawful killing'. This might have put an end to the speculation about what actually happened, but attempts by sections of the press and by the government to disparage the evidence of some witnesses helped to keep speculation alive. The government tried to stop the showing of *Death on the Rock* and some newspapers went out of their way to blacken the character of one particular witness, Mrs Carmen Proetta, who lived in a flat overlooking the site of the McCann and Farrell shooting and, according to her evidence, saw the whole thing take place.

In her evidence, Mrs Proetta said that she was sitting at her window when her attention was attracted to events across the road when she saw two people putting their hands in the air. 'These people were turning their heads to see what was happening and when they saw these men with guns in their hands, they put their hands up. It looked as if the man was protecting the girl because he stood in front of her, but there was no chance.' According to her evidence the soldiers 'jumped in with their guns in their hands and just went and shot these people. That's all.' Another witness claimed that Farrell and McCann were shot again while lying on the ground.

This evidence contradicts that given by the SAS troopers, who claimed that all three terrorists either put their hands to their pockets or, in Farrell's case, into her handbag. Thinking they were reaching for weapons or the bomb trigger, the soldiers opened fire. Why all three should do this is remarkable, since they did not have weapons or a bomb trigger and had nothing to reach for.

A more natural reaction at such a moment of surprise would be to raise their hands in the air and, according to Mrs Proetta, that is exactly what Farrell and McCann did. Clearly, the sight of two people suddenly thrusting their hands into the air is more likely to attract attention from a lady idly watching the Sunday afternoon passers-by from her window than a hand reaching into a handbag or a pocket. It is worth adding that those British newspapers that attempted to dismiss Mrs Proetta's evidence by making attacks on her private and personal repu- tation were later obliged to pay heavy sums in damages.

*

This incident left many people more than a little unhappy about the use of the SAS in a plain-clothes, counter-terrorist role, and such incidents and arrests might have been better handled by the police. The city streets of Gibraltar are not like the fields of South Armagh, the jungles of Borneo or the jebels of Oman, places where ambush is an acceptable tactic. Most democratic states now take steps to counter terrorist activity in the streets of their towns or at their airports, but the role of eliminating such groups is usually entrusted to specially trained police units.

Every American police force contains a SWAT team, and the German police and the French gendarmerie have successfully wiped out terrorist gangs. As recently as Christmas 1994 the French GIGN successfully ended an aircraft hijack at Marseilles airport, and over the same Christmas period in 1994 'armed-response' units of the British police shot and killed two people carrying firearms in the streets of Britain. Why the SAS regiment CRW team should be deployed in the streets is less easy to understand, and too many unarmed or totally uninvolved people have died in the SAS–IRA feud for this question to remain unanswered.

Counter-terrorism is clearly one role the SAS wish to retain and develop, but this role needs careful control and can take the military rather too close to the political and intelligence establishment and on to the fringes of the law. US Special Force units in Vietnam fell into this trap. Britain does not need hit-squads, but this is the abyss that has engulfed SF units in other countries and needs to be guarded against.

The IRA campaign in Northern Ireland and elsewhere poses a number of questions about the use of SF troops. Clearly, there is a role for such troops, partly to reduce the impact of conventional cordon-and-search operations on the uncommitted civilian population, partly in the surveillance, intelligence-gathering and ambush role, where SF units have the training and the expertise. However, once past that point, their use is more debatable. There is a clear danger of SF units usurping the police role and using excessive force in a manner which provides propaganda victories to the enemy and reduces the effect of 'heart and mind' actions. Victory for democracy in the counter-terrorist war in Northern Ireland can come only when a political solution is found which the local communities will accept and support, abandoning their centuries-old hatreds and turning out the terrorists. Anything which erodes progress, however slow, towards that goal is counter-productive.

A winning tactical combination in the meantime is the collection and analysis of background intelligence and surveillance information from all available sources, and – if the police feel unable to tackle the terrorists without support – the use of combined police–army teams to ambush the enemy and subdue or arrest them. There is a vast difference between an ongoing, counter-terrorist guerrilla war, as fought in Malaya, Vietnam or Central America, and a sporadic, urban-guerrilla campaign, fought in the streets of European cities, and this difference must not be eroded simply to provide SF units with fresh fields for action.

Royal Marines badge

Chapter Thirteen

The Falklands War 1982

You can nearly always force an invasion, but you can't always make it stick.

Omar N. Bradley, General of the Army

The Falklands War, the South Atlantic campaign of April, May and June 1982, was the largest military operation Britain had mounted since the Suez landings of 1956. This was a war in which the training and fighting ability of the British Commando and Parachute units made them more than a match for the Argentine invaders, who greatly outnumbered them but could not compete with their professional standards in the field.

The Argentine invasion of the Falkland Islands came as a total surprise to the British government, but it is some indication of the speed and mobility of the British armed forces, and in particular of 3 Commando Brigade, Royal Marines, that the first elements of the Task Force sailed from Portsmouth within three days and the Argentine forces had been totally defeated and evicted from the Falklands by 14 June, just ten weeks after an Argentine Special Forces unit, the Buzo Tactico, attacked the Royal Marine barracks at Moody Brook.

In that time a British Task Force of sixty-five warships and transports had been mustered, sailed 12,000 miles to San Carlos Bay, landed two SOF assault infantry units, 3rd Commando Brigade and 5th Airborne

Brigade, fought off constant air attacks from the Argentine mainland, marched fifty miles across the wet and windy moorland of East Falkland, fought five battles, and repeatedly defeated an Argentine force that outnumbered them by at least two to one in any engagement. It was, by any military standard, a great feat of arms.

The credit for winning the Falklands War goes largely to the men of the SF and SOF forces who took part: the Royal Marine Commandos, the Parachute Regiment, the Special Air Service and the Special Boat Service, with due acknowledgement to the Scots Guards who took Mount Tumbledown and the men of the 1/7th Gurkha Rifles, whose very presence in the Falkland Islands struck gloom into the hearts of the Argentine soldiers. The core of that force was 3 Commando Brigade, Royal Marines, the only unit in the British armed forces fully trained in amphibious warfare.

'The Brigade is always at seven days' notice to move,' says Major-General Julian Thompson, who commanded 3 Commando Brigade in 1982, 'and as the rumours of Argentine actions in the South Atlantic grew stronger we brought that down to seventy-two hours, and then we actually did move, not least by loading 4,500 tons of first-line ammunition.' By 1982, 3 Commando Brigade had changed a great deal from that force of lightly armed infantry that had landed at Port Said and fought in the Radfan mountains and the jungles of Borneo. The Brigade was now a little amphibious army, a small replica of its mighty cousin, the United States Marine Corps. Apart from the three Commando units, 40, 42 and 45 Commandos, each around 1,000 strong, there was 29 Commando Regiment, Royal Artillery, 59 Commando Squadron, Royal Engineers, an Air Defence Troop equipped with Blowpipe missiles and an Air Squadron with Gazelle helicopters. Above all there was the Commando Logistic Regiment, the 'Loggies'.

'Don't forget the "Loggies",' says Julian Thompson, 'because without the "Loggies" the war could not have been won. Since the war some people have implied that we should have swarmed out of the beachhead and moved on to Stanley in the first couple of days. That is total rubbish; this was a real war, involving artillery, air power, ships, submarines, missiles, not the sort of war that can be won by men equipped with fifty rounds of ball ammunition and a bag ration. We had to get ashore, seize a bridgehead and hang on to it, built up our supplies, recce the ground and wear the enemy down. Then, and only then, could we advance on Stanley. That was the way we actually won the war, and without the support of the "Loggies", who supplied five battalions in the field, 12,000 miles from home, with all they needed to fight and win, it simply could not have been done.'

When the Argentine forces seized the Falkland Islands in 1982, the Falklands had been a British colony for almost 150 years and contained a British population of some 1,800 people, mostly sheep farmers, all of whom wanted to remain British. Argentina had been laying claim to the islands – known in Argentina as Las Malvinas – since 1811, after the collapse of the Spanish-American Empire, but the British claim predates the Spanish one. The islands were first claimed for Britain in 1690 by a sea captain, John Strong from Plymouth in Devon, who named them after Viscount Falkland, the Secretary of the Royal Navy. French seamen from Brittany arrived in 1698 and, not knowing of the British claim, named the islands after their home port of St Malo; the name 'Malvinas' is a corruption of the Breton 'Malouins'.

During the 150 years of British occupation the Argentines made constant claims to the sovereignty of the 'Malvinas', and there had been several attempts to negotiate a settlement. All these attempts foundered because the Argentines would only agree to a settlement in their favour. Negotiations were also hampered by the UN insistence on the rights of any colonial people to 'self-determination'.

'Self-determination' had been written into the UN Charter to enable any subject nation to slip the colonial yoke; it had never been envisaged that a nation would exercise its right to self-determination by choosing to remain a colony. So the dispute throbbed on down the decades until, in the South Atlantic autumn of 1982, thinking that the British were uninterested in defending the islands, and needing some sort of military victory to bolster their sagging popularity at home, the Argentine junta, that group of generals then ruling – or misruling – Argentina, without warning or a declaration of war sent a task force to seize the islands and drive the British out.

The defence of the Falkland Islands depended on Naval Party 8901, three officers and a platoon of thirty-three Royal Marine Commandos, which made up the permanent garrison of the islands. These Parties came on a one-year-tour, but two detachments were changing over in April 1982, so there were more than sixty Commandos on the islands when news of the impending invasion reached them. This small force, armed only with 7.62mm self-loading rifles, a few machine-guns and 66mm rockets, was reinforced by eleven men from the Royal Navy Antarctic survey ship HMS *Endurance* and twenty-three members of the local Defence Force. One heart-warming addition was Jim Fairfield, an ex-Royal Marine who had married a local girl and settled in the islands. Claiming that 'There is no such thing as an ex-Marine,' Jim turned up at the Moody Brook barracks, where he was given a rifle and sent to join the troops defending Government House.

The Falklands War employed a number of British SF and SOF units, but Argentine Special Forces were in action during the invasion phase. Argentine Special Forces are organized in Commando companies under the umbrella of Halcon 8, which acts as a cadre for all Argentine Special Forces including the Buzo Tactico, a Commando-trained assault company of the Argentine Navy. All the Argentine services, Army, Navy, Air Force and Coastguard, maintain SF units, many created in the 1960s and 1970s to handle counter-terrorist work within Argentina, with instructors supplied by SF units in the USA and Israel. Their quality varies, but the Buzo Tactico and the Army Commando Companies are the elite. Commando Company 601, normally stationed in Buenos Aires, was airlifted to the islands on 27 April, and Commando Company 602, raised especially for the Falklands campaign, arrived at the end of May in time to take part in the last battles around Stanley.

The Argentines sent a large force to seize the Falkland Islands, with over 600 Marine Infantry, the 25th Regimiento de Infantería and the Buzo Tactico in the assault wave. These came ashore by night near Stanley in Amtracs, amphibious tanks, and met a stout resistance from the garrison. The first attack came in at 0615 on 2 April, when the Buzo Tactico attacked the Royal Marine barracks with machine-gun fire and grenades. Fortunately, the Marines were already deployed in Stanley, the island capital, and when the Argentines sent in a 'snatch squad' to seize the Governor at Government House, they met alert Marine sentries in the garden, where three Argentine soldiers were killed in the first exchange of fire.

Firing and grenade explosions then began to be heard all over Stanley. Amtracs bringing more Argentine troops from the beaches were engaged with 66mm rockets, as were Argentine landing craft entering Stanley harbour. Even so, with odds that started at ten to one and were steadily rising, the Royal Marines were forced steadily back, and at 0830 hours the Royal Marine commander, Major Norman, told the Governor that his positions were being outflanked and he wished to fall back into the country and continue the fight from the hills. Negotiations began with the Argentines and the Governor ordered the Marines to cease firing at 0925.

Meanwhile, the Royal Marine Commando detachment at Grytvikyen in South Georgia, a small group of islands on the edge of Antarctica, twenty-two Marines under Lieutenant Keith Mills, had also come under attack. An Argentine frigate, the *Guerrico*, entered Grytvikyen harbour and ordered the Marines to surrender. Lieutenant Mills rejected this order and his men opened fire on the *Guerrico* with rifles, light machine-guns and 66mm rockets, at which the *Guerrico* withdrew out of range and began to shell the Marine positions with her 100mm gun.

The Royal Marines continued to resist even when the landing ship *Bahia Paraiso* appeared offshore crammed with Argentine infantry, and when an Argentine Puma helicopter overflew their positions, the Marines shot it down. Here, as on the main islands, the resistance against a vastly superior force could not be maintained for long, and, having given the Argentines a taste of what they were up against, Lieutenant Mills surrendered. All the British troops in the Falkland Islands and South Georgia were flown out to Uruguay within the next couple of days and repatriated to Britain, where they swiftly joined the British Task Force.

The initial Landing Force, tasked with seizing a bridgehead, was commanded by Brigadier Julian Thompson of 3 Commando Brigade, the cutting edge of the Task Force. Brigadier Thompson needed more men, and two battalions of the Parachute Regiment, first 3 Para and then 2 Para, were added to the landing force. In addition, Brigadier Thompson had under command men of the Royal Marine Special Boat Service and the Royal Marine Mountain and Arctic Warfare Cadre, a unit that specialized in snow warfare and cliff assault.

'The actions of the Cadre have been somewhat overlooked but they performed superbly in the Falklands,' says Major-General Thompson. 'In peacetime, as you know, they train cliff assault and snow warfare specialists for the Brigade, but in war they become the Brigade Commander's personal recce platoon. Apart from a useful raid on an Argentine forward position at Top Malo House, they acted as the recce and covering force on the left flank of the Brigade as we advanced on Stanley. Nothing escaped them, nothing got through their lines. While they were out there my flank was secure and I never had to worry about it ... they did a splendid job.'

Further units, including armour and artillery, came to join the Task Force, with the 5th Airborne Brigade, made up of the 1/7th Gurkhas, the Scots Guards and the Welsh Guards, coming along later. After 5 Brigade arrived, the entire Landing Force would be commanded by Major-General Jeremy Moore, another vastly experienced Royal Marines Commando officer, who had seen action in Malaya and Borneo and been decorated for his performance in both those places.

Another unit to join the Royal Marines was the 22nd SAS Regiment, eager to get a piece of the action in the South Atlantic. Lieutenant-Colonel Michael Rose, CO of 22 SAS, heard of the Argentine landings in the Falkland Islands on 2 April 1982, and immediately put the Regiment on standby. He then telephoned Brigadier Thompson at Stonehouse Barracks in Plymouth, knowing that, if the British were to retake the Falklands, then the Commando Brigade, the only British unit fully trained in amphibious warfare, would lead the assault.

The Falklands was clearly a Royal Marine 'show', but the SAS intended to be there and some tasks could surely be found for their talents, so Brigadier Thompson agreed to take them along. SAS soldiers were hastily summoned back from all parts of the world, from the Middle East, from patrols in the 'bandit country' of South Armagh, from scattered security operations in embassies and foreign capitals, all anxious to take part in a real war, one which should offer good scope for their raiding and reconnaissance skills.

Operations to retake the Falkland Islands began on the night of 21 April, less than three weeks after the Argentine invasion, with Operation Paraquat, the recapture of Grytviken, the port in South Georgia, a task executed by D Squadron, 22 SAS, the Royal Marine detachment from the destroyer HMS *Antrim*, part of M Company, 42 Commando, Royal Marines, and 2 Section, SBS, Royal Marines, making a total force of about seventy-five well-assorted fighting men. This force was commanded by a Royal Marine officer, Major Guy Sheridan, while D Squadron 22 SAS was commanded by another major, Cedric Delves.

Helicopters were to prove the key to successful operations in the Falkland Islands, and the Paraquat operation got off to a very bad start when the SAS took one helicopter and landed a troop of SAS in terrible conditions on the Fortuna glacier. After a night on the glacier the SAS commander decided to withdraw this force and sent three of the precious Wessex helicopters to extract them. Two crashed on the glacier and when the third helicopter, severely overloaded, finally made it back to the *Antrim*, it crash-landed on the deck. This loss of three helicopters for no useful purpose did not prevent Major Guy Sheridan from putting the rest of his force ashore and the Argentine garrison at Grytvikyen surrendered without firing a shot.

The swift recapture of South Georgia gave a great boost to public morale in Great Britain and to the fighting men in the Fleet now heading for the Falkland Islands. The SAS had not got off to a good start, but they redeemed themselves when, some days ahead of the main Task Force landings in San Carlos Bay, they carried out a raid on the Argentine airfield on Pebble Island. Lack of adequate air cover was a constant headache for the British commanders in the South Atlantic, who had just eighteen Harrier jump-jet fighters to protect the Fleet and the landing force against the entire Argentine Air Force, which was well equipped with Mirage and Dagger fighter-bombers and Pucara ground-attack aircraft. The more Argentine aircraft that could be destroyed on the ground the better, and every scrap of damage that could be done to their airfields in the Falkland Islands, would be of great assistance to the Task Force.

Pebble Island, with the airfields at Goose Green and Stanley on East Falkland, contained most of the Argentine aircraft based on the islands. Pebble Island was also believed to contain a sea-sweep radar that could detect the approaching Task Force. Admiral Sandy Woodward, commanding the Carrier Group from his flagship HMS *Hermes*, on which D Squadron were now embarked, therefore agreed to the D Squadron raid, a classic SAS operation which went in on the night of 11 May.

Pebble Island lies off the coast of West Falkland, the second of the two larger islands in the Falkland group. The garrison consisted of a small force from an Argentine infantry regiment, protecting a troop of Engineers who were preparing an airstrip for the use of Argentine Pucara ground-attack fighters and constructing a radar station. The recce for the raid was undertaken by the Boat Troop and Mountain Troop of D Squadron, and they began by inserting a party on West Falkland on the night of 11 May. Four men made the recce to Pebble Island and reported back that eleven aircraft and a quantity of bombs, ammunition and stores were on the airfield and open to attack.

The route planned involved transportation by helicopter from HMS *Hermes* to a remote promontory, Mare's Rock on West Falkland. From there they would round the peninsula in canoes and paddle across under cover of darkness to land on Pebble Island. It was about ten miles to the airstrip and this distance would have to be covered on foot.

There were, inevitably, a number of snags. The first was that heavy surf made it impossible to launch the Klepper canoes. The Boat Troop therefore recalled the helicopter and flew in towards their observation post on West Falkland where they set up an OP overlooking Pebble Island. When it grew dark, they launched their canoes safely and landed on Pebble Island before midnight. Here one patrol established a beach-head with a radio link to HMS *Hermes*, while the second four-man patrol moved out towards their objective, where they lay up till daylight. Sentries were plentiful, but the recce patrol could see all they needed to see. Abandoning their rucksacks they crawled away into dead ground and laid up there throughout the rest of the day, marching hurriedly back to the beachhead at night to signal the information to *Hermes*.

Major Delves' plan envisaged the SAS wiping out the entire garrison and destroying all the aircraft, but there was not sufficient time or strength available to put this into effect, for with every hour that passed the SAS recce group risked detection. The aircraft were the first priority, so the attack was scaled down and the recce group were joined that night, 14 May, by the rest of the Squadron, flown in by three helicopters from *Hermes*. This helicopter insertion was carried out without lights, in enemy-held territory and at wave-hopping height. Fortunately, the moon came to light up the scene after the raiders were landed and the approach march to the airfield was completed swiftly. Just before dawn, at 0700 hours, the raiders were in position.

The attack began with an impressive display of firepower from small arms and rockets, which destroyed several Argentine aircraft. The resulting confusion was kept going by the guns of HMS *Glamorgan*, which closed the shore and poured shells on to the airfield and the Argentine infantry positions. With the enemy heads well down, the SAS went onto the airstrip and set about blowing up any aircraft not destroyed by shellfire, plus all the ammunition, petrol and stores they could find. One man was injured by shrapnel, but by 0715 the airfield was ablaze and the SAS troops began to withdraw. By 0930 hours, on time to the second, naval helicopters swept in to lift the SAS away. This Pebble Island raid was a textbook SAS operation – but then came disaster.

On 19 May, the men of 19 Troop, D Squadron, were being transferred by night from the carrier *Hermes* to the assault ship HMS *Intrepid*, in preparation for another operation. Their Sea King helicopter was flying at about 400 feet when a seagull was sucked into the main engine. The engine faltered and the helicopter fell at once into the sea. A search began at once but no one could survive for long in the icy waters of the South Atlantic, and the SAS Regiment and their various supporting specialists lost twenty men in this one incident, the Regiment's largest single loss since the Second World War.

Replacements were on hand, for B Squadron were waiting on Ascension Island, the staging point for the South Atlantic campaign. Their orders to join the Task Force and strengthen D Squadron saved them from an operation which it would be charitable to call foolhardy.

Some bright spark, allegedly in the CO's Tactical HQ, had proposed embarking B Squadron in two Hercules aircraft and flying these aircraft directly on to Stanley airfield. Once there, the men of B Squadron, all sixty-four of them, would sally forth like Greeks from the Trojan Horse, and win the war. Exactly what the enemy would be doing at this time does not appear to have been considered but, fortunately for all concerned, this 'operation' was called off.

Meanwhile, the Task Force bringing the Commando Brigade and its supporting Parachute battalions was approaching the islands. At dawn on 21 May the first ships entered San Carlos anchorage and the troops went ashore after Argentine positions on Fanning Head, at the entrance to the anchorage, had been eliminated by a patrol of the Royal Marines SBS.

Argentine Special Forces were also active at this time, making recce patrols to possible invasion beaches and laying ambushes for the SBS and SAS men who might be carrying out recce missions before the main landing. After the landing 601 Commando Company was in action with British patrols near Mount Sussex and engaged British helicopters and ground-attack Harriers with Blowpipe missiles. They were then tasked to occupy Mount Kent, an important position on the road to Stanley, but when they moved up to it they were promptly ambushed by SAS and Marine patrols which were already in position, though the Argentine Company managed to withdraw for the loss of three men killed and two wounded.

Further losses were sustained to Commando Company 602 when nineteen men of the Royal Marines Mountain and Arctic Warfare Cadre (M&AW) under Captain Rod Boswell attacked a Commando Company position at Top Malo House. The Marines were flown up from San Carlos by helicopter and, landing some distance from the house, were able to move up and open fire before the Argentine Commandos knew they were even in the area. The Argentine soldiers put up a good fight but were defeated in what they later claimed to be a thirty-minute firefight, losing two killed, six wounded and the rest taken prisoner. The M&AW Cadre had two men wounded.

The choice of San Carlos for the landing was dictated by the need to find a place where the ships could anchor and discharge their stores and where the troops could seize an adequate bridgehead for the post-landing build-up. The snag was that San Carlos lay some fifty miles from Stanley and there was now a great shortage of helicopters, the necessary means of transport for men and supplies in modern war. Without sufficient helicopters, the British forces, and their commander,

Brigadier Julian Thompson, had a severe logistical problem.

Four helicopters had been lost, as already described, in SAS operations before the main landing and many more, including three of the giant Chinooks, were lost when the supply ship, *Atlantic Conveyor*, was hit and sunk by an Argentine Exocet missile. Brigadier Thompson called an O (Orders) Group of his battalion commanders to explain the situation governing the advance on Stanley, a meeting summed up by one officer who emerged from the O Group and remarked gloomily, 'I suppose that means we have to bloody well walk.'

Brigadier Thompson had other problems. The politicians in London wanted some swift action on the ground. There was a strong possibility that the UN would try to impose a ceasefire on the warring parties, which would leave the Argentines in a strong negotiating position since they currently held most of the islands and the capital, Stanley. If some blood was spilt, and the troops were fully engaged in battle, this call for a ceasefire would come too late, so some decisive military action was considered imperative. Brigadier Thompson was well aware of this but, unlike most of the people urging him on from London, he also understood the disciplines of assault landings and amphibious warfare.

His first task was to seize a bridgehead – which he had already done. Then he had to build up his stores and forces – which he was in the process of doing. Only then could he march on the crucial point in the battle area – Stanley, the island capital – and win the war. When Stanley fell, the war would be over, and any diversion from the attack on Stanley was a waste of effort.

Stanley, however, was a long way off, across inhospitable terrain and defended by 12,000 Argentine soldiers who were dug in behind minefields and supported by an active and aggressive air force that was already attacking and sinking ships in the San Carlos anchorage – and Thompson lacked helicopters, without which a swift advance was impossible. Most of the people in London, and some of the people in the beachhead, either did not understand these facts or chose to ignore them. That luxury was not available to Brigadier Thompson, who knew the whole picture and bore the burden of the field command.

Action was required from London and the eye of the planners lighted on the Argentine garrison on the airfield at Goose Green, sixteen miles from San Carlos. Brigadier Thompson was summoned to the radio and told to attack Goose Green; Thompson refused. 'I had already marked Goose Green down before the landing. Goose Green has an airfield, like Pebble Island, and we intended to have a go at it, nothing terminal, just a raid, to knock out any facilities and bugger off again. You can see why if you look at a map; Goose Green does not lie on the road to Stanley and the garrison there could easily be masked or contained from making a flank attack as we pushed out for Stanley; Goose Green stands on a narrow isthmus, a real bottleneck, so a raid on the airfield was all we needed. I was not at all opposed to attacking it if we could provide sufficient support.

'Then we lost a lot of helicopters, so I could not move the guns or ammunition to support the attacking battalion, so I called the raid off. Then Northwood HQ came on the line and told me to put it on again, or else, adding that the attacking battalion "did not need support". I was bloody furious, but they insisted on having their way; I can remember coming away from that telephone call, thinking, "I shall win this one for them, and then I will go." '

The battalion selected to attack the Argentine positions at Goose Green was 2 Para, commanded by Lieutenant-Colonel 'H' Jones. Support was provided by a frigate and two of the battalion's own 81mm mortars, but this support was not sufficient and the battalion needed a great deal more assistance, as Major Philip Neame, who commanded D Company of 2 Para, confirms: 'We had a lot of support on Wireless Ridge, later in the campaign, and that was a great help. Had we had something similar at Goose Green we would have walked it. As it was ... well...'

Goose Green lies at the tip of a narrow isthmus, with only room for one battalion to deploy. Halfway down the isthmus lies a long, low ridge, Darwin Hill, which held the main Argentine positions in front of the Goose Green area, which, being an airfield, is very flat. The main Argentine garrison at Goose Green came from the 25th Infantry Regiment, which had taken part in the invasion, and the 12th Infantry Regiment which had arrived later, the total number of defenders mustering around 600 men. There were also a large number of Argentine Air Force personnel, but they took little or no part in the fighting. In view of the flat ground Colonel Jones decided on a phased night attack, six phases in as many hours, during which he hoped to overwhelm the Argentine positions and get his battalion into cover. A daylight attack over open ground against dug-in positions would be suicidal, but the night attack soon fell apart.

Major Philip Neame again: 'We moved up from San Carlos to a lying-up area at Camilla Creek. While we were there, waiting to attack, we heard a BBC broadcast telling the world that a parachute battalion – us – was about to attack Goose Green ... which reduced most of us, including "H", to absolute fury. A track ran from our Start Line towards Darwin Hill and we advanced that night with A and C Companies on the left, B on the right, my D in the rear, in reserve and "H"'s in the centre. We soon started taking fire from the right, from B Company's area, and I found myself ahead of "H"'s Tac HQ, which he did not like at all. He went storming off up the track and my sections started to deal with the enemy.

'Within an hour of the attack starting it is fair to say that chaos was reigning. It was very dark, there was plenty of fire and the sections were being pulled in all directions, dealing with enemy trenches. We were doing that OK, but it took time and it was soon clear that "H"'s plan, a six-phase advance in the six hours before daylight, was simply not on.'

2 Para struck the main Argentine positions on Darwin Hill just before dawn and were soon in trouble on their left flank. The gun on the supporting frigate had jammed, so no support was coming from that direction and the battalion mortar teams had fired off all their bombs. It was now an infantry battle, the two Companies on the left flank, A and C, were meeting stiff resistance and their attack stalled. Colonel Jones therefore went up to examine the situation and ordered the A Company commander to make a frontal assault on the Argentine positions.

Major Dair Farrar-Hockley, commanding A Company, had already put in several frontal attacks and lost men in every one, without success. While the merits of another attack were being debated Major Neame of D Company came up on the battalion wireless net to tell Colonel Jones that he was now in position behind Darwin Hill and could see that the Argentine defenders on the right were abandoning their positions and fleeing along the seashore. Where they went, he could follow, and so outflank the stubborn defenders on Darwin Hill. 'This information was not well received,' says Major Neame. ' "H" told me – more or less – to wind my neck in and get off the air while he was fighting a battle. I could see it was going to be a very long day, so I told my blokes to brew up and get some food inside them. My porridge was just starting to bubble when we got the news that "H" had been killed.'

Colonel Jones was killed when, followed by his bodyguard Sergeant Barry Norman, he went off to outflank the Argentine position and was hit by Argentine fire. He was later awarded a posthumous VC, one of only two awarded during the Falklands campaign, both to the Parachute Regiment. The events on Darwin Hill have since proved very contentious, but clearly something went wrong. Two Companies were engaged in fruitless and costly assaults while another Company, a few hundred yards away, with nothing to its front and able to outflank the enemy position, was having breakfast.

The battalion Second-in-Command, Major Chris Keeble, then took over, and ordered Major Neame to advance as proposed, and D Company were soon advancing over the Goose Green airfield. Here they lost several men when an apparent Argentine surrender lead to the machine-gunning of some parachute soldiers, but an Argentine position in the school house fell after a couple of 66mm rockets had been fired into it. Argentine aircraft then attacked the battalion with bombs and napalm, one of them being shot down by D Company, and the battalion then took up positions around the airfield, ready to renew the battle against the remaining Argentine garrison. They had already had enough, and that night, some twenty-four hours after the attack began, the garrison of Goose Green surrendered to the 2nd Battalion of the Parachute Regiment.

From the strictly military point of view, Goose Green was an unnecessary battle and the battalion was not well handled. However, it achieved its political purpose in that there was no further talk of a ceasefire until the Argentines had been defeated. Moreover, the effect of Goose Green on public opinion at home and among the troops on the ground is hard to overstate. 'Goose Green set the tone for the whole war,' says Captain Ian Gardiner of 45 Commando. '2 Para showed the Argentines – and us – that we could defeat their forces any time, whatever the odds. 2 Para scored the first goal and after that we never looked back.'

With Goose Green taken and the politicians mollified, the war could go on with a major advance towards Stanley. The second main contingent, 5 Brigade, was now coming ashore at San Carlos, accompanied by Major-General Jeremy Moore, who took over command of the land operations and ordered Brigadier Thompson to proceed with his original plan, the advance on Stanley. The first step to that end was the capture of Mount Kent, a prominent feature halfway to the capital.

The Falkland forces seem to have contained a number of 'private armies', and Lieutenant-Colonel Nick Vaux, commanding 42 Commando, had already been somewhat surprised when, after Brigadier Thompson's O Group on 25 May, Lieutenant-Colonel Rose of the SAS allegedly took him on one side and suggested that 42 Commando might seize Mount Kent, which SAS patrols were currently recce-ing.

This matter had to be decided by Brigadier Julian Thompson, who was actually commanding land operations at that time, but he agreed that 42 should take the mountain. 42 duly went up on the night of 29 May and found the position empty of Argentine troops. The seizure of Mount Kent gave Major-General Jeremy Moore, the newly arrived Force Commander, a secure base for the investment of the capital, since Mount Kent lies just twelve miles from Stanley. The rest of the Landing Force were now coming up, by helicopter or on foot – 'yomping' as the Marines call it, 'tabbing' in the Parachute version – and the final battles for Stanley could now begin.

'Yomping' is a word that entered the English language after the Falklands War. It involves getting to war the hard way, carrying all the kit and ammunition needed for the battle, sleeping rough, putting up with whatever the weather and the enemy have to offer. Fortunately, the Commandos were well used to yomping and were soon up to their Start Lines on the slopes of the hills around Stanley. Though yomping into battle was hard work, the troops were spared the losses caused to the Welsh Guards of 5 Brigade who were being moved forward by ship and were waiting to disembark in the harbour at Fitzroy when Argentine aircraft bombed their landing craft, causing heavy casualties to the men of Support Company. This kept the Welsh Guards battalion out of the subsequent battles, though a number of their rifle companies were moved up to support the advance of 3 Commando Brigade.

The Argentines had some 8,000–9,000 men defending Stanley. These men were not well led or well trained, but they did not lack courage, had had weeks to dig in, had laid plenty of minefields and were well supplied with artillery and heavy weapons, including a quantity of heavy machine-guns. The Argentines used American equipment, much of it superior to that possessed by the British. The main British asset was the quality of their fighting men, and that factor was to prove decisive.

General Moore's plan for the final battles were based on a three- or four-phase elimination of all the enemy strongpoints, spread over three or four nights. A battalion would be deployed against each of the main Argentine positions and they would fall, like dominoes, as their mutually supporting systems were knocked away. On the first night, 11/12 June, three positions, Mount Harriet, Mount Longdon and Two Sisters, would be taken by 42 Commando, 3 Para and 45 Commando respectively. On the following night Mount Tumbledown would be attacked by the Scots Guards. Tumbledown overlooked Wireless Ridge and only when Tumbledown had been taken could 2 Para be recalled to the fray and sent against Wireless Ridge. The capture of Wireless

Ridge would put the British on the outskirts of Stanley, but if the Argentines continued to resist then the Gurkhas could unsheath their kukris and take Mount William and 45 Commando would advance on Sapper Hill. This was a sound, methodical plan, and it worked.

Lieutenant-Colonel Nick Vaux of 42 Commando had been recce-ing Mount Harriet for some days and, having discovered that the Argentine positions were fronted by minefields, elected to circle them and come in hard from the south side of the mountain. This meant a night march through 5 Brigade's area, and K Company then led the assault on the Argentine position. '42 Commando fought a lovely battle,' says Major-General Thompson. 'It was a crafty, skilful Commando battle that took the enemy completely by surprise and just rolled them up, infiltrating their positions and taking hordes of prisoners ... quite brilliant.'

K Company were well into the Argentine positions on Harriet before they were detected and, with the rest of the Commando coming in behind, they ran riot among the Argentine trenches with grenades, rifle fire and the bayonet. The Argentine positions straddled the top of the mountain and K Company had crossed the saddle on the top and were attacking positions on the far slope before they met serious resistance from heavy machine-gun fire and snipers using night sights. L Company of 42 met similar resistance on the eastern slope of the mountain, but after one persistent sniper was flushed out with a 66mm rocket, the Argentine position collapsed. 42 Commando took the position for the loss of one man killed and twenty wounded, killing twenty-five Argentine soldiers and capturing more than 300.

3 Para were doing equally well on Mount Longdon, where Sergeant Ian McKay won the Parachute Regiment's second posthumous Victoria Cross while attacking an enemy position. 3 Para took Longdon for the loss of eighteen men killed or wounded, while in the last battle of the night Lieutenant-Colonel Andrew Whitehead's 45 Commando swarmed over Two Sisters after one of the assault companies had become seriously delayed on the approach march. This unit, X Company, was commanded by Captain Ian Gardiner: 'We had done a lot of recce and I had been up on Mount Kent to see Two Sisters and study the ground. It is only about 1,000 feet above the surrounding ground, with two peaks on top separated by a saddle, but the ground is steep and difficult, a litter of rocks and great boulders. Our task was to put in the flanking attack on the south peak while the rest of the unit attacked the north one. I went for a three-phase attack, putting in the troops – a Commando troop is like an Army platoon – one after the other, with the mortar platoon of 40 Commando in support.

'The snag was that we had a great deal of kit to carry, at least 80lb apiece, and had the mortars along ... and we got lost. Eventually I broke radio silence and told the Colonel what was happening. He was lying up before the Argentine lines with the rest of the unit and was very calm, absolutely marvellous about it. He told me to get in position, sort ourselves out and let him know when we were ready. That is what we did and 45 Commando attacked together.'

45 raced up the Two Sisters hill, each Troop taking its objective and consolidating while the next Troop swept through to take the next one, the Commando rifle companies leapfrogging up the slopes. Colonel Whitehead, leading from the front as usual, was up with the forward troops: 'Let me say first of all that it took a great deal of character for Ian to break radio silence at that time. I was very worried – between you and me – and bloody glad to hear from him. The attack was supposed to be "silent", that is our mortars and artillery support followed a fire plan, altering the range and putting on the switches, but not pressing the button until I told them to, which would be when the Argentines knew we were there. This is nerve-racking, and at 0350 hours I could stand it no longer and told Gerry Ackhurst, our FCO [Fire Control Officer], to 'Switch to Noisy' and hammer them.

'It turned out to be perfect timing. The two Rifle Companies to my front opened up with all they had, just as Ian and his merry men ran into the enemy on the flank, so the whole unit went in together. We took the position at the cost of four killed and ten wounded, killing twenty Argentines and capturing about 200. I remember 45 in the South Atlantic as the "Can-do Commando", a band of brothers.'

45 Commando stayed on Two Sisters while the Scots Guards took Tumbledown and with that feature in British hands the next phase of General Moore's battle could take place – the capture of Wireless Ridge by 2 Para. Major Philip Neame again: 'We were the only unit in the Task Force to fight two battles and I cannot say we were very keen on the idea; any "gung-ho" had long since gone. We felt that we had done our bit for Britain at Goose Green and some other bugger could have a go. However, orders are orders. . . .

'We went up to Longdon and took a look at Wireless Ridge in the time before the Guards took Tumbledown. We had plenty of support this time, from naval guns on the frigate *Ambuscade* and artillery and Scorpion light tanks. We also had a new CO, Lieutenant-Colonel David Chaundler. The plan was for a night attack, with the bulk of the battalion taking the first half of the enemy position, a small hill in front of the main feature and covering D Company while we swept along Wireless Ridge proper. The ridge is fairly narrow, not large enough to deploy more than one Company and the attack went in at 0300 hours.

'At first all went well. We took the forward position without any trouble and were soon up on the main ridge. It was a cold night, very clear, and when we were about halfway along the ridge I told our FOO – Forward Observation Officer – in this case a Signals sergeant, to bring down some fire on the enemy position to our front. He duly got on the radio and called down thirty rounds of airburst, right on top of us.

'We had one guy killed and another injured by this "friendly fire" and shells were going all over the place. One gun was right off register and shelling B Company, so chaos was once again reigning. I also had the CO coming on the radio, demanding why I wasn't sending him sitreps and telling him what was going on. We finally got four guns firing on the enemy and we went in with that. I must add that the Scorpions were marvellous, just hosing the ridge with fire; we could have used them at Goose Green.

'Anyway, the enemy knew we were up there, but then someone let off a flare and that really gave the game away and a hail of tracer came up at us. We had lost our drive, the blokes went to ground and, frankly, I was shit-scared. The only thing to do at such a time is to run about shouting your head off, and that is what I did, yelling at the men to get up and get moving ... and they got up and started advancing again. We took the enemy position at the trot and once we got the Argentines on the move we managed to keep them that way, until we reached a line of telephone poles at the end of the ridge.

'I had been told not to go any further than that as the SAS were staging some sort of private party on the beach by Stanley, so we stayed up there and beat off a couple of counter-attacks. When dawn came I could see hundreds of Argentine troops streaming off the mountains heading back into Stanley. Then Chaundler and Thompson came up, asking about the battle and why we were not firing on Sapper Hill, but I just showed them the scene. It was obvious that the Argentines were jacking it in and the war was over.'

While D Company were attacking Wireless Ridge the SAS were putting in their last attack of the war, a seaborne raid on the oil tanks by Stanley Harbour. The attacking force consisted of a party of SAS and SBS, carried to the attack in four Rigid Raider assault craft of the Royal Marines Raiding Squadron. The purpose of this attack, according to the commander, Major Cedric Delves of Grytvikyen fame, was to divert the enemy's attention while the Paras attacked Wireless Ridge.

This assistance was unknown to Major Philip Neame, commanding D Company of 2 Para on Wireless Ridge, who only knew that his advance must halt at the end of Wireless Ridge.

Precisely why it was thought necessary to attack the oil tanks in Stanley, which the islanders and the British soldiers would need for their own use within a day at the most, is still not clear, but the raid was not successful. As the Rigid Raiders entered the bay, they encountered an Argentine hospital ship, which illuminated the boats with its searchlight and then, according to one account, opened fire on them with a machine-gun. Machine-guns on the shore then opened up and the SAS were clearly getting into serious trouble. 'They were not under my command,' says Julian Thompson, 'and the first we knew of their problems was when we got a wireless message telling us what was going on and asking me/us to divert 2 Para from their attack on Wireless Ridge and send the battalion to their assistance. I am afraid they got a dusty answer ... something to the effect that if they were big enough to get into trouble, they were big enough to get out of it.'

2 Para had enough on their hands on Wireless Ridge, and in the event the SAS got away safely and returned to base. All the Rigid Raiders were damaged and two men were injured, but otherwise no harm was done to either side, and with this last adventure the war ended, when, on the following morning, with the British occupying every feature around the capital, the Argentine commander, General Menendez, requested a ceasefire.

The South Atlantic Campaign – Operation Corporate – the Falklands War of 1982, ended on 14 June, just ten weeks after the Argentine invasion. Argentine losses exceeded 700 killed, while thousands were wounded and over 100 Argentine front-line aircraft were shot down. The British lost 255 men and had more than 700 wounded, with a number of ships lost and aircraft destroyed. The political cause of the war, the Argentine claim to the islands, has still not been resolved, but Britain and Argentina are at least on speaking terms – and the junta of generals which ordered this attack on a friendly power was driven from office soon after the war was over.

In the years since the war there have been a number of controversial books on the campaign, criticizing various aspects of the way it was fought. It was primarily a SOF campaign, with the bulk of the fighting falling to the Royal Marines Commandos and the Parachute Regiment, and all these units did extremely well. Some Army commanders have complained that the Marine officers who commanded the Corporate operation were too slow in pushing ahead from San Carlos after the initial landing. The Royal Navy and the Royal Marines have pointed out that an ignorance of 'amphibiosity' – the art of making and maintaining an amphibious assault – or a reluctance to accept the disciplines of such warfare caused a number of unnecessary problems, and contributed in no small measure to the disaster that befell the Welsh Guards at Fitzroy.

Few complaints have come from the men who fought in the Falkland Islands. The war was won, at no great cost in lives, and when all the risks are taken into account that alone is a minor miracle. The main contribution of SF and SOF soldiers to the Falklands War was in the provision of first-class, well-trained troops, who could fight and win against heavy odds and in inhospitable terrain at the end of a long logistical trail. Without such troops, and a knowledge of their abilities, the retaking of the Falkland Islands would have been impossible and could not have been seriously contemplated.

The war had been a risky venture but final victory went to the side that fielded the best fighting men. Field-Marshal Lord Bramall summed that aspect up in an interview with the author in 1995: 'We sent the First Team down there, the Royal Marine Commandoes, the Parachute Regiment, the Guards, the Gurkhas, the SAS ... but it had to be done, of course. If we had let the Argentines get away with it, it would have sent out the wrong kind of signals to all sorts of people and the government of the day would have fallen. We must just be thankful that we had the right men to do the job, and do it so superbly well.'

AK47 rifle

CHAPTER FOURTEEN

The Gulf 1958–1991

> Those who know war do not wander when they
> move and do not become exhausted when they
> climb. When you know yourself and your men,
> Victory is not in doubt.
>
> *Sun Tzu*, The Art of War, *1st century* AD

From the end of the Second World War to the present day, the Western powers have been plagued by problems in the Middle East. As a result Special Force units have been constantly involved in the area, propping up pro-Western leaders, training indigenous forces, staving off invasions or providing support to the local armies. It is a sensitive area, where an overt Western military presence is rarely welcomed and one where covert forces can play a useful role. Western leaders might have preferred to stay clear of the Middle East entirely, but one factor requires that the British and the Americans maintain forces in the region and play a part in Arab affairs. That overriding factor is oil.

Much of the hard work defending Western interests in the region has been left to Special Forces and Special Operating Forces, which have managed to protect Western interests and support the West's allies without upsetting fragile local sensibilities or providing ammunition for those who criticize Arab rulers for supporting Western interests. This support has ranged from the provision of small training teams and military assistance to stave off coups, as in Jordan in 1958, to an all-out war with Iraq over Kuwait in 1990–1. All this effort, over many decades, has not secured tranquillity in the region or prevented the rise of new, authoritarian, anti-Western regimes.

The Suez débâcle of November 1956 which marked the end of Britain's imperial pretensions and was widely regarded as a triumph for Colonel Nasser, encouraged other Arab groups or countries in the Middle East to try their luck against the British and their allies. In 1958 Colonel Nasser formed a short-lived United Arab Republic (UAR) consisting of Egypt, Syria and the Yemen. The UAR was backed by the Soviet Union, which supplied vast quantities of arms, plus training teams for 'on the ground' technical support. This eventually led to fresh threats against Israel, but the first to take the brunt of UAR subversive activity were the pro-Western rulers in Iraq, Jordan and the Lebanon.

In July 1958, the Iraqi Army staged a coup against the Iraqi Royal Family, who, with their pro-Western Prime Minister, Nuri-es-Said, were all murdered. The British Embassy was sacked by a Baghdad mob, and UAR-inspired demonstrations in other Arab states indicated that more trouble would follow.

The United States, though vehemently opposed to the Anglo-French operation at Suez two years before, had now realized the truth about Nasser and foiled the next coup in the Lebanon by landing a strong force of US Marines at Beirut in 1958, thus starting a long US involvement with that unhappy country. In Jordan, where King Hussein had sacked Glubb Pasha, the British Commander of the Arab Legion, a call for help was swiftly answered by the despatch from Cyprus of the 16th Independent Parachute Brigade, which took up positions around Amman and succeeded in overawing any pro-Nasser forces. John Grebby of 2 Para was one of those sent to Jordan: 'The quick airlift move of the 16th Independent Parachute Brigade Group to Cyprus in 1956, to Jordan in 1958 and British forces to Kuwait in 1961, including our 2nd Battalion, were all "Force Projections" to bring immediate military and political stability to those areas. They certainly succeeded in the last two cases. In today's world, a lot of the Third World countries have modern armed forces and Britain's future intervention would have to be in coalition with other Allied forces as in the Gulf War, but in the 1950s Britain still had a political will and military clout.

'Practically every day during our time in Jordan Hunter jet fighters of 208 Squadron RAF used to roar off the airfield, four at a time. The Parachute Brigade were stationed around the airfield, close to the city of Amman. The spectacle of these Hunters, as they went almost supersonic at the end of the runway, was a thrill to watch. Even the Arabs admired it. In times like that one was proud to be a member of the British forces overseas.

'Jordan was a very hot, dusty and sandy climate to be stationed in. Tent space was not available for everyone and most of the battalion were on standing patrols around the capital city or down south at the one and only port of Aqaba. I had to sleep in a crate. Today's necessities, like sun lotion, even sunglasses, were luxuries or unobtainable in those days. For most months in Jordan it didn't rain at all. After a few weeks in Jordan, our food improved, and we had at least one two-course meal a day, consisting of fresh vegetables and meat. I am sure that our QM [Quartermaster] sent the MT Platoon around the Arab markets in Amman to get fresh supplies instead of us eating hard-tack rations all the time.

'On our return from Jordan in October/November 1958, the units of the 16th Independent Parachute Brigade Group started re-equipping. All units had to be ready for operations in a jungle or desert environment. For this reason, I think the British Army of today is more versatile and demands higher standards than in the early post-war days. Back then the Army recruiting officers would grab you if you had only a few years at a secondary school; now they can pick and choose.'

British involvement in the Middle East and the Gulf was to continue until the end of the 1960s, during which time a force of Royal Marine Commandos was kept at sea off the Gulf or somewhere in the Indian Ocean, embarked on two helicopter-equipped Commando carriers, fleet carriers transformed into the troop-carrying role.

Nasser, however, was not the only one causing trouble in the Middle East. In July 1958, while the Parachute Brigade were settling in around Amman, the Saudi Arabian princes, already in dispute with Britain over the oil-rich Burami oasis, decided to incite a rebellion in the Oman. When the local forces could not contain this rebellion, the Sultan of Muscat and Oman asked for British help and received in return the Malaya veterans of the SAS Regiment. In 1958 the Sultanate of Muscat and Oman was to all intents a medieval kingdom ruled by the Sultan Sa'id, a despotic ruler who kept the country in a tight grip, resisting all moves towards democracy and the introduction of all Western inventions other than arms. His son, Qaboos, was eventually sent to the British military academy at Sandhurst and returned home with some democratic notions which eventually led to the overthrow of his father and the reorganization of Muscat and Oman into a fairly modern state. But all that lay in the future in 1958.

Britain needed to protect its oil supply from the Gulf and this need obliged the British to support the Sultan Sa'id. Therefore in November 1958, D Squadron of 22 SAS arrived from Malaya and became involved in a stiff campaign against the main dissident chieftain, Ghalib bin Ali – the 'Lord of the Green Mountain' – who was established on a high plateau, the Jebel Akhdar. The local defence force, the British-officered Trucial Oman Scouts, had already tried to storm the Jebel Akhdar, which is set on the top of steep cliffs that soar up for 6,000 feet from the surrounding plain. This attack failed. Even a battalion attack on the Jebel had been driven off with loss, for there was not enough room to deploy large forces on the narrow tracks leading to the top. Estimating that there were at least 600 armed dissidents on the Jebel, the local commander, Colonel David Smiley, an ex-SOE officer, then requested the help of British troops, specifying that he wanted fit, professional troops and needed 'either a Royal Marine Commando or a Parachute battalion'.

These units were not available and their deployment might have been regarded as provocative by the Saudi government, so, at the suggestion of Major Frank Kitson, who was then serving at the War Office in London, Smiley was sent an SAS Squadron from Malaya under Major Anthony Deane Drummond, with instructions that they must take the Jebel Akhdar with the utmost despatch, the minimum of public fuss and no casualties. The difficulty of tackling this formidable position was brought home to the SAS soon after they arrived, when one of their corporals, scouting the routes up the escarpment, was killed by a single shot from a sniper on the cliffs above.

In view of the dissidents' expertise with weapons it was decided that the SAS should only move on to the Jebel at night. In December, Captain 'Red Rory' Walker led an SAS troop up to the top, using an ancient, single-file pass known as the 'Persian Steps' passing unoccupied dissident sangars – small, stone emplacements – on the way and taking up a defensive position on the top. There was no sign of the enemy, so over the next few days the rest of the Squadron came up and began to push patrols out across the plateau. This was already a considerable feat, for the Jebel Akhdar position had been regarded as impregnable, as indeed it would have been had the enemy been on the alert.

Patrolling activity continued, and eventually the main dissident base was located in the south of the plateau and attacked by two SAS

Troops, one led by Captain Peter de la Billière, who was to command the British forces in the 1991 Gulf War. This two-troop attack was met with a hail of fire from sangars and concealed positions. It became apparent that the position was too strong to be taken and the SAS would have to pull out. Extraction was aided by rocket attacks from British Venom jet fighters, and the SAS withdrew for the loss of one man killed.

The dissidents were now aware that the SAS were on the Jebel, and bickering between the SAS and the enemy intensified, with the SAS positions enduring constant sniper fire and mortar attacks. Nevertheless, they kept up the pressure on the enemy and by acting aggressively managed to cling on to their position at the top of the Persian Steps, forty SAS men standing off some 600 dissidents.

Heavy weapons, including 3-inch mortars, were brought up to the escarpment and an attack was launched against the enemy's Akhbat position, a collection of caves and stone sangars which penned in the SAS position and barred the route to the centre of the plateau. This attack went in on the night of Christmas Eve 1958, the SAS troopers played into the attack by 'Red Rory' Walker's bagpipes. By dawn the Akhbat position had been taken and the dissidents were falling back.

D Squadron now had a firm footing on the Jebel and were in no danger of being pushed off, but more troops would be needed to clear the entire plateau. A Squadron were therefore sent over from Malaya, a force commanded by one of the original SAS desert soldiers of the Second World War, Major John Cooper, who had served as an NCO with David Stirling. A Squadron arrived in January 1959 and replaced D Squadron on the Jebel. D Squadron, which had been fighting up on the Jebel for six weeks then withdrew for a brief rest before rejoining A on the summit for the final push.

The key to the Jebel Akhdar was a two-summit mountain which the SAS codenamed Sabrina, after a certain well-endowed British actress of the period. These peaks dominated access to the last rebel stronghold, and A Squadron was tasked with taking them. This was a diversion but it had to be a convincing one, to conceal the main SAS attack on the rebel position in the village of Saiq, which would be mounted from the plain below. Cooper's attack was made over rough mountainous ground on 26 January and required the support of rocket-firing fighters and bombing by RAF Shackleton aircraft before the Sabrina position was taken.

Cooper's men then hurried down the mountain to join A Squadron.

All the SAS men then piled into trucks, drove rapidly round the base of the Jebel and began a night-climb to the top of the escarpment, 8,000 feet above. They reached the top at dawn, arriving close to the rebel base at Saiq, and immediately went in to the attack. The outlying rebel positions were overrun for the loss of two men killed and one wounded, and the startling appearance of this strong force of SAS troops – actually no more than 100 men – in the heart of his stronghold was too much for the Lord of the Green Mountain. He abandoned his fortress and fled over the frontier to Saudi Arabia, and the SAS were able to march into Saiq without meeting further resistance.

This first Oman adventure was a neat little campaign, a textbook example of what Special Forces can do. The SAS force never numbered more than 100 lightly armed men, while the opposition were numerous, well-armed, good shots, in well-prepared positions on top of a natural stronghold, and knew the ground. Nevertheless, in less that eight weeks, the SAS were able to put down and disperse a force that had previously beaten off battalion-sized attacks and held the Jebel Akhdar for years. On the political front it demonstrated that even after Suez the British still had the means and the will to support their friends in the Middle East and protect their vital interests.

This resolve was tested further in June 1961 when General Kassim, the new ruler of Iraq, announced his intention of annexing the oil-rich state of Kuwait. Kuwait had been a British protectorate since 1899, and the British had only given up the Protectorate on 19 June, six days before General Kassim decided to annex it. The Emir of Kuwait immediately called for a renewal of British assistance. Within a few days two British units, 42 and 45 Commando, Royal Marines, had arrived and, with supporting tanks and artillery, were deployed in the desert along the Iraqi frontier. Further troops arrived, including a Parachute battalion, and although the total force landed was not more than 5,000 men it was enough to deter the Iraqis from crossing the frontier.

45 Commando then returned to a task that would keep it occupied for most of the 1960s, attempting to curb an outbreak of terrorism in the Crown Colony of Aden, where the next major outbreak requiring the skills and fitness of Special Force troops had already begun.

Aden was a British colony at the foot of the Red Sea, a hot and humid spot endowed with a large airfield and a splendid natural harbour. After the British left the Canal Zone, Aden became one of the major links in Britain's oil supply line and a base from which forces could be deployed to protect British interests in the Gulf or the Indian Ocean. Aden

Town was surrounded by Aden Colony, and that in turn by the Aden Protectorate, a group of sheikhdoms straddling a 100,000 square mile mountainous region bounded on the north by the Yemen and Saudi Arabia.

Daily life in the Protectorate was not unlike that on the North-West Frontier of India in the days of the British Raj, a mixture of casual raiding and banditry among the tribesmen, who subsidized their frugal lives by collecting tolls from caravans coming into Aden down the Dhala road. The British in Aden Colony kept a light rein on the activities of the Protectorate sheikhs, controlling them when necessary with a local defence force, the Aden Protectorate Levies, a unit composed of Arab soldiers commanded by officers of the RAF Regiment.

The stresses affecting the rest of Arabia had an inevitable effect in Aden, but the main source of disaffection was the Yemen. The Yemenis had long laid claim to the Aden territory and in 1962 a Nasser-inspired coup overthrew the ruler of the Yemen, Al Badr. Al Badr was not killed in the attack on his palace and, having escaped to the mountains, he organized a resistance against the rebels, who were led by the former commander of the Yemeni Army, General Sallal. Both sides then received reinforcements, General Sallal getting two divisions of the Egyptian Army. Al Badr received Major John Cooper, now retired from the SAS, and three 'unofficial volunteers' on unpaid leave from the SAS Regiment in Hereford.

Major Cooper and his men soon began to make soldiering in the Yemen a most trying experience for the untested soldiers of the Egyptian Army. Exactly how Major Cooper got involved in this affair is still a mystery, but the first contact came from David Stirling, and permission was given on the quiet by the British government. The arms and money came from the Saudi princes, who did not relish seeing hereditary rulers overthrown so close to their borders.

Cooper and his men began with a careful recce of the Egyptian garrisons and troop movements, while organizing the Yemeni fighters into groups of five or seven men, designated as 'gun sections' or 'killing groups'. That done, Cooper mounted his first operation, an ambush in the Wadi Thoul, a valley east of Sana'a, the Yemeni capital. Into this wadi came a large force of Egyptian troops, including a parachute battalion and several batteries of artillery, and Cooper let them get well into the wadi before he ordered his men to open fire. This sudden ambush threw the Egyptians into complete confusion. Their tanks started firing in all directions, mostly into the ranks of their own infantry, the infantry stayed in formation to be raked by machine-gun fire from the hills, and at the end of the day, when the Egyptians fled back towards Sa'ana, they left behind eighty-five dead and a great quantity of arms and equipment, which was swiftly gathered up by the gleeful Yemeni irregulars.

Cooper's next venture was an equally successful mortar attack on a strong Egyptian position and, satisfied with these opening moves, he then sent his three SAS men reluctantly back to Brecon and ordered the Yemeni irregulars to carry on harassing the enemy while he went out to Aden to report on the first phases of the fight. He then returned to the Yemen and there he stayed, training the irregulars, treating the sick in the approved SAS 'hearts and minds' fashion, surviving various attempts on his life by the Egyptians, who were well aware of his existence and even used chemical weapons in an attempt to eliminate him.

Cooper was then joined by Sergeant Cyril Weavers of 21 SAS, the SAS territorial unit, and Lieutenant David Bailey, an enthusiast for the Yemeni cause. These three stayed in the Yemen for another three years, fighting with the Royalist irregulars until a ceasefire was agreed in 1965 and Al Badr agreed to go into exile in Saudi Arabia. During all this time, and for some years after it, the British Army and in particular the Parachute Regiment and 45 Commando, Royal Marines, were fighting a nasty little war in Aden.

The political background to the Aden troubles can be briefly explained. The British at first wanted to retain the Aden colony as a means of protecting their oil interests in the Gulf and as a base for action in the Indian Ocean. The Protectorate sheikhs relied on British protection and were alarmed by the revolutionary, pro-Egyptian rebellion in the Yemen. Into this mix stepped two local independence parties in Aden, the left-wing, Communist-inspired National Liberation Front (NLF), which intended to take over both Colony and Protectorate, driving out both the British and the sheikhs and setting up a pro-Communist state in the Yemen. The other was the Aden-based People's Socialist Party (PSP), which began as a Yemeni-controlled trades union front, and developed into a terrorist organization.

Both parties competed for Egyptian and Yemeni support and briefly formed a popular front, FLOSY, the Front for the Liberation of Occupied South Yemen – South Yemen being their name for the Aden Colony and Protectorate. Then the NLF broke away from this arrangement, and FLOSY and the NLF began to fight among themselves in what time they could spare from the terrorist campaign against the British. The opening round in this campaign came in December 1963 when a grenade was thrown at the British High Commissioner at Khormaksar airfield, killing an Indian woman and the Commissioner's ADC as well as wounding thirty others. A state of emergency was declared the same day, and the Aden conflict had begun.

The little war in Aden can be divided into two main phases, the Radfan campaign astride the Dhala road of 1963–4, and the terrorism campaign in Aden Colony – by then Aden State and *en route* for independence – which ended in the British withdrawal in November 1967. Bob Strickland of the Parachute Gunners arrived in Aden at the end of 1956 when the troubles were just beginning and gives a descriptive account of frontier warfare in a British colony as the Empire ended: 'An infantry battalion, the Cameron Highlanders, had already been in action on the Yemen border and had quite a few casualties. A detachment of artillery had been requested and my Troop (C Troop of 97 Parachute Field Battery) had been elected to go out in support. The only problem was that the guns we were to use in Aden were 75mm howitzers and we were all trained on 25-pounder field guns. The 75mm howitzer is a good gun, ideal for stripping down and packing on camels for transporting through the mountains of Aden. Our training was very intensive with a lot of gun drills and it did not take long before we were 100 per cent efficient and ready for action.

'One hundred men of C Troop, under the command of Captain Steptow, flew out to Aden on 14 February 1957. Our journey in a Hastings aircraft was a very long flight, taking some twenty-nine hours; no jet airliners for the troops in those days. The flight took us from Lyneham in Wiltshire to an airfield in Tunisia (night stop), across to El Adam in Libya (night stop), then north over Turkey and through Iraq to Habbaniya near Baghdad (night stop), down to Bahrain, then along the Persian Gulf and around the Arabian Peninsula to the port of Aden.

'After arriving in Aden we quickly set up camp on Khormaksar airfield. For the first few days we went out on exercises to fire the guns for the first time. Our Troop was split into two sections; one section was sent to the east of the country and our section went in Land Rovers, towing the guns along very rough tracks up into the mountains, via the Dhala road to the Yemen border, where we camped with the Cameron Highlanders.

'We went out on many sorties with the Highlanders and APL [Aden Protectorate Levies] seeing action against the Yemenis, but we often had problems with the APL because the Arab families were tribal and family members could serve in both armies. You would end up with one brother fighting in the APL and another brother fighting in the

Yemeni army – or in the forces the Yemen was sending across the border to attack the Dhala road (the Dhala Road was the scene of fighting until we left the Radfan for good). On some occasions, fathers, sons and cousins were involved from the various Yemeni and Adeni tribes. So we would end up with a soldier in the APL saying he could not fight today because someone of his family was fighting in the military unit we were about to engage, but he was quite willing to fight if the action was in another area where a different tribe lived and none of his family was involved.

'A lot of the rifles used by the Yemenis were home-made but were very accurate over long distances. On one occasion we were in a battle and a Yemeni fired his rifle at a Venom jet fighter, hitting his fuel tank. Unfortunately the aircraft crashed, killing the pilot. The RAF lost several aircraft in the mountains of Aden. They would dive down and fire on Yemeni targets and then steeply climb up to try and clear the mountain tops. But some of the mountains were so steep that the pilots just did not make it.

'The dissidents in Aden were known to us as the "Blue Men". The "Red Wolves of the Radfan" came later. All the mountains in Aden are very dark rock and the local people had perfected a blue dye which was identical with shady rocks and they dyed all their clothes and even their skin the same colour. They only had to go a few feet and you could not see them because they blended with the rocks. The airfield in Dhala was a very dodgy place to land on, because you could only approach it in one direction through the mountains, and the locals had the approach taped and would fire on the aircraft. The aircraft which supplied us with most of our supplies was the old Beverly twin-boom freighter and parachute aircraft. This is a very large aircraft and on landing it had to reverse its engines quickly in order to stop. On one occasion the pilot reversed his engines too hard and the aircraft landed eighteen inches shorter than when it had taken off. All the plates on the fuselage were buckled and the Air Force had to fly three more aircraft up and strip the damaged aircraft down to return it to Khormaksar airfield.

'Aden Colony itself was a very depressing place. Although it was very hot up-country in the Radfan we did not really feel the heat because there was no humidity, but it was a place where we had to drink a lot otherwise we would very quickly dehydrate. All our water was drawn from the wells. All fresh meat had to be cooked and eaten immediately after the animal had been killed. There were plenty of sandstorms out there and they always seemed to appear when we were having our meals, so our food always had a film of sand on it and you had to watch out for the hawks which would swoop down and snatch the food off your plate. A delicacy for the Arabs was locusts. The locusts would fly over in huge swarms from somewhere in Africa and devour everything in sight, but the Arabs would pluck them from the air as they flew over, pull off their wings and eat them alive.

'We departed from Aden on 18 November 1957 on the troop ship *Oswestry*. Our journey home brought us back via the Suez Canal and on our trip through the Canal we were told not to wear our red berets on deck in case the people on shore got a bit anti, remembering the Port Said landings of the previous year. We still wore our berets, and there were no problems from the locals – in fact they cheered us. One thing we noticed on passing El Cap, the place where we had dug in our guns during the Suez operation, was that the camouflage nets were still covering the pits. We also noticed that de Lesseps' statue at the head of the Canal had been removed and replaced with a statue of an Egyptian soldier holding British and French paratroopers by their 'chutes.'

The Dhala road ran from Yemen across the Protectorate and into the Colony and was being used by the NLF as a supply route for arms and explosives. To stop this traffic meant sending a large force up to Dhala, and the arrival of the British Army, represented by 45 Commando and later by the 3rd Battalion, the Parachute Regiment, was seen by the locals as a good excuse for a spot of target practice. The local tribesmen – the Red Wolves – were soon mining the Dhala road and keeping the British garrison in Dhala under sporadic rifle fire.

In January 1964, Brigadier James Lunt, commanding the former Aden Protectorate Levies, a force which had now become the Army of the newly formed South Arabian Federation, mounted Operation Nutcracker against the tribesmen of the Radfan, using three SAA (South Arabian Army) battalions, supported by light tanks and helicopters from HMS *Centaur*. This operation lasted a month and drove the Red Wolves away from the Dhala road, but the effort could not be sustained in the face of the rising unrest in Aden State and, when Brigadier Lunt's forces were withdrawn, the Red Wolves returned. The only solution was to invade their stronghold in the Danaba basin, and this task was given to three British units, 45 Commando, 3 Para and a troop of SAS men commanded by Captain Robin Edwards.

The plan called for a night advance by 45 into the Danaba basin from Thumier on the Dhala road, a move preceded by a drop by B Company, 3 Para, on to a position in the Wadi Taym, where they would land on a DZ seized by the SAS. This operation began on the night of 30 April

1964 and swiftly ran into trouble. Captain Edwards' ten-man patrol infiltrated towards the Wadi Taym without difficulty, but at dawn they were detected by the local tribesmen, who came swarming out of their villages and soon had the SAS pinned down in a set of hastily erected sangars and under heavy and accurate fire. Edwards and his radio operator were killed, and the patrol was only saved from destruction by ground strafing from a constant 'cab rank' of RAF Hunter jet fighters attacking the Arab positions.

Since the DZ had been compromised, the parachute drop was called off and the entire weight of the attack was placed on the Marines of 45 Commando, now marching fast for Danaba. Their CO, Lieutenant Colonel Paddy Stevens, takes up the tale: 'The Radfan is murderous country but since it is above the 4,500-feet mark, at least the climate is a relief from the muggy humidity of Aden. It was very clear after Nutcracker that the Danaba basin could only be taken on foot by very fit troops, so the first task was to get the unit very fit indeed. Since there was damn all to do in Aden but play sport this was not hard, but there was a low ridge behind the refinery at Little Aden that provided an endurance course. I put my kit on and went over it, to set a time which everyone in the unit had to better; everyone flung themselves over this in full kit two or three times a day and before long the fitter Marines were putting up some amazing times. All this paid off when we started to march into Danaba.'

As a result of their training and in spite of the fact that most of them were carrying 80lb – or more – of kit and ammunition 45 sped into the Radfan that night, hearing on the way that the parachute drop had been called off and that B Company, 3 Para, had come up to Thumier and were heading out after them. The operation was compromised and Paddy Stevens was told to establish his men on two features called Coca Cola and Sandfly, and wait there for the paratroopers and further orders. Coca Cola was a high steep mountain and was eventually scaled with the help of ropes carried to the top by Major Mike Banks and some former members of the Commando Cliff Assault Wing.

By dawn on 1 May, 45 Commando were on these hills and overlooking the Danaba basin, where the local tribesmen were still sniping at the remains of Edwards' patrol. This patrol was eventually extracted but had to leave behind the bodies of Captain Edwards and his radio operator. The Arabs decapitated the two dead men and their heads were later exposed in the market place at Sana'a.

Over the next two weeks 45 hung on in the Radfan and were steadily reinforced. When the next phase began the British forces in the area amounted to all of 45, the complete 3rd battalion of the Parachute Regiment and two conventional infantry battalions, the King's Own Scottish Borderers and the 1st Royal Scots, supported by light tanks and armoured cars as well as helicopters and the invaluable Hunter ground-attack fighters. All this was only just enough to carry the tribesmen's positions. It required a four-day fight to clear the Bakri ridge, which was taken by 3 Para and X Company of 45, after which the force moved on to take another rebel stronghold in the Wadi Dhubsan. In early June the East Anglian regiment and a battalion of the Federal Army took the Wadi Misra and the Radfan tribes were finally crushed by a full-day battle at the village of Shaab Sarah.

From that time on there were no major engagements in the Radfan, though mining and sniping went on until the British Army withdrew from the Radfan in June 1967. The focus of attention then shifted back to Aden State, the former Aden Colony, where riots, grenade attacks and sabotage became daily occurrences. The last years in Aden are a sorry tale, for the British had decided to leave the East of Suez theatre completely and now had no need of the Aden base. This left the Protectorate sheikhs unprotected against the Yemeni and Egyptian forces pressing in from the north and the NLF and FLOSY enemies in Aden State. The final years were spent by the British, including 45 and 1 Para, which had replaced 3 Para after the Radfan campaign.

1 Para, commanded by Lieutenant-Colonel Mike Walsh, were based at Radfan Camp on the outskirts of Aden Town. Here Sergeant Tom Godwin recounts what happened: 'Radfan Camp was by Khormaksar airfield, and from there we sent out patrols and endured grenade attacks, sniping and ongoing riots. We were "blooded", as it were, on 6 June 1967, the anniversary of D-Day, when the local wogs made a co-ordinated attack on our camp. This was daft of them for sniping is one thing but fighting is another and we were pretty good at it. We killed eight of the opposition and wounded a good many more, and our only casualty was the CSM [Company Sergeant-Major] of one rifle company who got concrete splinters in his arse when the wogs fired a rocket through a wall.'

The fighting in Aden had now attracted the attention of the anti-colonial caucus at the United Nations, who sent three representatives to Aden in April 1967, one each from Mali, Venezuela and Afghanistan. They stayed for five days, lurking in a downtown hotel, while the streets outside were torn apart by the most sustained rioting that the town had yet endured, most of it orchestrated for their benefit. By the time the UN representatives left eight rioters had been shot dead and eighteen British soldiers had been wounded. In June 1967 the NLF declared a no-go zone in the Sheikh Othman district, which was smashed by 1 Para, who entered Sheikh Othman and took the NLF on. After a day in which six terrorists were killed and twenty injured, 1 Para opened the district again for police and Army patrols.

A few days later came the famous 'Crater' incident. The forthcoming British withdrawal, now scheduled for November, was unnerving the local police and units of the Federal Army. On 20 June there was a small mutiny at the SAA camp near Khormaksar and when the mutineers saw a lorry full of British soldiers passing their camp they thought it was aiming to break up the mutiny and fired upon it, killing or wounding sixteen British soldiers, who were actually heading back to their barracks after some range practice and had no aggressive intentions towards the Federal Army.

The mutineers then opened fire on the Lancashire Regiment, based in Dhala Camp just across the road, and while the Lancashires were firing back and suppressing this mutiny, the Aden Armed Police in Crater, a part of Aden Town, alarmed by the sound of firing, and hearing rumours that the British had attacked the SAA camp, opened fire on two Land Rovers containing men of the Royal Northumberland Fusiliers and the Argyll and Sutherland Highlanders. Both vehicles were set on fire and seven more British soldiers were killed. A patrol led by Lieutenant Davis of the Fusiliers, which went into Crater to find out what was going on, was also attacked and overrun. Lieutenant Davis and his men were never seen again and were probably murdered when they ran out of ammunition.

The garrison commander decided to leave Crater to cool down, a decision that did not please Lieutenant-Colonel Colin Mitchell, commanding officer of the Argyll and Sutherland Highlanders. On 3 July, covered from the heights around Crater by men of 45 Commando and led by their battalion pipers, the Argylls re-entered Crater and subdued any members of the local population looking for a fight. That event, the retaking of Crater, was a small success in an otherwise sorry story.

In early September the NLF claimed that they would take over when the British left, and in November the British government accepted this 'ultimatum'. This NLF announcement in September was followed by a pitched battle in Sheikh Othman between the NLF and FLOSY, a battle fought out under the bemused eyes of the 1 Para soldiers, who were ordered not to interfere. The NLF won and spent the next few weeks rounding up FLOSY supporters, again under the eyes of the

British troops, taking them into the desert in trucks commandeered from the Federal Army and machine-gunning them to death. Colonel Joe Starling of the Parachute Regiment recalls this time: 'It was sickening, and the men did not like it, not at all. A patrol from 1 Para found a great grave at Dar el Said, filled with bodies which the pi-dogs and vultures were feeding on. We had pulled back to a defence line, the Scrubber Line, and truckloads of FLOSY were taken through every day and out of sight, though we could hear long bursts of machine-gun fire as they were finished off. We protested to higher authority but back came the order: "It's no longer our business, do not interfere." Sometimes obeying orders is not easy.'

The British withdrew from Aden in November 1967, the last man out being Lieutenant-Colonel Dai Morgan of 42 Commando, Royal Marines. Aden was a tale of military success brought to nothing by a failure of political will, and the lesson to be learned from it is that unless the political will is there, no solution is possible short of a pull-out, with all that that involves, including public humiliation and the abandoning of allies – in this case the Protectorate sheikhs, who had relied on the promise of British protection and were simply left to their fate. Some were murdered with their entire families, others were lucky enough to flee into exile in Saudi Arabia. Aden became part of the People's Republic of South Yemen, a savage Marxist state, briefly an Arabian base for the Soviet fleet and a place locked since the early 1970s into sporadic civil war. Shortly after the British left Aden, more trouble in the Gulf brought the SAS back to the Oman.

Very little had changed in the Oman since the Jebel Akhdar campaign in the 1960s, though the British presence in the country had expanded, with more British units in the area, regular training teams and 'advisers' at work, commanding small garrisons of Baluchi mercenaries in frontier forts. Most of these 'advisers' were Heavy Weapons-trained NCOs of the Royal Marine Commandos detached from the 3rd Commando Brigade.

Sultan Sa'id was still in power, the country remained a medieval anachronism and those Omanis who were rich enough had fled abroad to more liberal climes, where some became involved in liberation movements. Rebellion therefore simmered in the Oman, notably in the mountainous southern province of Dhofar, which lay on the border with the Communist-controlled republic of South Yemen. The Dhofaris were fervent, even fanatical Muslims, who despised the 'decadent' West and deplored any attempts to Westernize their country.

Sultan Sa'id, who might well have shared this view, was finally overthrown with help from the West in July 1970 and replaced by his son, Qaboos, who eventually transformed Muscat and Oman into one of the most pleasant and progressive of all the Arab states. Qaboos entered into his dangerous inheritance with revolt simmering everywhere, most notably in Dhofar, where the newly formed Dhofar Liberation Front were mustering men and gathering arms, and sent for the assistance of the SAS, who at once began a campaign which combined a version of their Malayan 'hearts and minds' operations with military training for the Sultan's irregular forces, most of them from Dhofar, who were mustered in small bands known as *firqats*. The Dhofari opposition were referred to as the *adoo*.

The first unit to campaign in Dhofar was A Squadron of the 22 SAS, commanded by Major Tony Jeapes, and in January 1971 Jeapes mounted an amphibious raid against the rebel-held town of Sudh. The force was conveyed to the beach in dhows and overran the town inside an hour without firing a shot. This operation was followed a few weeks later by an assault by helicopter into the hills of Dhofar, which saw a little more action, when three armed *adoo* were ambushed and killed. The rebels then brought up an 81mm mortar, and some hectic mortar and counter-mortar fire than took place, killing six more *adoo* before the SAS and the *firqats* withdrew. Operations continued, mounting in size and number, and it was soon clear that to wind up this campaign would take far longer than the one in the Jebel Akhdar. After another three-day engagement in the Jebel Aram, which escalated until it involved a battalion of the Sultan's army, at last the *adoo* were soundly defeated and driven off. A Squadron then returned to the UK and were replaced by B Squadron, who were soon to be joined by G Squadron.

B Squadron's strategy was to establish and hold a base in the Dhofari Mountains, and in October 1971 they entered the hills with a large force amounting to around 1,000 men, including five *firqats* and the Omani battalion. This force finally took up residence at Jibjat on the Dhofari plateau, a camp which became known to the SAS as White City, and from here SAS and *firqat* patrols began to attack Yemeni camel trains supplying the *adoo* from across the Yemeni border. This action continued for the rest of the year, with plenty of patrol activity, and might have gone on a good deal longer had the *adoo* not decided on a major trial of strength against the SAS by attacking their base at Mirbat, a small town on the coast of Oman, not far from Salala, the capital of Dhofar.

In July 1972, the group of eight SAS soldiers from B Squadron, commanded by Lieutenant Mike Kealey, who made up the British Army Training Team (or BATT) in Mirbat were preparing to leave for England. They had spent three months in Mirbat, a drab little cantonment made up of a group of flat-roofed houses and two mud-walled forts. Mirbat was enclosed on two sides by the sea and though officially a training camp was still in the front line – in so far as there was a front line in Dhofar. The SAS BATT group had seen little action at Mirbat other than the periodic crash of a mortar bomb or the sudden arrival of an anti-tank missile; during the last week of May, and the first week of June alone, a total of twelve mortar bombs had fallen on Mirbat, followed on one occasion by three 74mm shells. Life in Mirbat was therefore typical of that found in any Special Forces location in a time of strife, sometimes busy, often boring, and occasionally danger-ous. In Mirbat, apart from the BATT team were a group of local armed police, the Gendarmerie, who lived in one of the forts. In addition to their small arms, the garrison of Mirbat could also employ a 25-pounder British field gun, an 81mm mortar and a .5 Browning machine-gun.

The SAS had spent their time training the local *firqats* and generally fostering goodwill among the local Dhofaris. Looming up near by, often hidden in the heat haze, was the long bulk of the Dhofar Mountains, and in mid-July a large group of *adoo* from the Dhofar Liberation Front assembled up there for a swift *coup de main* against the British advisers in Mirbat. The rebels had gathered more than 250 of their best men for this attack, all of them well armed with Russian Kalashnikov AK47 automatic rifles, grenades, machine-guns, mortars and Swedish Carl Gustav rocket launchers.

Once off the jebel, the *adoo* divided into smaller groups of ten and spread out into a wide circle surrounding the town. Some went past the town and down to the edge of the sea and fanned out along the beach, planning to attack the town from the seaward side. These men were well armed and clearly well trained, they had a good plan of attack, and before dawn the unsuspecting garrison was surrounded.

The main garrison in Mirbat consisted of thirty Gendarmerie – armed police *askaris* – from northern Oman, armed with British .303-inch rifles. These occupied a building close to the beach known as the Wali's Fort. Inside the town itself were about forty of the local *firqats*, whom the SAS were training, armed with FN762 automatic rifles and Bren light machine-guns. There was a further force of around twenty-five men of the Dhofar Gendarmerie, also armed with FN rifles and a single light machine-gun in the second fort just inside the enclave occupied by the small SAS training team. The British Second World War 25-

pounder field gun was positioned in front of this fort, commanding the town and the small airfield.

Eight gendarmes were on sentry duty at the airfield and it was their position which first came under attack by the rebels. The *adoo* crept up on this outpost just before dawn, but were spotted by the gendarmes and challenged. The gendarmes got off a single shot before the rebel assault line swept in, but in the fight which followed four of the gendarmes were killed. The rest managed to break out and get back to the cantonment, where they raised the alarm and turned out the SAS and their *firqat* trainees.

Having now lost the essential element of surprise, the rebels began their main attack by opening a rapid mortar fire on the fort and the town. The SAS returned fire with the 81mm mortar, putting down white phosphorus smoke to obscure their positions from the enemy's view. An SAS trooper opened fire with the .5 Browning, to cover the area between the two forts, while other SAS men fired on the groups of advancing rebels and mustered the *firqats*. Although the defence leaped into action quickly, they were still scattered and outnumbered by at least five to one. Lieutenant Kealey hurriedly sent an urgent message for reinforcements to the provincial headquarters at Salalah, and established radio contact with the crew of his heaviest weapon, the 25-pounder gun in front of the fort which was already in action. As the sun rose every weapon was firing and the fight for Mirbat really got under way.

Rebel troops had now advanced into the town, and bursts of machine-gun fire were raking the streets; mortar bombs were crashing down around the forts and bullets came slapping over the walls from the rear where the rebels were advancing from the seaward side. The garrison was completely surrounded and forced to beat off attacks from every direction. The SAS mortar crew were stuffing bombs down the barrel as fast as they could, plastering any group large enough to engage, while the 25-pounder, manned by an Omani, Walid Khamis, and two Fijian SAS men who had dashed from the fort to the gun at the beginning of the attack, was now engaging the *adoo* groups over open sights.

The rebels were suffering heavy casualties but continued to press home their attack. Gradually, as numbers told, they gained ground. Eventually they were within yards of the inner perimeter fence, from where they opened fire on the fort with their Soviet RPG-7 rockets and a Carl Gustav grenade launcher. The rockets soon had a shattering effect on the fort and the main tower collapsed, a pile of rubble sweeping down on the SAS men firing the mortar, the .5 Browning and the light machine-guns. These machine-gunners turned their fire on the rebels, who were now right on the perimeter wire and about to rush the fort. The rebels broke through the wire but heavy fire from the defenders prevented them overrunning the fort. Lieutenant Kealey, concerned about the lack of return fire from the Gendarmerie in the other fort and the field-gun post outside, decided to go out and take a look. This involved a 300-yard dash over exposed ground under heavy enemy fire and other men in the BATT volunteered to go with him, but he took only the medical orderly, Trooper Tobin.

Kealey and Tobin eventually reached the 25-pounder gun position, where they found the Omani gunner lying across the weapon, seriously wounded. The two Fijian SAS men were continuing to fight, although one was bleeding badly from a head wound while the other was trying to stop the flow of blood from a wound on his face. Both men had continued to load and fire the 25-pounder, which was now fully depressed and firing point-blank into the still-advancing enemy. From the 25-pounder position Kealey sent a radio message to Salalah calling for an immediate air strike. Just as he had sent it, one of the Fijians operating the 25-pounder was killed and Tobin had the lower part of his face shot away. With the *adoo* less than thirty yards away, the vital field-gun position was now manned by Captain Kealey and one wounded Fijian soldier, both under heavy fire. Kealey shot two rebels as they charged the gun pit with grenades and the wounded Fijian soldier managed to prop himself up on one elbow and fire at the rebels sweeping in from the left flank. A light machine-gun started spraying bullets close across the top of their heads and in came a shower of grenades, exploding close by but missing their target; one that rolled into the gun pit failed to go off.

Just as their position seemed quite hopeless, two Strikemaster jets swept overhead, almost at ground level, and their 500-pound bombs rained down on where the rebels were gathering for their last decisive push. This battle around the fort and gun position had been raging for an hour and a half when the Strikemasters came in, one knocking out the rebel machine-guns on the slopes of the Jebel Ali which overlooked the town, while the other attacked the rebels near the fort perimeter.

The air strikes provided a useful breathing space, but it was evident that substantial ground reinforcements would still be needed to beat the attack off. Fortunately, such help was at hand. The replacement training team from G Squadron, 22 SAS had arrived the previous day at Salalah and the G Squadron men were zeroing their weapons on the local firing range when the news of the attack on Mirbat came in. These

SAS men were immediately flown up by helicopter and landed on Mirbat beach under cover of a second air strike.

The first helicopter lift of eighteen SAS troopers moved inland in two groups and knocked out a rebel machine-gun and mortar position on a ridge overlooking the town. This SAS group was soon spotted by rebels near the fort, who opened fire on them with machine-guns and rocket grenades, but meanwhile the second helicopter lift was landing more SAS soldiers on the beach. These troops were soon engaging rebel positions on the southern and seaward side of the town and sweeping on into the cantonment. Before long the rebels were in full retreat and by mid-morning they had been driven back to the jebel by the *firqats*.

The defenders' total casualties turned out to be mercifully small: four dead and three wounded – the wounded Fijian SAS soldier insisting on walking out to the helicopter – while the rebel count showed at least thirty dead and many more wounded. This attack on Mirbat was the largest assault mounted by the Dhofari rebels; they never recovered from this defeat or attempted a similar assault again. Lieutenant Kealey was awarded the DSO for this epic defence, and Trooper Tobin, who died of his wounds, received a posthumous DCM. Sadly, a few years later, in 1979, Kealey, by then a major, died from exposure during an SAS exercise in the Brecon Beacons.

While the British were aiding the West's friends in the Gulf the US forces were suffering further losses in the Middle East. American involvement in the Lebanon civil war caused further trauma, for in April 1983 seventeen US diplomats were killed in a bomb attack on the US Embassy in Beirut. This was followed in October of the same year by a suicide-bomb attack on the US Marine barracks in Beirut, when an Islamic fanatic drove a truck-load of explosives into the Marine compound and set it off, killing himself and 243 Marines; another attack killed forty-eight French servicemen, mostly Foreign Legionnaires.

Beirut continued to be the scene of attacks on US citizens. In June 1985 a TWA jet, Flight 847, was hijacked to Beirut and while it was on the ground there the Arab hijackers identified and beat to death a US Navy SEAL, Robert Stethem, who was one of the passengers. The Syrian Army eventually took over the Lebanon, stamped on the warring militias and imposed a peace, but the country is still used for attacks on Israel by Muslim fundamentalist groups and is still inherently unstable.

These 'alarms and excursions' in Arabia and the Gulf were to continue throughout the 1980s. It was with a certain amount of relief that those involved in these thankless semi-clandestine operations turned on a more visible enemy when the dictator of Iraq, Saddam Hussein, invaded Kuwait and precipitated the last or latest of the Special Force wars, the Gulf War – Operation Desert Storm – of 1990–1.

SAS Land Rover

CHAPTER FIFTEEN

Desert Storm 1990–1991

Two kinds of military leader have been praised.
The first is the one who accomplishes great deeds
with an already organized army. The second is
one who has first to produce a good and well-
disciplined army.

Fabrizo Collona, Condottori General of the
Florentine Republic, 1516

The Gulf War of 1990–1 – codenamed Operation Desert Storm – began on 2 August 1990, when the dictator of Iraq, Saddam Hussein, invaded the tiny sheikhdom of Kuwait. This was not the first time that the Iraqis had attempted to make good their claim to Kuwait by force of arms for, as previously related, in June 1961, after claiming that Kuwait had once been part of the Ottoman province of Basra, the Iraqis threatened to invade. On that occasion they were deterred by a small force of British Commandos and parachute troops hastily deployed along the Mutlah Ridge, north of Kuwait City. In August 1990, the Iraqis invaded without warning and overran the oil-rich little sheikhdom in a matter of hours, and once again Special Forces, from the USA and Great Britain, were on hand to get them out.

When UN commands to leave were ignored by Saddam Hussein it was the United States, leading a large coalition of forces under the banner of the United Nations, which took on the task of expelling

287

them. The build-up before the battle took months and, when the Coalition force was finally assembled, the US general in charge of Desert Storm, Norman Schwarzkopf, had more than half a million men under his command, from Britain, France, Egypt and many other Arab states, including Kuwait and Egypt, as well as an especially large contingent of troops from Saudi Arabia, from where Desert Storm was launched. Schwarzkopf's success in blending this disparate army together into a viable whole, while coping with the sensitivities of his Arab hosts and allies, was one of the most striking feats of the war.

The official reason for this overwhelming international response was to deter other dictators from similar acts and to introduce a democratic 'New World Order', following the collapse of the USSR and the familiar Cold War verities. The real reason was a determination by the Western powers to protect and secure the vast oil reserves of Saudi Arabia and repossess those of Kuwait, which together supply some 40 per cent of Western oil needs. Had Kuwait produced cucumbers, Saddam Hussein would be ruling there today.

Among Schwarzkopf's Army was a large contingent of Special Forces, US Green Berets and Navy SEAL, British SAS and SBS, and a number of US SOF units, including the 1st and 2nd US Marine Division and the 101st Air Assault Division (the Screaming Eagles). To their considerable chagrin, the British SOF units, the Royal Marine Commandos and the Parachute Regiment, were left out of the Coalition order-of-battle. This omission caused a certain among of *angst* among Britain's SOF contingents in Aldershot and Plymouth, where the Parachute Regiment battalions and the 3rd Commando Brigade, Royal Marines were waiting impatiently, anxious to be committed. One very senior Royal Marine officer remarked at the time that it was 'very bad manners for the Americans to give a war and not invite Her Majesty's Royal Marines'.

It was rather more remarkable that General Schwarzkopf permitted the deployment of so many Special Force units, for the General had seen Special Forces at work in Vietnam and was less than totally convinced that they were useful: 'wierdos and snake-eaters, who had to be rescued by regular "grunts" when their hare-brained schemes went awry' was one alleged description. It was also clear that the destruction of Saddam Hussein's Army was really a task for large conventional forces, especially air and armoured forces, a war in which SF activity would be at best peripheral.

Iraq's Army was very large and had been battle-hardened in the long war against Iran. But General Schwarzkopf was never in any doubt that his men could defeat Saddam's forces, though the cost in lives could be high if the Iraqis chose to make a fight of it. Schwarzkopf was also well aware that the American public would not support heavy losses. In the event, US technology and firepower, deployed here for the first time in modern war, was to reduce Saddam's ability to wage war so dramatically that Desert Storm petered out inside three days of the first ground attack.

The Special Force effort in the Gulf War was co-ordinated by SOCCENT (Special Operations Command, Central Command), commanded by a US colonel, Jesse Johnson. This was subdivided into Army Special Operations Task Force (ARSOFT), a Navy Special Warfare Task Group (NSWTG) and Air Force Special Operations Command (AFSOCCENT). These varied headquarters had some 7,000 troops under command, including 150 British SAS or SBS men, the 5th US Special Forces Group, various Special Service support battalions, SEAL Teams 1 and 2, plus French Special Forces, probably from the 2 REP of the French Foreign Legion, and Special Force units from the Arab nations, including Kuwait.

Forces started to deploy in Saudi Arabia within days of the Kuwait invasion, and the Coalition build-up continued as the UN and the USA tried every diplomatic ploy in an attempt to get the Iraqis out of Kuwait without a fight. These diplomatic moves were totally unsuccessful. In the weeks and months that followed the Kuwait invasion Saddam Hussein prevaricated and temporized, skilfully running rings round the leaders of the Western Coalition. It soon became evident that force would have to be employed, and the Gulf War finally started in earnest on Thursday 17 January 1991, though the ground fighting, Saddam Hussein's much vaunted and long-promised 'Mother of Battles', the Coalition Desert Storm offensive, did not begun until 0400 hours on Sunday 24 February after weeks of aerial interdiction that shattered Iraq's infrastructure and war-making capability.

The first phase of the air war consisted of massive aircraft and Cruise missile attacks on military targets in Baghdad and on Iraqi front-line positions and airfields, in an attempt to wear the enemy down and 'write down' his forces. These air attacks continued for some weeks, wrecking Saddam's military command network and pounding the Iraqi positions in the desert, while the Allied navies roamed up the coast, sinking Iraqi shipping, clearing mines and launching Cruise missiles at targets ashore. Only when the Iraqi forces had been severely pummelled from the air, and the Iraqi Air Force had been destroyed or forced to flee into Iran, did the ground war begin.

The air war was extremely successful, but it might not have gone so well, and with such small losses, had not the US Air Force Air Commando unit, the First Special Operations Wing, managed to destroy a large part of Saddam's air-defence radar. The US had been monitoring Iraq's defences for months, from satellites and aircraft, and failed to find a sure way to penetrate the air-defence shield until Colonel George Grey, commander of the First Special Operations Wing, told Schwarzkopf that his men could destroy it totally. Schwarzkopf accepted the offer provided that Grey could guarantee 100 per cent success. This is a tall order for any military operation, but Grey accepted the challenge.

The idea was to attack the ground-to-air missile sites and their radar control points around Baghdad by flying in at night and at low level, fifty feet above the desert, in Pave Low and Apache attack helicopters. The Pave Low helicopter is a version of the Sikorsky 'Jolly Green Giant' aircraft, packed with electronic equipment and used for detecting radar installations which the Apaches would then destroy. The task was entrusted to Major Bob Leonik's 'Green Hornet' helicopter squadron – Task Force Normandy – and their attack went in on the night of 17 January. Task Force Normandy consisted of two teams of six helicopters, two of the Pave Lows to guide the force and four Apaches to carry out the actual strike.

These attacks were totally successful, the radar and missile sites being picked up on the Pave Lows' sophisticated monitoring systems and wiped out by rocket and cannon fire from the Apaches; a hole had been punched in Saddam's shield around Baghdad and the Coalition air forces were soon swarming through it. Forty-one Iraqi aircraft were destroyed in Desert Storm, but the bulk of the Iraqi pilots refused to engage. Thirty-eight Coalition aircraft were shot down, all by missiles and ground fire, and in spite of great efforts by the US search-and-rescue squadrons, only three of sixty-four surviving aircrew were picked up before capture by the Iraqis.

When the ground war began the US Air Force's 8th Special Operations Squadron lent a hand to the United States Marines. The main obstacle to the USMC thrust was the minefields on the Kuwait border, and the Air Force offered to blast a path through these using a 15,000 pound bomb known in the USAF as a 'Daisy Cutter'. This bomb had been employed in Vietnam to level ground for airfields and, since its effects were awesome, the US Psy-Ops teams decided to tell the Iraqi infantry what was coming. Thousands of leaflets were dropped on the Iraqi positions telling them that unless they surrendered they would be attacked by 'the largest bomb in the world'. The bomb was duly dropped on the morning of 7 February, and the effect was such that a British SAS soldier, far out in the desert radioed a report to his base that 'The Yanks have just nuked Kuwait.' The Iraqi soldiers did not wait for a further demonstration; massive desertions flooded the UN lines with Iraqi soldiers, and among their possessions was a map showing all the Iraqi minefields on the Kuwait border, a useful piece of information for the US Marines moving up to the attack.

The ground assault took the form of three massive thrusts across the Iraqi border. In the east, the two divisions of the United States Marine Corps, denied an amphibious landing, struck north with all their power into Kuwait and began to thrust up towards Kuwait City.

The next phase, Operation Cobra, was a fifty-mile advance into Iraq by the 101st Air Assault Division, which flew across the border in more than 300 assault and transport helicopters. The first phase of this assault took place at 0725 hours on 24 February, when the 1st Brigade of the 101st flew ninety miles into Iraq and landed 2,000 airborne troops to establish a forward operating base, FOB Cobra. The Brigade found an Iraqi infantry battalion in position and spent the first few hours eliminating them using attack helicopters and artillery.

This Division, which was part of the US XVIII Airborne Corps, went into Iraq from the west and was tasked to sever Highway 8, the main road linking Baghdad and Basra, the two principal towns of Iraq. Backed by the massive Coalition airpower, these forces struck the Iraqis a terrible blow and Highway 8 was cut on 25 February. Twelve hours later Schwarzkopf committed his second wave, the VII Corps. The Iraqi front collapsed and a day later, on 26 February, the Gulf War was over. The ground war had lasted about ninety hours.

Victory in the conventional war was never in doubt, although many Western pundits foretold heavy losses among the Coalition ground forces, especially when their units encountered elements of Saddam's 'elite' Republican Guard – the word 'elite' was never omitted from their title by Western correspondents. In the event, the Republican Guard – troops much feared at home for their use in stamping out public dissent within Iraq – fled from battle with the Western forces as fast as their transport would take them. The success of Desert Storm was far more at risk from the attacks made on Israel by Iraqi Scud rockets, and it was in finding and destroying the Scud launchers which the Iraqis used to strike at Israel that the Special Forces of Britain and the USA made a major contribution to the UN victory.

The Scud is a medium-range tactical missile, produced in the Soviet Union and capable of carrying an explosive, chemical–biological or nuclear warhead. Fortunately, the ones deployed by Iraq against Saudi Arabia and Israel were of the conventional kind. Scuds can be fired from fixed sites or mobile transporters and have a range of between 100 and 175 miles. This was a useful piece of information for the Special Forces charged with their destruction, for it meant that to range freely against targets in Israel, the Scuds had to be launched from points in north-western Iraq and could not be hidden in fixed bunkers all over Iraq.

On the night the air war began, Saddam launched eight Scud missiles against Israel. Two hit Haifa and four landed in Tel Aviv, causing considerable damage and more than 100 civilian casualties. Within minutes, war planes of the formidable Israeli Air Force were in the air and heading for Baghdad, and they turned back only when the US President, George Bush, promised to deploy Patriot anti-missile systems in Israel and send troops to find and destroy Iraq's Scud launchers. Israel had kept out of the war so far, but had no intention of letting the Iraqis rocket its cities with impunity, and that posed a grave political problem for the leaders of Desert Storm, both political and military.

One of the main problems facing the West throughout Desert Storm was keeping the other Arab nations from supporting Hussein. Saddam Hussein is a murderous brute and head of a repressive regime which is extremely unpopular in the Arab world, but throughout the six months of the Gulf War crisis Arab and Muslim communities all over the world – including those in the UK – largely supported him. They saw Saddam as a champion of Islam, their leader in the fight against the decadence and ungodliness of the West, and especially against those Western countries which supported Israel. Whatever their leaders, rulers and politicians might feel, many ordinary Arabs regarded Hussein as a hero. Saddam's support among the Arab nations would increase ten-fold if he could present his war as part of the struggle against the arch-enemy, and carry the war into Israeli territory.

This is one reason why the Western Coalition powers chose to fight without any assistance from the Israelis. But, following the Scud attacks, the Israelis made it plain that if the West failed to put a stop to the Scud attacks they would do so themselves. If Israel did enter the war, most of the Arab nations – including Saudi Arabia and Jordan – would feel obliged either to support Saddam or, at the very least, to bow out of the fight against him, or risk a revolt among their own people. Saddam therefore had every reason to provoke Israel, and the Scuds were the way he chose to do it. The Scuds had to be found and eliminated as soon as possible and the arm chosen to do it was the Special Forces, in particular the British SAS and the US Green Berets.

The SAS role in the Gulf War remains surrounded by a certain amount of mystery, other than those activities vividly described by Andy McNab in his bestselling book *Bravo Two Zero* and in accounts published since 1991 by other SAS men. What can be said is that the SAS saw more action, over a longer period, than most of the other ground forces involved and were out in the desert, behind the Iraqi lines, even before the air war began.

The SAS had gone out to the Gulf tasked with finding ways to rescue the Western hostages kept inside Iraq. Many of these were British citizens who had been working in Kuwait when the Iraqis invaded and had then been taken into Iraq for use as 'human shields', men, women and children kept at potential targets, power-stations, command centres and army bases, to deter strikes by Coalition aircraft. This hostage-rescue task was eventually abandoned, for the hostages were too widely dispersed to make any rescue attempt viable. In the event Saddam decided that using hostages as 'human shields' was counter-productive and let most of them go before the air war started.

The first Special Force action of the war was a small raid by Royal Marines of the Special Boat Service. On 23 January the SBS were carried deep into Iraq in two Chinook helicopters, landing at a point near Highway 8 where they dug up and severed a large section of the communication link between Saddam's bunker HQ in Baghdad and the Iraqi front-line positions. The SBS then rejoined their helicopters and returned safely to Saudi Arabia, bringing with them a section of Saddam Hussein's communication cable, which was presented to General Schwarzkopf 'with the compliments of the Royal Marines' – an action which brought a wintry smile to the General's face and may have slightly changed his views on the usefulness of Special Forces.

The SAS were born in the desert, fifty years before Desert Storm, so in many ways the regiment was returning to its birthplace in the Gulf War, albeit a few thousand miles further east from their old stamping grounds in the Western Desert of North Africa. The SAS were even equipped for this operation in a similar way. Long-wheel-based Land Rovers replaced the traditional Willys' jeep and the GPMG (general-purpose machine-gun) was mounted in place of the Bren gun or the Vickers 'K', but otherwise not a lot had changed since the desert campaigns of half a century before. The regiment had several squadrons in the desert by early December 1990, and the soldiers were presented with two important tasks. The first was to interdict the Iraqi MSRs (Major Supply Routes), and the second, and by far the most important, was to find and destroy the Iraqi Scud missiles.

The British Commander in Saudi Arabia was General Sir Peter de la Billière, a former SAS officer who had served with the Regiment in Malaya and the Oman. De la Billière had decreed that the SAS would be deployed only if there was a task suitable to their talents that could not be performed equally well by some other means, and if the SAS troopers, in the event that they were committed behind the Iraqi lines, could be safely extracted when their task was done. This last assurance was given by the US Air Force and by mid-January the SAS were already out in the Iraqi desert charged with attacking Iraqi road transport and communication links and creating all possible mayhem as soon as the war commenced. The air war began on 17 January 1991 and the SAS went into action three days later.

Six days later the SAS suffered a major setback when one of their patrols was located and attacked by the Iraqis and eight men went missing. But before that happened the SAS had become involved in the search for the Scuds. Fixed Scud missile sites could be found by radar and attacked by Coalition aircraft, which were now ranging at will above Iraq. A far more difficult task was to locate and destroy the mobile Scud missile launchers, and this task was given to the SAS and their colleagues in the American Special Forces.

The area where the Scuds were believed to roam was known as the 'Scud Box', and the SAS and the Green Berets divided the Box into two areas. The British concentrated on 'Scud Alley', to the south of the Baghdad–Amman road, and the Americans to the slightly upscale 'Scud Boulevard' to the north of it. The heavy Scud launchers tended to travel along the MSRs rather than roving on the open desert, and the tasks of interdicting the MSRs and finding the Scuds could often go hand in hand.

Roaming around the desert in vehicles, the Special Force teams began to locate the missile launchers. Once found, they were either attacked at once by the SAS and Green Beret teams or, if they were too heavily guarded, by air strikes. Passing on the necessary map co-ordinates and calling in the air strike often took time, and with the mobile missile launchers able to move within minutes, these air strikes were not as successful as they might have been. The SAS therefore took to engaging the missile launchers with heavy machine-guns or Milan anti-tank missiles as well as attacking the communication and radar installations controlling Scud missile operations. These attacks proved highly effective but merely confirmed what the Iraqis were beginning to suspect anyway: that the SAS and US Special Force teams were behind their lines and would have to be rooted out. They therefore sent strong mobile patrols into the desert, and began to track the SF and SAS patrols down.

Meanwhile, the SF and SAS soldiers were having problems with the weather. The deserts of Arabia are not always warm, sun-kissed, sandy regions and it was now mid-winter in northern Iraq. The teams were hit by a succession of blizzards and very low temperatures, mingled in with sandstorms and fog. This itself was very testing without the pressure brought on by having to avoid motorized Iraqi patrols. A number of SAS patrols had been inserted by helicopter but were attempting to operate on foot, and these slow-moving foot patrols became very vulnerable to the Iraqi motorized units.

The SAS were easier to find in Iraq than they were in the Western Desert during the Second World War, because to find their targets they were obliged to stay close to the Iraqi main supply routes – the metalled roads and firm tracks which were capable of supporting the passage of the heavy Scud missile transporters. Striking at the MSRs proved risky but very effective, and the Iraqis were unable to mount any missile strikes against Israel after 24 January. That is a measure of the Special Forces' success, though precise details of the raids and attacks made against the Scuds may not be known for a long time.

The main accounts concerning SAS involvement in Desert Storm come from those SAS men who were cut off during the course of these attacks and either made their way to friendly territory or were picked up by Saddam's troops and put through a harrowing ordeal. The full story of what happened to Andy McNab and his eight-man team has been told by McNab in *Bravo Two Zero*. Briefly, his foot-patrol team were spotted by an Iraqi child and then located by an Iraqi armoured patrol. Attempts to call in a helicopter extraction failed and the team were forced to disperse. Three of the soldiers were killed, and those captured, including McNab, were beaten and put through brutal interrogations before being handed over to the Red Cross on 5 March. Another SAS soldier from this patrol walked nearly 200 miles to safety across the enemy-thronged desert and got into Syria before being picked up and taken to the British Embassy in Damascus.

A similar fate was narrowly avoided by a Green Beret team led by Master-Sergeant Jeffery Sims. The Green Berets had been charged with surveying the desert ahead of the routes planned for the US armoured assault, taking core samples of the sand and bringing them back to base for analysis, to see if the ground would support massive armoured deployment. That done, the Green Berets put out recon teams to observe the Iraqi dispositions, one of them commanded by Master-Sergeant Sims. Sims and two of his buddies had been inserted behind the Iraqi lines and were lying up in a camouflaged hole when they were detected by a little girl. She ran to fetch her father and he raced off to fetch some Iraqi soldiers. Before long Sims and his team were surrounded by more than 100 Iraqi soldiers, holding them off with rifle fire and calling for urgent aerial assistance.

By the time this arrived in the shape of two F16 Falcon fighters and a Blackhawk helicopter, Sims and his men were on the verge of being overrun. The fighters swept the ground with cannon fire and the pilot of the Blackhawk, James Crisafulli, landed his helicopter between the Green Berets and the advancing Iraqis. His crew chief, Randy Stephens, opened up on the Iraqis with the helicopter's machine-guns as the three Green Berets broke from cover and swarmed aboard. The helicopter, though taking hits, soared away from the firefight, leaving nine Iraqi dead behind.

The Green Berets were constantly engaged throughout the rest of Desert Storm, attacking or detecting Scud missile launchers and cutting telephone lines and communication cables. One eight-man A Team, caught far behind the lines, fought off a 150-strong company of Iraqi soldiers for more than six hours before extraction, and on 27 February, as the Iraqis were preparing to surrender, a Green Beret patrol detected a force of no fewer than twenty-six Scud missile launchers being prepared for a last-gasp strike against Israel. The position was sent back to base and this group of missiles was attacked and destroyed by Coalition aircraft. After the ceasefire Schwarzkopf sent this A Team a congratulatory signal, thanking them for keeping Israel out of the war. Three Green Berets, all from Delta Force, were killed in Scud-hunting missions, the only Green Beret casualties of the Gulf War.

The US Navy SEAL carried out the only amphibious operation of the Gulf War on 23 February, the day before the ground war began, when a small force of just six men led by Navy Lieutenant Tom Dietz carried out a diversionary raid on the beaches of Kuwait. The Iraqis anticipated an amphibious landing by the US Marine Divisions, and Dietz and his men intended to convince them that such a landing was indeed taking place. The SEALs had been swimming ashore on to the Kuwait beaches for the last few weeks, finding them all heavily mined and defended by infantry, and this deception plan was not without risk.

The SEAL closed the shore in Zodiac dinghies and began by placing buoys off the beaches, hoping to convince the Iraqis that they were marking routes to the beach for landing craft.

Then they swam ashore, spread explosive charges along the waterline and set the timers. That done, they swam back to the Zodiacs and began to cruise along the shore, firing tracer at the Iraqi defences. Then the charges laid on the beaches and by the offshore buoys started to go off. Strafing the beaches, detonating charges, the SEALS lit up miles of the Kuwait coast, until the defenders were all awake, firing out to sea and calling for reinforcements. By the time the weary SEAL returned to base, the radio monitors could tell them that two Iraqi divisions had been pulled away from the border and were heading for the beaches, to fight off an anticipated landing from the US Marines.

The actual Gulf War did not last very long and the role of Special Forces was small. Their work was still extremely useful, especially in the detection or destruction of Scud missiles. Had the Scud attacks continued unabated, Israel would certainly have struck at Iraq and the war would undoubtedly have escalated to who-knows-what dimensions. As for SOF soldiers, their special skill and talents had not been required because the war ended before any behind-the-lines assault, on the beaches or by parachute forces, was considered necessary. The United States Marines were in the forefront of the battle, however, and demonstrated, not for the first time, that SOF forces, whatever their particular skills, can play a decisive role in a conventional war.

It might have been better if the Coalition forces had pressed on into Baghdad and toppled Saddam and his regime once and for all. However, the aim was to evict him from Kuwait and that aim was achieved, with an awesome use of military technology and the minimum cost in lives. The war also demonstrated that a few good men, if sensibly employed, can make all the difference to the strategic dimensions of the battle.

Rangers badge

CHAPTER SIXTEEN

The Twenty-First Century

Everything changed with the end of the Cold War.
Up to then we knew what we had to do and who
the potential enemy was and we could train and
prepare accordingly. Now it's all guesswork.

General Sir Peter Inge,
Chief of the Defence Staff, 1996

This book has traced the development of Special Forces with a
particular concentration on SF activity since 1945. It has also
explained what Special Forces are for and where they can be
used to the best effect. These pages have revealed that the use of Special
Forces extends far beyond the popular concept of the SF role, but they
have also pointed out that these forces have their limitations.

So much for the past; what about the future of Special Forces, now
that the Cold War is over and the possibility of worldwide conflict
seems to have receded? The historical perspective is useful for, while
a great deal has changed in the last fifty years, a surprising number of
things have remained constant. Clearly, the most significant use of
these highly trained Special Force soldiers is for battlefield reconnaissance, the gathering of information and intelligence by long-range
patrols, small-scale attacks and raiding, and the use and support of
guerrilla operations, often behind the enemy lines.

These were the tasks of Rogers' Rangers in the French and Indian

Wars of the eighteenth century and they remain the prime tasks of Special Force soldiers today. Technology – especially the use of satellites – has added greatly to the amount of information available to battlefield commanders, but no information is quite as useful as that gathered by the traditional method, a reliable man with a pair of fieldglasses. 'Nothing is so useful or so well worth having as information gathered by recce patrols,' said Lieutenant-Colonel Andrew Whitehead, who commanded 45 Commando in the Two Sisters battle during the Falklands War in 1982. 'The best instrument for a commander to use before an attack is the Mark 1 Eyeball ... so we sent a lot of recce patrols up to Two Sisters before we went in, and they told us all we needed to know, where the minefields were, where the enemy was ... and knowing that, I could plan the attack.'

One of the objects of this book is to explain what the SF soldier – and SF soldiering – is really like. It is probably fair to say that the true image of Special Force soldiering, the one presented in these pages by the soldiers themselves, is very different from the 'gung-ho', macho, 'one-man wave of destruction' impression imprinted on the popular imagination by the mass media and by certain former members of some SF units in their memoirs. Special Force soldiers are much more than that, but they remain front-line soldiers, a rare breed of fighting men. The question is, if the world can at last establish peaceful ways of settling disputes, is there still a role for such fighting men, or must they become as obsolete as the Greek hoplite or the Roman legionary?

Special Forces have survived and expanded over the last fifty years, especially since the late 1950s, either because they have been needed to fill a gap in conventional-force capability, or because the Special Force commanders have managed to find fresh roles for these units to fill. It seems likely that this process will continue, because whatever else the world has become at the end of the twentieth century it has not become any more peaceful. As these words are written there are over thirty wars going on in various parts of the world, from the former Soviet Union to Afghanistan and Africa, and there is plenty of potential for further conflict in the Balkans, Africa and the Middle East. Such conflicts breed insecurity, and wise leaders will not relax their watch or disband forces that are vital to their national security – or so we must hope.

That apart, the skills of Special Forces could be usefully deployed in other areas. Special Force commanders have suggested that among fresh fields of endeavour the drug cartels, terrorist groups, rogue states, piracy and the protagonists of Islamic fundamentalism may require their attention in the foreseeable future. Therefore, steps should be taken now to ensure that when the challenge comes – and whatever it is – the Western powers and their Special Force units are ready to meet it. One of the most pressing problems for the West is drugs – cocaine, crack and heroin – mostly supplied by the South American cartels, and against this foe the Special Forces are already in action.

Force Recon Marines and US Special Force units have been assisting the Colombian and Bolivian armed forces in anti-drug operations against the drug cartels for years, both in the provision of MTTs (Military Training Teams) to South American police and army units and by participating in operations against the drug producers, their fields and their refining centres. This activity is politically sensitive and has not been widely publicized, but it has certainly been taking place since President Reagan declared his International War on Drugs in 1988. US action against the drug producers has grown in intensity during the 1990s, especially in Colombia, where the actions and power of the Cali and Medellín drug cartels is a clear threat to the integrity of the Colombian state.

The Colombian drug cartels demonstrated their contempt for the elected authority by a series of car-bomb attacks in 1992–3. These attacks killed hundreds of people and were mounted only to demonstrate the impotence of the state compared with the power at the disposal of the cartels. A 500lb car bomb in a shopping centre near Bogotá in April 1993 killed fifteen people and injured a further 300. Eight car bombs went off in central Bogotá in the first four months of 1993, killing sixty people and injuring over 500, and so it continued. Responsibility for these attacks was claimed by Pablo Escobar's Medellín cartel and the Colombian government eventually asked the USA for assistance.

USMC Force Recon had been sending a training team – or 'mission' – to Colombia every year since 1990. The largest of these missions was in 1992, when the Colombian Marine Corps received technical assistance to create a Riverine Patrol Force using high-speed Piranha patrol craft. This mission was followed by an Infantry MTT which taught counter-insurgency tactics and advanced weapons-handling techniques to the anti-narcotics agents of the Colombian National Police. If this assistance seems excessive it has to be remembered that the drug cartels are both strong in numbers and heavily armed; their weaponry includes heavy machine-guns, rocket-propelled grenades and ground-to-air missiles for use against helicopters. Many of the cartel gunmen have received weapons training from the Cuban armed forces.

These specially trained Colombian anti-narcotics forces scored a major success in 1993 when one of the leading *narco-trafficantes*, Pablo Escobar, was hunted down and killed on the roof of his Medellín apartment by a force from the Colombian police. Escobar had spent a fortune on security equipment and his guards, who for increased security were mostly recruited in Cuba, had been trained and equipped by former members of the Israeli Special Forces.

It is alleged that one of these men returned to Tel Aviv and passed on details of Escobar's security arrangements to the Mossad, who passed it on to Washington; in this way Escobar's security arrangements became known in Colombia. By the middle of 1993 Escobar had laid plans to move away from Colombia and relocate his drug operations in Santiago, Cuba, from where the Medellín cartel intended to flood the USA with drugs via the large Cuban community in Florida, using midget submarines supplied from the Soviet Union to ship the drugs across to the American mainland. This plan was well advanced, for one such submarine was sold on to the Cali cartel and then captured by the Colombian Navy in September 1994, when loaded with three tons of refined cocaine. It was therefore necessary for the USA and the Colombians to get Escobar before he could flee to the greater security of Cuba and get this smuggling operation under way.

In late 1992, one of his henchmen, Brance Mosquera, was shot and killed by police agents from the Anti-Drugs Task Force in the streets of Medellín. In his pocket the police found a list of telephone numbers and computer codes which, with US assistance, were revealed as the key to the cartel's worldwide drug network. A further set of codes was found on another man shot dead by the Task Force, Alfonso Munoz. More of Escobar's followers were killed or arrested n 1992–3 and many of them talked, giving more vital information to the security forces. High-level contacts were also established between the USA and Fidel Castro, the Communist ruler of Cuba, and the Medellín's scheme to relocate in Cuba had to be dropped.

That US Special Forces were actively helping the Colombians suppress the cartels was now an open secret, as was the fact that the Americans and Colombians wanted Escobar dead. Many of the smaller drug barons wanted to surrender in return for an amnesty but no amnesty was offered to Escobar. On 2 December 1993, he made the mistake of using one of the phone lines known to police intelligence to set up a meeting with his family. The call was traced to an apartment in Medellín, the police and Special Force elements surrounded the building and after a violent gunfight Escobar was hit three times in the head and killed.

Escobar's death sent a clear warning to the drug barons that their old freewheeling days were over, but the drug problem is too big and the sums of money involved too large to permit a swift solution. The economies of entire countries, such as Afghanistan or Bolivia, or of regions like the Golden Triangle in South-East Asia, are almost entirely dependent on drug production, and some valuable cash crop must replace drugs before the local people will give up producing the raw coca leaf or poppy. There is also the matter of corruption. In 1994, six top Colombian military and police chiefs were dismissed from their jobs following allegations that they had been taking bribes from the drug cartels. The best that can be done at the moment is to wipe out the production centres and interdict the supply routes, and both of these tasks are ideally suited to Special Force deployment.

The USMC appears to have taken a lead in the creation of anti-drug forces in the US military and the Marine Corps Combat Development Command at Quantico, Virginia has already given a high priority to the war on drugs. Combating the drug trade is now one of the tasks of the USMC Warfighting Centre's Special Operations and Low-Intensity Warfare Branch. Since much of Colombia is as dangerous as any war zone such involvement makes good sense, but the drug barons are working closely with local guerrilla forces like the Elan Liberation National and FARC, the Revolutionary Armed Forces of Colombia, two left-wing groups aiming to overthrow the current Colombian regime. Working with local forces against these groups could bring the US military into the Colombian political arena, and create a far more contentious situation.

Anti-drug or anti-terrorist roles would appear to be police or intelligence functions, and if the military stray into these areas, for whatever reason, their role and their lines of command and responsibility will have to be reviewed. This is going to be necessary if Special Forces from democratic states are used to back up or train the counter-insurgency forces in friendly but essentially undemocratic states. The volatile nature of governments in Latin America and in other parts of the world tempts some Western governments to intervene, as happened in the Caribbean in 1983, when US forces, mostly drawn from SF and SOF units, invaded the island of Grenada.

This operation was described afterwards as a confidence-building operation for the US government after Vietnam, a chance to show the American public that military operations need not produce a large number of body bags. The loss of confidence that had gripped the United States in the aftermath of the Vietnam War was not due to any lack of fighting spirit in the American soldier. It arose from fear in Washington that the public would not stand for any more débâcles leading to a loss of American lives. Some small, successful operation was needed to restore public faith in American arms and that chance came in October 1983 when the United States invaded Grenada. For a small-scale affair, the success of the landing was greeted with a great public fanfare in the USA. After this operation, codenamed Urgent Fury, more than 8,000 awards and decorations were presented to the attacking soldiers, roughly one for every man taking part.

The background to the Grenada operation is as follows. On 12 October 1983, the elected government of Grenada, a left-wing junta led by Maurice Bishop, was overthrown in a coup by the New Jewel Movement, an even further left-wing organization led by General Hudson Austin and Deputy Prime Minister Coard. A week later, Maurice Bishop and several of his ministers were taken from their prison cells and murdered, and although the US government had no particular regard for Bishop, who had been a strong supporter of Fidel Castro, the Communist ruler of Cuba, this atrocity could not be tolerated in a country within America's zone of influence. President Reagan ordered his forces to invade Grenada and arrest Austin and Coard, and on 25 October the American forces went ashore.

Grenada is a very small island, just fifteen miles long and ten miles wide. The national 'Army' was the 3,000-strong Grenadian Defence Force, a militia armed with rifles, pistols and submachine-guns, backed by some 700 Cubans, who were described as 'construction workers', but seemed to go to work carrying Kalashnikov rifles instead of picks and shovels. Against this force the US threw the 22 Marine Amphibious Unit, a team of Navy SEAL, elements of the 82nd Airborne Division, a small fleet of warships and transports, a Tactical Fighter Wing and the First Special Operations Air Wing, from Elgin Air Force Base in Florida. The Americans got ashore without difficulty, but the fighting on the island went on for a week until some 100 of the Grenadian and Cuban defenders had been killed and over 300 wounded. US casualties were eighteen dead and fifty-seven wounded.

Following the Grenada invasion, 100 Special Force teams, each team consisting of eight Green Berets, were deployed in Grenada and the surrounding islands – St Kitts, Nevis, St Lucia, Barbuda – to train the local police and defence forces in counter-terrorist warfare.

The Grenada operation did a lot to restore America's confidence after the Vietnam trauma, and if the US government really felt that Grenada might become another Cuba such intervention becomes understandable as a preventive measure. Operations in Central America had a similar justification, but went much further, especially in Nicaragua and Salvador, two countries in the grip of civil war during the 1980s. USc intervention in Salvador between the left- and right-wing factions was revealed in 1985 when a grenade was thrown into a café, killing four US Marines, but US Special Forces had been in Salvador for at least six years. What the US Marines were doing in Salvador finally became apparent a month later when the White House announced that US 'advisers' from the USMC and Special Forces were operational in Salvador 'in support of the government'. The government of Salvador at this time was an unsavoury, right-wing, military junta, not unlike the one just ejected from power in Argentina, and one which employed death squads to eliminate – that is, murder – its political opponents and any liberal elements among the general population.

The situation in Nicaragua was different, but the US involvement was similar. Here the US was attempting to destabilize the elected left-wing Sandinista government, by supporting guerrilla activity organized by the right-wing 'Contras' in the mountains. US activity here even included mining Nicaraguan harbours in what amounted to an undeclared war on a small state, simply because the US government did not agree with that government's political complexion. Broadly speaking, the USA supported brutal, undemocratic right-wing regimes – usually described as 'authoritarian' – while deploring and attacking brutal, undemocratic left-wing regimes – usually described as 'totalitarian'. The long-suffering people who endured the rule of these regimes could not usually tell the difference.

Green Beret teams were also deployed in Honduras, Costa Rica and Guatemala, and this commitment to training 'counter-terrorist' forces or taking direct action to protect US interests in 'America's Back Yard' has not ceased in subsequent years. Neither has the involvement of at least some of these 'counter-terrorist' forces in anti-democratic actions against liberal elements in the civilian population, people who have no love of Communism or 'left-wing' regimes but who only wish for a more equitable distribution of their national resources for the common good. Such people are often targets for death squads in many Latin American countries and the support of the US for anti-liberal regimes, and the training supplied by US Special Forces to such 'counter-terrorist' forces – a euphemism for death squads – is an activity that should at least be reviewed and probably discontinued.

Special Forces are involved in most, if not all, of these activities and there lies a potential problem. Special Forces are increasingly secret and ever more secretive. This secrecy, it is alleged, is part of their 'mystique', one reason for their effectiveness, and this military reason is used to justify the concealment of their actions and activities. The trend is to shift Special Forces away from military control and public accountability into a shady area as the cutting edge of the intelligence community or the less savoury side of diplomacy.

Fortunately, many Special Force soldiers are well aware of this danger and take care to add instruction on human rights – or 'hearts and minds' – into the training they give to Third World units, where such concepts are all too often completely unknown. The US 7th Special Forces Group is the theatre group for the US Commander-in-Chief, South, the officer guarding US interests below the Rio Grande. This role brought the group in touch with the troubles in San Salvador, where Colonel J. S. Roach was employed as part of an operational planning and training team from 1984 to 1986: 'Human rights was not a separate one-hour block at the beginning of the day. You had to find a way to couch it into the training so that it wasn't just a moralistic approach. The Salvadorean military understood that they were not supposed to violate human rights, but they believed they were driven to it by extreme circumstances. When you could convince them in an operational context why human rights made sense, you started to get their attention. When the Salvadoreans started to see that "If we don't shoot the civilians we'll get their support and therefore be able to rout out the guerrillas," then they saw human rights from a pragmatic perspective.'

Officers and NCOs of the 7th Special Forces Group serving in Salvador clearly devoted a lot of time to inculcating the notion of 'hearts and minds' into their trainees, and this may have been the most useful part of their work. However, the US Ambassador in Salvador at the height of the trouble, Robert White, felt that the Salvador government did not need external support; neither did he acknowledge the existence of significant outside interference in El Salvador from the Communist bloc or Cuba, which the US government feared. He therefore did not see any need for Special Force 'advisers' and refused to allow the C-in-C South into the country.

Special Force soldiers finally went in on attachment to a normal MTT training team after the US C-in-C South felt that while the

Salvadorean military might hinder the progress of the right-wing government towards democracy – the understatement of the decade – a far greater threat to democracy in Salvador came from the left-wing dissenters. Why a US general feels qualified to make such decisions and then take actions affecting the political process in a foreign country, in defiance of the view of the resident Ambassador, the man representing the elected US government, is another matter.

Most nations will maintain the right to intervene in any country where law and order has broken down and the life of their nationals is threatened; and, if this action is open and for a good reason, it has to be supported. The French have always held that position and have not hesitated to deploy their troops in the intervention role, especially in Francophone Africa. The troops most frequently used for this purpose are those of the Foreign Legion, especially from the 2nd Régiment Etranger Parachutiste, the famous 2nd REP, the Legion equivalent of the SAS, which carried out a classic rescue operation in Zaire in May 1978, after a 12,000-strong force of Congolese rebels crossed from Angola and seized the town of Kolwezi in Shaba province, the former Katanga.

Kolwezi is a mining town and in 1978 it contained around 2,500 white technicians, with their wives and families. These were rounded up by the rebels, who then went on the rampage, raping and killing, setting fire to buildings and threatening to destroy the town. When the Zairean Army of President Mobutu showed itself incapable of intervening, the French decided to take a hand and the task was handed to Lieutenant-Colonel Erulin of the 2nd REP, who was told to fly into Kolwezi, drive off the rebels and get these people out. This order reached Erulin on the morning of 17 May; two days later the 2nd REP, using borrowed American parachutes and borrowed US aircraft, parachuted into Kolwezi, 2,000 miles south of their base in Corsica.

There were not enough aircraft available to carry the entire 700-man force for one drop, so only 450 Legionnaires flew in with the first wave. These took the outskirts of the town and secured the airfield, beating off heavy attacks for a full day before the rest of the regiment could be flown in to join them. It took another two days to drive the rebels back across the Angolan frontier, and on 4 June the REP were back in Corsica. This action cost the regiment five men killed and twenty-five wounded, but they had saved the lives of more than 2,000 people and killed over 250 rebels. Above all, they had demonstrated the long arm of the French military machine and the willingness of the French government and nation to use their military clout if the situation seemed to demand it. It is more than likely that similar situations will occur again in the years ahead and intervention like this will remain a Special Force task.

One traditional area of criminal activity that has reappeared in the last few decades is piracy. In 1994 the Lloyds Register reported ninety attacks on shipping in various parts of the world; by 1996 this figure had jumped to 226 and official sources believe that the actual total might be twice this figure. Not all attacks are reported, for some ships have simply disappeared. Pirates are now active in many parts of the world, from the Caribbean to the South China Sea and the Mediterranean, and appear to be growing bolder and more ruthless. Their attacks range from boarding and ransacking ships to seizing the vessel and killing the crew before steering the ship into some friendly port and removing the entire cargo. Yachts have been attacked off the coast of Corfu and around the coast of East Africa and the islands of the Caribbean, where the attackers have either murdered the passengers and crew or forced them overboard into shark-infested waters, selling the yacht later to some unsuspecting buyer.

Nor are these attacks confined to the high seas. Ships have been attacked in the harbour at Singapore and around the islands of Indonesia, which many Merchant Navy officers now regard as the most dangerous waters in the world. Boarding a high-sided, fast-moving ship at night calls for trained men and fast craft, both of which can be found in the Indonesian armed forces, though the official reply to that allegation is to claim the existence of a renegade pirate gang led and trained by ex-members of the British Special Forces.

Some of these attacks – perhaps the majority – are clearly carried out with the co-operation of the shore authorities. In March 1997, a Cypriot cargo vessel, the *Samir*, vanished off the coast of Libya and although it has since been located by satellite in a Libyan port the Libyan authorities deny that it is there – and there is no word of the crew. Four other vessels from different countries have also vanished off the Libyan coast since 1995.

Piracy has to be combated and the Special Forces, especially those trained in amphibious work, have the equipment, like fast patrol craft and helicopters, plus the relevant expertise to raise the cost of piracy, if means can be found to bring them into action. Commanchio Troop, Royal Marines, is already tasked with protecting and defending the North Sea oil rigs, and Royal Marines Commandos, embarked on Royal

Navy frigates, have abseiled from helicopters on to the decks of ships suspected of breaking the UN arms embargo off the former Yugoslavia. These techniques could easily be deployed to retake vessels seized by pirates, and the use of helicopter patrols would provide some protection for vessels anchored in dangerous harbours or unprotected roadsteads. Until the problem of piracy is tackled, it will continue to grow.

The use of Special Forces to tackle piracy is not a far-fetched notion, for some SF units have already established primary tasks outside a clearly military role. The main function of the 2,500-strong US Delta Force is hostage rescue and they train relentlessly for that task at their base in Fort Bragg, where the full range of SAS-style facilities, from helicopter pads, civil aircraft fuselages and CQB (Close Quarter Battle) 'Killing Rooms', are in constant use. The British have become accustomed to hearing that the SAS have been called in for anti-terrorist operations on the mainland of Britain or as far away as Peru, although in both places there are adequate numbers of armed police units available for such a purpose. The dividing line between the police function and military action by Special Force units has become blurred in recent years and is another one that needs to be redrawn.

Special Force units are not confined to the armies, paramilitary police forces or clandestine intelligence operatives of the Western powers. As the list of SF and SOF units in the Appendix reveals, even if most of the active units are found in the armed forces of the USA and Great Britain, many nations now maintain Special Force units and deploy them wherever their national interests seem to require it. Russian Spetznaz units, for example, have been closely involved in the brutal internal wars affecting the new nations within the former Soviet Union. In some countries, especially in the Third World, Latin America and the Arab States, SF units are a form of uniformed virility symbol, ranking with the international airport and the flag-carrying airline, organized more for impression than effect.

Nations create and maintain Special Force units today rather as they once created and maintained Guards regiments, as the cutting edge of their armies and an elite force. There are now so many Special Force units that they even hold international competitions to test their various skills and exchange ideas. In 1993 Delta Force took first place in an International Counter-Terrorist Competition – a bizarre concept in itself – an event that attracted thirty-nine teams from thirteen countries.

Special Forces are not a universal panacea for any military difficulty. This book has illustrated, not once but many times, that the first rule for any engagement, and especially any Special Force engagement, is that the task must have a definite achievable aim. This was not the case in the ironically named Operation Restore Hope in December 1992, an attempt by US forces to reinforce and protect humanitarian aid missions in the war-torn country of Somalia. This intervention was requested under UN Security Council Resolution 751, which authorized the UN Secretary General to deploy a security force in Somalia where the local warlords were terrorizing the citizens and making the distribution of aid impossible.

The first contingents came from Italy – the former colonial power in Somalia – and Pakistan, and before long some twenty-six nations had troops on the ground, in numbers ranging from Ireland with 80 to Italy with 2,600. The main Somali warlord, 'General' Aidid, at first agreed to the deployment of UN troops. Then he changed his mind and began to attack them, and the situation was deteriorating fast when the US forces, from the 1st Marine Division and the 10th Mountain Division, came ashore in the glare of TV arc lights on 9 December 1992, after the landing area had been checked out by Navy SEAL. The US forces in Somalia eventually numbered 24,000 men and women, and their military and logistical support was the best the USA could provide, but numbers and equipment could not contain the situation.

The first problem arose over the task the US troops were to perform. US orders were to secure the Somali capital, Mogadishu, and the main provincial town of Baidoa, guard the airfields and ports through which food aid was arriving to the starving population, and construct some fresh logistical facilities. They were also to guard the various relief teams and free them from the attention of the Somali gangs, who were charging the relief teams hard cash before they would permit them to function at all and stealing most of the food aid supplies to feed their own forces. With that much achieved, and the local clans duly overawed, the US soldiers would hand over to fresh UN troops and withdraw.

The UN Secretary General, Boutros Ghali, allegedly had other ideas. He wanted the US and other UN troops to disarm the warring clans and restore order to this ravaged country. To achieve this the UN would have had to take over Somalia and rebuild the country from the ground up. The leading warlords, and especially General Aidid, who was doing very nicely blackmailing the aid teams and buying arms with the money thus extorted, had no intention of letting this happen. There was also one factor that no one at the UN or in the USA had taken account of before the troops went in: the Somalia clan militias were heavily armed, skilled in guerrilla warfare, and more than willing to fight.

As a result, the US troops, tasked to carry out a humanitarian mission, were soon coming under fire. The airfield at Beli Dougle was captured only after a firefight involving Marine Cobra helicopter gunships, and though the US Marines and French Paras pushed the militias out of Mogadishu, fighting spread to the hinterland. The port of Kismayu was taken after an amphibious assault by the USMC and Belgian Para-Commandos, but the situation grew extremely tense on 11 January 1993 when Aidid refused to hand over his heavy weapons and machine-gun-equipped trucks – known as 'technicals' – to UN control.

The first US Marine was killed by the Somalis on the 12th, and the fighting, sniping and mine-laying then escalated by the day. On the 25 January there was a major battle in Mogadishu between Belgian Para-Commandos backed by US Marine gunships and the 'technicals' of another local warlord, 'General' Morgan. Meanwhile, the security situation in the capital was also deteriorating, with Somali mobs, incited by Aidid, attacking the US, Egyptian and French embassies. Those UN troops who believed they had been sent to Somalia to help feed starving people began to wonder what was going on here, for they seemed to be fighting a war.

The short answer was that Somalia was no longer a nation in any recognizable sense of the term. There was no law, no justice, no public administration. Schools, hospitals and police forces had all ceased to function. The territory known as 'Somalia' was simply a battleground between various rival clans, and anyone who got in the way of their private wars came under attack from every side. It was bad before the UN intervened and then it got worse. In June Aidid's forces ambushed a Pakistani contingent, killing twenty-eight soldiers and wounding another fifty, and it is some indication of the scale of the fighting in Somalia that it took a relief column of Italian tanks and infantry to get the survivors away.

On 20 June the Pakistanis opened fire on a rioting mob, killing twenty Somalis, and four days later, when the US sent in troops to arrest Aidid, the attempt led to an all-out battle in which large numbers of Somali civilians were killed, as well as six Moroccan soldiers serving with the UN. On 12 July, a US helicopter attacked one of the Aidid militia positions in Mogadishu, and in the riot which followed four Western journalists were beaten to death by the crowd. On 8 August, four US soldiers were killed by a mine. After that, with this state of affairs being shown nightly on US television, the President, Bill Clinton, sent for the Rangers and – or so it is said – for Delta Force, and tasked them to kill or capture Aidid, the man identified as the main source of the trouble.

The US Rangers were soon in action, but without conspicuous success. On 30 August they attacked a building believed to contain Aidid's headquarters, but found it contained only UN relief workers. A further raid, on 7 September, was equally unfruitful, and meanwhile Aidid or one or other of his rivals was attacking the UN soldiers and killing them in quantity. An ambush of Pakistani troops on 9 September led to further losses, including 100 Somalis killed when US troops engaged some of Aidid's militia sheltering behind a crowd.

Then came a major and tragic setback. On 25 September, a US Blackhawk helicopter was brought down in Mogadishu by ground fire and the surviving crewmen were attacked and killed by a vengeful Somali crowd. Pictures of burned and mutilated US soldiers being dragged through the streets behind a 'technical' were shown on US television and inevitably produced demands that the troops were achieving nothing and should be pulled out. Instead, the US administration ordered the Rangers to make another attempt to capture Aidid.

The Rangers elected to raid Aidid's headquarters and swamp it with men and firepower, putting a large force in by helicopter and seizing all the militiamen they could find. This raid duly went in and was met with a storm of fire from heavy machine-guns and rocket-propelled grenades from the Somali positions, which shot down two Blackhawks. One of the crewmen, Warrant Officer Michael Durant, was captured and held prisoner for nearly two weeks; Delta troopers and the Rangers were pinned down by Somali fire and twelve Rangers had been killed and eighty wounded before a relief force, which had to include tanks and armoured cars, broke through. Two of the Delta troopers, both snipers, Gary I. Gordon and Randall D. Shugart, were later awarded posthumous Medals of Honor for their attempts to rescue Durant and the rest of his crew after Durant's Blackhawk had been brought down by Somali ground fire.

The two men reached the crash site in the middle of Mogadishu in another Blackhawk, and, seeing movement inside the crashed aircraft down below, they volunteered to jump down and see what they could do. This was obviously hazardous as both aircraft were under fire and taking hits and the men could see armed Somalis on the roof tops and running through the streets towards the crash site. The Delta troopers were landed about 100 yards from the crash site and had to fight their way through streets and shanties to reach the aircraft. There they found all the crew severely injured, but they managed to pull both pilots and two crewmen from the wreckage and set up a defensive perimeter before the mob arrived. They kept the mob back by firing at anyone who broke cover, but numbers told and before long their position was being swept with fire from roof tops and alleyways, and they were getting short of ammunition. Meanwhile their own Blackhawk had been hit by an RPG missile and forced to break off the action and return to base. They were on their own.

Shughart was the first man to be killed, and Gordon then fought on alone, using weapons retrieved from the helicopter, even his Beretta pistol, as the mob rushed the wreck and finally overwhelmed him. Of the six Americans involved, four helicopter crewmen and two Rangers, only Durant survived, dragged from the scene, his leg broken, stripped of his clothes and forced to march through the streets of the city by a shrieking mob. When the Ranger relief force finally reached the scene, all the bodies had gone and only a pile of empty cartridge cases gave witness to what had happened.

Four Pakistani tanks were knocked out in the subsequent fighting, four Blackhawks were shot down, dozens of men killed and more wounded – and all this in the course of a supposedly humanitarian mission. The fighting went on and on, but it gradually dawned on the UN, and rather more quickly on the nations providing the UN with military forces, that there was no hope of establishing peace in Somalia until the local people wanted it, or until the UN were prepared to go in there mob-handed and wipe out the militias to the last man.

Since that was not an acceptable option, the UN forces began to pull out and the last US soldier left on 8 March 1993. Inter-clan fighting, which had never stopped, rose to a fresh intensity and still continues.

Restore Hope was not a military failure. The troops could have wiped out the militias and reduced the country to some form of order, but the political will to do that was not there. Moreover, there was no real understanding of the Somali people, and their wishes or aspirations. They may have wanted peace, but not if it was imposed on them by Western, Christian foreigners. The only outcome of the UN operation was to unite the Somali people against those soldiers who had come in to help them and the long-term result may be the establishment of an Iranian-backed, fundamentalist Muslim state on the Horn of Africa.

The most obvious lesson of Restore Hope is that in such a shambolic political situation the soldier's task is impossible. This is one lesson that the present century might pass on to the next one: that intervention without clear objectives is pointless. Such operations may be proposed in the future, perhaps in Africa or the Balkans, but unless clear lines of command and clear rules of engagement are laid down before the troops are committed success cannot be guaranteed, even by sending in large numbers of Special Force soldiers. The UN has no mandate for rebuilding countries ravaged by civil war or tribal fighting, but more and more such countries are coming to public attention, especially in Africa, where the fighting in Ruanda alone has cost millions of lives.

Committing troops without deciding on an achievable role is a cardinal error. So is the creation of Special Force units without an identifiable, legitimate function or the use of such forces without a clear, admitted legal aim. This point has been made before but it is worth repeating. In a large number of countries, especially in Latin America and the Third World, Special Force units have been trained and used, not to defend national territory against subversion and external aggression, but to suppress legitimate political dissent.

Even the US Green Berets have been involved in 'wet' operations, a euphemism for assassination, and in 1991 there were newspaper reports of US Green Berets assisting Kuwaiti soldiers to beat and kill Palestinian people in Kuwait City after it was recaptured from the Iraqis at the end of the Gulf War. The US Green Berets have certainly trained Special Force units from a number of Latin American countries, units that on returning home have become noted for brutality, torture and murder. Some of the actions of the British SAS – the Gibraltar killings, for example – have not escaped criticism.

There are those who approve of certain military units being used for such 'shoot to kill and no questions asked' purposes, but a question that ought to be asked and answered is: where does such conduct stop and where will it lead? Countries which operate by open, democratic principles and employ armies under the rule of law are in the minority in the present-day world, but even there clandestine Special Force units, operating outside the public domain, exist and flourish and declare themselves 'secret'. This trend needs to be curbed and it can be curbed without the slightest effect on operational capability; unless it is curbed it presents a danger to Special Force units in the years ahead.

Soldiers in democratic countries are first and foremost citizens of that country and are bound by the same laws as every other citizen. This is a fact that sometimes seems to be forgotten, though it was stated plainly for the British Army by the British Parliament as long ago as 1693, after the Earl of Argyll's Regiment had massacred the

MacDonalds of Glencoe: 'Though the command of an officer be absolute, yet no command against the laws of nature is binding; a soldier, retaining his commission, ought to refuse to commit any barbarity, for if a soldier should be ordered to shoot a man passing by innocently in the street, no such command will exempt him from the punishment for murder.'

There are those who feel that the moral case against the use of counter-terrorism tactics is one for wimps. Such people may be persuaded by the fact that treating the civilian population harshly, beating or torturing prisoners, running death squads or acting illegally does not work. The use of such tactics will end up by eroding the basis of the entire campaign and the authority of the government in power. Brigadier Robert Thompson, an expert in counter-terrorism, pointed that out during the Vietnam War: 'In dealing with terrorism there is a temptation for government forces to act outside the law, the excuse being that the normal process of the law is too cumbersome, that the safeguards of the law are not designed for an insurgency situation and that a terrorist deserves to be treated as an outlaw anyway. Not only is this morally wrong, but it will, over a period, create more practical difficulties than it solves and destroy the legitimacy of the government campaign.'

An American counter-terrorism expert, Robert Kupperman, has made much the same point: 'Secrecy can open the door to unacceptable behaviour – recall the recent Central American "how-to" assassination manual, or the mining of Nicaraguan harbours. We clearly undermine our position against international terrorism when we can be accused – correctly – of engaging in the tactics of terror ourselves. The notion that their terrorism is automatically immoral and our counter-terrorism is automatically moral will not stand much scrutiny.'

This is not a thinly veiled accusation against Special Force soldiers in general or any particular Special Force units, but these statements will hit home in certain places and provide a warning that as SF units become increasingly secretive, more involved with the intelligence community and less publicly accountable, so the risk arises that they may be used for purposes for which there is neither official sanction nor – rather more to the point – public approval. Dressing up in black balaclavas lest some far-off dictator learns what they look like is simply farcical, but refusing – and being allowed to refuse – to reveal their identities when brought before a court of law is not acceptable and should not be permitted in any democratic society.

SF lines of command are increasingly becoming blurred and in some cases – as with the US Delta Force and the British 14th Intelligence Company – their very existence is denied. This tactic might be accepted from these two units, but the secrecy is spreading to other Special Force units. This is potentially dangerous, as those who have taken part in training SF units for service in the Third World and Latin America must be all too well aware; the step from denying the existence of such units to disclaiming responsibility for their actions is a short one. The vague claim that 'it cannot happen here' is not sufficient. All military units, even Special Force units, must fit into the military framework and act within the law, and claims that personnel will be at risk if their names and actions are known should be justified rather than simply accepted.

As they are used more and more in clandestine operations, outside the context of open war, so SFs become liable – to put it delicately – for uses which are not acceptable in democratic societies. This may not yet have happened, but the danger is there. In November 1995, John Deutch, the Director of the CIA, in a speech on 'The Future of Intelligence', began by describing two challenges facing the intelligence community. The first was to deploy considerable resources against the most pressing security threats of the post-Cold War era. The second was to be accountable: 'We must carry out our intelligence operations in an efficient and responsible manner and we must maintain an efficient service ... and we must carry out our duties with integrity.' Deutch then listed what the CIA sees as the main challenges of the post-Cold War world:

1. The proliferation of chemical, biological and nuclear weapons of mass destruction.
2. The activities of countries like North Korea, Libya, Iraq and Iran.
3. The growing threat of international crime, terrorism and narcotics trafficking.

These three challenges have also been identified by various Special Force units, and such units have expanded massively in recent years. To give one example, the United States Special Forces organization, popularly imagined by the general public as a few Green Beret A Teams or SEAL Teams, is actually a vast, inter-service Command, numbering tens of thousands of men and women, deploying a gigantic budget and extending into all three services.

The US Air Force Special Operations Command, based at Hulburt Field in Florida, has an establishment of 12,187 men, charged with 'unconventional warfare, delivering Special Operations combat power "anytime, anywhere"; special reconnaissance, counter-terrorism, counter-narcotics and foreign internal defence support', and this an Air Force unit, not a Commando force. The US Army maintains an even larger Special Forces Group, based at Fort Bragg in North Carolina. This numbers no fewer than 30,000 effectives, men and women, and includes the Green Berets, the Rangers, a covert-attack helicopter unit and psychological warfare (propaganda) and civil affairs experts. The Navy has its SEAL teams based at Coronado, California, a unit which now covers the functions of the old UDT teams. This force is estimated at around 4,000 effectives, consisting of SEAL, Special Boat Squadrons and SEAL delivery teams, the latter operating small submarines and aircraft. There is also the Joint Services Force, which specializes in counter-terrorism and comprises the Navy's SEAL 6 Team and Delta Force. Delta Force is believed to number about 1,300 effectives. The total comes to some 45,000 troops, the equivalent of three full-strength infantry divisions, a far cry from the small British commando units of the Second World War, the ones who set this Special Force concept going.

However, as this history has illustrated, Special Forces have a cyclic life span. They usually begin as the British Commandos began in 1940, as small units of very fit, highly trained soldiers, charged with a specific role or task. Then, gradually, they grow, to become battalions, brigades, even divisions, or entire commands. Heavy equipment, artillery, engineers, service elements, a logistical back-up gradually become necessary, until the Special Force unit is not unlike any other conventional force – at which point a smaller Special Force, not unlike the original concept, is found necessary and created, often spun off from the present formation. And so the whole process begins again.

As the next millennium looms, the future looks bright for Special Forces, provided the trends identified above can be contained. Every country of any size has at least one Special Force unit and more will undoubtedly appear. Anti-terrorist Special Forces on the SAS–Delta–Green Beret model need to be kept in being, even if they are not in current use, and this may be a problem, for their size and training does not equip them for more general use: the SAS cannot be used to face down a rioting mob in Belfast, for example, or capture a strong position like Goose Green. Special Forces cannot be cobbled together at the last minute and tasked to do any job that comes along. Their equipment and their transport must always be on hand and primed for instant use and this will be expensive, but the alternative is to surrender the initiative to the enemy, the terrorist, the urban guerrilla, the man with the bomb and the cause. The main internal task for these units will be to keep their role tightly defined, and stay away from any attempts to use them in a police or paramilitary role, or as the hard edge of the intelligence services.

Special Operating Forces have also expanded in recent years and few countries are now without their Commando units and Parachute brigades. These SOF forces are conventional forces charged with a special role: a parachute battalion is fundamentally an infantry battalion that goes into battle by parachute. Once the paratrooper is on the ground and out of his harness he takes up a normal infantry role, but one which these units handle extremely well.

The specialization of such men lies in the fact that they may be cut off behind the lines or tasked to hold a bridgehead for some days before conventional ground forces can join them, so such men are exceptionally well-trained and resolute soldiers. The same is true of US Marine and Royal Marine Commando units, and all such units offer the advantage of being able to fight a conventional war as well as fulfilling their special operating task. A Royal Marine Commando unit or a Parachute Regiment battalion *can* quell a riot in the streets of Belfast, or fight a full-scale action on Two Sisters, as well as spearheading an assault. These soldiers and Marines are cost-effective, for they can take on a wide range of tasks and are particularly suited to the rapid-reaction role, a role that may become increasingly important if the current instability affecting many parts of the world spreads and intensifies.

There is a military dictum which states that 'A company in the right place today will contain a situation that a brigade cannot handle tomorrow,' and there is some truth in that assertion. A comparison between the Iraqi threats to Kuwait in 1961 and 1990 is a good indication of that rule. In 1961, the British were able to rush some SOF units to the area in a few days, and the Iraqis held back. In 1990, Saddam Hussein sent his tanks in without any warning and it took half a million men and a full-scale war to get them out. Getting an adequate number of men on the ground quickly is going to be ever more important, and hence the creation of rapid-reaction forces, notably in the UK, France and the United States, which has had one since March 1980 when President Carter ordered the US Marines to form a Rapid Deployment Force. The first was established at MacGill Air Force base in Florida under the command of a USMC general, P. X. Kelley.

In the United Kingdom, the Rapid Reaction Force formed in 1996 will be a light division of two brigades, 3 Commando Brigade, Royal

Marines, and 5 Airborne, with a common Command and Headquarters at Northwood, near London. New assault ships have been ordered for the Royal Marines, adequate numbers of transport aircraft have been allocated to the paratroopers and their force-enhancing helicopter allocations are being increased. In France the rapid-reaction force is already in being, based around 2 REP and a Cavalry (Light Armoured) unit of the French Foreign Legion.

These forces will be expensive to maintain and will be effective only if they have clear direction and are backed up with good intelligence. The Royal Marine Commandos and Paratroopers reacted quickly to the Argentine invasion of the Falkland Islands; but, had British intelligence been adequate, the original Argentine invasion could have been anticipated and so prevented, or met with superior force on the beaches. In future, it will not be enough to *react*, it will be necessary to *anticipate*.

It is likely that an expanding role of SOF forces will be to bridge the gap and hold the ground between the insertion of Special Force teams and the arrival of large conventional units, between, say, the advance recon carried out by a Green Beret A Team and the arrival of an armoured division. This role had been anticipated by the US Army with the creation of Special Operations Command and Control Elements (SOCCE). These elements are based on the notion that, as the US gets involved in operations just short of war, deployed units and SOF forces will have to work together closely. A SOCCE will therefore be attached to a conventional headquarters whenever the operational command covered by that headquarters overlaps with a SOF operational area – all good common sense, but an area often overlooked. This role has already been tested in Bosnia and Croatia in 1995, when US Navy SEAL were deployed around Orašje, to feel out the extent of potential opposition and check on river bridges before the arrival of a 1,500-strong battalion of Combat Engineers and further US forces. And so it goes on, as Special Forces follow their star, from a glorious history into an unpredictable future.

This book has charted the course of Special Forces since their inception in the eighteenth century, with a close look at their development since 1945. This has revealed a different picture of Special Forces from that portrayed in the cinema or in some of the more lurid memoirs published in recent years. The role of the Green Berets in training the CIDG forces in Vietnam, the US Marines of the CAP platoons, the British paratroopers stoutly serving on the housing estates of Ulster or plugging on in the dark across the tracer-swept ground of Goose Green are all light-years away from the actions of John Rambo. The Special Force soldier emerges from this history as a tough, well-trained but essentially human figure, the sort of soldier that has come down through history as a recognizable type, the kind that can be found in any Army, at any time. He is, quite simply, a fighting man and wars cannot be won without him.

The great bond between such men finds expression in the units that contain them, the units to which such men eventually gravitate. Take, as a final example of this unit spirit, the words of John Cooper, one of the original SAS soldiers: 'Looking back on the years between 1941 and 1960 in the SAS, I consider it to have been more of a club or a family, with no great emphasis on the physical toughness that is often attributed to it today. We were carrying out David Stirling's insistence that small patrols of three or four men could do enormous damage to an enemy owing to their ability to penetrate behind the lines, and we proved that in the early days. This was coupled naturally to the ability to change methods to changing circumstances and the enemy response; it was this flexibility that kept us ahead of the Afrika Corps and those same principles have stood us in good stead ever since.'

The curious thing is that throughout their lengthening and colourful history, the true role of Special Forces has not really changed. They are the eyes of the Army, the source of sound, reliable intelligence. They work with indigenous people in the jungles and mountains of the world, teaching these people how to defend themselves. They are the small-scale raiders, happy to work in squads or teams rather than battalions, they are the ones who come from the sea or the sky by night, to hold the ground and buy the time. They are the ones who demonstrate by their exploits in the field that even in the ever-more technological world of modern warfare, a good man with a rifle can still make a difference.

APPENDIX
The World's Special Forces 1997

Argentina
601 and 602 Commando Company
Marine Brigade
'Buzo Tactico'
Halcon 8 ('Falcon 8') of the Argentine Army (GSG9 type)

Austria
Jagdkommando (Rangers)
Gebirgsjägerbattalions (Mountain Warfare)
Gendarmerie Einsatz Kommando (GEK) ('Cobra') (GSG9 type)

Australia
Special Air Service Regiment (SASR)
* A, B, C Squadron
* HQ Squadron
LRRP-type
* Norforce Regiment
* Pilbara Regiment
* Far North Queensland Regiment
Navy Clearance Divers
1 Civil Affairs Unit (Psy-Ops type)
Australian Protective Service (APS) (VIP Protection)
Australian Federal Police (AFP) CT/Hostage Rescue Unit

Bahrain
U-Group

Belgium
1st Special Reconnaissance Company
Escadron Special d'Intervention of the Gendarme Royal (ESI)

Bolivia
Special Forces Training Centre

Brazil
1º Batalhão de Forças Especialis (1st Special Forces Battalion)
Grupo de Mergulhadores de Combate (GRUMEC) (Combat Divers Group)
Comandos Anfíbios (COMANFI) (Amphibious Commandos)

Comandos de Reconhecimento Terrestre (RECONTER) (Land Recon Commandos)
Grupos de Operações Especiais (Special Operations Groups)
PARASAR (Parajumpers)

Bulgaria
Mountain Warfare Unit

Canada
Special Service Force
* Canadian Airborne Regiment (1/2/3 Airborne Commando), disbanded February 1995; reconstituted as follows on 12 April 1995:
  – 1 Airborne Commando: attached to Royal Canadian Regiment
  – 2 Airborne Commando: attached to Princess Patricia's Canadian Light Infantry
  – 3 Airborne Commando: attached to Royal Vingt-Deuxième Regiment
* Airborne Service Commando
Emergency Response Teams, RCMP

Chile
Escuela de Paracaidistas y Fuerzas Especiales (School of SF of the Chilean Army)
Buzos Tacticos del Ejercito (Army SF Commandos)
Buzos Tacticos de la Armada (Navy SF Commandos)
Unidad Anti-Terroristes (UAT) of the National Police Force ('Cobra')
GOPE (Grupo de Operaciones Especials) of the National Police
FACH (part of the Chilean Air Force)

China (People's Republic of China)
6th Special Warfare Group
8th Special Warfare Group
12th Special Warfare SF Detachment

Colombia
Grupos Especiales de Operaciones (GEOS) (Special Operations Group) of the National Police Force (GSG9)
GAES (Anti-Extortion and Kidnapping Groups of the Colombian Army)
GADJA Teams (part of Colombian Air Force)

Commonwealth of Independent States (ex-USSR)
Naval Infantry
103rd, 104th, 105th Airborne Guards Divisions (VDV)
Independent Battalions

Independent Assault Brigades
Alfa Brigade (FSB anti-terrorism)
Delta Brigade (FSB anti-terrorism)
OMON ('Black Berets')
MVD (Interior Ministry Troops)
Kondor Division of MVD (anti-terrorism)
Spetznaz (SPETZialnoje NAZnachenie)
* 'Razvedchiki': one battalion/division divided into two companies (one for LRRP, one for Airborne operations)
* 'Rejdoviki': brigade-sized: operate in battalion- and company-sized units in an independent recon role
* 'Vysotniki': brigade-sized: operate in eleven-man units and are the closest to US SF/UK SAS

Czech and Slovak Republics
22nd Vysadkova (Airborne) Regiment

Denmark
Jaegerkorpset (LRRP)
Froemanskorpset (Frogman Corps)
Saerlige Efterretning Patruljer (SEP) (Special Intelligence Patrols)
Sirius Patruljen (Sirius Patrol)
Patruljekompaniet Ved Jydske Division
Politiets Efterretningstejeneste (PE) of the State Police Intelligence Service

Dominican Republic
6th Regular Battalion (LRRP)
Six Special Forces Companies

Ecuador
Puma Unit (Army SF)

Egypt
* Army
  Unit 777/'Sa'aga/'Thunderbolt Force'
* Navy
  UDT/SEAL-type unit (designation unknown)
* Paramilitary
  'Special Operations Troops' of the Central Security Forces (a branch of the Ministry of the Interior) (VIP protection, SWAT-type etc.)

Federal Republic of Germany
Fallschirmjäger (Parachutists)
Fernspäh Kompanies (SAS-type/LRRP)

Kampfschwimmerkommando (German SEALs)
Gebirgsjäger (Mountain Warfare troops)
Grenzschutzgruppe 9 (GSG9, Counter-Terrorism)

Finland
Laskuvarjojaakarikoulu (Airborne Ranger school)
Laivaston Erikoistoimintayksikko (Navy Special Operation unit)
1 Rannikkojaakarikomppania (1st Marine Commando Company)
Sissikomppaniat (Ranger/Guerrilla Warfare Companies)
Osasto Karhu ('Bear Unit') of the Helsinki Police Department (counter-
   terrorism)

France
1er Régiment Parachutiste d'Infanterie de Marine (1er RPI Ma)
   (Para-Commandos – nearest French equivalent to SAS/SF etc.)
Force d'Action Rapide (Rapid-Reaction Force)
* 4ème Division Aéromobile (4th Airmobile Division)
* 6ème Division Légère Blindée (6th Light Armoured Division)
* 9ème Division d'Infantrie Marine (9th Marine Light Infantry Division)
* 27ème Division Alpine (27th Alpine Division)
Foreign Legion
* 1er Régiment Etranger
* 2ème Régiment
* 3ème Régiment d'Infanterie
* 4ème Régiment Etranger
* 1er Régiment Etranger de Cavalerie (1e REC)
* 2ème Régiment Etranger de Parachutiste (2ème REP) (NB Also a part
   of 11ème Division Parachutiste (11th Parachute Division))
* 5ème Régiment Mixte du Pacifique
* Detachment Légion Etrangère de Mayotte
* 13ème Demi-Brigade Légion Etrangère
* 13ème Régiment Dragoons de Parachutiste (LRRP)
Groupe de'Intervention Gendarmerie Nationale (GIGN)
RAID (counter-terrorist)

Greece
Alpine Raiding Company
Dimoria Eidikon Apostolon (DEA) (Special Mission Platoon) of the Athens
   City Police (counter-terrorism)

Honduras
Army SF Commandos

Commando de Operaciones (COE) of the Honduras Army SF Commandos (counter-terrorism)

Hong Kong
Police Special Duties Unit (SDU) of the Hong Kong Police

India
Special Frontier Force
Special Services Group of the Special Frontier Force
India–Tibetan Border Police

Indonesia
Marines
Police Mobile Brigade (PMB)
Special Warfare Command
Satgas Gegania (Counter-Terrorist Task Force) of the Indonesian National Police
Satgas Atbara (Counter-Terrorist Task Force) of the Indonesian Air Force
Detachment 81 of the Army Special Forces (Delta Force type)
Kesatuan Gurita of the Indonesian Navy (SEAL type)

Iran
23rd Special Forces Brigade

Iraq
Republican Guard
Special Forces Brigade ('Green Berets')

Ireland, Republic of
Irish Army Ranger Wing

Israel
Sayaret Almond (LRRPs)
Sayaret Mat'kal (attached to General Staff) (SAS type)
Sayaret Shakad (incorporated into Sayeret Golani)
Each branch of the IDF also has/had its own Sayaret units, for example:
    Sayeret Sherion (attached to Armour)
    Sayeret Golani (was attached to the old Golani Brigade)
    Sayeret T'zanhanim (attached to the Parachute Brigades) etc.
Naval Commandos (Shayet 13)

Italy
'Folgore' Airborne Brigade
Alpine Brigades

Brigata Alpini Torinese
Brigata Alpini Orobica
Brigata Alpini Tridenta
Brigata Alpini Cadore
Brigata Alpini Julia
Comsubin
Incursori (SEAL type)
Carabinieri Parachute Battalions
NOCS (Nucleo Operativo Centrale di Sicurezza) (counter-terrorism)
GIS (Gruppo di Intervento Speciale)

Japan
Police Special Action Units

Jordan
Special Forces
Spcial Security Groups
101st Special Forces Battalion

Kenya
General Service Unit (GSU) of the Kenya Police

North Korea
Twenty-two Commando Brigades

South Korea
1, 2, 3, 4, 5, 6, 7 Special Forces (Airborne) Brigades
707th Special Mission Battalion (Delta Force type)
ROK Marine Corps
Counter-terrorist Special Attack Unit of the National Police

Lebanon
Maokataha of the Lebanese Army

Malaya
Unit Timpaan Khas (Special Strike Unit) and
Unit Indak Khas (Special Action Unit) of the Royal Malaysian Police

Morocco
Gruppe Intervention Gendarme Nationale (GIGN) (counter-terrorism)

Netherlands
7th (NL) Special Boat Squadron
Korps Commando Troepen

BBE (Bijzondere Bijstands Eenheid) (GSG9 type)
BSB (Brigade Speciale Beveiligingsopdrachten)

New Zealand
1 New Zealand SAS

Norway
Marinejegertroppen FKN (Naval Commando Troop) (northern Norway)
Marinejegerlaget FKS (Naval Commando Team) (southern Norway) (reserve unit)
Fallskjermjegerkommandoen (Parachute Ranger Commandos)
FSK (Forsvarets Spesial Kommando) (Special Commando of the Defence) (anti-terror unit)
Beredskaptrop of the National Police ('Delta') (Counter-terrorism)
Heimevernets Spesialstyrke (Special Force of the Home Guard)

Oman
Sultan's Special Force

Pakistan
Special Services Group
Rangers

Peru
Six Special Commando Companies

Philippines
Army Special Warfare Brigade
Special Operations and Group of the Army Special Warfare Brigade
AVESCOM (Aviation Security Commando)
Light Reaction Force of the Philippines Constabulary
Integrated National Police Field Force

Poland
7th Lujcyka Naval Assault Division
4101st Paratroop Battalion (LRRP)

Portugal
Marine Commandos
Army Commandos
Airborne Commandos

Romania
One Naval Battalion
Two Mountain Infantry Brigades

Saudi Arabia
Special Forces
Special Security Force

Singapore
1 Commando Battalion (Airborne)
10 Commando Battalion (Airborne, Reserve)
Naval Divers
Police Tactical Team

South Africa
1, 2, 4, 5 REECE, Reconnaissance Commandos (SAS type)
1, 2 (CF), 3 (CF) PARA, Parachute Battalion
SAN Combat Divers (SEAL type; although 4 RECCE has similar role)
SAPS Special Task Force (GSG9 type)

Spain
Spanish Army
* Brigade de Paracaidistas – Legion España (BRIPAC) (LRRP)
* Spanish Legion
    – 1 and 2 Tercio: Ceuta and Mellila
    – 3 Tercio and 4 Tercio combine to form basis of RDF unit in Spanish
      armed forces with BOEL (see below)
* BOEL (Brigade de Operaçiones Especiales Legion)
* GOE II (Gruppo Operaçiones Especiales)
* GOE III and IV (non-regular SF, like 21 SAS etc.)
Spanish Air Force
* Escuadrilla de Zapadores Paracaidistas (EZAPAC) (LRRP, FAC, CT,
  CSAR etc.)
* Escuadrilla de Ayuda al Despliegue Aereo (EADA) (Pathfinders)
Spanish Navy
* Unidad Especial de Buceadores de Combate (UEBC) (SEALs)
* Unidad de Operaçiones Especiales (UOE) (Spanish Marines SF)
Guardia Civil
* GEOS (Grupos Especiales de Operaçiones) (GSG9)
* UEI (Unidad Especial de Intervençion)
* GAR (Grupos Antiterroristas Rurales)

Sri Lanka
Army Commando Squadron

Sudan
144th Counter-Terrorist Unit (CTU)

Sweden
Fallskaermjaegere (Parachute Ranger Company)
Kurstjaegerskolan Attack Divers (Coastal Ranger Company)
SAFR (Swedish Air Force Rangers)
Rangers (LRRPs)
122/Lappland Jaeger Regiment
K4/Norrland Dragoons
National Rescue Unit (part of the Stockholm Police Department) (counter-
    terrorism)

Switzerland
Para-Grenadiers
Stern Unit (based in Berne) (GSG9 type)
Enzian Unit (based in Zurich) (GSG9 type)

Taiwan
Long-Range Amphibious Reconnaissance Commandos
Para-Frogmen

Thailand
Royal Thai Army 1st Special Forces (Airborne) Division
* 1, 2, 3, 4 Special Forces (Airborne) Group
* Psy-Ops Battalion
* LRRP Company
Royal Thai Navy SEAL
Special Unit of the Royal Thai Air Force

Tunisia
Groupement de Commando of the Garde National (GCGN)

Turkey
Special Warfare Department
Ozel Inithar Kommando Bolvya (colloquially dubbed the 'Jandara Suicide
    Commando Companies')

United Kingdom
Special Forces Brigade
* 21 (TA) (Artists Rifles) Special Air Service (SAS)

* 63 (TA) (SAS) Signals Squadron
* 22 Special Air Service
  - Sabre Squadrons (A, B, D, G, R Squadrons)
  - Royal Corps of Transport Motor Pool
  - Army Air Corps S Flight
  - 262 (SAS) Signals Squadron
  - Operations Research Wing
  - Operations Planning and Intelligence Wing ('The Kremlin')
  - Demolitions Wing
  - Training Wing
  - Counter-Revolutionary Warfare Wing
* 23 (VR) Special Air Service
* Special Boat Squadron, Royal Marines (SBS)
* Special Forces Flight (No. 47 and No. 70 Squadrons, RAF)
148 (Meiktila) Commando, Forward Observation Battery, Royal Artillery
  (Para- and Commando-trained FACs)
The Honourable Artillery Company (HAC), Forward Observation Battery,
  Royal Artillery (TA equivalent of 148 Battery)
14 Intelligence Company, Intelligence Corps
3rd Commando Brigade
* Brigade HQ and Signals Squadron, RM
* 539 Assault Squadron, RM
* Tactical Air Control Parties, RAF
* Air Defence Troop, Royal Artillery
* 40, 42, 45 Commando RM (Royal Marines *per se*)
* Commando Logistic Regiment
* Commando Air Squadron
* 29 Commando Regiment, Royal Artillery
* 59 Commando Squadron, Royal Engineers
* 845, 846 Naval Air Squadrons, Royal Navy
* Mountain and Arctic Warfare Cadre (M&AWC)
* Special Boat Squadron (SBS)
5th Airborne Brigade
* Brigade HQ and Signals Squadron
* 89 Intelligence Section Intelligence Corps
* Air Force Liaison Section, RAF
* Two Para Battalions from the Parachute Regiment
* One Infantry Battalion (Guards Independent Para Company)
* One Gurkha Battalion
* Pathfinder Platoon
* Blues and Royals or Life Guards Armoured Recce Regiment
* 658 Aviation Squadron, Army Air Corps
* 613, 614 Tactical Air Control Parties, RAF
* 63 Squadron, Royal Corps of Transport

* 82 Ordnance Company, Royal Army Ordnance Corps
* 10 (Para) Field Workshop, Royal Electrical and Mechanical Engineers
* 23 (Para) Field Ambulance, Royal Army Medical Corps
* 160 Company, Royal Military Police

(3rd Commando Brigade and 5th Airborne Brigade now form the UK's rapid-reaction force)

Brigade of Gurkhas
* 2 King Edward VII's Own Goorkha Rifles
* 6 Queen Elizabeth's Own Goorkha Rifles
* 7 Duke of Edinburgh's Own Goorkha Rifles
* 10 Princess Mary's Own Goorkha Rifles (amalgamated into 3 Battalion Brigade in 1995)

D–11 of the London Metropolitan Police (GSG9 type)

United States

US Army Special Forces (Green Berets)
* 1, 3, 5, 7, 10 Special Forces Group (Airborne) (Regular Army)
* 3/7th Special Forces Group (Airborne) (Regular Army)
* 1/10th Special Forces Group (Airborne) (Regular Army)
* 19, 20 Special Forces Group (Airborne) (National Guard)

US Army Delta Force (SF Operational Detachment Delta)

US Army Rangers
* 1/75th Infantry, 2/75th Infantry, 3/75th Infantry

US Army Long-Range Surveillance Units (LRRP)
* 82 Airborne Division LRSD
* F Company 425th (LRS) Michigan National Guard
* G Company 143rd Infantry (LRS) Texas National Guard
* 143rd Infantry Detachment (LRS)
* 18th Airborne Corps LRS Company

US Joint Services Special Operations Command (JSSOCOM)
* 1, 3, 7, 10 Special Forces Group (Airborne) (Green Berets)
* 4th Psy-Ops Group
* 1, 2, 3/75th Infantry (Rangers)
* 96th Civil Affairs Battalion
* 160th SOAR (Special Operations Aviation Regiment)
  – Two Battalions at Fort Campbell, Kentucky
  – One Battalion at Hunter Army Airfield
  – 617th Special Operations Aviation Detachment (Panama Canal Zone)
  – 1/245th Aviation Battalion (National Guard, Oklahoma)
* NAVSPECWARDEVGRU (SEAL)

US Marines Corps
* 1st–4th ANGLICO (Air–Naval Gunfire Liaison Company)
* 1st–4th Marine Battalion Recon (LRRP)
* 1st–4th Marine Force Recon (SBS/SEAL type)

* Search and Target Acquisition Platoon (one per regiment in USMC) (snipers)
* Radio Reconnaissance Platoon (one for the Pacific fleet, and one for the Atlantic fleet)

US Air Force
* Tactical Air Control Parties
* 23rd Air Force, USAF

US Naval Special Warfare Groups
* NAVSPECWARGRU ONE
  - SEAL Team 1, 3, 5
  - SEAL Delivery Vehicle (SDV) Team One
  - Naval Special Warfare Unit One (NAVSPECWARUNIT–ONE) based in Guam, and a detachment in Kodiak, AK (NAVSPECWARGRU–ONE DET KODIAK)
* NAVSPECBOATRON-ONE (Coronado, California)
  - Special Boat Squadron One (SPECBOATUNIT 11 (Reserve) 12)
* NAVSPECWARGRU TWO
  - SEAL Team 2, 4, 8 (Naval Special Warfare Units (NAVSPEC-WARUNIT) 2, 4, and 8, located in Scotland, Puerto Rico and Panama respectively)
  - SEAL Delivery Vehicle (SDV) Team Two
* NAVSPECBOATRON TWO (Little Creek, Virginia)
  - Special Boat Squadron Two (SPECBOATUNITS 20, 22 and 26) (located in New Orleans, Louisiana, Little Creek, Virginia and Panama respectively)
* NAVSPECWARDEVGRU (under the joint authority of US Special Operations Command (USSOCOM) in Tampa, Florida, and Commander, Naval Special Warfare Command (COMNAV-SPECWARCOM) in Coronado, California

FBI Hostage Rescue Teams
Other units with the US Marshall's Service, National Parks Board and Department of Energy (NEST – Nuclear Emergency Search Team)

Venezuela
Special Intervention Brigade

Vietnam
'Dac Cong' (Special Forces)

Zimbabwe
Parachute Brigade
Zimbabwean Special Air Service (possible?)

SELECT BIBLIOGRAPHY

What follows is a small selection of books on Special Forces and Special Force operations. Among other publications consulted, the *Globe and Laurel* (journal of the Royal Marines), *Pegasus* (the Parachute Regiment magazine), *Behind the Lines* (the US Special Forces magazine) and the US *Marine Corps Gazette* proved particularly useful.

Anderson, Ellery, *Banner over Pusan (Special Forces in Korea)*, Evans, 1960

Arthur, Max, *Men of the Red Beret: Airborne Forces, 1940–1990*, Hutchinson, 1990

Asprey, Robert B., *War in the Shadows: A History of Guerrilla Warfare*, Little Brown, 1994

Bank, Colonel Aaron, *From OSS to Green Berets: The Birth of Special Forces*, Presidio Press, 1987

Beckwith, Colonel Charles A., *Delta Force: America's Super-Secret Counter-Terrorist Unit*, Fontana Books, 1985

Biggs, Colonel Bradley, *The Triple Nickels: America's First All-Black Paratroop Unit*, Archon, 1986

Black, Robert W., *US Rangers in World War II*, Ivy Books, 1992

Black, Robert, *US Rangers in Korea*, Ivy Books, 1989

Bosdiljevac, T. L., *SEALS: Udt–Seal Operations in Vietnam*, Paladin Press, 1990

Bullock, Brigadier Christopher, *Journeys Hazardous: Gurkha Clandestine Operations in Borneo, 1965*, Square One Publications, 1994

Carver, Field-Marshal Sir Michael, *War since 1945*, Weidenfeld & Nicolson, 1980

Chambers, Larry, *Recondo: LRRP in the 101 Airborne*, Ivy Books, 1992

Coogan, Tim Pat, *The IRA: A History*, Roberts Reinhart, 1994

Cooper, Lieutenant-Colonel Johnny, *One of the Originals: A Founder Member of the SAS*, Pan, 1991

Cowles, Virginia, *The Phantom Major: David Stirling and the SAS*, Collins, 1959

Crockett, Anthony, *Green Beret, Red Star: The RM Commandos in Malaya*, Eyre & Spottiswode, 1954

Deacon, Richard, *The Israeli Secret Service*, Sphere Books, 1979

De la Billière, General Sir Peter, *Storm Command: A personal Account of the Gulf War*, HarperCollins, 1993

Delta Group, *Ranger Training and Operations*, Desert Publications, 1982

Department of the Army, Washington DC, *Special Forces Handbook*, 1965

Dewar, Michael, *Brushfire Wars: The Minor Campaigns of the British Army since 1945*, Hale, 1984

Dickens, Peter, *SAS: Secret War in South-East Asia*, Ivy Books, 1983

Eshel, David, *Daring to Win: Special Forces at War*, Arms and Armour Press, 1992

Farran, Roy, *Winged Dagger (SAS at War)*, Fontana Books, 1948

Gabbett, Michael, *The Bastards of Burma: Merrill's Marauders and the Mars Task Force*, 1989

Geraghty, Tom, *Who Dares Wins: The Story of the SAS, 1950–1980*, Fontana Books, 1985

Green, Colonel T. N., *The Guerrilla and How to Fight Him: Selections from the Marine Corps Gazette*, Army Publishers, New Delhi, 1962

Grover, Colonel G. W. M., *A Short History of the Royal Marines*, Gale & Polden, 1959

Hastings, Max, *The Korean War*, Michael Joseph, 1987

Herbert, Anthony B., *The Making of a Soldier*, Hippocrene Books, 1982

Horner, David, *SAS, Phantoms of the Jungle: A History of the Australian SAS*, Allen & Unwin, 1989

Jackson, General William, *Withdrawal from Empire*, Batsford, 1986

Karnow, Stanley, *Vietnam: A History*, Viking Press, 1983

Katz, Samuel M., *Israeli Special Forces*, Motorbooks, 1993

Kelly, Francis J., *The Green Berets in Vietnam, 1961–71*, AUSA Books, 1991

Kemp, Anthony, *The SAS: Savage Wars of Peace*, John Murray, 1994

Kitson, General Sir Frank, *Gangs and Counter Gangs (Kenya and Mau Mau)*, Barrie & Rockcliffe, 1960

Klare, Michael T. and Kornbulh, Peter, *Low-Intensity Warfare*, Methuen, 1989

Lanning, Michael Lee, *Inside the LRRPs: Rangers in Vietnam*, Ivy Books, 1988

Lanning, Michael Lee, *Inside Force Recon: Recon Marines in Vietnam*, Ivy Books, 1989

Laqueur, Walter, *Terrorism*, Abacus Books, 1978

Larsen, General Stanley R. and Lawton Collins, General James, Jr. *Allied Participation in Vietnam*, Department of the Army, 1975

Lewis, Jon E., *The Elite Forces*, Robinson Books, 1993

Linderer, Gary A., *Eyes behind the Lines: L Company Rangers in Vietnam, 1969*, Ivy Books, 1991

Linderer, Gary A., *The Eyes of the Eagle: F Company, LRPs in Vietnam, 1968*, Ivy Books, 1991

Lodwick, John, *The Filibusters: The Special Boat Service in World War 2*, Methuen, 1947

Lucas Phillips, General C. E., *The Greatest Raid of All: St Nazaire, 1942*, Pan Books, 1958

McClintock, Michael, *Instruments of Statecraft: US Guerrilla Warfare, Counter-Insurgency and Counter-Terrorism, 1940–1990*, Pantheon Books, New York, 1992

Macdonald, P. G., *Stopping the Clock: Bomb Disposal in the World of Terrorism*, Hale, 1977

McNab, Andy, *Bravo Two Zero*, Corgi Books, 1993

Melma, Yossi, *The Master Terrorist, Abu Nidal*, Avon Books, New York, 1986

Neillands, Robin H., *By Sea and Land: The Royal Marines Commandos, 1942–1982*, Weidenfeld & Nicolson, 1987

Neillands, Robin H., *A Fighting Retreat: The Military Campaigns in the British Empire, 1947–1997*, Hodder & Stoughton, 1996

Neillands, Robin H., *The Raiders: The British Army Commandos, 1940–1945*, Weidenfeld & Nicolson, 1988

Neillands, Robin H., *True Stories of the French Foreign Legion*, Virgin Books, 1997

Neillands, Robin H., *True Stories of the SAS*, Virgin Books, 1995

Norton, G. G., *The Red Devils: From Bruneval to the Falklands*, Arrow Books, 1971

Paddock, Alfred H. Jr., *US Army Special Warfare: Its Origins*, National Defense University, 1982

Peniakoff, Colonel Vladimir, *Popski's Private Army*, Cape, 1953

Pisor, Robert, *The End of the Line: The Siege of Khe Sahn*, Norton, 1982

Reid Daly, Colonel Ron, *Selous Scouts: Top-Secret War*, Galego Books, Johannesburg, 1982

Reitz, Denys, *Commando: A Boer Journal of the Boer War*, Faber & Faber, 1955

Rottman, Gordon L., *US Army Special Forces, 1952–82*, Osprey, 1985

Ruby, Marcel, *F Section, SOE*, Grafton Books, 1990

Russell, Lee E., *The US Marine Corps since 1945*, Osprey, 1984

St George Saunders, Hilary, *The Green Beret: Commandos at War*, New English Library, 1959

St George Saunders, Hilary, *The Red Beret: The Airborne at War*, New English Library, 1958

Santoli, Al, *Everything We Had: An Oral History of Vietnam*, Ballantine Books, New York, 1981

Spencer Chapman, F., *The Jungle Is Neutral*, Chatto & Windus, 1950

Steenkamp, Willem, *Borderstrike: The War with Swapo*, Butterworth, Johannesburg, 1983

Stevenson, William, *90 Minutes at Entebbe: Operation Thunderbolt*, Bantam Books, 1976

Stirling, Clare, *The Terror Network*, Berkeley Books, New York, 1986

Thayer, Charles W., *Guerrilla*, Michael Joseph, 1961

Thompson, Leroy, *US Special Forces, 1941–1987*, Blandford Books, 1987

Walker, Greg, *At the Hurricane's Eyes: US Special Forces from Vietnam to Desert Storm*, Ivy Books, 1994

Wert, Jeffry D., *Mosby's Rangers*, Simon & Schuster, 1990

Windrow, Martin and Wayne Brady, *French Foreign Legion Paratroops*, Osprey, 1985

Wood, Ernest, *The SAS and Other Special Forces*, HarperCollins, 1996

Index

Note. Military personnel are given the most senior rank mentioned in the text even though they may have subsequently attained higher rank.